Measuring Data Quality for Ongoing Improvement

Measuring Data Quality for Ongoing Improvement
A Data Quality Assessment Framework

Laura Sebastian-Coleman

AMSTERDAM • BOSTON • HEIDELBERG • LONDON
NEW YORK • OXFORD • PARIS • SAN DIEGO
SAN FRANCISCO • SINGAPORE • SYDNEY • TOKYO
Morgan Kaufmann is an imprint of Elsevier

Acquiring Editor: Andrea Dierna
Development Editor: Heather Scherer
Project Manager: Anitha Kittusamy Ramasamy
Designer: Alan Studholme

Morgan Kaufmann is an imprint of Elsevier
225 Wyman Street, Waltham, MA 02451, USA

Library of Congress Cataloging-in-Publication Data
Application submitted

British Library Cataloguing-in-Publication Data
A catalogue record for this book is available from the British Library.

ISBN: 978-0-12-397033-6

For information on all MK publications
visit our website at *www.mkp.com*

Printed and bound by CPI Group (UK) Ltd, Croydon, CR0 4YY
Transferred to digital print 2012

For George
"Wherever we travel, we're never apart."
– Bob Dylan

Contents

SECTION 1 CONCEPTS AND DEFINITIONS

SECTION 3 DATA ASSESSMENT SCENARIOS

SECTION 6 THE DQAF IN DEPTH

Online Materials:

Acknowledgments

"O Lord, that lends me life,
Lend me a heart replete with thankfulness!"
—William Shakespeare, Henry VI, Part II (1591)

Writing a book is at once a very personal and a very social experience—personal because you spend a lot of time in your own head, sorting through ideas and tossing around words that give those ideas a shape; social because you realize how much of what you know, understand, and accomplish depends on other people.

I am grateful to Andrea Dierna and Heather Scherer at Morgan Kaufmann for the opportunity to do this project and for the unrealistic deadlines that ultimately made it a reality. And to Alan Studholme and Anitha Kittusamy Ramasamy for their work in finalizing the end product.

Many people at Optum and UnitedHealth Group provided direct and indirect input to the framework: Dave Albright, Jeff Alexander, Derryl Bell, Morgan Berkus, Danita Born, Toni Bozada, Linda Briere, Tanya Bruzek, Tom Carey, Nancy Couture, Laura Cullen, Karen Davis, John Drake, Sharon Ehrlich, Jerry Enright, Dave Fallert, Bill Franzen, Celia Fuller, Lisa Groothausen, Rick Hauritz, Joe Herron, Lisa Hodne, Rose Knott, Shawna Jarzabek, Jon Lindquist, Jim Locke, Michelle Love, Peggy Magness, Eric Mellum, Vinnie Mercer, Cheryl Middlekauff, Roselle Monsalud, Kathi Mohr, Bob Naughton, Steen Poulsen, Jim O'Connell, Pam Opulski, Omkar Patel, Krishna Reddy, Jim Reitter, Sara Rekow, Janice Richardson, Ansh Sarkari, Roy Scott, Varjesh Shah, John Shin, Dave Stumpf, Ralph Tartaglione, Barb Turner, and Diana Walter. Including the current UDW and UCG-DQAF implementation teams: Jim Aronson, Debasis Acharyya, Vignesh Asaithambi, Sreeni Barla, Nagender Bethy, Mary Ellen Cash, Igor Gitlevich, Kishore Kolanu, Bhuvanesh Kumarsomu, Dan Pahl, Anand Ramasamy, Bhanu Rayapaneni, Kanwar Singh, Kurt Skepper, Ron Smith, Vijay Tadepalli, Bindu Uppuluri, and Bill Wood. I sincerely hope I have not missed anyone.

In particular I am grateful to Tim Holt for encouraging me to formulate these ideas into a framework and for providing valuable feedback on the white paper that grew into this book; to the original DQAF team: Rich Howey, Greg Kozbauer, Gary Mersy, and Susan White; to Donna Delvecchio for her work on the Galaxy implementation project that made me see aspects of the framework I had not originally recognized; and to Kent Rissman for his insight, feedback on the manuscript, and continuous encouragement of the project. Special thanks to Eric Infeld, for launching me on my data quality journey, providing feedback and insight on the manuscript, and engaging with me in an ongoing conversation about data quality over the last nine years.

Optum Insight's generosity has enabled me to attend conferences at which I have been exposed to leading thinkers and my fellow practitioners in the field of data quality. This book has grown from seeds planted at the MIT's International Conferences on Information Quality and Industry Symposia, as well as IAIDQ and DGO conferences. Through these events, I have learned from extremely smart, engaged people who work hard to make data better. My thanks to David Loshin, Danette McGilvray, Tom Redman, and Lwanga Yonke, all of whom generously provided feedback on the proposal and manuscript. I cannot thank Danette enough for her overall encouragement of this project, her close and thoughtful reading of the manuscript, and her friendship. Any errors or omissions are my own.

I am fortunate also to have had encouragement and support from my friends and family.Mom, Dad, Karen, Maura, Lisa, Amanda, thanks for your well-timed phone calls and encouragement. My sister-in-law, Virginia Janzig, and her husband, Dick Janzig, closely read the manuscript and shared their expertise in writing as well as decades' worth of experience in the information technology industry. My husband, George, and my children, Janet and Richard, put up with my late nights, early mornings, and occupied weekends with no complaints and complete confidence in my ability to finish. Thanks, guys.

Foreword

It was in 2007 that I first became aware of Laura Sebastian-Coleman. While listening to her comments in a general session at the MIT Information Quality Industry Symposium, I noted what an articulate person she was. That first impression has not changed and has strengthened over time. The following year at MIT we met directly when we were both invited to present at the conference. Once again I was impressed by her thoughtfulness and ability to express her ideas clearly and coherently. We continued to interact at subsequent conferences at MIT and for IAIDQ (International Association for Information and Data Quality). Each time I looked forward to hearing about her data quality accomplishments in the health care sector. With this book, now all of us have the opportunity to learn from her.

In fact, I have been eagerly awaiting her book ever since I heard that she had plans to publish. For those of you familiar with my book *Executing Data Quality Projects: Ten Steps to Quality Data and Trusted Information*™ you know that my methodology fills a space in our body of knowledge between higher-level concepts and the deep-dive detail of certain slices of the data quality pie. Step 9 of my Ten Steps is called "Implement Controls." With Laura's book, we now have the deep-dive detail for implementing controls.

This book is the go-to manual for how to do in-line measurement, which takes place in conjunction with the processing of data. Her Data Quality Assessment Framework (DQAF) was originally developed to solve the following problem: "How do we establish an approach to data quality measurement that will work across data storage systems, provide measurements that are meaningful, and contribute to efforts to improve data quality?" The DQAF, as outlined in this book, has succeeded in answering those questions.

Laura was part of a team that originally created and implemented the framework at Optum Insight. She recognized there wasn't a book published that addressed one of the biggest challenges for data quality practitioners, which is how to measure the quality of data over time. Much has been written about the need to measure and about practices related to profiling, data discovery, and inspection, but not about the ongoing monitoring of data to ensure it continues to meet requirements. Improving data quality depends on the ability to continuously measure whether data meets business expectations. Laura starts with the context for data quality measurement and moves ultimately to the detail necessary for implementation. Her practical experience, along with her educational background, makes her well qualified to write this book. It is an important addition to our data quality literature, and I believe it is destined to become standard reference material for data professionals.

From that time five years ago when I first heard Laura and now as my trusted colleague and friend, I continue to pay attention to what she says. With a nod to a commercial from many years ago, when Laura Sebastian-Coleman talks—everybody should listen. Here is your chance! Learn and enjoy!

Danette McGilvray
Author of *Executing Data Quality Projects: Ten Steps to Quality Data and Trusted Information*™
(Morgan Kaufmann, 2008);
President and Principal Consultant of Granite Falls Consulting, Inc.
Fremont, California, 2012

Author Biography

Laura Sebastian-Coleman, a data quality architect at Optum Insight, has worked on data quality in large health care data warehouses since 2003. Optum Insight specializes in improving the performance of the health system by providing analytics, technology, and consulting services. Laura has implemented data quality metrics and reporting, launched and facilitated Optum Insight's Data Quality Community, contributed to data consumer training programs, and has led efforts to establish data standards and to manage metadata. In 2009, she led a group of analysts from Optum and UnitedHealth Group in developing the original Data Quality Assessment Framework (DQAF) which is the basis for *Measuring Data Quality for Ongoing Improvement.*

An active professional, Laura has delivered papers at MIT's Information Quality Conferences and at conferences sponsored by the International Association for Information and Data Quality (IAIDQ) and the Data Governance Organization (DGO). From 2009 to 2010, she served as IAIDQ's Director of Member Services.

Before joining Optum Insight, she spent eight years in internal communications and information technology roles in the commercial insurance industry. She holds the IQCP (Information Quality Certified Professional) designation from IAIDQ, a Certificate in Information Quality from MIT, a B.A. in English and History from Franklin & Marshall College, and a Ph.D. in English Literature from the University of Rochester (NY).

Author Biography

Introduction: Measuring Data Quality for Ongoing Improvement

Data Quality Measurement: the Problem we are Trying to Solve

One of the biggest challenges for data quality practitioners is defining how to measure the quality of data, especially as the uses of data evolve and the amount of data we depend on grows over time. The purpose of this book is to help people understand ways of measuring data quality so that they can improve the quality of the data they are responsible for. I am starting with the assumption that most people—even those who work in the fields of information quality and data management—find data quality measurement difficult or perplexing. For data, we do not yet have the physical tools of manufacturing—the caliper and micrometer—or the diagnostic tools of medicine—the thermometer and blood pressure cuff—to measure the basics of data quality. We don't even quite have consensus on what those basics would be. Beginning in the early 1990s, there has been an ongoing discussion about dimensions of data quality. There has also been advancement in tools and concepts related to data profiling. But it is not always clear how to apply these concepts and dimensions to data quality measurement and monitoring. Without an approach to the "how's" of ongoing measurement, efforts to improve data quality can be difficult to sustain over time.

Measuring Data Quality for Ongoing Improvement will try to reduce that difficulty by describing the Data Quality Assessment Framework (DQAF), a set of 48 generic measurement types based on five dimensions of data quality: completeness, timeliness, validity, consistency, and integrity. A DQAF measurement type is a category within a dimension of data quality that allows for a repeatable pattern of measurement to be executed against any data that fits the criteria required by the type, regardless of specific data content (e.g., completeness checks for files, timeliness of processes, validity of column content, consistency of population of related columns). The ideas presented here grew out of the efforts at Optum Insight to reformulate the "how's" of ongoing data quality measurement.

DQAF Measurement Types will be introduced in *Section Two: DQAF Overview*. Each measurement type is defined by six facets or sets of characteristics: A detailed definition, a set of business concerns that the measurement type addresses, a measurement methodology, a set of engineering or programming considerations, a description of support processes needed for the measurement type, and a set of logical attributes (models) needed to define specific metrics and to store the results of measurements. The facets of each type will be described in depth in *Section Six: The DQAF in Depth*.

The DQAF was originally developed to address in-line data quality measurement—measurement that takes place in conjunction with the processing of data within a data store or other application. Examples are measurements that are taken as part of an extract, transform, and load (ETL) process.

But it can also be applied to initial assessment such as profiling and inspection or assessment of data for specific analytical purposes, or periodic measurement activities, such as determining the integrity of data in an existing data store. These applications will be discussed in *Section Three: Data Assessment Scenarios*. Once the framework was defined, it became apparent that we could use it as part of the requirements definition process to better define expectations about data. In doing so, we could look to ways to build quality into data production, collection, processing, storage and use. These uses will be discussed in *Section Four: Applying the DQAF to Data Requirements*.

Recurring Challenges in the Context of Data Quality

Many of the DQAF characteristics can be understood as technical and process-oriented. Indeed, part of my intention is to provide guidance on how organizations can build data quality measurement into their processes. But, as often happens, the effort to make improvements in one area revealed related challenges that can influence an organization's ability to implement data quality measurement. These provide the context for much of the thinking that has gone into this book and is described in *Section One: Concepts and Definitions*.

Definitions of Data Quality

The quality of data is defined by two related factors: how well it meets the expectations of data consumers (how well it is able to serve the purposes of its intended use or uses) and how well it represents the objects, events, and concepts it is created to represent. In order to measure whether data meets expectations or is "fit for use," expectations and uses need to be defined. We usually equate expectations with requirements for particular uses, and, within most projects and systems, they are synonymous. However, we also have expectations about data in a wider sense. Living in the Information Age, we are influenced by prevailing assumptions about data—that it simply exists out there waiting to be used (or misused) and that it represents reality in a true and simple way. Early systems developers saw data in a different way, as the result of observation (always from a particular perspective) and instrumentation.

Throughout *Measuring Data Quality for Ongoing Improvement*, I will remind readers that data serves a semiotic function. Data are abstract representations constructed by people.[1] While data is not real—it does not represent reality in a simple or unproblematic manner—there are realities about data that we should acknowledge in trying to improve its quality. Data represents slices of reality in specifically defined ways. Data is produced by answering particular questions that enable an organization to function. Because of our dependence on electronic capture and storage of data, characteristics of the data we collect are related to the system through which it is captured. While data can be separated from its originating system, it will still bear some of the lineaments of its formation within a particular system. Its origins remain with it. There is an intimate relationship between data, as a representation of some facet of reality, and the design of systems that enable people to access and use data. System design is critical to understanding what data represents and how it effects its representation; it is therefore critical both to creating high-quality data and to understanding the quality of data (Wand & Wang, 1996, p. 88; Ivanov, 1972).

---

[1]In Latin and in English, *data* is a plural noun. Generally, I will follow this contemporary usage of data as a collective noun, grammatically singular. However, I will also use *data* as a plural when necessary for clarity's sake, as in "Data are abstract representations."

Expectations about Data

To measure expectations about the quality of data, it is necessary to know what those expectations are. We usually talk about expectations as being defined by data consumers, but doing so assumes a model of production and consumption that is far simpler than most of us live with. Most often data is *not* originally created *for* data consumers; rather, it is created *by* data "producers" for reasons of their own or as a by-product of other processes. Once it exists, it may be consumed for multiple uses. Over time, as new uses emerge, so do new expectations.

While most organizations document data requirements, few articulate expectations related to the expected condition or quality of data. Articulating expectations is difficult because we rarely question our assumptions about how data is produced, stored, and used. The process of unpacking assumptions and expectations about data often uncovers obstacles to meeting those expectations. Obstacles have a range of causes. They may be related to the completeness of data; for example, a transactional system may not even collect the data desired. Or they may be related to the structure of the data; for example, a system may not capture data at the granularity, atomicity, or precision required by data consumers. Or they may be associated with other factors influenced by the choices through which data is produced. In *Section Four Applying the DQAF to Data Requirements*, I will describe how to use DQAF categories to define data quality requirements in a consistent and understandable fashion, so that you can determine the degree to which these requirements have been met. The problem of measuring data quality is one of how to measure an abstract concept. For measurements to be effective, people need to understand what they represent and why they are important. All measurement involves a comparison between the thing being measured and the object against which it is measured. Data quality is measured against some form of expectation about the condition of data.

Risks to Data

Other obstacles to data quality can be characterized as risks posed by the business or technical processes that produce, transport, transform, or store data. If these processes produce unexpected results or do unexpected things to the data, the data may no longer meet requirements. Put another way: our expectations about data include not only what the data should represent and the structure through which the representation is effected, but also the things that happen to the data: how it is collected, stored, and moved. So when unpacking assumptions about data, it is important to identify potential risks associated with the data process or movement. Risks can be measured. In fact, measuring risk points in a data stream is often a way of preventing downstream data problems. In *Section Six: The DQAF in Depth*, I will describe how the DQAF measurement types can be leveraged to measure data risks as well as data expectations.

The Criticality of Metadata and Explicit Knowledge

In descriptions of challenges in knowledge management, data is described as input to higher levels of understanding: information, knowledge, and wisdom. This way of thinking about data interferes with our ability to manage data and improve its quality because it fails to recognize that data is created based on decisions about how to represent the world. There can be no data without knowledge.

Metadata is explicit knowledge about data. It is documented and shared to enable a common understanding of an organization's data, including what the data is intended to represent (data definition and business rules), how it effects this representation (data definition and system design), the limits of that representation (what it does not represent), what happens to it in its life cycle, particularly what happens to it as it moves through processes and systems (provenance, lineage, and the information chain), how data is used and can be used, and how it should not be used. Throughout the book, I will emphasize that metadata is necessary for the effective use of data.

The Business/Information Technology Divide

Organizations must remove cultural obstacles to high-quality data. One of the biggest of these obstacles is the challenging relationship between people who work directly in information technology (IT) roles and those who work in business-oriented roles. In today's data-driven world, most people recognize that data is not only valuable (even if they don't know quite how to value it) but essential for operating a business. But because IT manages data and the systems that house it, many organizations still perceive data as the province of IT. This perception gets in the way of important conversations about business requirements for data and makes it difficult to build the kinds of systems and processes that will enable the production of high-quality data. Throughout the book, I will emphasize the need for a shared responsibility in the improvement of data quality. This relationship will be the focus of **Chapter 2: Data, People, and Systems**.

Data Quality Strategy

If data is the lifeblood of today's organizations,[2] and the desire to measure the quality of data affects not only documentation practices but also organizational relationships, funding decisions, and everything in between, then it cannot be addressed in isolation. True, lasting improvements in the quality of data require organizational commitment that can only be attained through a well-articulated strategic vision. *Section Five: A Strategic Approach to Data Quality* will situate data quality measurement within the wider context of data quality strategy and data governance.

DQAF: the Data Quality Assessment Framework

While this book will address the recurring challenges related to data quality, at its heart is a description of the DQAF itself. The DQAF unpacks the dimensions of completeness, timeliness, validity, consistency, and integrity in order to define repeatable patterns through which specific measurements can be taken in a consistent manner. DQAF measurement types can be thought of as generic business requirements for taking repeatable kinds of measurements—just as a thermometer may be thought of as a generic means of measuring temperature. Discussions about data quality measurement describe dimensions of data quality, but they do not necessarily describe how to apply them. Consequently, many people charged with measuring data quality focus on specific measurements that pertain only to known challenges with their data. They do not necessarily see similarity between their measurements;

---

[2] The DAMA Book of Knowledge begins with the assertion that "Data and information are the lifeblood of the 21st century economy. In the Information Age, data is recognized as a vital enterprise asset" (2009, p. 1).

nor do they collect and process measurement results in the same way. The DQAF presents this opportunity and with it, an approach to data quality measurement and data management that will better enable business and IT people to work together to improve data quality.

Once you have the ability to measure, it is tempting to start measuring anything you can. A working assumption behind the framework is that data quality measurement should be purposeful and actionable. It should be directed at identifying anomalies, mitigating risks, and surfacing opportunities for improvement. Using the framework includes establishing criteria for critical measures and applying those criteria consistently within the system or systems where measurements are being taken. It also includes formulating strategies for using the measurement types not only directly for measurement, but also for defining requirements and engineering processes to produce data of higher quality.

Overview of Measuring Data Quality for Ongoing Improvement
Section One: Concepts and Definitions

Section One: Concepts and Definitions discusses a set of terms that are significant to data quality and data management and that will be used throughout the book.

Chapter 1: Data presents an extended definition of *data* that emphasizes data's semiotic function, as well as its existence as the product of definable processes and input into analyses. Data represents things other than itself. How well it does so influences perceptions of its quality.

Chapter 2: Data, People, and Systems defines a set of roles related to data and data management and discusses challenges connected with the relationship between information technology (IT) and businesspeople.

Chapter 3: Data Management, Models, and Metadata presents a set of concepts related to data management that have a direct bearing on data quality and the process of data quality measurement.

Chapter 4: Data Quality and Measurement introduces the concept of data quality dimensions as a means through which data quality can be measured and defines several general concepts associated with data quality assessment and some specific terms used by the DQAF.

Section Two: DQAF Overview

Section Two: DQAF Overview describes why the DQAF was created; outlines the assumptions, definitions, and governing ideas of the framework; and presents a short description of its 48 measurement types.

Chapter 5: DQAF Concepts describes the scope of the DQAF: to define a set of measurement types, based on objective aspects of the dimensions of quality that can enable basic IT stewardship of data. The chapter defines these dimensions: completeness, timeliness, validity, consistency, and integrity. It also discusses related concepts: objects of measurement, assessment categories, and functions of measurement (collect, calculate, compare).

Chapter 6: DQAF Measurement Types describes how the DQAF was originally formulated. It provides a high-level description of each of the 48 measurement types. It includes diagrams of several basic processes that enable readers to envision what a comprehensive data quality measurement system might look like.

Section Three: Data Assessment Scenarios

Section Three: Data Assessment Scenarios describes this wider context of data assessment.

Chapter 7: Initial Data Assessment describes goals associated with and input to such an assessment and delves into the "how to" details of profiling data (column profiling, structure profiling). Initial data assessment produces valuable metadata about the content, structure, and condition of the data being assessed. Initial assessment should also produce a set of recommendations for data quality improvement and for ongoing measurement and control.

Chapter 8: Assessment in Data Quality Improvement Projects describes the relation of measurement to data quality improvement projects. It includes a table of root causes and approaches to improvement.

Chapter 9: Ongoing Measurement presents general principles related to how ongoing measurement (in-line data quality measurement, controls, and periodic measurement) can be used to sustain data quality. It discusses the input needed to define ongoing measurement (an understanding of data's critical and risk), the need for automation of such measurement, and the deliverables associated with the process of ongoing measurement.

Section Four: Applying the DQAF to Data Requirements

The purpose of *Section Four: Applying the DQAF to Data Requirements* is to demonstrate how DQAF categories can be used to formulate data quality requirements so that in-line data quality measurements, controls, and periodic measurements can be specified.

Chapter 10 Requirements, Risk, Criticality reviews the concept of data quality requirements in the context of business requirements and for the purpose of identifying characteristics of data that can be measured. It describes how risk and criticality can be assessed to identify specific data and rules to be monitored on an ongoing basis through in-line measurements, controls, and periodic measurement.

Chapter 11: Asking Questions presents a set of questions that can help data consumers to articulate their assumptions and expectations about data quality characteristics, as well as to identify critical data and process risks. Their answers can be used to determine how to measure particular data elements and rules. From the exchange, analysts have input for the definition of specific data quality metrics to be taken in-line, as well as those that might be taken periodically.

Section Five: Data Quality Strategy

Section Five: Data Quality Strategy provides context and an approach for defining a data quality strategy.

Chapter 12: Data Quality Strategy defines the concept of data quality strategy so that it can be understood in relation to an organization's overall strategy and to other functions (data governance, data management, systems strategy) that also contribute to the effort to produce better data. It discusses the different kinds of decisions that need to be made as part of the information life cycle. It proposes a set of general considerations for data quality strategy.

Chapter 13: Directives for Data Quality Strategy presents a set of 12 directives for establishing an organization's data quality strategy. It describes how to assess organizational readiness for such a strategy. The directives break down into three sets. The first focuses on the importance of data within an enterprise. The second applies concepts related to manufacturing physical goods to data. The third focuses on building a culture of quality in order to respond to meet the ongoing challenges of strategic data management.

Section Six: the DQAF in Depth

The purpose of *Section Six: The DQAF in Depth* is to present the DQAF with a level of detail to enable an organization to determine which parts of the framework to implement. The introduction to the section provides an overview of these components.

Chapter 14: Functions of Measurement: Collection, Calculation, Comparison describes the process of taking in-line measurements, including what raw measurement data needs to be collected, what calculations need to be made with it (i.e., how it needs to be processed), and what comparisons need to be made to produce measurement results. The purpose of describing these common functions is to acclimate readers to the detail and to reduce redundancy in the detailed descriptions of the measurement types.

Chapter 15: Features of the DQAF Measurement Logical Model describes features in the DQAF measurement logical data model (LDM) that are common to many of the measurement types and provides general information related to the structure of tables that define specific measurements using DQAF measurement types and store measurement results. It discusses optional fields that might be included in these tables and describes additional features of a system to automate in-line data quality measurement.

Chapter 16: Facets of the DQAF Measurement Types describes each of the DQAF's 48 measurement types in relation to the six facets of the DQAF: definition, business concerns, measurement methodology, programming, support processes and skills, and the measurement logical data model. For in-line and some periodic measurements, the chapter includes tables from the measurement LDM. The chapter presents information that a team would need to implement any of the measurement types.

Intended Audience

This book is intended primarily for people directly engaged in improving and sustaining the quality of data and for leaders of staff who have these responsibilities. Depending on the organization, such people will have different names:

- Data quality practitioners charged with improving data quality, who want a practical approach to data quality measurement they should read the whole book to understand the context, the general approach, and the specific measurements.
- Managers of teams charged with monitoring data quality, investigating data issues, and working on data quality improvement projects, who want a comprehensive approach to measurement and a means of understanding improvement within their organizations.
- Business analysts, working on project development or operational project teams, who map data relationships and define data issues and gaps, and who want an approach to defining data quality requirements. Business analysts are sometimes called systems analysts. Under either name, they are expected to be able to translate business needs into technical requirements.
- Programmers (software developers and engineers) and managers of teams of programmers, who want to better enable their business counterparts to have a high level of confidence in their data.

In addition, IT executives who want a high level of confidence that the data their teams manage will meet strategic business needs, and business executives who want a high level of confidence in the data their teams use and who want to be able to leverage data effectively as new business needs arise, may also want to read parts of this book. It offers a different view of data than many people in business see. Its approach to assessing strategic readiness for data quality initiatives is intended to help organizations figure out how to take advantage of the other content in the book.

I hope readers will benefit at several levels from the ideas in this book. My intention is to enable a deeper understanding of data quality measurement and a practical approach to applying that understanding. The DQAF will create a common vocabulary—across IT and business—for approaching the general challenges of data quality measurement and for understanding the meaning of specific measurements. By using the categories in the DQAF, I hope readers will be able to clarify and address the challenges specific to their own organizations, and that they will have an approach to measurement that will enable them to meet those challenges. I also hope people will gain from the wider context I have presented. We are deep into the Information Age, but we still retain a relatively naïve view of data itself. A little skepticism may take us a long way.

What Measuring Data Quality for Ongoing Improvement Does Not Do

In setting expectations for what I hope readers will get out of this book, it is important also to point out what the book will not do. It does not, for example, present "code" for implementing these measurements. Although it contains a lot of technically oriented information, it is not a blueprint for a technical implementation. In defining requirements for measurement types, it remains business-oriented and technology independent.

It also does not advocate for the use of particular tools. I have separated the DQAF from discussions of particular tools because too often a focus on tools prevents teams from actually defining the problems they are trying to solve. When I was first engaged in the project to define data quality measurement, some members of our team saw the primary goal of our discussions to be the selection of a data quality tool—before we even had agreement on what we meant by measuring data quality. Based on conversations I have had with people at conferences and symposia, we were not too different from teams in other companies. Many people want to buy tools before they define their goals for measuring. I feel very strongly that people need to know what they are trying to accomplish before they use a tool. (I also have not yet seen a tool that measures data quality in-line in the way described by the DQAF without a significant amount of customization).

One benefit of the DQAF is that it will help you understand what, why, and how to measure the data that is critical to your organization. Once you have defined your requirements, the taxonomy can provide criteria for tool selection. And many organizations will indeed want to purchase tools, since data quality measurement should be as automated as possible. Because the ideas presented in the book will allow you to define data quality expectations more clearly, they should enable you to get more out of any tool you might adopt or build.

The book will not address in detail either how to conduct process analysis, manage issues, or conduct root cause analysis. I will refer to these topics, since they are critical to data quality improvement. However, they are covered very well in other books.[3] It is important that anyone wishing to improve data quality knows and can execute these processes. As importantly, people who are working on issue management should understand that measurement is critical both to identifying problems and to understanding the impact of root cause remediation.

The book will also not address how to measure the value of data or the costs of poor data quality. Both of these topics are well covered in other books. On the companion web site, I have summarized the thinking of key thought leaders on this topic. I will take as a starting point the idea that data is valuable because it is required for a wide range of purposes and that most of these purposes assume the data represents what it is expected to represent. Like issue management and root cause analysis, understanding the costs of poor quality data is critical to data quality improvement efforts and data quality practitioners need to know how to do it. What this book does cover—measuring the quality of data—is a prerequisite to measuring the impact of poor quality data.

Why I Wrote Measuring Data Quality for Ongoing Improvement

As is the case with many people working in data and information quality, I feel a deep commitment to ensuring that data is clear, complete, and usable. That said, my path to the field was not exactly straight and narrow. Although I have worked in information technology for the past decade and a half, I am not a technologist. My formal education is in the humanities. In college, I majored in English and History. My doctoral thesis focused on how the autobiographical writings of an eighteenth-century Irish revolutionary, Theobald Wolfe Tone, were edited and published during the nineteenth and twentieth centuries. While I would not have used these words at the time, that analysis was my first in-depth exploration of the sensitivity of data presentation to context, as well as of the relation between information quality and fitness for purpose. It also provided me with an education in semiotics, the limits of language in representing the world, and the importance of understanding the perspective of the observer in an observation.

My IT career began because I was in the right place at the right time with the right people. When the insurance company I worked for launched its Internet site, they needed a "content provider" (an interesting synonym for *writer*) to produce company success stories— one-page vignettes about how we had helped our clients improve their safety practices. IT tapped me, a lowly corporate communications specialist and ghost writer of the company newsletter. To get this work done, I partnered with the Web development team. Through a fortunate series of events, the VP who headed this team brought me into his organization to manage the effort to build our intranet.

I did not immediately recognize what a remarkable company this was. It sold workers' compensation insurance bundled with safety engineering services. This seemed like pretty dry stuff, on the surface. Our product, marketed as Zero Accident Culture (ZAC), was more expensive than those of many other insurance carriers. We sold to organizations that had poor loss experience—poor safety records, lots of workers compensation claims, high premiums. But many could not get insurance through other carriers no matter what they were willing to pay. This situation might sound like one in which an insurance carrier could take advantage of a business, but the opposite was the case. We promised to

---

[3] See Tague (2005), *The Quality Toolbox*, for a discussion on quality tools in general. English (1999, 2009), Redman (1994, 1996), Loshin (2001, 2010), and McGilvray all discuss process analysis and root cause analysis in relation to information and data quality improvement.

work with clients to improve their loss experience and help make their workplaces safer. Reducing the number of claims was a win-win-win situation. It would benefit our clients, our clients' employees, and our company's bottom line.

How did it work? Sales staff and safety engineers assessed the client's physical plant, critical processes, and claim history (in other words, claim data) in order to identify the root causes of employee injuries. From these findings, they proposed a program of improvement. Improvements usually included aspects of the physical setup of a manufacturing plant, nursing home, or office (changes could include everything from ensuring stairs had reflective tape to bringing in safer equipment), along with worker training on safety (safe lifting, ergonomics, use of personal protective equipment, etc.). We backed up our recommendations with data related to the success of other clients in the same industries. And we visited clients on a regular basis to monitor their implementation of and ensure compliance with our recommendations. We worked with them to remove any obstacles to their ability to comply. And we provided continuous feedback in the form of their own claim data.

It takes about three years to improve a workers' compensation loss ratio. But we immediately began to measure the effects of our recommendations on the factors that would bring overall improvement to the loss ratio—these were the situations I wrote success stories about. One tool we used for both assessment and improvement was a simple data-mapping diagram. It mapped three years of claim data to a schematic image of a human body; we dubbed this the ZAC Man. Each claim related to a wrist injury would map to the ZAC Man's wrist; each claim related to a back injury would map to the back; shoulder to shoulder, and the like. This data mapping provided a very clear picture of the frequency of specific kinds of injuries. It also illustrated the collective pain caused by those injuries. In doing so, it surfaced opportunities for improvement and reasons for pursuing those opportunities. It could also be used to illustrate the beneficial effects of safety process improvements.

Clients who followed our recommendations saw clear results in very short periods of time. These results showed up (or better stated, were no longer showing up) not only on ZAC Man, but also on the quality of life for employees. We helped reduce the total number of accidents and, with them, the number of lost workdays. Our nurses supported a transitional return to work program that reduced the average number of days any individual employee was out of work. Since many of our clients' employees were hourly workers, getting back to work was critical to them and their families. Transitional return to work balanced this need with the corresponding need to reduce the risk of re-injury, which of course would be costly to all three parties. As the clients improved their safety records, their premiums went down, which had a direct impact on their financial success. Because these companies also showed they cared about their employees, employee morale went up, which also had an added effect on the bottom line.

Working for this company provided many lessons in the connection between process improvement, efficiency gains, and cost reduction. I have been a believer ever since. Data was the key ingredient.

But the most remarkable thing about working for the company was this: To a person—from the sales force and safety engineers who met with clients and set up programs to improve their safety records to the nurses who focused on enabling injured workers to return to their jobs, to myself in corporate communications who wrote up the success stories, to the programmers and IT analysts who managed the data that was the foundation of our ability to help clients—the employees of our company were committed to the company's vision and mission: We saved life and limb. Why? Because the mission itself was important, because we actually achieved it (we had the data to prove it), and because each person understood how he or she contributed to that mission.

The second most remarkable thing was this: the IT team and the business team were partners; they were not in conflict or competition. They recognized each other as part of one team, striving for the same goal. Some of the credit for this relationship goes to the individuals involved. But a lot of it resulted from the clarity of the company's mission and the centrality of data to that mission. Businesspeople wanted the data and relied on IT to make it available in a usable form. IT knew what the business was trying to accomplish and understood how data helped meet business goals. And they understood the data itself: where it came from, what it represented, how and why it changed over time, how it was used to create other data.

This first exposure to working directly with data amazed me. I was fascinated at how much it could show about the way processes worked; and how data focused on one thing—injuries that workers had sustained—could be used to surface improvement opportunities for something completely different—a manufacturing process or the layout of a nursing home. The availability and use of appropriate and reliable data had direct and positive effects not only on organizational success for our company and our clients, but also on the quality of life for individual people. The job also left me naïve and therefore idealistic about the best relation between business and IT—a topic I'll get into again later in the book. And it made me a data geek. In my current role in health care, I continue to be impressed by what data can show us.

But the longer I work with data, the more I realize the importance of words in enabling data to do its magic. The intention of this book is to help people get a better understanding of how to measure the quality of data. The first step in doing that is to get the right words in place to understand what it means to measure the quality of data. So the book will also contain recommendations about metadata and requirements definitions, as these are directly related to data quality measurement. It is also critical, on an ongoing basis, to be able to define goals around the improvement of data quality. Some of these goals will be expressed in numbers, but reaching them needs to be understood through words. What follows are my words. I hope other people can benefit from them.

Concepts and Definitions

"Does not any analysis of measurement require concepts more fundamental than measurement?"
—John Stewart Bell, Irish Physicist, 1928–1990

The purpose of Measuring Data Quality for Ongoing Improvement *is to help people understand ways of measuring data quality so that they can improve the quality of the data they are responsible for. A working assumption is that most people—even those who work in the field of information quality—find data quality measurement difficult or perplexing. The book will try to reduce that difficulty by describing the Data Quality Measurement Framework (DQAF), a set of 48 generic measurement types based on five dimensions of data quality: completeness, timeliness, validity, consistency, and integrity. The DQAF focuses on objective characteristics of data. Using the framework requires a wider context than just these dimensions. Effective data quality measurement requires building knowledge of your organization's data: where it comes from, where it is stored, how it moves within the organization, who uses it, and to what ends.*

Section One defines a set of foundational concepts related to data, the ways it is managed within organization, and how we understand and measure its quality. These concepts provide the context for the other subjects covered in the book, so they are explored in depth. Concise definitions are captured in the glossary. While this section introduces most of the basic concepts, it does not describe requirements (these will be covered in Section Four), strategy (see Section Five), or statistics (see Section Six). Each of these concepts is covered in the sections focused on those topics. Section One includes four chapters.

Chapter 1: Data *presents an extended definition of data that emphasizes data's semiotic function. Data represents things other than itself. How well it does so influences our perceptions of data quality. The chapter defines information as a variation on the concept of data and discusses the relation of both to knowledge. A primary implication of the chapter is that there cannot be data without knowledge.*

Chapter 2: Data, People, and Systems *defines a set of roles related to data and data management: data producer, data consumer, data broker, data steward, data quality program, and stakeholder. In many organizations individuals play multiple roles. It is not always people who fill these roles, however. Systems also produce and consume data. The chapter also addresses the sometimes challenging relationship between people who work in information technology (IT) and businesspeople.*

Chapter 3: Data Management, Models, and Metadata *presents a set of concepts related to data management, data models, and metadata, as these have a direct bearing on data quality. Data management implies the need for particular kinds of knowledge about data: what data represents, how much there is of it in an organization, how it is organized and maintained, where it resides, who uses it and the like. Knowledge about data captured in data models and metadata is necessary input for the process of data quality measurement.*

Chapter 4: Data Quality and Measurement *introduces the concept of the data quality dimension as a means through which data quality can be assessed. It presents a definition of measurement, discusses the challenges associated with establishing tools for or systems of measurement, and presents characteristics of effective measurements. It then defines several general concepts associated with data quality assessment and some specific terms, such as the measurement type, used by the DQAF.*

This book is about data quality measurement. That means it is about four things: how we understand data, how we understand quality, how we understand measurement, and how the first three relate to each other. Understanding each of these requires breaking through assumptions and preconceptions that have obscured the reality of data and our uses of it. When we acknowledge the representational aspects of data, we can leverage it more effectively for specific purposes. We can also better understand how to measure and improve its quality.

A note on the definitions: My starting point for definitions of common words and their etymologies is the New Oxford American Dictionary, *Second Edition (2005) (cited as NOAD). For terms specific to data and information quality, I have synthesized dictionary definitions and definitions in published works on the subject. In most cases, the definitions I have adopted do not differ significantly from other published definitions. However, I have defined them in relation to how they applied to the DQAF.*

Data

1

"The spirit of Plato dies hard. We have been unable to escape the philosophical tradition that what we can see and measure in the world is merely the superficial and imperfect representation of an underlying reality."
—**Stephen Jay Gould,** *The Mismeasure of Man*

"Data! Data! Data!" he cried impatiently. "I cannot make bricks without clay."
—**Sherlock Holmes, "The Adventure of the Copper Beaches"**

Purpose

This chapter presents an extended definition of the concept of *data*. Understanding what data is and how it works is essential for measuring its quality. The chapter focuses on data's role in representing objects, events, and concepts. It also discusses the relation between data and information.

Data

The *New Oxford American Dictionary* defines data first as "facts and statistics collected together for reference or analysis." The American Society for Quality (ASQ) defines data as "A set of collected facts. There are two basic kinds of numerical data: measured or variable data, such as '16 ounces,' '4 miles' and '0.75 inches;' and counted or attribute data, such as '162 defects'" (ASQ.org). And the International Standards Organization (ISO) defines data as "re-interpretable representation of information in a formalized manner suitable for communication, interpretation, or processing" (ISO 11179).

The term *data* (plural of *datum*)[1] derives from *dare*, the Latin past participle of *to give*.[2] Its literal meaning is "something given." Despite this generic root, the term has a strong association with

---

[1] Data plural versus Data singular. In Latin and in English, *data* is a plural noun. Its singular form is *datum*. However, in common contemporary usage, it is also a collective noun and therefore often grammatically singular. Generally, I will follow this contemporary usage of data as a collective noun. However, I will also use *data* as a plural because doing so is sometimes necessary for clarity's sake. For example, in defining *data*, "it is important to recognize that all data are representations of characteristics of the real world, rather than asserting that data (the collective) is a representation of characteristics of the real world". To me, the second assertion is confusing.

[2] Definitions of *data*, *datum*, and *fact* are from the *New Oxford American Dictionary (NOAD)*, Second Edition, (New York: Oxford University Press, 2005). The *NOAD* will be the source for all dictionary definitions cited in this book unless otherwise indicated.

numbers, measurement, mathematics, and science. Seventeenth-century philosophers used the term to refer to "things known or assumed as facts, making the basis of reasoning or calculation." A singular *datum* provides "a fixed starting point of a scale or operation." We often think of data in relation to computing, where *data* refers to "the quantities, characters, or symbols, on which operations are performed by a computer, being stored and transmitted in the form of electrical signals and recorded on magnetic, optical or mechanical recording media" (*NOAD*) (although as we enter the age of "big data," we may even have grown beyond the boundaries of this characterization).[3]

Today, we most often use the word *data* to refer to facts stored and shared electronically, in databases or other computer applications.[4] These facts may be measurements, codified information, or simply descriptive attributes of objects in the world, such as names, locations, and physical characteristics. Because they are stored electronically, we can more quickly understand aspects of their content. The definition of *data* I will use throughout this book highlights not only data's existence as part of information systems, but also data's constructed-ness: Data are abstract representations of selected characteristics of real-world objects, events, and concepts, expressed and understood through explicitly definable conventions related to their meaning, collection, and storage.

Data as Representation

Each piece of this definition is important. The adjective *abstract* means "existing in thought or as an idea but not having a physical or concrete existence" (*NOAD*). As a verb, *to abstract* has several definitions, all of which include the concept of separating things from each other—for example, abstracting an idea from its historical context, or producing a summary (an abstract) of a book or article. Data enable us to understand facets of reality by abstracting (separating) and representing them in summary form (an abstract) (Peirce, 1955, p. 98). This ability works with facts based on well-known criteria (for example, birthdates based on the Julian calendar) as well as with facts based on more complex formulas, such as the performance of stocks on the New York Stock Exchange.

Data are always representations. Their function is primarily semiotic. They stand for things other than themselves (Chisholm, 2010; Orr, 1998). These things can be objects (people, places, things) or events or concepts. They can even be other data. Data functions as a sign of the thing it represents in the real world (semantics). It is rare that there would be one and only one way of representing the same thing. To be understood, any piece of data also operates within a system of signs, the meaning of which is dependent on each other (syntactics). And, finally, it is used for specific purposes and has particular effects (pragmatics) (Semiotics, Chandler, 2009).

---

[3] Because we store so much stuff electronically, it is tempting to call everything "data"—for example, the multitude of files and input referred to in discussions of "big data" and "unstructured data." I think we need another word for this stuff. From early on (as far back at least as Walter Shewhart), people have recognized that data is meaningless without context. I would say that data are not data without at least a minimum context that says what the data are supposed to represent. See Konnikova (2012).

[4] In *Developing High Quality Data Models* (2003) Matthew West points our that as we rely more and more on electronic storage of information, we have changed our way of "holding" information: "The trend is to hold information as data because this enables increased computer support, for example, 'intelligent' drawing packages. The intelligence comes because having information in a structured form means the computer can have knowledge of what the information is about and can therefore act to support the user based on that knowledge."

Data represent only *selected characteristics* of the objects, events, and concepts. In this sense, data is a model of reality.[5] We will talk about data models in Chapter 3. Models play an important function in our ability to understand the world. As Emanuel Derman asserts in *Models Behaving Badly*, "The world is impossible to grasp in its entirety. We can focus on only a small part of its vast confusion. ...Models project a detailed and complex world onto a smaller subspace" (Derman, 2011, pp. 58–59). But, he continues, "Models are simplifications and simplification can be dangerous" (Derman, 2011, p. 59). The primary risk in using models is that we may believe in them. "The greatest conceptual danger," writes Derman, "is idolatry. ...Though I will use the models. ...I will always look over my shoulder and never forget that the model is not the world" (2011, p. 198). Data presents a similar risk. In *Data and Reality*, his comprehensive exploration of the limits of data, William Kent observes, "A model is a basic system of constructs used in describing reality. ...[It] is more than a passive medium for recording our view of reality. It shapes that view, and limits our perceptions" (Kent, 2000, p.107). Kent's book delineates all the choices that go into representing "amorphous, disordered, contradictory, inconsistent, non-rational, and non-objective" reality in data models. Deciding what is an entity (what equals "one" of the things you are representing), what is an attribute, a category, the right level of detail in a description, what is the system, what is a name—all of these decisions contribute to selecting the parts of reality we choose to understand through data. Despite the impossibility of reaching an "absolute definition of truth and beauty," Kent concludes that we can share a common and stable view of reality (p. 228). At the root of this shared reality is shared language (p. 226) (though he sees, as any semiotician would, that language itself participates in the problem of models).

I will give two examples to illustrate the kinds of decisions that are made when we structure data. The first has to do with the concept of "one" thing—even for a familiar concept. When we talk about a pair of shoes, are we talking about one thing or two things? The answer depends on definition and use. For most people, a pair of shoes is one thing. But for someone who has orthopedic problems, a pair of shoes means two things: a left shoe that may need one kind of alteration to be usable and a right shoe that may need another kind of alteration.

The second example is about the arbitrariness of representation. As any high school student who has written a research paper knows, a necessary part of research is compiling a bibliography. There are different conventions for presenting information about the sources used in research. The American Psychological Association (APA) represents books like this:

Talburt, J. (2011). *Entity resolution and information quality*. Boston, MA: Morgan Kaufmann.

whereas the Modern Language Association (MLA) represents them like this:

Talburt, John R. *Entity Resolution and Information Quality*. Boston, MA: Morgan Kaufmann, 2011. Print.

And the *Chicago Manual of Style* (CMS) has yet another variation:

Talburt, John R. *Entity Resolution and Information Quality*. Boston, MA: Morgan Kaufmann, 2011.

These citations present the same basic facts about the same book—author, title, publication date, publisher, and place of publication—but the conventions of representation differ between them.

---

[5] We will talk about data models in Chapter 3. Here I am talking about the general concept of a model, "a representation of a person or thing or of a proposed structure, typically on a smaller scale than the original" (*NOAD*).

Undoubtedly, thought went into these choices so I assume there is some significance to them. But that significance is not apparent within the representation itself. (Why does the APA not capitalize all the nouns in the title? Why does MLA include the medium of publication while APA and CMS do not?) To almost anyone using them, they are simply conventions of representation.

The Implications of Data's Semiotic Function

One implication of the semiotic function of data is that data do not simply exist; they are created. Another implication is that any given data model is only one way of representing reality. Data are thus both an interpretation of the objects they represent and themselves objects that must be interpreted.

We tend to use words that imply otherwise.[6] Recognizing data's representational function is another way of saying that data cannot be understood without context, but it goes a bit further than just that assertion. To be fully understood, data must be recognized within the particular context of its creation (or production). Most work on data quality emphasizes whether the data meet consumers' requirements (whether data is "fit for use").[7] Ultimately, however, understanding whether data meet requirements requires understanding where the data come from and how they represent reality. Data always must be interpreted. In some situations, such as the presentation of financial reports to lay audiences or the description of scientific assertions to students, the need to describe context is recognized. Such data are presented with a full context. But in business, we often skip this step. Even for relatively straightforward data, it is important to remember that data are created through a set of choices about how to represent reality. Underlying these choices are assumptions about what constitutes reality in the first place.

Data are formal and contextual. Their meaning depends on how they are structured as well as on what they represent. Context includes explicitly definable conventions of representation. These conventions translate characteristics into numbers, identifiers, codes, or other symbols based on decisions made by people.[8] To understand the meaning of a piece of data, one must understand not only what

---

[6]Bugajski (2009), "Foundations of Data Governance," states that data governance is the most effective means for senior executives to ensure "that the information they obtain using IT systems is reliable, *authentic*, accurate, current, and useful" (emphasis mine, p. 4). Larry English (1999) defines data as "an *equivalent reproduction* of something real. If all facts that an organization needs to know about an entity are *accurate*, that data has inherent quality—it is an electronic reproduction of reality" (emphasis in the original, p. 22).

[7]Malcolm Chisholm's blog on *Information Management*, Data Quality Is Not Fitness for Use, was published as I was finishing this manuscript (August 16, 2012). His assertions there are very similar to mine in this book. While my understanding of semiotics is based on my graduate school experience, in applying these concepts to data, I have been greatly influenced by his 2010 book, *Definitions in Information Management: A Guide to the Fundamental Semantic Metadata*, which I would consider essential reading for anyone working in data quality.

[8]I formulated this definition before discovering a similar one by H. H. Wellisch: Data are "the representation of concepts or other entities, fixed in or on a medium in a form suitable for communication, interpretation, or processing by human beings or by automated systems" (quoted in Zins, 2007). Wang and Strong (1996) recognize this aspect of data quality through the category of Representational Data Quality. Representational DQ is understood as the extent to which data is presented in an intelligible and clear manner. The category implies that a system must present data in such a way that it is easy to understand (represented concisely and consistently) so that the data consumer is able to interpret the data. Representational dimensions of quality include interpretability, ease of understanding, representational consistency, and concise representation. Redman (1996) also recognizes the representational aspects of data, defining a data item as a representable triple: a value, from the domain of an attribute, within an entity.

the data are supposed to represent, but also the conventions of representation they employ to convey meaning. For example, measurements (classic instances of data) that consist of numbers and units of measure represent characteristics such as height, length, width, weight, and density. They can be understood in relation to a system of measures whose conventions we know or can learn. Because they represent discrete characteristics (attributes) of the objects, events, or concepts, data are usually thought of as *pieces* of information (e.g., facts, measurements, statistics, names, characterizations, observations). If these conventions are not applied effectively when data are created or collected, or if they are not well understood by people using data, then the data themselves will not be understood in the way intended. They may also be perceived as being of low quality (See Figures 1.1–1.4).

Many discussions of data quality refer to large datasets in data storage applications or data as it is moving through a set of systems within an organization. But data's representational function and formal nature pertain to all data: the old-fashioned kind (measurements written down in a notebook

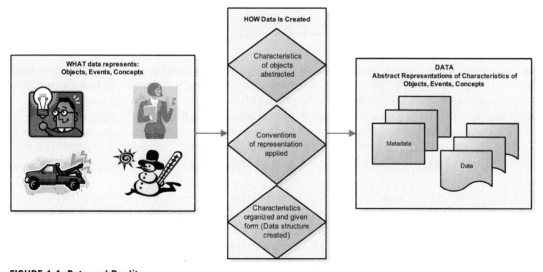

FIGURE 1.1 Data and Reality

Data is created by observing and representing a subset of characteristics from the infinite possible set of characteristics that could be represented, applying to these conventions of representation, and organizing these representations so that they can be understood. The observer who creates data may be a person or a machine. The decisions about what subset of characteristics to represent and how to represent them may be made with differing degrees of consciousness. Reinterpretation can also involve different degrees of consciousness. Creating data involves the use of cognitive structures to transmit information about the objects, events, and concepts so that they can be understood by someone else. Using data is a process of reinterpreting it. Metadata is required for this purpose. Like data, metadata can be simple or complex. Data is considered to be of high quality if it meets the expectations of data consumers. Those expectations can be clearly defined and known, or they can be based on unarticulated assumptions about what data represents and how data effects its representation.

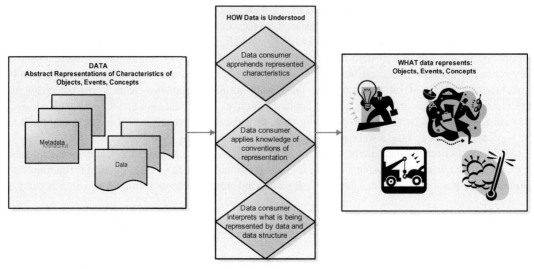

FIGURE 1.2 Reality and Data

The process of creating data is a process of interpreting reality through a particular lens. It depends on making decisions about how to represent an object, event, or concept—that is, decisions about which characteristics to abstract and what conventions of representation to apply to make them suitable for communication, interpretation, or processing. The process of interpreting data is similar to that of creating data. A data consumer (who can be a person or a system) must first apprehend the characteristics represented by the data. Then the data consumer applies knowledge of conventions of representation to associate characteristics with his, her, or its existing knowledge of objects, events, and concepts and interprets what the data represents.

as part of a high school science lab) and high-tech kind (biometric readings taken via an iPad application and transferred to a computer in a hospital). In both cases, the questions behind the data—those that identify which characteristics of the objects, events, and concepts are to be represented, and the manner in which the data are collected and stored—both imply how the data will be structured and how data will effect their representation. I am using the verb *effect* in its primary meaning "to cause (something) to happen; to bring about" (*NOAD*).

Semiotics and Data Quality

Data are created under specific conditions (often, but not always) for particular purposes. Those conditions always include an observer, as well as the thing observed and the conditions of observation, such as the perspective adopted by the observer and instrument used to make the observation. This assertion may seem overly complex and scientific for much of the data we store today. We know what we mean by things like names, addresses, birthdates, product codes, and transaction details. These common data elements do not seem to require an observer and an observed or an instrument of observation. They are implicit nevertheless. We are so familiar with much of what we call data that we do not always think about what goes into creating it. The instrument of observation may be an order form. The conditions of

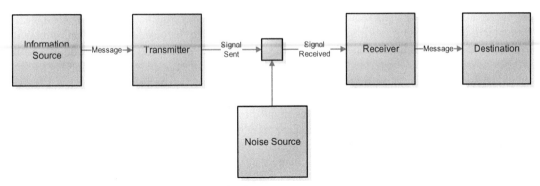

FIGURE 1.3 Shannon's Schematic for Communication

C. E. Shannon's 1948 schematic diagram of a general communication system described an information source having a message to send; a transmitter sending a signal to be received; and the message arriving at its destination. Shannon recognized that a noise source can interfere with the signal and reduce the clarity of the message. Improvement in communications entails reduction of the effects of noise on the message. The schematic provides both a way to assess an actual communications system and a metaphor for the challenges of communication itself.

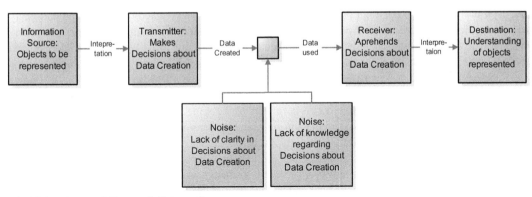

FIGURE 1.4 Data and Shannon's Schematic

The process of data creation and interpretation can be understood using C. E. Shannon's 1948 schematic diagram of a general communication system. The objects to be represented are a source of information. The transmitter makes decisions about how to represent them. Creating data is a way of interpreting the world. They are received by a data consumer who must apply an understanding of the decisions related to data creation in order to understand the objects represented. Understanding data is another process of interpretation. Noise can be due to two general conditions: a lack of clarity about how to create data and a lack of understanding about how it was created. Data is considered to be of high quality if it meets data consumers' expectations. Those expectations are often based on unarticulated assumptions about what data represents or poorly understood assumptions about how data represents the real world. Lack of knowledge about data is an obstacle to its effective use.

observation are defined by input requirements for the order form, the sequence in which fields appear, the graphic user interface or the color of the paper of the form, and the place where the order form is filled out. The observer is the person filling out the form. Add to this the idea that data input on a form may then be compiled and aggregated in a database and used as input for analysis of buying habits and you will begin to see some of the ways in which systems are designed to observe (See Figures 1.1–1.4).

Before they land in a database, data are created through a set of requirements about what needs to be represented and a series of assumptions about how to represent reality and how reality was assumed to be represented in source systems. Data may be filtered through many lenses, such as the questions that were used to collect it and the means of collection and storage. Many data consumers ignore this aspect of data production, just as many data producers are often unaware that their data will be used in ways they had not anticipated.

Recognizing that data are only one of many ways to represent reality and that they are created through human choices is fundamental to understanding data quality. When we evaluate the quality of data, we are evaluating how and how well data represents the objects and events they are designed to represent. Data quality is judged by how well data perform their semiotic function. *How* data represent reality directly influences *what* we understand is being represented. Many of the expectations we associated with the quality of data are directed at the *how* of representation.

It is relatively easy to find examples of data that do not represent reality in the way that we imagine they should. At the 2010 MIT Information Quality Industry Symposium, crime statistician Daniel Bibel described the conditions under which much crime data is collected (Bibel, 2010, p. 494). Police are charged with maintaining order, but data in the reports they file are aggregated regionally and nationally and can therefore influence national perceptions of crime. The data collection in the field presents many challenges, from a lack of standardization about locations (instead of providing a street address, one report documented a location as "at the 7–11 near the high school"—while this was understandable to the local police, it was not understandable to anyone not familiar with the town); to classifications of crimes (in Massachusetts, breaking into a car is considered a burglary. Crime statistics in the town of Agawam, Massachusetts, included more than two dozen burglaries at the same address, the parking lot of the Six Flags amusement park); and the lack of provision for updating records when new details are discovered (for example, a case in which an event eventually ruled a homicide was first reported as an accidental death and remained on the record as an accidental death). These types of conditions create "inaccurate" or "incorrect" data. But they point to a bigger problem: In many cases, there are discrepancies between the reality the statistics are meant to represent and the capacity of the categories to represent it.

The other risk of data's semiotic function is that we will forget that data do not come into existence on their own. People create them. Stephen Jay Gould's history of the development and use of measurement related to "intelligence," *The Mismeasure of Man*, provides a set of object lessons in the relation between assumptions about the structure of reality, methods of measuring those assumptions, and the interpretation of data to support conclusions that confirm those assumptions. In his deconstruction of arguments central to biological determinism, Gould demonstrates how measurements were designed and executed to "prove" predetermined conclusions about racial, sexual, and class differences. His analysis of the choices scientists made shows the extent to which cultural setting can influence the definition and use of data. He also continually reminds his readers of the fallacy of reification, "our tendency to convert abstract concepts into entities (from the Latin *res*, or thing)." His explanation of how we reify intelligence into a unitary thing summarizes the problem of believing that the concepts we create have an existence outside of our conceptual models of them: "We recognize the importance of mentality in our lives and wish to characterize it, in part so that we can make the divisions and distinctions among people that our culture and political systems dictate. We therefore give the word 'intelligence' to this wondrously complex and multifaceted set of human capabilities. This shorthand symbol is then reified and intelligence achieves its dubious status as a unitary thing" (Gould, 1996, p. 56).

Gould's analysis serves as an additional warning against the assumptions that data are simply "out there," in an understandable form, waiting to be used, and that data represent reality in a true, direct, and unproblematic way. In emphasizing these characteristics of data—that data are constructed based on choices that we make about how to represent reality—I am not saying data are not meaningful or useful. In fact, I am asserting just the opposite. They are very useful, provided one understands what they are intended to represent and how they effect their representation. If data consumers do not have this understanding, they risk misinterpreting and thereby misusing data. These assumptions can also be obstacles to the work of explicitly defining assumptions about data and, through them, expectations related to the quality, as well as the qualities, of data.

Data as Facts

With a general notion of data as pieces of information, it is worth taking a closer look at what is most often implied by the term *data* when we associate it with *facts*. The concept of a *fact* implies both truth and objectivity. A fact is a piece of information that is "indisputably the case," and that is "the truth about events *as opposed to an interpretation*" (emphasis added). Facts usually come to us in full sentences, assertions that contain the context of the fact. By itself, "July 4, 1776" is not a fact. It becomes one only when it is part of an assertion, such as, "The date recorded on the Declaration of Independence of the United States is July 4, 1776." Sometimes it appears that facts do not require interpretation. But that is largely because we already know the conventions through which they are presented to us. Still, there are limits. While most Americans understand 7/4/1776 to mean July 4, 1776, in many other parts of the world, 7/4/1776 signifies April 7, 1776.

Data often comes to us in small pieces—numbers in fields in a database, for example. In order to understand a piece of data, even a "fact" like a date, we need to understand its context, part of which consists of the conventions supporting its representation—for example, its structure (in the example, the sentence containing the assertion) and context (the association of a specific date with an event). In a database, metadata ("data about data," defined more fully in Chapter 3 on Data Management) provides much of this context. Metadata explains how data represents the world. Of particular importance is metadata describing the data model that conveys meaning through its own conventions, structuring data into tables and columns and defining data elements in relation to each other.

Data as a Product

Many data quality practices are rooted in quality control and assurance practices developed for manufacturing.[9] These are based on the idea that data should be treated as a product of the business

---

[9]MIT established its TDQM (Total Data Quality Management) program in the late 1980s based on the concept of Total Quality Management. English (1999), Redman (1996), Loshin (2001), and McGilvray (2008) all participate in this tradition.

processes that create it. As we will discuss in more detail in Section Five, managing data like a product means managing its overall life cycle. It includes understanding and documenting the processes that produce it (through process flows and information product maps), measuring it against specifications, and addressing data quality issues at their root causes.

The need to treat data as a product is driven also by the alternative: If data is not treated as a product, it is treated as a by-product. A *by-product* is "an incidental or secondary product made in the manufacture or synthesis of something else … a secondary result, unintended but inevitably produced in doing something or producing something else" (*NOAD*). By-products are not managed in the same way as products. Managing data as a product focuses on the data and its life cycle. Managing data as a by-product means managing the systems in which data resides, not managing the data (Lee, Pipino, Funk, & Wang, 2006).

One consequence of describing data as a product is that we adopt other terms from manufacturing to understand other aspects of data management (data producers, data consumers, and the like, as will be discussed in Chapter 2). Another consequence is that quality of data is defined by two related factors: how well it meets the expectations of data consumers and how well it is able to serve the purposes of its intended use or uses. Both ideas are rooted in manufacturing quality. Thomas Redman's description of data quality addresses both factors by focusing on customer needs: One data collection is of higher or better quality than another if it meets customer needs better. He recognizes that this formulation is inherently subjective and that customers "are the final arbiters of quality" (Redman, 1996, p. 19). Larry English also focuses on customer perceptions of quality when he asserts that information quality means "consistently meeting knowledge worker and end-customer expectations," (1999, p. 24). He then takes the concept of intended purpose to its logical extreme. "Quality is *not* fitness for purpose. …Quality is fitness for *all* purposes made of the data, including the likely future uses" (English, 1999, p. 16, emphasis in original).

Given my definition of *data* (Data are abstract representations of selected characteristics of real-world objects, events, and concepts, expressed and understood through explicitly definable conventions related to their meaning, collection, and storage), I question whether this possibility—fitness for *all* purposes—is even desirable. There are many reasons why specific data (in the form of specific information products) may be fit for one purpose and not for another. The key to making decisions about fitness for use is knowing what the data are intended to represent and how they effect their representation.

Data as Input to Analyses

The purposes for which data need to be fit can vary. In science, data are needed to build knowledge, test hypotheses, and advance ideas. In business, data are used to make decisions, characterize outcomes, and inform stakeholders. Scientists, businesses, and individuals use data to solve problems. Each of these data uses depends on an assumption or an assessment of whether the data are appropriate to the purpose of the analysis. In many cases, the uses to which data are put themselves produce more data. If the input data are not appropriate, then the data produced through the analysis will be questionable. Our understanding of data quality is complicated by the idea that the same data can be both product and raw material and that, in either case, data quality depends in part on *how* data represent objects, events, and concepts. These complications remind us that using data requires knowledge of data's origins as well as data's current condition.

Data and Expectations

What we understand data to be has a direct bearing on how we assess its quality, especially when we make assertions such as, "Data quality is determined by customer expectations." To *expect* something is to regard it as likely to happen, or likely to do or be something; an *expectation* is "a strong belief that something will happen or be the case in the future" (*NOAD*). When we refer to expectations related to data quality, we mean a set of assumptions related to the condition of the data. Expectations may be based on very little knowledge of the data (sometimes, mere hope for its existence), or they may derive from a thorough understanding of data content, structure, and limitations. Expectations are usually connected to intended uses of data. But even these intentions can vary from the germ of an idea to a fully planned system. Expectations can also be connected to what the data are supposed to represent regardless of how they will be used. Expectations may be well articulated and even documented (for example, a simple data definition may imply a set of expectations), or they may not have even been identified. In short, the concept of expectations is broad and amorphous. People are not always aware of their expectations; sometimes people identify them only when they are not met.

Further, expectations are intertwined with *requirements* (things or actions that are necessary to fulfill a purpose) and *standards* (acknowledged measures of comparison for quantitative or qualitative values, criteria). We will discuss requirements in more detail in Chapter 10. Here we will take a moment to explore the relation between standards and expectations. A *standard* is something "considered by an authority or by general consent as a basis of comparison, an approved model" (*NOAD*). Or it is a rule or principle that is used as a basis for judgment. Standards embody expectations in a formal manner. To *standardize* something means "to cause it to conform to a standard; or to choose or establish a standard for something" (*NOAD*). In manufacturing, we associate standards with tolerances for variation from a specification. A *tolerance* refers to "an allowable amount of variation of a specified quantity, especially in the dimensions of a machine or part"—for example, a tolerance of one one-thousandth of an inch (*NOAD*). *Data Standards* are assertions about how data should be created, presented, transformed, or conformed for purposes of consistency in presentation and meaning and to enable more efficient use. Data standards can be defined as the value (column) or structure (table) or database levels. They have an impact on technical processing and storage of data, as well as on data consumer access to and use of data. *Data quality standards* are assertions about the expected condition of the data that relate directly to quality dimensions: how complete the data is, how well it conforms to defined rules for validity, integrity, and consistency, as well as how it adheres to defined expectations for presentation. In other words, standards often pertain directly to the conventions of representation that we expect data to follow.

General data standards and data quality standards address common situations. They are put in place largely to ensure a consistent approach to common problems (e.g., defaulting, use of the NULL or empty value in a data field, criteria for establishing data types, naming conventions, processes for maintaining historical data). Standards for a given system must be cohesive; they should not contradict each other. They should also be enforceable and measurable. They should be understood using similar criteria for measurement. Standards differ from requirements. They generally apply to how requirements are met, rather than being requirements themselves.[10] That said, some requirements

---

[10]Thanks to Bill Franzen for input on the concept of data standards formulated here.

may be expressed in terms of standards. For example, a national standard for performance within the health care system is the Healthcare Effectiveness Data and Information Set (HEDIS), developed by the National Committee for Quality Assurance (NCQA).[11] The need to meet HEDIS requirements measures can drive a set of requirements related to the content and storage of health care data.

Information

Often the concept of *data* is contrasted with the term *information*.[12] The two concepts are usually presented as points along the continuum or as parts of a pyramid (the knowledge pyramid or Data Information Knowledge Wisdom or DIKW hierarchy) that is used as a model for people's relationship to how they understand what they know. Data is the base; information and knowledge comprise the middle sections; and wisdom is the pinnacle of this pyramid. Data are also seen as providing the raw material—simple facts—for the information product[13] or the building blocks for information. Within such a paradigm, data are of little use in and of themselves and need to be converted to information. Thus, information is data endowed with purpose. Thomas Davenport and Laurence Prusak assert, "[T]here is no inherent meaning in data. …Unlike data, information has meaning. …Not only does it potentially shape the receiver, it has a shape: it is organized to some purpose. Data becomes information when its creator adds meaning. We transform data into information by adding value in various ways" (1998, p. 4).

While experts in knowledge management make a strong distinction between data and information, the dictionary does not. The first definition of *information* is very similar to that of data: "facts provided or learned about something or someone" (*NOAD*). However in its root, the Latin verb *informare*, meaning "shape, fashion, describe" allows us to understand the basis of the perceived difference. Information requires that data be synthesized—formed—to a usable state, for a specific purpose. From there, according to the DIKW model, information leads to knowledge and knowledge leads to wisdom.

The distinction between data and information allows us to comprehend information as something people create and thus something that can be evaluated as useful or not useful, credible or incredible, depending on the circumstances under which it is created. However, the emphasis on information as a product and data as the raw material has at least one implication that can be an obstacle to our understanding data quality. It can be taken to mean that data simply exists out there in the real world as raw material.[14] But that is not the case. Like information, data are products of human thought—they are

---

[11] HEDIS measures the performance and outcomes from a range of health care entities (providers, health care plans, etc.). NCQA provides national benchmark measurements against which any individual entity can measure its performance. A HEDIS audit is a form of assessment that identifies improvement opportunities for medical protocols and practices. These improvements are aimed at both reducing costs and improving outcomes (NCQA.org).

[12] The series of places where data is contrasted with information, including English (1999), Zins (2007), DAMA-BOK (2009, 2).

[13] English (1999): "If data is the raw material, information is a finished product. Information is data in context. Information is usable data. Information is the meaning of data so facts become understandable" (19).

[14] This implication that data simply exist out there is probably a direct result of adopting the DIKW hierarchy from its origins in education, where data were defined as symbols or signs representing stimuli or signals; in this sense, data require a degree of formalization before they can be understood at all. What we most often think of when we use the word "data" today is a set of facts that can be electronically stored and shared. In order to be stored at all, data are already formalized to a large degree—they are the result of asking specific questions or of otherwise meeting requirements for specific pieces of information.

created based on a series of choices about how to represent reality. The process of creating data gives them shape, organization, and purpose.

The DIKW hierarchy is a model of the educational process that is used to describe organizational learning and approaches to knowledge management. The model uses the term *data* as a metaphor for gathering basic information or input into other forms of learning; a primary characteristic of data is that it is not yet synthesized (Allee, 1997, p 110). Peter Drucker's characterization of the relationship between information, data, and knowledge gives a twist to the hierarchy: "Information is data endowed with relevance and purpose. Converting data into information thus requires knowledge" (Drucker, 1991, p. 5). I would argue that the opposite is also true. Converting information from the world into data that can represent that information is a way of compressing knowledge into a usable form. I'll use the example of the thermometer (which we will touch on again in Chapter 3). To develop the thermometer required a significant amount of knowledge and creativity. Once it was created, it became an everyday object, simple to use. One data point, say today's temperature, implies the existence of a whole lot of knowledge. Because we have learned the concept of temperature, we do not need to know its history to use a thermometer. The challenge in many organizations is that people have not learned or do not have access to the meaning of their data. So we need to capture explicit knowledge about data in order to use data effectively. Thomas Stewart refers to explicit knowledge as that which is contained and retained "so that it becomes company property … structural capital … the knowledge that doesn't go home at night" (Stewart, 1999, p.108).

Concluding Thoughts

There have been numerous discussions about the relation of *data* and *information* and where to draw the line between them. (There have been far fewer discussions on the relation between *data* and *knowledge*.) To me, they are variations on the same concept. While data are generally understood as smaller than information, even the question of size is relative. Whether a datum is information or a piece of information itself depends on context in which it is presented or used. One person's data are another person's information. Throughout this book, I will use the term *data* to refer to facts stored in databases and shared electronically and *information* to refer to collections or uses of data. But the focus is on data. The content-focused measurement types in the Data Quality Assessment Framework (DQAF) describe measuring the quality of data—the smallest level of fact that we store and share electronically. The measurement types are cast in terms of databases and the processes used to move and store data. They depend on a data model that defines data elements and the relations between them. In that sense, the framework adopts is a technically oriented perspective on data that recognizes data's formal characteristics, the conventions of data's representation. The DQAF focuses on these characteristics because they are fundamental to other uses of data. It is necessary to have clear expectations about what characteristics of the real world particular data elements represent and to understand the relations between data elements, if we are to have the level of data of the quality needed for more complex purposes.

Data, People, and Systems

2

*"Still a Union that can be maintained by swords and bayonets, and in which strife and civil war
are to take the place of brotherly love and kindness, has no charm for me."*
—General Robert E. Lee (1861)

*Some men enjoy the constant strife
Of days with work and worry rife,
But that is not my dream of life:
I think such men are crazy.*
—James Weldon Johnson, Lazy (1917)

Purpose

This chapter defines a set of roles related to data and data management. Much of the vocabulary of data quality has its origins in quality control processes in the manufacturing sector. The central metaphor of data as a product describes roles related to data in terms similar to those used in manufacturing: *data producer, data consumer, data broker, data steward, data quality program*, and *stakeholder* (Strong, Lee, & Wang, 1997). In many organizations individuals play multiple roles. A person can function as a data producer in one situation and a data consumer in another. As importantly, it is not always people who fill these roles. Because systems also produce and consume data, we will also explore, very briefly, some general considerations about their relation to quality. The chapter will also address questions related to data ownership and the sometimes challenging relationship between people in information technology (IT) roles and those in business (nontechnical) roles.

Enterprise or Organization

Here the terms *enterprise* and *organization* are used interchangeably to refer to businesses or other organizations that produce and use data to accomplish their goals. In today's world, that includes nearly every business, large or small, along with nonprofits, educational institutions, and parts and subparts of the government. I favor the term *organization* as the more generic. *Enterprise* should work better than it sometimes does to signify a comprehensive view of a given organization. But, people often refer to subparts (usually to their own subparts) of an organization when they use the term *enterprise*.

Because data crosses organizational boundaries, improving data quality requires thinking holistically about an enterprise. Doing so can be challenging because many of today's organizations are large and complex.

17

IT and the Business

Most organizations distinguish between technical and nontechnical functions and departments. Information technology (IT) refers to anyone in a technical role (including database administrators, programmers, IT-based business analysts, and managers of information systems). The term *the business* should refer to people who do work directly related to achieving an organization's business goals, as opposed to those in supporting roles, such as working in a department focused on developing or maintaining technical systems. In practice, *the business* is often used as IT-speak for anyone who does not work directly for an IT part of an organization.[1]

The relationship between IT and the business is a source of tension in many organizations, especially in relation to data management. This tension often manifests itself in the definition of data quality, as well as the question of who is responsible for data quality (Klein & Callahan, 2007; Pipino, Lee, & Wang, 2002).

While data is recognized as critical to the success of most organizations and IT is responsible for managing data and the systems that house it, IT is often perceived as (and often perceives itself as) separate from the business. Such an assertion is comparable to seeing the circulatory system as separate from the body. Yes, the circulatory system is a thing in itself, and its parts and pieces can be understood as parts and pieces of itself. But it cannot exist outside the body, and the body cannot exist without it. More importantly, its purpose for existing at all—to keep blood moving through the body—is integral to the body.

The Data Management Association (DAMA) asserts that data management overall should be a shared responsibility (DAMA-BOK, 2009). But many organizations struggle with how to make it one. On the question of data quality, most experts agree that businesspeople (rather than IT people) need to define what constitutes high-quality data. This idea is often phrased in terms of *ownership*, as in "the business should own the data." However, businesspeople need help to improve the quality of data inside the systems where data is stored. IT staff are responsible for those systems. Information systems and the data they contain are integral to running today's organizations. IT exists because organizations require technology to operate. IT needs to see itself in closer relation to the business processes it supports. This relation includes having a better understanding of data content so as to ensure a higher level of data quality.

Philosophically, it seems legitimate to ask, "Isn't IT always part of a larger enterprise? Shouldn't all parts of the enterprise work together for the greater good?" The answer would of course be "Yes." But the relationship between IT and the business is frequently formed along organizational lines that involve decisions about budgets and other resources. Such decisions can be highly political and present obstacles to improving data quality. In *Data Driven*, Thomas Redman identifies 12 barriers to effective management of data and information assets. Among these barriers are the politics of data sharing and data ownership, the misalignment of management and data flow, and commingling the management of data and information with that of technology (Redman, 2009, p. 161).[2]

---

[1] As a side note: The line between IT and the business is blurry at best. My own role as data quality architect is an example. I report through an IT organization. People whom I see clearly as businesspeople perceive me as "technical." However, more directly technical people within my own reporting structure see me as *the business*. Even within technical and nontechnical roles, additional distinctions arise—for example, between *data people* and *other people*.

[2] Redman (2009) Chapter Seven.

The practicality of measuring also needs to be taken into account. While expectations about data should come from data consumers, it is sometimes difficult for consumers to articulate these expectations in terms that lend themselves to establishing measures. This difficulty sometimes results in the assertion that IT should not or cannot measure the quality of data. Dr. Matthew West observes that "[W]hat distinguishes information from other products is that there are certain properties that determine its quality that are independent of what the data is about" (West, 2003, p. 6). Among those he identifies are accuracy, timeliness, completeness, and consistency. He further asserts, "[E]verything we do in IT and information management is about delivering information quality" (West, 2003, p. 7), emphasizing the fact that data producers share with their data consumers the responsibility for understanding the quality of their products. In the case of dimensions of data quality that rely on data processing, IT is far more capable of measuring than are data consumers. In such cases, it is important that data consumers understand why the measures are in place so that they have a basis for confidence in the data. But it is equally important that IT take responsibility for data stewardship during the production process.

References to *IT* and *the business* in this book will distinguish between people in technical roles and those in notechnical roles. Improving data quality requires both technical and business expertise. The most relevant question is not, "Who is responsible for data quality, IT or the business?" It is "In what ways does the business contribute to improving data quality, and in what ways does IT contribute?"

The terms defined below—*data producer, data consumer, data broker*—are intended to describe different relationships to data. In this sense, they point to functions that cross departmental lines and they are best understood within a data chain or information life cycle. A data consumer in relation to one dataset may be viewed as a data producer in relation to another dataset.

Data Producers

Data producers are people and systems that create data. Data producers may create data expressly for the purpose of making data available for use or they may generate data as a by-product of another process. Although producers have control over what they create, they do not have control over the uses to which their data may be put. They may create data for one purpose that is subsequently used for other purposes.

A critical subset of data producers are business owners of processes that create data. Whether data is consumed immediately or fed to downstream processes, business process owners are critical links in the information chain. They have knowledge of the purposes and functions of processes they own. They can modify processes to ensure they produce data that better meets the needs of data consumers.

Data Consumers

Data consumers are people and systems that use data at any point in the information life cycle. I dislike the term *data consumer* because it seems to ignore an important characteristic of data, namely, that data is not actually "consumed" through use the way that other assets are. Multiple people or systems can consume the same dataset without preventing the others from doing so. However, the term well works in relation to the idea of an information life cycle in which data is created by data producers and used (applied) by data consumers. I prefer *data consumer* to the alternative terms *user, end user*, and *customer*. Confusion can arise between references to data customers and an organization's other customers. I have not adopted the term *knowledge worker* as a general term because knowledge workers are only one subset of data consumers (not all people who consume data are knowledge workers) and because the concept of *data consumers* includes both people and systems.

Data Brokers[3]

The concept of a *data broker* is sometimes overlooked in the producer/consumer paradigm. *Data brokers* are middlemen in data management. They do not produce data, but they enable others to consume it. They are similar to distributors of manufactured goods. It is important to recognize brokers because they are part of the information chain and can influence data content and the formal structure of data, as well as its availability and timeliness, and thus its quality.

Data Stewards and Data Stewardship

The term *stewardship* is defined as "the management or care of another person's property" (*NOAD*). *Data stewards* are individuals who are responsible for the care and management of data. Although they are essentially synonyms, the term *data steward* is preferable to *data custodian* since for many people the term *custodian* is synonymous with *janitor*, rather than simply meaning someone who looks after something. Ideally, stewardship implies an engaged role—the "management or care" part of the term. Good stewardship involves an understanding of data content, as well as of the role, uses, and value of data in an organization. Stewards should understand data, help others understand and use it, and support improvement of the condition of the data.

DAMA defines stewardship as a purely business role. While data management professionals are "curators and technical custodians of data assets ... data stewardship is the assigned accountability for business responsibilities in data management" (DAMA, 2009, p. 5). There is little benefit in drawing a line between business *stewards* and IT *custodians* or *curators*. IT has a stewardship role. This role includes pure data management functions, such as database administration, but it also carries with it an obligation to have at least a working understanding of data content and uses. One of the reasons the DQAF was developed was to help articulate specifics related to IT's stewardship role.

All of that said, one wishes there were another word for this role of care and management because, unfortunately, the concept of stewardship is not well understood. People don't know exactly how to be good stewards, and most organizations do not empower stewards effectively. Depending on the nature of the enterprise, data stewards almost always have other roles. They may be primarily producers, consumers, or part of a data quality program team. They may be part of a formal data governance structure, or they may simply be good, diligent people trying to make their organization's data more reliable and understandable. Ideally, all people who have a stake in the success of a given

---

[3] Thanks to Jim Locke for the observation on data brokers. Gartner also uses the term *data handlers* to discuss a role associated with ensuring that data remains secure as it is moved between systems and uses.

enterprise should be good stewards of an enterprise's data, just as they should be good stewards of all other assets belonging to an organization, from paper clips, to departmental budgets, to time.

Data Owners

Since stewards look after the property of other people, it is logical to ask about data owners. The concept of a *data owner* is challenging for most organizations. Data is not tangible, and it is not always understood as an asset. When it is recognized as an asset, it is generally recognized as an organizational asset but this perception can end up meaning that no one is taking care of it. Most other organizational assets do not have owners per se. Facilities Administration may be responsible for a physical plant but does not own it. Similarly, the Accounting Department is responsible for the general ledger but does not own it. Assets are owned by the organization itself. The difference between data and other assets is that there is clear accountability for (rather than ownership of) other assets, and it usually resides in one department or function within the organization. In contrast, data moves between departments and functions (Redman, 2008). And while IT clearly is responsible for systems that house data, IT has historically disavowed responsibility for data in those systems.

The desire to identify data *owners* can be seen as the desire for a solution to a problem—specifically, to the fact or perception that an organization's data is not meeting its needs. When people perceive that their organization's data is insufficient, inconsistent, or chaotic, they look for an owner to bring data under better control. Like other organizational assets, data needs to be managed. Management includes knowing what data an organization has, using data to advance the goals of the organization, and minimizing any risks associated with data use. Data can be difficult to manage because it is not only intangible but also very easy to reproduce, and because many organizations do not define a clear line between managing data and managing the systems in which data reside.

The often conflicted relationship between information technology people and businesspeople makes the boundary between data and systems even fuzzier. Because people can clearly see the costs of IT systems but do not always see the benefits of their organization's data, it can be quite difficult to balance costs and benefits when making decisions about data management. A natural conclusion is this: If only we had a data owner! All our questions would be answered and managing data would be easy. Unfortunately, there is not a simple solution to the complex challenges of data management. However there are effective approaches. One of them is to have clear accountability for data within an organization, throughout the information life cycle. If it is helpful for organizations to name this accountability *data ownership*, then they should.

Data Ownership and Data Governance

Gwen Thomas of the Data Governance Institute points out that the goals of data governance include enabling better decision making, reducing operational friction, and protecting the needs of data stakeholders—all things aimed at improving the overall performance of an enterprise. Data governance should also contribute to operational efficiencies by enabling repeatable processes, common approaches, and coordination of efforts—in other words, by simplifying what the organization has to do (Thomas, 2011). Data governance should work a lot like other forms of governance. But with regard to data management and data governance, most organizations are still in the political theory stage. There is not always agreement on how to implement governance concepts, and some people are afraid of their implications. Instead of perceiving data governance as a way to mitigate risk, people often reacted to it as another form of risk. When it is mandated from the top without an assessment of existing practices, governance can look like a set of outsiders imposing an unrealistic model on processes that may be working pretty well to meet local goals and may even be able to contribute to enterprisewide strategies, if there were some effort at alignment. When data governance is imposed, it foregoes the opportunity to gain the commitment of employees and can breed distrust because it is not clear who will benefit from it, who will pay for it, or what the new regime will look like.[4]

In other words, data governance can incite a power struggle. As Thomas Redman points out, "Data and information give rise to heated passions and brutal politics. …Veterans know that it is not the hard, technical issues that stymie an organization's efforts to better manage and utilize its data and information assets, but rather the soft organizational, political and social issues" (Redman, 2008, pp. 159–160).

IT, the Business, and Data Owners, Redux

Redman's observation brings us back to the question of the relation between IT and the business: At a fundamental level, data governance efforts try to mediate this relationship. Mediation is not a simple thing, because both the business and IT are complex entities—organizations performing and coordinating multiple functions that should be aligned to common goals, but often are not, and are always competing for limited resources (which means data governance also needs to mediate between different parts of the business, as well as between business and IT). Data ownership becomes a point of contention because different stakeholders have different goals related to data and therefore different ways of controlling and making decisions about data. David Loshin summarizes factors that complicate discussions of data ownership in his discussion of different concepts of data value, the relation of data and privacy, turf wars, fear, and bureaucracy (Loshin, 2001, pp. 28–30).

Loshin also provides a logical and common-sense approach to data ownership by breaking the question down into manageable parts and allowing us to see how the pieces relate to each other. He recognizes that the question of ownership "is essentially a control issue—control of the flow of information, the cost of information, and the value of information" (Loshin, 2001, p. 28). He outlines the different roles people play in the creation of information. "Actors in the information factory" include data suppliers, acquirers, creators, processors, packagers, delivery agents, consumers, and different levels of management who ensure people are doing their jobs, systems are working, and decisions support the organization's overall goals and strategy (p. 26). He then details the responsibilities of data ownership. These include defining data, securing data, enabling access, supporting the end-user community, packaging data, maintaining it, measuring data quality, and managing business rules, metadata, and standards, as well as managing data suppliers (pp. 31–33).

Given these roles and responsibilities, Loshin describes different paradigms for ownership itself. Each paradigm is based on the ways value is associated with or derived from information. Data can

---

[4]This risk of data governance is one reason why I like Robert Seiner's "nonintrusive" approach.

be owned by its creator, consumer, complier, enterprise, funding organization, decoder, packager, reader, subject, purchaser/licenser, or everyone is the owner. What Loshin's model recognizes is the reality of a set of different relationships to data, each of which includes some degree of control, decision-making responsibility, or other authority over data. Without using the word *governance*, he recommends creating a data ownership policy that articulates the different relationships, clarifies responsibilities, and provides criteria for settling disputes among stakeholders (pp. 38–40). His approach makes so much sense that it is surprising that organizations are still fighting the battle of ownership. But as noted, many organizations are still in the political theory stage of data governance. Turf, fear, and bureaucracy continue to trump common sense.

It is a simplification, but generally true, that businesspeople desire "ownership" of data because they benefit from controlling data. But if they do not "own" the systems that process and house the data, then they do not feel a sense of control over data. IT people disown data ownership because they do not control data content and do not want to be held accountable if data content does not meet business needs. At the same time, they are responsible for the systems that process and house the data, and, by virtue of this fact, IT has a significant amount of control over the data in any given system, as well as the movement of data between systems. And this horizontal movement of data makes data ownership even more slippery. As data moves along the data chain, it can be copied and transformed into another dataset, potentially "owned," that is controlled by a system other than by its originating system or by a team other than the team originally responsible for it (Redman, 1996, p. 235). The questions of ownership and governance break down into two interrelated concerns: control and decision making. One of the benefits of data quality measurement is that it provides a particular kind of knowledge about data that allows an organization to understand whether or not their data is under control. Data that is under control is more likely to be trusted and less likely to be the object of political struggle.

Data Quality Program Team[5]

The term *data quality program team* (abbreviated as *DQ team*) refers to people formally charged with data quality activities. Data quality activities include data assessment and measurement, data quality issue management, and a range of strategic and tactical activities that drive improvement of the data and contribute to the creation of an organizational culture directed at producing high-quality data. In this sense, DQ team members always play a stewardship role, but not all data stewards are part of the DQ team. In a best case, DQ program team members are focused on implementing data quality strategy, either directly as hands-on analysts or indirectly as propagators of and subject matter experts in the data quality methodology. Not all organizations will have a data quality program, and not all teams working toward these goals will have the words *data quality* in their names. However, in order to make significant headway on data quality management, it is better to have individuals assigned to lead these efforts.[6]

---

[5] Redman (1994) uses the term *data keeper* to refer to people "responsible for implementing several data quality functions common to a given database. For example, the data keeper should manage and administer edits" (p. 292).
[6] See Pierce (2003), Redman (1994, 2007), English (2008), and Yonke, Walenta, and Talburt (2011).

Stakeholder

The term *stakeholder* refers to the collection of people, teams, and roles that are affected by the quality of an organization's data. Stakeholders include all the people mentioned here: direct and indirect data producers, consumers, brokers, and stewards, from both business and technical teams, data quality program team members, along with company management and owners. As should be clear from the preceding discussion, stakeholders have a wide range of relationships to data. When stakeholders are interacting with each other, especially when they are making decisions about data, they should know each other's roles and understand each other's perspectives.

Systems and System Design

As noted earlier, systems also produce and consume data. *The New Oxford American Dictionary* defines *system* as "a set of interconnected things or parts forming a complex whole." More abstractly, a *system* is "a set of principles or procedures according to which something is done; an organized scheme or method" (*NOAD*). Quality pioneer W. Edwards Deming defined a system as "a network of interdependent components that work together to try to accomplish the aim of the system. A system must have an aim. Without an aim, there is no system. The aim of the system must be clear to everyone in the system" (1994, p. 50). Deming's formulation emphasizes that systems must be purposeful. If they are not, they are just a collection of components.

Technical systems are created to meet particular purposes, sometimes referred to as applications of the system. Any human-created system is based on a set of assumptions that can be called its *model*—a paradigm of what the system is supposed to do and how it is supposed to do it (Weinberg, 2001). As we will discuss in Chapter 3, models are always simplifications, and therefore depending on a system presents the risk that it may be missing something. Part of a system's success depends on how well thought out it is; if it does not have a robust and detailed model that accounts for the ways it will be applied, the system may fail to meet its aims.

Kristo Ivanov, in his 1972 discussion on information quality, addresses challenges caused by inadequate models of systems. He points out the need for correspondence and alignment between the system and the world it interacts with (that is between the objects in the real world for which a system must account and the way in which the system accounts for them). When these are not aligned in an information system, it is often more challenging to change the system than to "force reality to fit the model" (Ivanov, 1972, p. 3.9). Consequently, people responsible for entering information into the system will work around the limitations of the system in order to keep work moving. Work-arounds cause the information in the system to be out of alignment with the objects, events, and concepts it is supposed to represent.

Other inadequacies of a system model can cause the creation of poor quality information. Ivanov asks whether the information created by such work-arounds is inaccurate because of the people who enter it or because of the system that does not allow them to account for it in any other way. He recognizes that even an apparently simple question (What is the true value?) cannot be answered outside of the context of the definitions within a specific system (Ivanov, 1972, p. 4.23). His point is that poor system design—an inadequate model—can contribute to low-quality information as much as human factors such as data entry errors do. He goes so far as to say that the quality of information expressed in error rates "may be an important indicator of the adequacy of system design or of the model. Up to now, it has been regarded as an indicator mainly of the coding [data entry] and observation process itself" (Ivanov, 1972, p. 3.13). Ivanov's ideas are more fully summarized on the companion website. For now, I want to emphasize his basic observation: System adequacy directly affects data quality. A system may be inadequate in its aims (the aims of the system and the aims of the organization may be misaligned) or in its functions (functionality may be missing or formally incorrect).

Concluding Thoughts

Living in the Information Age, we can all agree that electronic data is critical to the work of most organizations, yet we still struggle to meet the goal of producing high-quality data. The Business/IT divide makes it hard to build systems that handle data in a manner that meets evolving business needs. But if we are better able to articulate and document expectations about data, and we have a shared purpose to produce higher quality data, then we can make organizational decisions that contribute to the production of higher quality data. As is the case with other products, we should be able to build quality into the systems that produce and collect, process, store, and make data available for use.

Business and technical teams have a shared responsibility for data quality, and that data quality measurement provides a means through which they can successfully fulfill this responsibility. They have a shared responsibility simply because both are part of the same organization and, more importantly, because for most enterprises, organizational success depends on high-quality data. Achieving a level of cooperation is not easy, and it will not follow the same model in every organization. But just as in the creation of any model, organizations need to make conscious decisions about how they formulate the relationship between their constituent parts.

Data Management, Models, and Metadata

"Management of many is the same as management of few. It is a matter of organization."
—Sun Tzu, *The Art of War* (6th century BC)

Purpose

This chapter presents a set of concepts related to data management in order to ensure a common understanding of these terms throughout the book. It includes discussion of *data management* itself, along with the various kinds of data assets that require management. Data management implies the need for particular kinds of knowledge about data: what data represents, how much of it there is in an organization, how it is organized and maintained, where it resides, who uses it and the like. The chapter includes an extended discussion on data models and on metadata, as these have a direct bearing on both data management and data quality.

Data Management

The New Oxford American Dictionary defines *management* as "the process of dealing with or controlling … [and] having responsibility for." But management goes beyond "dealing with." To be successful, management must be a purposeful activity. It includes knowing what resources exist for meeting specific goals, organizing those resources, and planning and executing activities to meet those goals. (See the discussion later in this chapter on the Data Chain and Information Life Cycle.) Measurement is critical to all these functions of management, ranging from understanding what resources you have to work with to determining how successful the work has been (the degree to which goals have been met).

The Data Management Association (DAMA) defines data management as "the business function that develops and executes plans, policies, practices, and projects that acquire, control, protect, deliver, and enhance the value of data" (DAMA, 2011, p. 78). DAMA advocates that data management be a shared responsibility between data management professionals within information technology departments and business data stewards (DAMA-BOK, 2009, p. 5). Data management responsibilities are wide-ranging. They include everything from traditional data administration to data architecture, metadata and reference data management, security management, data warehousing, operational management, data security, and data governance. From the DAMA perspective, data quality management is a function within the overall scope of data management.

Although DAMA advocates a shared responsibility between businesspeople and information technology people, the definition still recognizes that there are "data management professionals" and that most of these are in IT departments. By recognizing the need to engage businesspeople in data management, the definition points to the struggle many organizations experience in trying to "manage" data. Discussions of data management often focus on the "data" rather than the "management" part of it.

Although the goal of data management may be to "enhance the value of data," data management is not an end in itself. It always takes place within a wider organization. Tony Fisher defines data management as "a consistent methodology that ensures the deployment of timely and trusted data across the organization" (Fisher, 2009, p. xvi). The goal of delivering data and information assets is to enable the use of data to bring value to an organization. Like other aspects of data management, data quality management requires measurement. It is important to assess the condition of data when you start a data quality program and to have a means of measuring improvement to judge the success of the program.

Database, Data Warehouse, Data Asset, Dataset

The term *database* was coined in the early 1960s "to capture the sense that the information stored within a computer could be conceptualized, structured, and manipulated independently of the specific machine on which it resided" (Committee on Innovations in Computing and Communications, 1999). The dictionary defines a *database* as "a structured set of data that is held in a computer, especially one that is accessible in various ways" (*NOAD*). Databases can be of various sizes. In the 1960s and 1970s, large databases were generally referred to as *data banks*.

A *data warehouse* is a large database or a collection of databases: "a large store of data accumulated from a wide range of sources within a company and used to guide management decisions." Warehouses became commercially viable in the 1980s, based largely on the concept of the relational database (as formulated by British computer scientist Edgar F. Codd in 1970). They changed the way that we store and access data.

Warehouses not only "accumulate" data; most also integrate data from different sources. Most contain data from a wide range of subject areas or data domains (e.g., customer, product, sales). From a technical perspective, the definition of data warehouse can be expanded upon. Warehouse data can be structured according to different meta models (star schemas, hierarchies, fact/dimension) that demand differing degrees of normalization. In all cases, data is understood in terms of tables and columns. The warehouse's data model provides a concise visual representation of data content of a warehouse.

The term *data asset* focuses on the value data brings to an organization, rather than on the form in which data is stored. Section 1.1 of the DAMA Body of Knowledge (DAMA-BOK) recognizes that "assets are resources with recognized value under the control of an individual or organization." Assets help organizations achieve their goals. Data is widely recognized as an enterprise asset. Organizations that used to produce data as a by-product of their work now see data as something they can consume to improve their operational effectiveness (Fisher, 2009. p 4).

While DAMA is clearly focusing on data *as an asset*, the term *data asset* is often used to refer to any system that contains data and is managed to ensure effective use of that data. Data assets are differentiated from other systems that may produce data but that do not store data and make it available for analysis and decision making. Even in this usage of the term, however, data is seen as separable from the system that houses it. Data can be moved from one data asset to another, and it remains the same data. (Of course, data movement is not as simple as such an assertion implies. As it moves between systems, data is changed both by the technical requirements of the target system and the business requirements driving its movement).

In this book, the general term *database* is used to refer to any collection of structured data and *data warehouse* to refer to a large database organized into data domains whose data content is defined by a data model. As originally developed, the Data Quality Assessment Framework (DQAF) measures were focused on data warehouse content. However, they can be applied to all databases and potentially to other applications as well. The term *data asset* is used to stress the data content itself and the value it can bring to an organization.

Data exists in different forms (files, tables, messages) and in different places (source systems, databases, data warehouses). And it can be measured at different points in the data chain. Many of the DQAF's measurement types are taken in-line as part of data processing. Source data arrives at a database or other application and is processed so that it can be stored in and accessed via database tables. The term *dataset* is a generic way of referring to a collection of data that will be measured.

Source System, Target System, System of Record

Databases are most often target systems. They store data from other sources. In its most general definition, a *Source System* is a transactional system, application, or data store that provides data to another system. Source systems are usually distinguished from *target systems*, those systems that receive data from a source. However, the term *source system* is relative. A system from which data is directly consumed by one functional area may be a source system for another data store.

Most data warehouses contain data from multiple transactional or operational source systems. Transactional systems allow business interactions (transactions) to take place. They perform functions such as establishing records for customers, processing orders, and paying bills. It is generally not the purpose of these systems to store historical data for use in analysis and decision making (although sometimes they do); instead, their function is to enable business transactions to take place.

Databases receive data from multiple sources. Data usually arrives via a complex data chain. It is therefore beneficial to distinguish between different kinds of sources: for example, a *system of origin* (where the data was originally created) and a *direct source system* (the system from which the data warehouse actually receives the data). In between, there may be other systems through which the data has passed. The term *source data* as used here refers to data that has not yet been processed in a data warehouse, and the term *data* (without a qualifier) to refer to data in a database.

A *system of record* is a system that is charged with keeping the most complete or trustworthy representation of a set of entities. Within the practice of master data management, such representations are referred to as *golden records*, and the system of record can also be called the *system of truth*. *Master data management* refers to "control over master data values to enable consistent, shared, contextual use across systems of the most accurate, timely, and relevant version of the truth about essential business entities" (DAMA-BOK, 2009, p. 171).[1] David Loshin's definition of master data objects is very

---

[1] Given my definition of *data* in Chapter 1, I find the terms *golden record* and *system of truth* problematic. All the previous caution about the need for clear definition is redoubled when we start to use this kind of language. However, those concerns are not the subject of this book. These terms have a good deal of currency, especially in discussions of master data.

useful: "Master data objects are those key 'things' that we value the most—things that are logged in our transactional systems, measured and reported on in our reporting systems, and analyzed in our analytical systems ... customers, vendors, suppliers, parts, products, locations, contact mechanisms, profiles, accounting items, contracts, policies" (Loshin, 2011, p. 329).

Data Models

A *data model* is a visual representation of data content and the relationships between data entities and attributes, created for purposes of understanding how data can be (or actually is) organized or structured. Data models include entities (understood as tables), attributes (understood as columns containing characteristics about represented entities), relationships between entities, and integrity rules, along with definitions of all of these pieces.[2] Because data models define data structure and content, they are tools for understanding data content, as well as for enabling the storage and access of data. They contain much of the metadata necessary for data use.

As noted, the term *database* captures the sense that the information stored within a system should be independent of the specific system in which it is housed. The concept of the relational database, described in abstract mathematical terms by Codd in 1970, drives our modern understanding of data structure and modeling.[3] A relation (or table) is made up of tuples (rows) that share the same attributes (columns). Each row represents one instance of an entity (the concept represented by the data).

Relational data is based on set theory, which can be used to describe the rules for how datasets and subsets can interact with each other. Depictions of these rules are included in relational data models. Not all data is organized relationally. However, the concept of data stored in tables, where columns represent attributes or characteristics of the entity represented on the row, provides a means of understanding a wide array of data quality questions. The relational approach (largely) defined data as we now know it. Databases are made up of tables. Often these are organized into *data domains* or *subject areas* containing tables with related content. A table is made up of columns that represent individual characteristics of the concept (entity) represented in the table. Each row represents the detailed characteristics of one instance of the entity represented on the table.

These terms can be somewhat confusing because of how they are used in different contexts. For example, in conceptual modeling, an *entity* is a concept that is being modeled. Because of this use, *entity* is sometimes used as a synonym for *table*. In the process of entity resolution, an *entity* is "a real world person, place, or thing that has a unique identity that distinguishes it from all other entities of the same type" (Talburt, 2011, p. 205). There are specific differences between the meaning of an *attribute* (which represents a characteristic of an entity), a *data element* (which is a component piece of

---

[2]The term *entity* in modeling should not be confused with the concept of entity in the process of entity resolution (ER). In another reminder that data's primary function is representational, John Talburt states, "In the ER context, entities do not exist in the information system—they exist in the real world. ... Information systems store and manipulate references to entities, not the entities" (Talburt, 2010).

[3]One of the significant advantages of Codd's approach is that it removed the burden of navigation from data consumers by allowing the data to be understood independently of the system itself. It opened the door for SQL and other query languages that removed the need for a programmer to access records for less technical people.

a data used to represent an entity), a *field* (which is part of a system used to display or intake data), and a *column* (which is a place in a table to store a defined characteristic of a represented entity, i.e., to store values associated with data elements). There are also differences between *entity* (a thing or concept about which an organization captures information) and *table* (a two-dimensional collection of data consisting of rows in which instances of entities are represented and columns in which characteristics of those entities are associated with data values).[4] I will do my best to use these terms precisely, while keeping in mind that loosely speaking, *attribute*, *data element*, *field*, and *column* are often understood as synonyms.

To create a model of a concept, one needs to define what one instance of the concept looks like—what characteristics need to be associated to understand it as one thing. These choices have implications for the technical implementation of a database as well as the business uses of a dataset. The set of attributes (columns) that define an instance of an entity comprise the table's *primary key*. Attributes that enable tables to join to each other are referred to as *foreign keys*.

Types of Data Models

Different types of data models depict data at different levels of abstraction. *Conceptual data models* present the entities (ideas or logical concepts) that are represented in the database and have little if any detail about attributes. *Logical data models* include detail about attributes (characteristics in columns) needed to represent a concept, such as key structure (the attributes needed to define a unique instance of an entity), and they define details about the relationships within and between data entities. Relationships between entities can be optional or mandatory. They differ in terms of cardinality (one-to-one, one-to-many, many-to-many). *Physical data models* represent the way that data are physically stored in a database. They describe the physical characteristics of data elements that are required to set up and store actual data about the entities represented. In addition to models that differ by levels of abstraction, there can also be models of data consumer-facing views of the data. Technically, a *view* is a dataset generated through a query that produces a virtual table. A more mundane definition is that a view is what a data consumer sees. At its simplest, a view can have exactly the same structure as a physical table. Views can also be used to display a subset of data from a table, to aggregate data within a table, or combine data from multiple tables. As with other data models, models of views enable data consumers to understand how data is organized.

The process of data modeling involves a series of decisions about how to represent concepts and relate them to each other. Data modeling uses tools and conventions of representation that convey meaning in a consistent way, regardless of the content of the data being modeled. Like all forms of representation, data models are limited. They can be articulated to different levels of detail for different purposes. They focus on representing those aspects of the things represented that are important to a particular purpose of the representation (West, 2003).

To understand the implications of purpose and representation in data modeling, let's consider how these choices affect other kinds of modeling. All models are built for particular purposes and must be understood in light of those purposes. A house in a subdivision will be depicted differently in different representations or models built for different purposes. In a street plan for the subdivision, it will be represented as a box on a parcel of land. The purpose of such a plan is to convey information about

---

[4] Definitions formulated based on Hay (2006).

the size and shape of the subdivision and the location of houses and lots to each other. Such a plan might be shared with a town planning commission charged with making decisions about land use or with potential buyers wanting to understand the general characteristics of a neighborhood. In architectural drawings, the house will be depicted in a set of views showing the size, shape, and details of its structure. The purpose of an architectural drawing is to enable people to see what the house would look like and to make decisions about how it will be built. The accompanying floor plan, another model of the house, contributes to the process of understanding the size and shape of the house and is also necessary input to building the house. It contains details such as room sizes, the number of windows and doors, and the like that will influence the construction of the house. None of these models is the house itself, but all of them depict the house. Each represents a subset of characteristics important to the purpose of the representation. The same idea applies to data models.

When working with data models, it is important to recognize that there is not one-and-only-one way to model any given dataset. Put this way, models present a kind of chicken-and-egg problem: Do data define models, or do models define data? The answer is both. To be understandable at all, data require context and structure. Data models provide a means of understanding this context. In doing so, they also create context. If data stakeholders find that models are understandable representations of data, then they can become a primary means of defining data.

For most databases, especially data warehouses, models are critical to data management. The conceptual and logical models allow data managers to know what data resides in the data asset. The physical model has a direct bearing on how data is moved within the database, as well as how it is accessed.

Physical Characteristics of Data

Physical characteristics of data include data type, format, field length, and key constraints. While data itself is intangible, data is captured and stored in particular forms (data values with meaningful formats; data fields of defined sizes), in relation to other pieces of data (data models, fields in an application), and these days largely through systems (databases and applications) designed to perform particular functions. Data is embedded in these systems. The way the system is set up will establish a set of requirements for how data is formatted, how keys must be defined, and how datasets can be maintained. Its expression can change as it moves from system to system or from use to use, but data always has some shape and that shape can be understood in relation to the system in which it exists. The quality of data depends to a large extent on how it is presented in these systems and how well people are able to understand the context and conventions of its presentation. To understand the significance of the presentation of data, we need to understand the systems in which it is captured and stored and from which it is accessed. Data quality measurement also depends on these things.

Metadata

Metadata is usually defined as "data about data," but it would be better defined as explicit knowledge documented to enable a common understanding of an organization's data. Ideally, metadata describes what data is intended to represent (definition of terms and business rules), how data effects this representation (conventions of representation, including physical data definition [format, field sizes, data types, etc.], system design and system processing), the limits of that representation (what the data does not represent), what happens to the data in systems (provenance, lineage, data chain, and information life-cycle events), how data is used, and how it can be used.[5] Metadata is a general category. Like other structured data, metadata contains data elements that are governed by conventions of representation. Standard database metadata includes table and column names and definitions, data types and lengths of specific columns, and rules governing data relationships (mandatory vs. optional) and their cardinality (one-to-one, one-to-many, many-to-many).

Business terms are often identified as metadata, but there is a difference between definitions of business terms and definitions of data elements. The difference is rooted in the relation between data and what it represents. Business concepts need to be defined in order for business to be conducted. They can be instantiated in data in different ways. Take the concept of a person's name. Each of us has a name, and common sense allows us to understand what another person's name is. But when we try to break a name down into data elements, we can bump into challenges in definition. One step in transforming the concept of a name into data elements is to try to determine how many data elements are needed. In most cultures, people's names have (at least) two component pieces: a "given name" (or "first name") and a "family name" (or "last name"), both of which convey different meaning. Another step in transforming a concept into data elements is to name them appropriately. In some parts of the world, what Westerners think of as "first name" does not come first when people refer to themselves. Definitions of data elements must describe not only the concept being represented but also the way in which the concept is represented, synonyms for the concept, and so forth.

The National Information Standards Organization (NISO) describes metadata as "structured information that describes, explains, locates, or otherwise makes it easier to retrieve, use, or manage an information resource" (NISO 2007). Writing largely for library sciences, NISO defines three types of metadata: descriptive, structural, and administrative. Descriptive metadata enables an information resource to be identified; structural metadata describes a resource's features; and administrative metadata is used to manage the life cycle of and access to information resources. NISO's types align with data warehousing categories of business, technical, and operational metadata. Business metadata describes data content. Technical metadata describes its structural features. Operational metadata enables understanding of the movement of data within a system and is necessary for management of the information lifecycle (Zhu, et. al, 2011).

Because metadata can be thought of in terms of what it represents, or where it comes from, or who uses it, it can be organized and stored in different ways. It is easy to get caught up in questions of metadata definition and categorization. (It is almost impossible not to.) However, it is more important to ensure that necessary metadata is available in a usable form.

Metadata is critical to data management, data use, and data quality. Without it, an organization will not know what data it possesses. Still, many organizations function with inadequate metadata. They are able to do so because knowledgeable individuals are able to help novices navigate through systems. While tacit knowledge is part of organizational success, the lack of explicit, structured, accessible information related to data and the systems that store it poses significant risks to organizations. The idea that data must be understood is another way of saying that you need a foundation of useful, usable metadata to use data at all. An organization that does not know its own data is at risk of misusing that data. Such

---

[5] Kimball (1998) defines metadata as "all of the information in the data warehouse environment that is not the actual data itself" (p. 22). He later describes "back room metadata" as largely process-related and "front room metadata" that is largely descriptive (p. 435). Of course, the sets overlap.

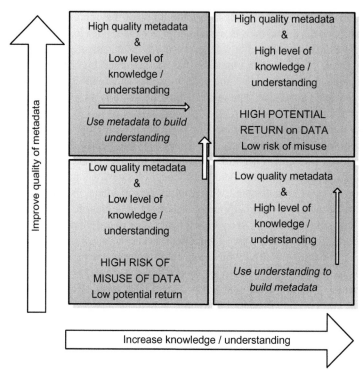

FIGURE 3.1 Metadata, Risk, and Return on Investment in Data

Metadata is explicit knowledge documented to enable a common understanding of an organization's data. Robust metadata reduces the risks associated with data use. Without it, organizations depend on the tacit knowledge of individuals. Inadequate metadata diminishes an organization's ability to benefit from its data. Improving the quality of metadata and the level of organizational understanding of its data will create optimal conditions for gaining value from organizational data.

an organization also risks underutilizing its data by missing opportunities to gain advantages from its data. Metadata itself does not remove these risks. People still must use and understand metadata to make better decisions when they select data for specific purposes. Nor does metadata remove the need for data analysis, such as profiling and measurement, which enable characterization of the actual (as opposed to documented) condition of the data. Organizations will get the most out of their data when they have robust metadata, knowledgeable employees, and processes such as in-line measurement and periodic assessment that keep them continually informed about the condition of their data.

Metadata is critical to measuring data quality. It is necessary simply to understand most organizational data, and it is input into the process of defining measurements. Even if it does not contain explicitly formulated expectations, metadata holds foundational information needed to understand common-sense assumptions about data; thus it provides a starting point to defining expectations related to data quality. Dimensions of data quality focus on measuring data's representational effectiveness (how well people understand what it represents), characteristics of its presentation, and its suitability for particular purposes. The better defined each of these is, the clearer the expectations about data and therefore, the clearer the criteria for measurement.

	LOW DATA KNOWLEDGE	HIGH DATA KNOWLEDGE
CLEAR EXPECTATIONS	Consumers in this quadrant know what they want, but do not know the data well enough to know whether it will meet their needs. When they identify an issue, there is a medium risk of a problem requiring technical changes or that a business-related change has unexpectedly changed the data.	Consumers in this quadrant know the data very well and they have clear requirements for use. When they identify a data issues, there is high likelihood that something is wrong with the data – could be caused by technical or business-related changes
UNCLEAR EXPECTATIONS	Consumers in this quadrant are under-prepared to use data effectively; they need training in business uses of the data and on data structure. When they identify a data issues, there is a low risk that something is actually wrong with the data and a high Risk that the problem is based in a misunderstanding of the data.	Consumers in this quadrant know the data but need to clarify intentions for use to see if the data will meet those needs. When they identify a problem, there is a medium risk of a problem requiring technical changes or that a business-related change has unexpectedly changed the data.

FIGURE 3.2 Knowledge, Expectations, Risks

The need for robust metadata is directly related to its function as explicit knowledge. A data issue is any condition of the data that is an obstacle to a data consumer's use of the data, regardless of its origin. Some issues originate from the data consumer's assumptions about the data. The combination of high data knowledge and clear expectations can help to identify flaws and gaps in data and programming.

Data is valuable because of what people can learn from it and how they can use it. Its value depends largely on how successful people are in applying it for particular purposes, sometimes multiple purposes. Inherently, this means how well-suited it is to those purposes. Practically, it means how understandable it is to data consumers. The more knowledgeable data consumers are about what data represents and the conventions of its representation and the better they understand the systems in which data is captured, stored, and used, the better able they will be to interpret data and to make decisions about which data to use (see Figure 3.1 and Figure 3.2).

Metadata as Explicit Knowledge

Discussions of knowledge management distinguish between *tacit knowledge* and *explicit knowledge*. *Tacit knowledge* is the knowledge that is inside people's heads. It is informal and often includes things that people do not know they know. *Explicit knowledge* exists in an objective form. It is written down so that it can be shared. Metadata is explicit knowledge about data.

Because most often we do not question our assumptions about data, we also miss the opportunity to capture what we actually do know about data and the systems that make it available for use. Most of the data we depend on exists in and is made available through technical systems that are complex and perceived as difficult to understand. Sometimes we attribute this difficulty to their inherent complexity or our lack of specific technical knowledge. We shouldn't. People are quite capable of understanding complex systems—if they have the tools and guidance they need to do so. The primary tool for understanding systems is documentation about how they are built and guidance on using them. It is not necessary that everyone know all the details about a given system. But it is reasonable that data consumers have a working understanding of how a given system functions if they are to use it effectively. We would not expect every person who drives a car to know how to fix an engine, but we would expect them to know that there is an engine, that running it requires fuel, and that keeping it in good condition requires a periodic oil change.

Despite the fact that they know data is critical and systems are complex, most organizations do not do a good job of capturing—in writing, for all to see—what they know about data and the systems that store it. Without this explicit knowledge, it becomes harder to use data over time, especially as business needs evolve and expectations change. Throughout this book, I will emphasize the importance of metadata and other documented knowledge to the ongoing use of data and to understanding its quality. As noted the DQAF will provide guidance on capturing expectations about data in a consistent and understandable manner. A working assumption should be that nothing related to system design or data is intuitive. Data and the systems that house it are not natural. They are artificial constructs. Knowing their construction is very helpful—in some cases, essential—for using them. They need to be learned or explained to be understood.

Data Chain and Information Life Cycle

The terms *data chain* and *information chain* refer to the sets of processes and systems that move data from one place to another within or between organizations for different uses. (*Data stream* and *information stream* are synonyms for *data chain* and *information chain*.) The metaphor of the chain is a useful one. As it implies, processes and systems are linked together. If one link in the chain breaks, there are negative repercussions for the entire chain. Its disadvantage as a metaphor is the implication that any given dataset is a link in only one chain. If we were to diagram the data chain for most organizations, our picture would likely resemble a web with multiple linkages. Perhaps, the *data mesh* would be a more accurate way to describe these relationships.

The *data chain* is different from the *data* or *information life cycle*, which provides a way of looking at how data is managed. The concept of the *information life cycle* describes data as a resource that, like other resources, is managed in phases. These phases including planning, acquisition, application and maintenance, and disposal (English, 1999, pp. 200–209; DAMA 2009, pp. 3–4). When thinking about data, it is helpful to recognize an additional phase of storing and sharing as part of the application of data as a resource. This phase is critical. One characteristic that differentiates data from other resources (such as money, time, and equipment) is that it can be shared without losing value. Therefore, I have adopted Danette McGilvray's formulation of the information life cycle: plan, obtain, store & share, maintain, apply, dispose, referred to as POSMAD (McGilvray, 2008, pp. 23–30).

Data Lineage and Data Provenance

Data lineage is related to both the data chain and the information life cycle. The word *lineage* refers to a pedigree or line of descent from an ancestor. In biology, a lineage is a sequence of species that is considered to have evolved from a common ancestor. But we also think of *lineage* in terms of direct inheritance from an immediate predecessor. Most people concerned with the lineage of data want to understand two aspects of it. First, they want to know the data's origin or provenance—the earliest instance of the data. (The word *provenance* in art has implications similar to lineage; it refers to a record of ownership that can be used as a guide for a work's authenticity or quality.) Second, people want to know how (and sometimes why) the data has changed since that earliest instance. Change can take place within one system or between systems.

Understanding changes in data requires understanding the data chain, the rules that have been applied to data as it moves along the data chain, and what effects the rules have had on the data. *Data lineage* includes the concept of an origin for the data—its original source or provenance—and the movement and change of the data as it passes through systems and is adopted for different uses (the sequence of steps within the data chain through which data has passed). Pushing the metaphor, we can imagine that any data that changes as it moves through the data chain includes some but not all characteristics of its previous states and that it will pick up other characteristics through its evolution.

Data lineage is important to data quality measurement because lineage influences expectations. A health care example can illustrate this concept. Medical claims submitted to insurance companies contain procedure codes that represent the actions taken as part of a patient's health care. These codes are highly standardized in hierarchies that reference bodily systems. Medical providers (doctors, nurses, physical therapists, and the like) choose which procedure codes accurately reflect the services provided. In order to pay claims (a process called *adjudication*), sometimes codes are bundled into sets. When this happens, different codes (representing sets) are associated with the claims. This process means that specific values in these data fields are changed as the claims are processed. Some changes are executed through rules embedded in system programming. Others may be the result of manual intervention from a claim processor. A person using such data with the expectation that the codes on the adjudicated claims are the very same codes submitted by a doctor may be surprised by discrepancies. The data would not meet a basic expectation. Without an understanding of the data's lineage, a person might reasonably conclude that something is wrong with the data. If analysis requires codes as submitted and only as submitted, then adjudicated claim data would not be the appropriate source for that purpose.

Concluding Thoughts

This chapter has discussed some key concepts related to data management. Among these concepts are data models and metadata. The general idea that data can be managed—that we need to plan for it and control it—is central to data quality. Data management implies the need for particular kinds of knowledge about data: what it represents, how much there is of it in an organization, how it is organized and maintained, where it resides, who uses it, and the like. Much of this knowledge is captured in data models and metadata, both of which are necessary input for the process of data quality measurement and improvement.

Data Quality and Measurement

4

"Weights and measures may be ranked among the necessaries of life to every individual of human society. They enter into the economical arrangements and concerns of every family. They are necessary to every occupation of human industry. ...The knowledge of them, as established in use, is among the first elements of education, and is often learned by those who learn nothing else, not even to read and write."
—**John Quincy Adams, *Report on Weights and Measures*** (1821)

"It doesn't matter what temperature the room is, it's always room temperature."
—**Stephen Wright**

Purpose

This chapter introduces the concept of data quality dimensions as a means through which data quality can be measured. It presents a definition of *measurement*, discusses the challenges associated with establishing tools for and systems of measurement, and presents the characteristics of effective measurements. It then defines several general concepts associated with data quality assessment and some specific terms used by the DQAF.

Data Quality

Many people use the words *data quality* as if they are referring to an object, as in "We need data quality!" I wish instead they would say, "We need high-quality data!" All data has some level of quality, even if that level is not acceptable. Whichever way they phrase it, people really mean, "We need data that looks like we expect it to and acts like we expect it to. Data that is as compete and accurate as we expect it to be. And it needs to be accessible when we expect to use it."

The confusing use of the word *quality* in relation to data probably stems from conflation of its two meanings. *The New Oxford American Dictionary*'s first definition of *quality* reads: "the standard of something as measured against other things of a similar kind; the degree of excellence of something; general excellence of a standard or level." The second definition refers to quality as "a distinctive attribute or characteristic possessed by someone or something." When people say they want high-quality data, they expect data to meet a standard of excellence. Meeting a standard implies the data has particular, distinctive characteristics (qualities) that meet individual facets of such a standard.

By either definition, data quality is about whether data meets implicit or explicit expectations of people who will use the data. How someone judges the quality of data depends on what that person expects from the data. Expectations can be complex. They are based not only on what the data is supposed to represent, but also on why a person needs the data and how he or she intends to use it.

The definition of *data quality* used throughout this book is similar to those definitions used by other data quality practitioners: The level of quality of data represents the degree to which data meets the expectations of data consumers, based on their intended uses of the data. Data quality is thus directly related to the perceived or established purposes of the data. High-quality data meets expectations to a greater degree than does low-quality data.[1] However, data is also a representation of objects, events, and concepts. (It serves a semiotic function, acting as a sign of something other than itself.) One factor in how well it meets the expectations of data consumers is how those consumers perceive data's ability to represent what it purports to represent.

Data Quality Dimensions

Data and information quality thinkers have adopted the word *dimension* to identify those aspects of data that can be measured and through which its quality can be quantified. While different experts have proposed different sets of data quality dimensions (see the companion web site for a summary), almost all include some version of accuracy and validity, completeness, consistency, and currency or timeliness among them.

If a quality is "a distinctive attribute or characteristic possessed by someone or something" then a data quality dimension is a general, measurable category for a distinctive characteristic (quality) possessed by data. Data quality dimensions function in the way that length, width, and height function to express the size of a physical object. They allow us to understand quality in relation to a scale and in relation to other data measured against the same scale or different scales whose relation is defined. A set of data quality dimensions can be used to define expectations (the standards against which to measure) for the quality of a desired dataset, as well as to measure the condition of an existing dataset.

Measuring the quality of data requires understanding expectations and determining the degree to which the data meets them. Often this takes the form of knowing data's distinctive characteristics and assessing the degree to which they are present in data being measured.

Put in these terms, measurement seems simple. But there are at least two complications: First, most organizations do not do a good job of defining data expectations. Very few make clear, measurable assertions about the expected condition of data. Second, without clear expectations, it is not possible to measure whether the data meets them. This doesn't mean you need measurement to know you have poor quality data. As David Loshin has pointed out, "the definition of poor quality data is like Supreme Court Justice Potter Stewart's definition of *obscenity*: We know it when we see it" (Loshin, 2001, p. 101).

Let's take the first complication. In defining requirements, many information technology projects focus on what data needs to be made available or what functionality needs to be put in place to process or access the data. Consequently, data requirements often focus on data sources, modeling, source-to-target mapping, and the implementation of business intelligence tools. Very few projects define requirements related to the expected *condition* of the data. In fact, many people who work

---

[1] English (1999), Redman (1996), and Wang (1998) all use variations on this theme, as do Loshin (2001) and McGilvray (2008).

in information technology (IT) think the content of the data they manage is irrelevant to the system built. With limited knowledge of the data, they have no basis for knowing whether or not the data meets expectations. More challenging still, data can be used for different purposes. Each of those purposes may include a different set of expectations. In some cases, expectations may be in conflict with one another. It is risky not to recognize these differences. Failure to do so means that data might be misused or misunderstood.

The second complication goes to the purpose of this book: It can be hard to measure expectations, but it is impossible to measure them if you cannot define them. Data is not a thing with hard and fast boundaries (Redman, 2007), but data does come to us in forms (records, tables, files, messages) that have measurable characteristics. Fields are specified to contain particular data. Files are expected to contain particular records. We can align these characteristics with the expectations of data consumers or the requirements of representation. From the combination, we can establish specific measurements of these characteristics.

Measurement

We are so surrounded by measurement that we sometimes forget what it means to measure. The first definition of the verb *to measure* reads, "to ascertain the size, amount, or degree of something by using an instrument or device marked in standard units or by comparing it with an object of known size" (*NOAD*). We usually understand measurement in this sense, associating numbers with objects or situations. However, the term *measure* also has a more figurative meaning. Measuring someone or something against another person or thing means to judge them in comparison to a standard, or to scrutinize them in order to form an assessment. In both senses, measurement involves comparison— either to a physical standard (a ruler, tape measure, or barometer) or to a poetic standard ("Too long a sacrifice / Can make a stone of the heart. O when may it suffice?"[2]).

Measurement exists in all societies for very practical reasons.[3] It enables communication by providing a common language for quantities, sizes of things, or distances between them. It is also necessary for commerce.[4] When we sell or purchase goods, we need to know how much we are getting and how much it costs, as well as how long it is expected to last, how far it will travel, and the like. In science, measurement enables us to understand or build knowledge about things and processes, as well as to gain control of those things and processes by reducing uncertainty about them or increasing

---

[2] W.B. Yeats, "Easter 1916."

[3] The importance of measurement standards was, for example, embedded in the U.S. Constitution (Art. I, Sec.8 [cited in Crease, 2011, p. 109]). Both Thomas Jefferson and John Quincy Adams wrote extensively on the potential economic and social benefits of greater standardization. The emergence of modern science during the Renaissance led to the effort to understand nature—the clockmaker's world—through measurement. Especially in the eighteenth and nineteenth centuries, men of science were bent on discovering the mathematical laws of nature. Such discovery drove efforts to improve the instruments and processes of measurement itself.

[4] People who argued against adoption of the metric system cast their arguments in religious terms, the metric system being seen as the dangerous product of rampant atheism, and the Anglo-Saxon inch, a cousin of the Pyramid Inch, was a God-given reflection of true cosmic relations (Crease, 2011, p. 154). When it came, the adoption of the metric system had more to do with commerce, industrialism, and the development of international trade than it did with the search for scientific (or religious) truth.

their predictability. In business, especially data-dependent modern business, measurement is needed for all of these functions.

The history of measurement tells us a lot about the creation of data. Take, for instance, the idea that, once upon a time, there were no thermometers and therefore, no temperature. Of course, there was a concept of hot and cold. People understood that some objects and environments were warmer or cooler than others, but they did not understand these differences in the way we have for the last four hundred or so years: as something that can be measured along a scale and can be expressed in numbers. So they had no way of saying how hot or cold a thing was in any absolute or consistent way. Nor could they express the difference in heat or cold between two different objects or places. In the modern world, we take for granted our ability to measure temperature and to understand its meaning. Today most first graders understand that 98.6 degrees Fahrenheit (or 37 degrees Centigrade) is considered normal body temperature—no reason to stay home from school. But the Greeks thought of heat as something different, a quality of the air, and of fevers and chills as signs of "morbid processes" (Pearce, 2002).

It's not necessary to understand the history of the thermometer to understand how to use one, anymore than it is necessary to know the history of the automobile in order to drive a car. But the history of the thermometer is instructive nevertheless for those who are interested in data quality, because of what it tells us about the challenges of measuring an abstract concept. It took many years, much intellectual effort, and a lot of false starts before people were successful in measuring degrees of heat.[5] Ultimately, scientists came up with a relatively simple tool—consisting of an element to sense temperature and react to it and a scale to assign a numeric expression to that reaction—to present consistent results in a manner that is comprehensible and reproducible, and allows for comparisons between measurements between objects and across time.[6]

In doing so, they achieved the primary goal of measurement: to enable different people to have a common way of referring to, and through this referent, a common way to understand, the thing being measured (NASA, 2005). To define temperature, scientists had to express an abstract concept—a quality of the air—in concrete terms—marks along the side of a tube, numbers on a scale. As long as the thing they needed to take the temperature of could be compared to those numbers on a scale, they could understand its temperature relative to scale itself and, through that, to any other thing whose temperature could be taken.

Measurement as Data

What we think of as *data* does something similar to what measurement in general does. It provides us with a way of understanding large or abstract concepts—changes in the population of a city over

---

[5]In 1593, Galileo Galilei invented a thermoscope (a thermometer without a scale) which detected changes in temperature. Nearly 20 years later Santorio Santorio put a scale on his thermoscope, creating the first thermometer. The first thermometer using liquid enclosed in glass was invented by Ferdinand II, the Grand Duke of Tuscany, in 1654. Daniel Fahrenheit invented his mercury thermometer and set a standardized scale 60 years later, in 1714. Anders Centigrade established his scale in 1742. Lord Kelvin invented his "absolute" scale more than a century later, in 1848. The first practical medical thermometer was created by English physician Sir Thomas Allbutt in 1867 (Bellis, 2011).

[6]As demonstrated in philosopher Robert P. Crease's history of the metric system, *The World in Balance: The Historic Quest for an Absolute System of Measurement* (2010), even for the measurement of physical objects, the road to consensus about a system of measurement was bumpy and winding.

time; the effects of smoking on the population; the average value of the stock market for a given day, month, or quarter; the impact of an economic crisis; the relative performance of a baseball player—by condensing those concepts into things we can understand: generally numbers, but sometimes other representations based on those numbers—graphs, charts, maps. In fact, much data in our world is measurement data. One definition of data is, after all, "facts and statistics collected together for reference or analysis." The American Society for Quality associates data directly and solely with measurement, defining *data* as "a set of collected facts. There are two basic kinds of numerical data: measured or variable data, such as '16 ounces,' '4 miles' and '0.75 inches;' and counted or attribute data, such as '162 defects'" (ASQ.org).

In *How to Measure Anything*, author Donald Hubbard clarifies our understanding of the purpose of measurement: To reduce uncertainty through observation. Using this concept, we can consider any observation that increases our understanding of an object or situation a measurement of that object or situation. The process of measurement allows us to understand a characteristic of one thing in terms of a characteristic of another thing.

The results of measurements of physical characteristics of physical objects are data. They are numeric representations of specific characteristics of an object being measured. The conventions of physical measurement include not only the object being measured, but also the instrument (ruler, tape measure, defined standard, etc.) being used to take the measurement and the means (scale) by which the results are expressed (inches, centimeters, pass/fail). There are analog conventions for more abstract measurement: an object being assessed (a personality, the quality of a bottle of wine) and an instrument through which to make the assessment (past experience interacting with people, past experiences with wine, or a set of criteria for evaluating wine), and a means through which to express the results (a characterization of personality type, a conclusion, "This is the best wine I've ever tasted). The results of these more abstract measures are not numbers, but instead are reasonable conclusions or inferences about the object or situation being measured.

Physical measurements of size (length, width, height) are referred to as dimensions. The more general meaning of the word *dimension* is "an aspect or feature of a situation, problem or thing" (*NOAD*). Dimensions are measurable categories for distinctive characteristics of an object, event, or concept. Dimensions can thus serve as analytical categories.

Physically, dimensions allow us to understand aspects of size from which we can build additional knowledge, such as shape, volume, and weight. Because measurement simplifies, by expressing an aspect of an object through a defined set of conventions, including in many cases, scale, we can make comparisons between objects measured in the same manner—an inch, a foot, a yard, or a mile. If we have knowledge of the relation between scales of measurement, we can compare across scales: meters to yards, kilometers to miles, and so on. Because of these characteristics of measurement itself, we can use measurement to understand an object in front of us—the size of a room in relation to its furniture, for example—and to set expectations for other objects—the new couch we want to buy or the table we want to move.

Data Quality Measurement and the Business/IT Divide

Despite recognition of the metric system's rational construction, it took nearly a century for it to be widely adopted in Europe. The history of developing systems of measurement is sobering. It makes clear how challenging it is to establish general, agreed-upon ways of measuring anything, even physical objects. Whether they give it a lot of thought or take it for granted, most people grasp that our systems of measurement are critical to comprehending the world. Some people even recognize how culturally embedded such systems are. Most people do not readily embrace new approaches to measurement. Doing so can require a change in world view, in addition to changes in tools and an adjustment of estimating skills.

The problem of measuring data quality is, in part, a cultural one. Sometimes people do not think they can measure quality, or they do not want to do so. The two groups involved with data quality measurement, IT and businesspeople, are often perceived as culturally distinct. At one extreme of this cultural divide is IT, thinking it is powerless over data content and can only cleanse data, and even that process depends on the business supplying exact rules. And they think that if someone starts measuring data quality and finds out how poor it is, then their systems will get blamed (Olson, 2003, pp. 9–10). At the other side is the business, believing data can and should be perfect and therefore not quite comprehending the need for measurement at all. Why not just get it right in the first place? Neither of these positions is conducive to establishing useful measurements.

The history of measurement is also a useful reminder about why we measure in the first place. Lord Kelvin's oft-quoted remark, "When you can measure what you are speaking about, and express it in numbers, you know something about it; but when you cannot measure it, when you cannot express it in numbers, your knowledge is of a meager and unsatisfactory kind" was made in an 1883 speech to the institute of Civil Engineers—a group that combined the interests of both business and science at the height of the search for definitions of the natural laws that governed the physical universe (Crease, 2011, p. 207; Hubbard, 2010, p. 3). For both business and science, measurement serves a purpose: It has to be useful. A primary criterion for usefulness is knowledge gained about the thing measured. In most cases, this knowledge is directed at being able to assess and, in business, make decisions about or, in science, draw conclusions about the thing measured.

Characteristics of Effective Measurements

Measurements turn observations into numbers that are comprehensible and reproducible, and enable us to make comparisons between objects and across time. We see these characteristics in everyday measurements, in gas mileage, for example. When we know how many miles our car can travel on a gallon of gas, we have a basic criterion for a range of decision making, whether we are faced with a simple problem (Should I stop for gas on the way to work or should I get it on the way home?) or a more complex one (How can I reduce my carbon footprint?). To be effective in helping solve problems, measurements must also be purposeful: They must provide answers to questions that help us reduce uncertainty. To be comprehensible and reproducible and to allow for comparisons, a single measurement can be thought of as a system, in the way that a single question can be thought of as a system.

Measurements must be Comprehensible and Interpretable

To be effective, measurements themselves must be comprehensible. If people cannot understand what characteristic is being measured, the measurement will not help reduce uncertainty or be useful, even if the object being measured is very important.

Consider again the thermometer. Can you remember not knowing what it was? If so, you were probably a child of five or six who suddenly realized that whenever you complained of feeling sick, your mom would put her hand on your forehead and, after a moment of thought, go to the medicine cabinet with and get this little glass stick in a plastic container. She's shake it a bit, put it in your mouth and tell you to sit still while she gazed at the clock. A minute or two later, she'd pull it out, peer at it. If she was satisfied, she'd announce that you would be going to school after all. If she was not, she might give it another shake and put it back in your mouth. What did it mean? I remember my mother explaining to me that the alcohol in the bulb of the thermometer expanded when it got warmer and pushed its way up the inside of the tube until the thermometer itself was the same temperature as the inside of your mouth. Then the alcohol inside stopped expanding. Whatever number it landed at was your temperature. If your temperature was 98.6 then you were normal. If it was higher, then you had a fever and needed to stay home. What happens if it is colder than 98.6? No answer. If your temperature was much above 100 degrees, then you might need to go to the doctor.

My mom was not a scientist. But part of her role as a parent was to be able to make decisions about who went to school and who did not; as well as under what conditions one of us kids needed to be taken to the doctor. It helped that she understood enough about how a thermometer worked to be able to explain it to a five-year-old child. But the main thing she knew was how to interpret the body temperature measurement itself. To a parent with a sick child, being able to measure body temperature is critical. It works as a triage mechanism, in part, because parents understand what it means and what they should do with the information.

If you measure something critical in a manner that no one understands, your measurement is not going to be effective; it is not going to help people increase their knowledge of the thing or situation being measured. People will not be able to use measurements they cannot understand to make decisions or draw conclusions about the things measured. Measurement is a communications tool, as well as an analysis tool.

The need to ensure that measurements are comprehensible and interpretable is another reminder of the criticality of metadata. Measurements are another set of data that must be supported with metadata. In addition to understanding what the data they are measuring represents, data consumers must also know what the measurements represent and have enough context to understand how to interpret them.

Measurements must be Reproducible

It may seem unnecessary to state that measurements should be reproducible. The main reason for focusing on the instruments of measurement (rulers, scales, and the like) and the conditions of measurement (temperature, age, etc.) is to produce consistent measurement results and to understand any factors that might introduce variability into the measurement. If we cannot trust the consistency of the instrument or make allowance for variables in conditions, then we cannot trust the measurements themselves. Or they simply may have very little meaning. Measurement always involves a degree of comparison. If we are comparing to an abstract standard (the official meter stick), then we won't get far enough, unless we also understand that our measurement of an object's size (say our child's height) will be measured consistently over time and that what we understand about one object is, in a sense, transferable to any other object that we might need to measure for similar purposes or under similar conditions (the height percentile of all children of the same age and gender as our child).

To make comparisons that allow us to understand change or lack of change requires a consistent approach to measurement and confidence that any individual measurement is reproducible. Within the manufacture of physical products, can you imagine how consistent we would be if everyday, we had a new instrument by which to measure tolerances? We all recognize the challenges we would face if we suddenly changed our measurement system itself ("Conversion" is the dirty word in such a case). In science, reproducibility is extremely critical. In everyday life (taking our weight in the morning or measuring a cup of flour), tolerances are a bit wider. In data quality, we need to be able to measure the same data in the same way if we are going to show improvement or deterioration. Thus not only is reproducibility a question of instrumentation, but it is also connected to the conditions and objects of measurement.

Measurements must be Purposeful

People often say, "You can't compare apples and oranges." What they mean is that apples and oranges are so different from each other that it is not productive to compare them. This implies that, in order to measure, you should have two objects that are "the same" and meaningful measurement will characterize the differences between them. That sort of makes sense—until we think about the line between "the same" and "different." In fact, there are several obvious similarities between apples and oranges: They are both round fruit, generally about the size of a baseball; both have seeds, both have skin, and so on. There are also differences: One is orange; the other can be red, green, yellow or a mixture. But an orange can also be green if it is not yet ripe. So what are we comparing them for anyway? And that is the right question. We need to have a reason for measuring the things we measure.

The history of measurement tells us that everyday measurements emerge in order to solve problems in everyday life. Science has evolved measurements to answer new questions that continuously emerge out of advances in our knowledge of how the world works. Businesses have developed financial and performance measurements in order to make decisions about what skills to look for in employees, where to make long term investments, and how to prepare for future opportunities.

Data Quality Assessment

To *assess* is to "evaluate or estimate the nature, ability, or quality" of something, or to "calculate or estimate its value or price." *Assess* comes from the Latin verb *assidere*, meaning "to sit by." As a synonym for *measurement*, *assessment* implies the need to compare one thing to another in order to understand it. However, unlike *measurement* in the strict sense of "ascertain[ing] the size, amount, or degree of something by using an instrument," the concept of *assessment* also implies drawing a conclusion—evaluating—the object of the assessment (*NOAD*).

Arkady Maydanchik defines the purpose of data quality assessment: to identify data errors and erroneous data elements and to measure the impact of various data-driven business processes (Maydanchik, 2007, pp. 23, 25). Both components—to identify errors and to understand their implications—are critical. Data quality assessment can be accomplished in different ways, from simple qualitative assessment to detailed quantitative measurement. Assessments can be made based on general knowledge, guiding principles, or specific standards. Data can be assessed at the macro level of general content or at the micro level of specific fields or values. The purpose of data quality assessment is to understand the condition of data in relation to expectations or particular purposes or both and to draw a conclusion about whether it meets expectations or satisfies the requirements of particular purposes. This process always implies the need also to understand how effectively data represent the objects, events, and concepts it is designed to represent.

While the term *data quality assessment* is often associated with the process of gaining an initial understanding of data, within the context of the DQAF, the term is used here to refer to a set of processes that are directed at evaluating the condition and value of data within an organization. These processes include initial one-time assessment of data and the data environment (metadata, reference data, system, and business process documentation), automated process controls, in-line data quality measurement, and periodic reassessment of data and the data environment. Process controls and in-line data quality measurement are defined briefly later in this chapter. They and the other assessment scenarios will be explored in more depth in Sections Two, Three, and Six as we unpack the framework.

Data Quality Dimensions, DQAF Measurement Types, Specific Data Quality Metrics

As noted in the discussion of data quality, the word *dimension* is used to identify aspects of data that can be measured and through which data's quality can be described and quantified. As high-level categories, data quality dimensions are relatively abstract. The dimensions explored in the DQAF include completeness, validity, timeliness, consistency, and integrity. Data quality dimensions are important because they enable people to understand why data is being measured.

Specific data quality metrics are somewhat self-explanatory. They define the particular data that is being measured and what is being measured about it. For example, in health care data, one might have a specific metric that measures the percentage of invalid procedure codes in the primary procedure code field in a set of medical claim data. Specific measurements describe the condition of particular data at a particular time. My use of the term *metric* does not include the threshold itself. It describes only what is being measured.[7]

The DQAF introduces an additional concept to enable data quality measurement, that of the *measurement type* (See Figure 4.1). A measurement type is a category within a dimension of data quality that allows for a repeatable pattern of measurement to be executed against any data that fits the criteria required by the type, regardless of specific data content. (I will sometimes also use the noun *measure* to refer to measurement types.) Measurement types bridge the space between dimensions and specific measurements. For example, if it is valuable to measure the percentage of invalid procedure codes in a set of medical claims, it is probably also valuable to measure the percentage of invalid diagnosis codes or invalid adjustment codes. And these can be measured in essentially the same way. Each value set is present on a column or columns in a table. The valid values for each are contained

---

[7] As will be discussed in Chapter 10, both Redman (1996) and Loshin (2001) associate thresholds with data quality requirements and the measurements that show those requirements are met. Specific metrics can have a threshold, if they are measuring an aspect of data to which a threshold applies—for example, the level of defaulted records. But in many cases, especially for consistency measurement types, they are measuring a set of values, each of which is associated with a percentage of records, so there is not one threshold for the overall set. There is instead an expectation of consistency.

| DIMENSIONS
The WHY of measurement	Completeness	Timeliness	Validity	Consistency	Integrity
MEASURE-MENT TYPES
The HOW of measurement	Compare summarized data in amount fields to summarized amount provided in a control record	Compare actual time of data delivery to scheduled data delivery	Compare values on incoming data to valid values in a defined domain (reference table, range, or mathematical rule)	Compare record count distribution of values (column profile) to past instances of data populating the same field.	Confirm record level (parent /child) referential integrity between tables to identify parentless child records, (i.e., "orphan") records
SPECIFIC DATA QUALITY METRICS
The WHAT of measurement	Total dollars on Claim records balances to total on control report	Claim file delivery against time range documented in a service level agreement	Validity of Revenue Codes against Revenue Code table	Percentage distribution of adjustment codes on Claim table consistent with past population of the field	All valid procedure codes are on the procedure code table

(Right margin, vertical text:) Decreasing abstraction, [increasing specificity, concreteness]. Closer proximity to data

(Right margin, vertical text:) Increasing ability to understand and interpret measurement results

FIGURE 4.1 Dimensions, Measurement Types, and Specific Metrics

The figure illustrates the relationship between data quality dimensions, DQAF measurement types, and specific data quality metrics. Dimensions are central to most discussions about data quality. They describe aspects of data quality that can be measured and provide the *why* of measurement. Measurement types are central to the DQAF. Describe generic ways to measure the dimensions—the *how* of measurement. They bridge the distance between dimensions and specific metrics that describe what particular data will be measured—the *what* of measurement.

in a second table. The sets can be compared to identify valid and invalid values. Record counts can be taken and percentages calculated to establish levels of invalid values.

A measurement type is a generic form into which specific metrics fit. In this example of diagnosis and adjustment codes, the type is a measurement of validity that presents the level (expressed as a percentage) of invalid codes in a specific column in a database table. Any column that has a defined domain or range of values can be measured using essentially the same approach. The results of similar measures can be expressed in the same form. Measurement types enable people to understand any instance of a specific metric taken using the same measurement type. Once a person understands how validity is being measured (as a percentage of all records whose values for a specific column do not exist in a defined domain), he or she can understand any given measure of validity. Just as, once one understands the concept of a meter, one can understand the relation between an object that is one meter long and an object that is two meters long.

Measurement types also allow for comparison across datasets. For example, if you measure the level of invalid procedure codes in two different sets of similar claim data, you have the basis of a comparison between them. If you discover that one set has a significantly higher incidence of invalids and you expect them to be similar, you have a measure of the relative quality of the two sets.

Data Profiling

Data profiling is a specific kind of data analysis used to discover and characterize important features of datasets. Profiling provides a picture of data structure, content, rules, and relationships by applying statistical methodologies to return a set of standard characteristics about data—data types, field lengths, and cardinality of columns, granularity, value sets, format patterns, content patterns, implied rules, and cross-column and cross-file data relationships, and cardinality of those relationships.

Profiling also includes inspection of data content through a column profile or percentage distribution of values. Distribution analysis entails counting all the records associated with each value and dividing these by the total number of records to see what percentage of the data is associated with any specific value and how the percentages compare to each other. Understanding the percentages is useful, especially for high cardinality value sets and for datasets with a large number of records. Unless you calculate proportions as percentages of the total, it can be difficult to comprehend differences between the individual measurement results.

Profiling results can be compared with documented expectations, or they can provide a foundation on which to build knowledge about the data. Though it is most often associated with the beginning of data integration projects where it is used for purposes of data discovery and in order to prepare data for storage and use, data profiling can take place at any point in a data asset's life cycle. Most data assets benefit from periodic re-profiling to provide a level of assurance that quality has not changed or that changes are reasonable given the context of changes in business processes. Section Three will discuss periodic measurement and reassessment of the data environment as one of the three assessment scenarios supported by the DQAF.

Data Quality Issues and Data Issue Management

Profiling and other forms of assessment will identify unexpected conditions in the data. A *data quality issue* is a condition of data that is an obstacle to a data consumer's use of that data—regardless of who discovered the issue, where/when it was discovered, what its root cause(s) are determined to be, or what the options are for remediation. *Data issue management* is a process of removing or reducing the impact of obstacles that prevent effective use of data. Issue management includes identification, definition, quantification, prioritization, tracking, reporting, and resolution of issues. Prioritization and resolution depend on data governance. To resolve a problem means to find a solution and to implement that solution. A resolution is a solution to a problem. Issue resolution refers to the process of bringing an issue to closure through a solution or through the decision not to implement a solution. Any individual issue will have a specific definition of what constitutes its "resolution."

Reasonability Checks

Depending on the nature of the data being profiled, some results may provide reasonability checks for the suitability of data for a particular data asset, as well as its ability to meet requirements and expectations. A *reasonability check* provides a means of drawing a conclusion about data based on knowledge of data content rather than on a strictly numeric measurement. Reasonability checks can take many forms, many of which use numeric measurement as input. All such checks answer a simple question: Does this data make sense, based on what we know about it? The basis for judging "reason-ability" ranges from simple common sense to deep understanding of what the data represents.

Reasonability checks are especially necessary during initial data assessment when little may be known about the data. The answer to the question of whether the data makes sense determines the next steps in any assessment. If the data does make sense, you should document why and continue through the assessment. If it does not make sense, then you should define why it does not and deter-mine what response is needed.

Because measurement adds to knowledge about the object being measured, what is "reasonable" may change as measurement produces deeper understanding of the data. For many consistency measurements, where the degree of similarity between datasets is being measured, initial reasonability checks can evolve into numeric thresholds. If, for example, historical levels of defaulted data range from 1 to 2% and the rea-sons for defaults being assigned are documented and understood, then 2% defaults might be considered a reasonable level and 2.5% might be cause for investigation. Even with such numbers in place, it is always the role of the data quality analyst to ask the question: Does this data make sense?

Many of the DQAF measurement types are characterized as reasonability measures. They com-pare one instance of measurement results from a dataset with the history of measurements of the same dataset in order to detect changes. Changes do not necessarily mean the data is wrong. They indicate only that it is different from what it had been. Within the framework, reasonability checks are contrasted with controls which can produce measurement results that confirm data is incomplete or incorrect. Controls can be used to stop data processing.

Data Quality Thresholds

A *data quality threshold* is a numeric representation of the acceptable limit of a measurement. Thresholds may be established in several different ways. For example, they may be set manually, based on reasonable levels. They may also be automated based on a calculation (such as the mean or median) of historical data.

In large databases, it is difficult to detect data quality problems through direct comparisons. But problems can be detected indirectly through measures that define expected patterns in the data and then identify changes in those patterns. Changes in trend are indicators of change in the data (just as the change in a person's body temperature is an indicator that something has changed in a person's body—he has an infection, or he has been exercising, etc.).

Thresholds are usually not raw numbers. Most are based on data being "flattened" through a math-ematical function, such as a percentage of total rows, average dollars per customer, or the like, before being compared to previous instances of the measurement. Such flattening is required to ensure that the com-parisons are between like entities and for the sake of comprehension. It would be difficult, for example, to compare a set of distinct procedure codes on a million medical claim records to a set of distinct procedure codes in a set of ten million records without first representing both as percentage distributions.

Thresholds function as controls. They provide feedback from the system, upon which action can be taken. Thresholds are effective when they are established based on a stable process with stable data. If neither the data nor the process is stable, then the threshold will not do much good and can even do some harm because it might be interpreted as "real" and cause analysts to forget that they must always ask the question, Does this data make sense?

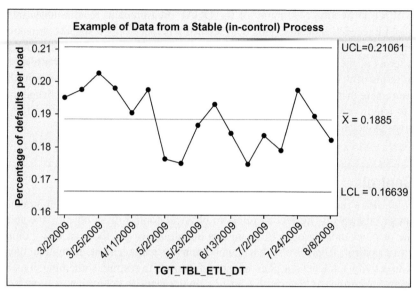

FIGURE 4.2 Example Data from a Stable Process

A control chart, a time sequence graph with the upper and lower control limits (UCL and LCL) presented at three standard deviations from the historical mean of the set of readings, is a primary tool used in statistical process control. A process is *in statistical control* when measurement points fall within the upper and lower control limits, and the points graphed on a control chart do not display any nonrandom patterns. *In control* means that any differences between the readings are affected only by *normal* or *common cause* variation (variation inherent in the process being measured) and there are not any *special causes* affecting the process. An in control process is stable and predictable.

The use of thresholds is best illustrated through a control chart, a primary tool for statistical process control measures. A control chart is a time sequence graph with additional features that identify data out of expected limits. In a typical individual/moving range statistical process control chart, the upper and lower control limits (UCL and LCL) are three standard deviations from the historical mean of the set of readings.

If the measurement remains within the upper and lower control limits, then the process is in control. *In control* means that any differences between the readings are affected only by *normal* or *common cause* variation (variation inherent in the process being measured). A process is in control when measurement points fall within the upper and lower control limits, and the points graphed on a control chart do not display any nonrandom patterns.[8] (See Figure 4.2.)

---

[8] Nonrandom patterns include: (1) One point more than three standard deviations from the center line. (2) Nine points in a row on the same side of the center line. (3) Six points in a row, all increasing or decreasing. (4) Fourteen points in a row, alternating up and down. (5) Two out of three points more than two standard deviations from the same side of the center line. (6) Four out of five points more than one deviation from the same side of the center line. (7) Fifteen points in a row within one standard deviation of either side of the center line (8) Eight points in a row more than one standard deviation from either side of the center line (Source: Ingenix SPC Tool Guide, 2003).

As you will see in Section Six, many of the DQAF measurement results tables include a field named Threshold Exceeded Indicator. This field records whether or not a specific measurement result is greater than the established data quality threshold. The DQAF measurements describe problems in two ways: in terms of the level of an undesirable characteristic of data, such as a level of defaulted records; or in terms of a significant change from past history, such as difference from the historical mean. A measurement that is greater than the threshold indicates a problem or a change that is significant enough to require investigation. Section Six also includes a discussion about some of the common calculations associated with measurement types.

Process Controls

The word *control* has a range of meanings. Its first definition reads: "the power to influence or direct people's behavior or events." The second refers to physical control of an object: "the ability to manage a machine or other moving object." From this definition we get the idea that a thing can be in control or out of control. *Control* also has connotations of management through setting limits: the restriction of an activity, tendency, or phenomenon; the power to restrain something; a means of limiting or regulating something. As a verb, *to control* a thing means to determine or supervise its behavior or to maintain influence or authority over (*NOAD*). These facets of control point to its function in mitigating risk. As noted, in statistical process control, a process is considered *in control* if the only variation in the process is the result of common causes. In information technology, the concept of controls is associated with both general controls that apply to how systems are changed and application controls that refer to how processes work within an application or system (input/process/output controls). These include controls on how data moves through the system.

The ASQ defines a *process control* as "the method for keeping a process within boundaries; the act of minimizing the variation of a process" (ASQ.org). Joseph Juran defined control as the "managerial act of comparing actual performance to standards and acting on the difference."[9] The development of controls in industry has a complex history (Andrei, 2005), but the basic concept is straightforward. A control is a form of feedback built into a system to keep it stable. A control has the ability to detect conditions that indicate a lack of stability (most often in the form of a measurement) and initiate action based on this observation. With automated controls, action may involve stopping the system or taking action that mitigates the condition (such as adjusting another variable within the system). The classic example of a control is a thermostat which, when it detects that temperature had fallen out of an acceptable range, will activate or deactivate a heating unit.

With regard to data, controls can be applied at different points within the information life cycle to test the quality of data and its suitability for the system in which it will exist. For example, data entry edits can be put in place to prevent unacceptable data from getting into a system to start with. Similar checks can be established as data moves between systems or within a system. In the warehouse in which I currently work, there is a system of controls we refer to as ABC's—audit, balance, control. The system includes checks of files sizes, comparisons to arrival times, and the like to monitor the flow of data and to detect when data is out of balance. In such situations, the control stops data

---

[9]Redman (1994).

processing. A subset of DQAF measures are controls designed to detect unacceptable conditions in the data.

In-line Data Quality Measurement and Monitoring

In-line data quality measurement is ongoing measurement of data that is integrated into data processing (for example, into an ETL—extract, transform, load—process) that prepares data to be loaded to a database. In-line measurements use many of the same techniques as data profiling; for example, they can include validity tests or reasonability tests based on the distribution of values. But in-line measurement applies them differently. Data profiling is usually done once, comprehensively, across a dataset in preparation for bringing data into a database. It is focused on discovering or confirming physical and content characteristics of data. Depending on the size and complexity of the data you are managing and the frequency at which it is updated, in-line measurement will most likely be targeted at a subset of critical data and relationships. If it is not, then managing and using the measurement results can present challenges. Profiling results, along with other output from initial assessments, including analysis of business and technical processes and evaluation of data criticality, provide input into decisions about which measurements to take in-line measurements.

For a stable process, the purpose of in-line measurement is monitoring. To *monitor* something is to "observe or check [its] progress or quality over a period of time; keep under systematic review" (*NOAD*). The goal of regular data surveillance is to identify any significant changes in data patterns that might be caused by a quality problem in the data. In such cases, monitoring should have a built-in control that can detect when a process is not in control and have the ability to impact the process.

Results from data monitoring can also be used to detect pattern changes that are caused by business process evolution about which staff running a database may otherwise be unaware. Information gathered about these changes should be used to update metadata and ensure that it clearly represents aspects of business processes that influence how data is used. For an unstable process, monitoring will provide input data that may help in determining the causes of instability.

Concluding Thoughts

The general purpose of data quality measurements is to help us understand and characterize, using consistent terms, the difference between expectations for data and the actual condition of the data. Data is intangible, but it is created and stored in contexts that enable us to measure it. For example, data domains can be defined, rules can be established describing under what conditions fields should be populated, and various sets of records can be compared with each other to determine whether the data they contain makes sense. Measurement always involves comparison. To measure data quality requires both the expectations for data and an instrument for observing the degree to which data meet those expectations. As we will explore in Section Two, the DQAF provides a structure and a set of processes (the instrument) through which data can be observed so that such comparisons can be made. With both in place, measurements can be made that are comprehensible and interpretable, reproducible, and purposeful, and that reduce the uncertainty associated with the condition of data, especially as its uses evolve.

DQAF Concepts and Measurement Types

Section Two describes why the DQAF was created and outlines the assumptions, definitions, and governing ideas of the framework before presenting the framework's 48 measurement types. I tell the story of developing the framework because it is a story about how to think about data. Knowing it may help you understand the framework better. The section contains two chapters. The first introduces a set of concepts associated with the framework, and the second presents the measurement types themselves.

The original DQAF was created by a team of analysts at Optum. Chapter 5: DQAF Concepts describes the problem we were trying to solve in creating the DQAF and our approach to solving it. We wanted to establish an approach data quality measurement that could work across data storage systems, provide measurements that are meaningful, and contribute to efforts to improve data quality. Such an approach would enable us to measure the quality of data in an automated way (in-line as part of data processing) and over time. It would also represent a basic level of IT stewardship of data.

The team took into account several challenges associated with data quality and data management (including the sometimes amorphous concept of quality and the organizational tension between IT and businesspeople); defined our scope based on criteria for objective measurement; focused a limited number of dimensions of quality; and began asking basic questions about measurement itself. As we formulated the measurement types, we recognized the need for categories in addition to the dimensions. These include objects of measurement and assessment categories. And we observed some of the other factors that influence an organization's ability to measure quality, such as the quality and scope of available metadata. Finally, we saw a basic pattern common to all the automated, in-line measurements we were proposing: that of collecting raw measurement data, executing a set of calculations against it to make it comprehensible, and comparing it to a standard or threshold to gain insight into the quality of the data.

Chapter 6: DQAF Measurement Types presents our answers to the basic questions about measurement in the form of high-level descriptions of the DQAF's measurement types. These are categorized in terms of objects of measurement, the measurement and control activities associated with data flow from a source to a target system, and the data quality dimensions of completeness, timeliness, validity, consistency, and integrity. The measurement types we originally proposed were reviewed with other teams, combined and compressed to produce a clarified set presented at the end of the chapter (and discussed in depth in Section Six). Chapter 6 also includes diagrams of several basic processes that enable readers to envision what a comprehensive data quality measurement system might look like.

DQAF Concepts

5

Purpose

This chapter describes the scope of the DQAF: To define a set of measures that enable basic IT stewardship of data, based on objective aspects of the dimensions of quality. The dimensions defined are completeness, timeliness, validity, consistency, and integrity. The related concepts are objects of measurement, assessment categories, and functions of measurement (collect, calculate, compare).

The Problem the DQAF Addresses

The DQAF was originally developed to solve a problem: establishing an approach to data quality measurement that would work across data storage systems, provide measurements meaningful to data consumers, and help improve data quality. This solution required establishing common vocabulary to bridge the distance between the conceptual dimensions of data quality and measurements of specific data. This chapter describes why the DQAF was created and outlines the assumptions, definitions, and governing ideas of the framework, including the dimensions of quality that it measures, the objects that it measures, and the categories of assessment it enables.

Several years ago, I was involved in a project focused on establishing a common approach to data quality measurement. The goal of the project was to establish a systematic, reusable approach to data quality measurement, one that produced measurement results people could understand across systems. But at the beginning of the project, we were not even speaking the same language. People tended to talk about data quality measurement in one of two ways: either in reference to dimensions of data quality as described by data quality experts or in terms of specific data quality problems they had encountered and wanted to prevent in the future.

Both approaches make sense. If you are trying to solve a problem, it's smart to research how other people have solved it and bring to bear their expertise on your own situation. And if you are aware of a risk that has been costly in the past, you would be unwise not to prevent its recurrence. However, neither of these approaches enabled an extendable approach to data quality measurement. The first was too abstract. It is important to understand dimensions of data quality, but these do not immediately lend themselves to enabling specific measurements. So people were saying, "We need to measure data completeness" or "We need to ensure we have accurate data," but they could not say how to measure completeness or accuracy. The second approach was too concrete. Measurements to detect specific, known problems are useful for managing those specific problems, but they do not help mitigate risks associated with other data. In some of our systems, the second approach led to a pile of inconsistent "control reports" that were understood only by the people who implemented them. They were not reusable, and, in some cases, the purpose of the measurements was not discernible from the reports themselves.

The team that defined the original DQAF included a data modeler, a technical architect with expertise in metadata, a programmer, a business representative, and me, a data quality analyst. While the team consisted largely of IT people we had a range of perspectives on data management. We were not looking to define new dimensions of data quality; rather, we drew on published paradigms of such dimensions. Our aim was to drill into these dimensions in order to establish measurement types—although we did not call them that at first. As defined in Section One, a *measurement type* is a category within a dimension of data quality that allows for a repeatable pattern of measurement to be executed against any data that fits the criteria required by the type, regardless of specific data content. We drew on successful data quality measurement practices within our company, as well as within other industries, and we identified ways to make them generic and therefore more extendable and reusable. Because most of the data assets we were responsible for were large relational databases, we explained these practices in terms of established data quality dimensions and the ways relational data is structured. The result was a set of measurement types that can be applied to data in warehouses, marts, and other data stores, as well as to any dataset that might require assessment.

Data Quality Expectations and Data Management

Most discussions on data quality will assert that businesspeople should drive data quality efforts and that IT people should not. I agree with the fundamental principle that the data consumer is the judge of quality—who else could be? That said, it is not easy for most people (business or technical) to define requirements and expectations related to data quality, and without these, it is not possible to measure quality. Part of the challenge in doing so stems from the nature of data itself. While data can be (and has been) viewed as a "product" of the processes that create it, data is also a representation of other things (things we think of as "real") and as such, has embedded in it the knowledge associated with how it represents those things, as well as with its creation, including its collection and storage (Chisholm, 2009; Loshin, 2001). If we already know how specific pieces of data work (what they represent and how they represent it), we may take that knowledge for granted and not recognize that other people do not understand the data. Or we may not be able to articulate what we expect of data; we just know when it is wrong. Two other challenges present themselves in trying to measure data quality: the concept of quality and the relation between IT and business functions in many organizations.

As described in Section One, *quality* is both "the standard of something as measured against other things of a similar kind" and "the degree of excellence of something; general excellence of a standard or level." People expect high-quality data to meet a standard of excellence. Despite the idea of a "standard," quality is also understood as subjective. What seems excellent to one person may not seem so to another. Data consumers have expectations about data, but those expectations may be so self-apparent to them that they do not articulate them. Or consumers may be able to see that data is wrong once they see it, but they have trouble describing what is necessary for data to be right before they see it. A quality is "a distinctive attribute or characteristic possessed by someone or something." Meeting a standard of excellence also implies that the data has particular, distinctive characteristics (qualities) that can be compared to individual facets of that standard. The idea that data has particular qualities helps get us closer to measuring its overall quality.

The often enforced separation of business and IT functions also creates a challenge to measuring data quality. Modern thinking about data encourages seeing it as separate from the systems that store it (Codd, 1970). This idea is often implicit in assertions such as, "The business owns the data. IT owns the system." And it is true that managing systems themselves (their architecture, hardware, and software) is different from managing the data in those systems. But serving organizational goals requires that both be managed. Data is collected, stored in, and accessed through technical systems. The construction of those systems influences how the data is understood and how it can be used—both of which directly influence its quality—as well as how it can be managed (Ivanov, 1972).

The primary tool we have for understanding data separate from the systems that house it is the representation of data structure in a data model, a visual representation of data content, and the relationships between data in a database, created for purposes of understanding how data is organized, and ensuring the comprehensibility and usability of that organization.[1] Because they enable people to see relationships between business entities and attributes, data models also enable people to identify expectations related to some dimensions of quality, such as completeness, consistency, and validity.

Generally speaking, people who work in information technology understand data structure better than businesspeople. They also understand the ins-and-outs of data processing and storage. This fluency allows them to propose likely rules and ways of measuring. Because of their relationship to the systems that store data, technically-oriented business analysts, programmers, modelers, and database administrators bring knowledge and a technical perspective to data quality measurement that can help businesspeople understand options for ensuring quality.

IT people also have a fundamental responsibility to manage the data in their systems. As is true of managing in general, managing data requires understanding its life cycle, knowing how much you have of it at any point in its life cycle, reducing risks associated with that life cycle, and deriving value at appropriate pints in the life cycle. Unfortunately, very little IT work is focused on managing the information life cycle. Most centers exclusively on managing data in individual systems, often with very little attention even to the movement of data between systems (the links in the data chain). This focus is unfortunate because, conceptually, organizational information should be highly interconnected, but often technically it is disconnected.

Although business uses of data what bring value to an organization, those uses are largely dependent on technical systems making the data available. Technical teams support those applications and need to be directly involved with other phases of the information life cycle (planning, obtaining, storing & sharing, maintaining, and disposing of data) for organizations to get value from their data. Success requires technical as well as business management. Much higher quality data could be achieved if IT people owned these responsibilities for data (not just systems) up front.

---

[1] See Redman (1996), who approaches data quality dimensions from the perspective of data modeling. A data item is defined as a representable triple: a value, from the domain of an attribute, within an entity. This abstraction is a useful reminder of data's constructedness. Dimensions of quality can thus be associated with the component pieces of data (i.e., with the data model as well as with data values). Redman identifies 15 characteristics of models and from them, boils out six quality dimensions related to the model: content, scope, level of detail, composition, consistency, and reaction to change.

Such ownership helps with measurement because, in addition to a common vocabulary, technical solutions require bridging the distance between conceptual dimensions of data quality and measurements of specific data.

The Scope of the DQAF

Since the work effort in "defining data quality measurement" was very broad, we narrowed our scope in several ways. First, we wanted to define *objective measures*—those that measured task-independent characteristics of data. Objective measurements can be taken without knowledge of how the data is being or will be applied (that is, without information about the context of its use). Measurement of subjective dimensions (believability, relevancy, etc.) requires input from data consumers (via a survey or other instrument) who have specific uses of data in mind. Subjective data assessments "reflect the needs and experiences" of data consumers (Wang et al. 2002).

In focusing on objective measures, we were not rejecting the idea that data quality is defined by data consumers. Instead we recognized that most data must meet certain basic conditions to be suitable for *any* uses. For example, it must first be present. It must also effectively represent what it purports to represent in the way it should (e.g., once a domain is defined, valid values should be used to populate records). We looked for ways to measure these conditions first.[2]

Objective data quality measurement involves at least one of two basic comparisons: Data can be measured either in comparison to a clearly defined standard (as instantiated in other data or as expressed in a threshold) or against itself over time (where there is an expectation of consistency in terms of data content or a data process). Most objective data quality metrics must involve one of these comparisons. More complex measures may combine both types. Specific metrics can be understood in terms of their relative complexity: how many data relationship measurements they take into consideration, the nature of the calculations required to take the measurements, and the kinds of comparisons being made.

If the quality of data is defined objectively in relation to a standard or as consistent over time, and data consumers are not satisfied with its quality, then there is a data quality issue, such as a genuine gap between the data and their expectations. Resolving such an issue requires work effort to improve the data or the processes that produce it. The measurement process itself can contribute to the definition of expectations by identifying the need for a stricter standard, a reduction in the level of inconsistency, or the imposition of higher consistency in data inputs. Measurement can help data consumers articulate assumptions and risks. It can also provide guidance in formulating the expectations themselves.

As a simple example, consider that in the United States, ZIP codes (postal codes) are defined as five digit codes. In order to have a chance of being valid, any value populated in a ZIP code field

---

[2] Jim Harris, in his blog Obsessive Compulsive Data Quality, makes the distinction in this memorable way: "Mass is an intrinsic property of matter, based on the atomic composition of a given object, such as your body for example, which means your mass would therefore remain the same regardless of whether you were walking on the surface of the Moon or Earth. …Using these concepts metaphorically, mass is an intrinsic property of data, and perhaps a way to represent objective data quality, whereas weight is a gravitational force acting on data, and perhaps a way to represent subjective data quality" (Harris, 2012-03-19). In a follow-up post, Harris extends the analogy. When we use data "data begins to slow down, begins to feel the effects of our use. We give data mass so that it can become the basic building blocks of what matters to us. Some data is affected more by our use than others. The more subjective our use, the more we weigh data down. The more objective our use, the less we weigh data down" (Harris, 2012-07-12).

needs to have five digits. Any value that does not meet this basic, objective criterion cannot be correct. A more complex example involves rules for specific data aggregations. Some analytic uses of medical claim data aggregate data based on a time period, a medical condition, or demographic characteristics (age, gender, location) of a population of people being assessed. In each case, in order for the findings to be usable, the data must meet defined conditions. For example, a dataset must contain records representing a specific time period, or there must be a sufficient number of records related to the medical condition or population being assessed. These requirements for input can also be assessed as measures of data sufficiency for a specific purpose.

Our first scope limitation was to focus on objective characteristics of data. In order to measure objective characteristics, we identified ways of measuring that could be taken largely through reference to data in a database itself. For example, validity measures require defined data domains within the database (in a reference table, for example) or within the metadata (where a valid range of values could be defined). We extended this concept to include data quality measurement results themselves as references against which comparisons could be made. For example, many of the consistency measurement types depend on comparisons to previous measurements of the same dataset. In some cases, historical data quality measurements can provide a benchmark for any instance of the same measurement.

Next, we defined assessments that IT could use for purposes of overall data management. These included basic controls that confirm receipt of data, measures of the efficacy of technical processes in the data chain, and measures of the quality of data content. Such measurements represent a reasonable expectation for IT stewardship of data. Through process measures and controls, IT should know how much data systems were processing, how long it took to process the data, and how successful the processing was. Through content measures, IT should have a reasonable understanding of the completeness, consistency, and validity of the data. Because IT had responsibility for data modeling, IT was also in a position to measure the integrity of data relationships. As did the requirement for objective measurement types, this goal narrowed our choice of data quality dimensions from which measurements could be established.

Finally, and most importantly, we wanted to establish in-line measures—those taken in conjunction with the processing of data within a data store or other application for example, measurements that are taken as part of an extract, transform, and load (ETL) process. We wanted the ability to measure the quality of large amounts of complex data in an automated manner for purposes of monitoring and providing continuous quality assurance. By measuring defined characteristics in the same way each time data was loaded, measurements would enable us to understand trends in the data. They would also need to be designed to detect unexpected conditions or unexpected changes to data.

While we were thinking largely in terms of measurements for a data warehouse, it became clear that the measurement types could apply to other data stores and applications as well. So as we formulated them, we tried to express the types in generic language, referring to data sets, fields/columns, and data processes or processing rather than to structures specific to a data warehouse.

DQAF Quality Dimensions

As a result of these considerations, the DQAF focuses on a set of objective data characteristics associated with five dimensions of data quality: completeness, timeliness, validity, consistency, and integrity.

Completeness

Conceptually, *completeness* implies having all the necessary or appropriate parts; being entire, finished, total. The first condition of completeness is existence. Data must exist before it can be understood as complete. This need is so obvious that it is sometimes overlooked. But in many organizations, expectations about data cannot be met because they are based on the assumption that certain data already exists which does not, or that data exists in a usable form and it does not exist in that form. The discussion that follows is based on the assumption that the condition of existence has been met, that suitable data exists and therefore can be measured.

A dataset is compete to the degree that it contains required attributes and a sufficient number of records, and to the degree that attributes are populated in accord with data consumer expectations. For a dataset to be complete, at least three conditions must be met: the dataset must be defined so that it includes all the attributes desired (width); the dataset must contain the desired amount of data (depth); and the attributes must be populated to the extent desired (density). Each of these secondary dimensions of completeness is measured differently. Completeness can also be understood in relation to data processing, for example, having all necessary or appropriate data to begin processing and ensuring that data is not dropped from a dataset when it is processed. Finally, data completeness can be understood in relation to the overall sufficiency of data content to meet organizational needs.

Timeliness

In its most general definition, timeliness refers to the appropriateness of when an event happens. In relation to data quality content, *timeliness* has been defined as the degree to which data represent reality from the required point in time (English, 1999). With regard to processing, timeliness (also referred to as *latency*) is associated with data availability, the degree to which customers have the data they need at the right time. Measures of timeliness can be made in relation to a set schedule or to the occurrence of an event. For example, timeliness is the degree to which data delivery from a source system conforms to a schedule for delivery. In large data assets, data is made available once processing is complete. Unsuccessful processing can result in delays in data availability. The timeliness of events within data processing itself can be a measure of the health of the data delivery mechanisms.

Data lag (the time between when data is updated in its source and when it is made available to data consumers), *information float* (the time between when a fact becomes known and when it is available for use) and *volatility* (the degree to which data is likely to change over time) all influence the perception of data currency and timeliness. Given these factors, for most people it's clear that data can be "timely" according to a schedule and still not meet the needs of data consumers. In that case, the thing that needs to be changed is the schedule itself (for example, to reduce data lag), not how we objectively measure timeliness. As with other aspects of data, metadata about data timeliness—schedules and update processes—needs to be shared with data consumers so that they can make better decisions about whether and how to use data.

Validity

Validity is the degree to which data conform to a set of business rules, sometimes expressed as a standard or represented within a defined data domain. Validity is differentiated from both accuracy and correctness, each of which requires comparison to real-world objects to confirm. Validity is limited to measuring against substitutes or surrogates for real-world objects. These substitutes can be instantiated as data, allowing validity to be measured directly from within a dataset in a way that accuracy and correctness cannot be.

Consistency

Consistency can be regarded as the absence of variety or change. As with any measurement, assessing consistency requires comparison. There are several ways to think about consistency in relation to data and data management. It can be understood in relation to a standard or rule (in which case it resembles validity), in relation to other data in a database (internal consistency of data as a synonym for data integrity), in relation to data in other systems, or in relation to the results from a different instance of the same data production process.

To establish in-line measurement types, we focused on the consistency of data over time. Consistency is the degree to which data conform to an equivalent set of data, usually a set produced under similar conditions or a set produced by the same process over time. Consistency measures may involve built-in conformance to business rules (dependencies that can be established technically if logic can be clearly expressed), or they may reveal logical patterns created within the data that reflect the connections between the real-world situations that the data represents.

Integrity

Integrity refers to the state of being whole and undivided or the condition of being unified. Integrity is the degree to which data conform to data relationship rules (as defined by the data model) that are intended to ensure the complete, consistent, and valid presentation of data representing the same concepts. Because integrity represents the internal consistency and completeness of a dataset, it encompasses these other dimensions. We reserved the term *integrity* for cross-table relationships.

The Question of Accuracy

Accuracy is usually the first concept people think of when they try to describe high-quality data. *Accuracy* is defined as data's correctness or truth in representation. Accurate data is true and correct. Unfortunately, measuring accuracy is not simple. Doing so requires comparing data to the real-world entity it represents or to a surrogate representation that itself has been validated for accuracy. In taking in-line measures in a large database, it is not possible to measure accuracy through direct comparison. It is possible to set criteria for determining that data is inaccurate or incorrect, but it is not possible to determine what the correct or accurate data is (unless it can be compared to—i.e., validated against—other data in which there is 100% confidence of correctness). In cases where records representing the same real-world fact contain different data (for example, when different records for one person show two different birth dates), we can conclude logically that at least one of them must be incorrect. But it is not possible to determine the correct real-world fact (birth date) without reference to an outside source or standard that establishes that fact. If that source is available, then data can be validated directly against it (thus changing the measure to one of validity). In the absence of such a source, it is possible to identify records that are probably incorrect, but not to identify how to correct them. In any instance where direct comparison to a source is possible, a validity measure can be taken.

We used the concept of validity to describe (more accurately) the dimension of quality that we could measure. There are obvious limitations to doing so. Just because a data value is valid (meaning it is included in a domain of values associated with a data element) does not mean it is correct. For example, the ZIP code for Unionville, Connecticut is 06085 and one of Chicago's ZIP codes is 60685. An address record for Unionville containing a ZIP code of 60685 would be incorrect, even though 60685 is itself a valid ZIP code. While validity is not accuracy (valid values can be incorrect), there is still knowledge to be gained by measuring validity (invalid values cannot be correct).

Defining DQAF Measurement Types

The approach we took to defining measurement types was simple. We asked ourselves some basic questions about what it would mean to measure each dimension of quality we had identified at any point in a generic process of moving data into a data warehouse. For example, in what ways could we measure data completeness? What would measures of completeness look like? What examples of completeness measures did we already have? How could these be extended?

Answering these questions for each of the five quality dimensions, we collected a set of potential approaches to measurement and control. Our focus was on measurements that could be used to detect unexpected conditions or changes in data content that might indicate a problem with the quality of data. But we also recognized controls that might be used to stop data processing if specific adverse conditions were detected (for example, balance controls on files).

We tried to define each measurement type discretely in order to understand the individual functions required to take it. In some cases, there was more than one way of looking at a type. For example, some completeness measures, and even complex validity measures, can also be understood as integrity measures and vice versa. Because a goal of the project was to establish a common vocabulary and (to the degree possible) to limit redundancy in the framework, we made decisions about which dimension to associate with each type and we moved on.

Since our definition process involved thinking through how data moves from a source system to a target system, there is a general movement in the proposed types from data receipt through data processing and storage to consideration of the overall condition of data within a database. In addition, we considered how the types might be applied to different categories or facets of data. So there is also a general movement from simple to more complex variations on the types. The measures are presented in terms of an individual data store. However, many of them can be applied along the data chain; for example, as data moves from transactional systems to a data warehouse or from there to data marts. In fact, the measurement types could be applied within an application or, logically extended, across the entire data chain.

Metadata Requirements

Our identification of types made clear why any approach to data measurement requires metadata that describes data content, structure, and processing. Specifically, measurement requires knowledge of

- Business concepts represented by the data.
- Business and technical processes that create data.

- Business and technical processes that maintain, update, or delete data.
- The data model in the target system (i.e., where data will be measured).
- Data processing rules for the target system.

Although each of these subjects can be understood separately, knowledge of all five is needed to understand the data chain. Knowledge of business concepts is the foundation for measurement. It includes not only the concepts themselves but also how the concepts are represented and the relationships between. Data is created through business and technical processes. Knowledge of these processes is necessary to understand risks related to data and, ultimately, to identify ways of improving data quality. Data does not always stay in its original form. It may be changed (updated, deleted) as it is maintained. The data model and associated metadata are critical tools for understanding how data content is stored within a system and for identifying and refining expectations related to data. Likewise, it is necessary to know the rules used to process data within the system being measured in order to understand both risk points and measurement opportunities.

Saying that such metadata is needed is not the same as saying it is available and well documented. Metadata management is a challenge for most organizations. Many organizations, for example, do not have a documented data model. The model exists (in a sense) because data is "structured" in applications and data stores. However, without documentation, data structure is difficult to discern and requires a significant amount of analysis. As will be described in Section Three, if metadata does not exist to support data quality assessment, then it will need to be created as part of the assessment.[3]

Objects of Measurement and Assessment Categories

As we began to describe the measurement types in more detail, we recognized that measuring data quality sometimes involved measuring data content and, other times, data processing. Some types were associated with particular kinds of content (date fields, amount fields, etc.). So we characterized the types in relation not only to dimensions of quality, but also to data content, structure, and database processing. We called this characteristic of the measurement types *objects of measurement* (an awkward but functional term for awkward but functional categories). In our working listing, the types were associated with

- *The data model:* Activities for assessing facets of the data model related to the consistency within the data model, including the application of data standards.
- *Receipt of data:* Activities for ensuring the correct receipt of data of data for processing.
- *The condition of data upon receipt:* Activities for inspecting the condition of data upon receipt.
- *Data processing:* Activities for assessing the results of data processing data as well as for understanding the quality of process execution. (e.g., adherence to a schedule)
- *Data content:* Various activities for assessing data content.
  - Validity, including cross-column validity

---

[3]Olson (2003) describes the chicken-and-egg problem of metadata and asserts that part of data quality improvement is metadata improvement.

- Consistency, including the consistency of particular kinds of data content, such as
  - Amount fields and aggregated amount fields.
  - Date fields, aggregated date fields, and chronological relationships.
- *Cross-table content:* Activities for assessing the integrity of cross-table content, including parent–child relationships.
- *Overall database content:* Activities for assessing overall database content.

These categories provide some of the organizing principles for the next chapter. Alignment is not exact, however, because the primary organizing principle of the DQAF remains the dimensions of data quality.

As stated earlier, our focus was on in-line measurements. However, in order to explain them, we broadened the discussion to include a wider context. Significant assessment of the data and the data environment should take place before in-line measurement is established. Other measurements should take place periodically because they cannot suitably be taken in-line (many integrity measures, for example). And, once measurement is established, it will produce a set of data that needs to be managed. So, just as assessment of the data environment is necessary to establish measurement, it is also necessary, periodically, to assess the effectiveness of specific metrics and of the processes that support measurement.

To further clarify the measurement types, the refined DQAF also includes the concept of an *assessment category*. Assessment categories pertain to both the frequency of the measurement (periodic or in-line) and the type of assessment involved (control, measurement, assessment). They include: initial assessment, process control, in-line measurement, and periodic measurement. Figure 5.1 illustrates the relationship of assessment categories to the goals of data management (top row) to each other (second row) and to a set of assessment activities (middle boxes).

Functions in Measurement: Collect, Calculate, Compare

In developing the DQAF, we also wanted to describe how to take measurements. With this information, the DQAF could provide a draft set of specifications for an overall system of measurement. The basis for describing how to execute each measurement type was a simple paradigm: Collect, Calculate, Compare. The ways of collecting raw measurement data can be understood largely in terms of what features of the data need to be counted (file sizes, process duration, record counts, group-bys, etc.). Calculations applied to raw measurement data help to make it comprehensible (percentages, averages, etc.) In order to draw conclusions about data quality, the results of these calculations need to be compared to a signifier for that quality (e.g., a threshold or other standard, such as the results of past measurements in a stable process).

The *how* of each measurement type will be discussed in depth in Section Six. This concept has been introduced in this chapter because it is integral to the overall in-line measurement process. Figure 5.2 illustrates the approach. During the measurement requirements definition process, expectations are defined and associated with measurement types (see Section Four). In-line measurement involves the collection of measurement data so that calculations and comparisons can be made and notifications sent. Use of the results requires having analysts respond to unexpected measurement results. The illustrations of basic validity and consistency measures in the next chapter also draw on the collect, calculate, compare paradigm. (See Figures 6.2 and 6.3.)

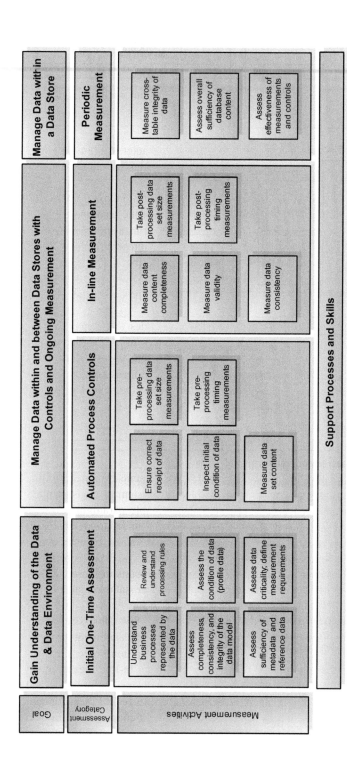

FIGURE 5.1 DQAF Overview–The Context of Data Assessment

The goal of the DQAF is to provide a comprehensive approach to data assessment. The top row represents the primary data management goal of each assessment category. For example, the goal of initial one-time assessment is to gain an understanding of the data and its environment. The second row contains the assessment categories. Assessment categories pertain to both the frequency of assessment (one-time, ongoing, or periodic) and the type of assessment (control, measurement, assessment). The small boxes in the third row represent a set of assessment activities related to objects of measurement and measurement types. Objects of measurement categorize the measurement types in terms of whether they focus on process or content, or on a particular part of a process (e.g., receipt of data) or kind of content (e.g., the data model). Measurement types are categories within a dimension of data quality that allow for repeatable patterns of measurement: to be executed against any data that fits the criteria required by the type, regardless of specific data content. The bottom row, support processes and skills, provides the foundation for the framework. Successful data quality measurement depends on having knowledgeable people in place to analyze results and respond to findings. *Note:* While some measurement activities are type-specific, measurement types are not detailed as a category in this figure, because including all of them would make the schematic very dense. In Section Six, each measurement type is associated with an assessment category and an object of measurement (as well as a dimension of quality).

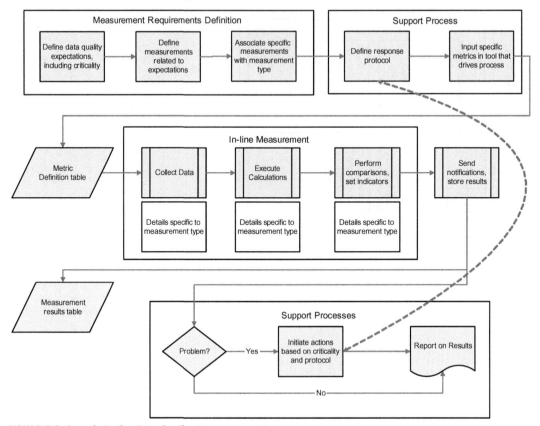

FIGURE 5.2 Generic In-line Data Quality Measurement Process

All in-line measurements follow a similar form: collect raw data, execute calculations against it to make it comprehensible, and compare the results against a threshold or other standard to make them meaningful. The figure depicts the processes and inputs needed to establish effective metrics in an overall system of measurement. First expectations related to data must be defined and associated with measurement types. As part of this definition, metrics should be rated on a scale of criticality and response protocols should be defined. Specific metrics can then be set up in the definition tables. These drive the collection of measurement data, which provides input into a set of calculations and comparison based on the measurement types. The comparison process assigns indicators based on defined thresholds (usually automated and, for a stable process, based on the history of past results). If the measurements produce unexpected results, notifications will be sent and response protocols initiated. All results will be stored in results tables for trend analysis and reporting. Response protocols should be revised continuously as more is learned about how best to respond to findings.

Concluding Thoughts

This chapter has described the context in which the DQAF was initially developed. I have described the problem we were trying to solve when we started the project and some of the challenges related to establishing an approach to measurement; how we limited our scope in order to focus on objective dimensions of quality; and how we introduced additional organizational categories that allow further understanding of the options for measurement. We now have a picture of the overall context of data quality assessment and one of the basic functions of in-line measurement. The next chapter will describe the initial formulation of the DQAF measurement types.

DQAF Measurement Types

Purpose

This chapter describes the DQAF as it was originally formulated and provides a high-level description of the DQAF's measurement types. They are categorized in terms of objects of measurement, the measurement and control activities associated with data flow from a source to a target system, and the data quality dimensions of completeness, timeliness, validity, consistency, and integrity. The chapter includes diagrams of several basic processes that show what a comprehensive data quality measurement system might look like. We ultimately combined and compressed the initial set to the 48 types summarized at the end of this chapter and discussed in depth in Section Six. Walking through the process of formulation will enable you to understand how the pieces came together and how they comprise an overall approach to data quality measurement.

Consistency of the Data Model

Consistent application of data model standards contributes to overall data consistency. Data standards and naming conventions help ensure consistent representation of concepts. As a starting point to understand the quality of data in a database, it is necessary to assess the condition of the data model. In particular, it is important to know what standards exist for representing data and how effectively they have been enforced within the data model itself. The following conditions can be thought of as prerequisites to the overall ability to measure data quality. The ways that enforcement of data standards can show up in the model include the following:

- Consistent formatting of data within a field, including a consistent degree of precision within a field
- Consistent formatting of data within fields of the same type across a database, including a consistent degree of precision within fields of the same type throughout the database
- Consistent default value for fields of the same data type

If attributes are modeled in a consistent way, all subsequent assessments are easier. If they are modeled inconsistently, comparisons are more difficult. To take a simple example, suppose in a database that contains address data, there is not a standard default value for ZIP code. On some tables, unknown or missing ZIP codes are left blank; on others, they are populated with 00000; and on a third set, they are populated with 99999 or just plain 0. Understanding the level of invalid ZIP codes in any individual table requires knowing or determining the range of ways invalids are represented. To understand the relationship between invalids between any two tables requires a similar level of knowledge and the ability to reconcile differences. One standard default would simplify both assessment and ongoing maintenance.

Ensuring the Correct Receipt of Data for Processing

Problems with data processing can be costly and risky. Any time a process is stopped and restarted there is a risk that undetected changes to the data may adversely affect its quality. Ensuring that the data is in its expected condition when it is delivered reduces these risks related to processing. The simplest of these activities ensure that the dataset is complete. They include the following:

- Dataset completeness/availability—Confirm all files are available for processing (with version check if possible)
- Dataset completeness—For files, compare record counts in a file to record counts documented in a control record; for other methods of delivery, count the rate of delivery (e.g., the rate of messages delivered)
- Dataset completeness—Compare summarized data in amount fields to summarized amount provided in a control record
- File completeness—Reasonability check comparing size of input file to size of past input files for the same process

Not all of these activities apply to all situations. Which to use in a particular system depends on data content and system design. If your data includes financial attributes that are expected to balance, then summarized amount fields can be used as a control. If the number of records received for a particular process is expected to be similar each time the process is run, then comparing the size of any instance of a file to the size of past instances can provide a reasonability check. (See Figure 6.1.)

Inspecting the Condition of Data upon Receipt

Specifications for data to be processed by a database embody expectations about the data. They detail conditions of the data necessary for technical processes to run successfully. Additional data inspection activities can confirm that aspects of the initial condition of data conform to expectations described in specifications. For example,

- Record completeness—Length of records matches a defined expectation based on file structure.[1]
- Field completeness—All non-nullable fields are populated.

---

[1] This process control was pointed out to me by the data delivery team on a warehouse project. Records that are of narrower than expected width may have been truncated; those that are wider may have been corrupted.

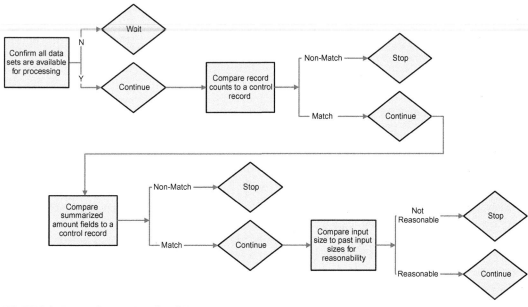

FIGURE 6.1 Ensure Correct Receipt of Data

The purpose of controls related to the correct receipt of data is to ensure that data is in condition to be processed and stored. The process includes a set of check points based on information provided by source systems, as well as a reasonability check based on past sizes of datasets.

- Dataset integrity—Duplicate records are identified and removed.[2]

In addition to the technical aspects, a set of reasonability checks can be established based on rules about data content that embody expectations about the business relationships inherent in the data.

- Dataset integrity reasonability check—Ratio of duplicate records to total records in dataset is consistent with a defined threshold or historical percentage for datasets for the same process
- Field content completeness—Number and percentage of records defaulted for critical fields in a source-provided field compared with defined threshold or historical number and percentage
- Dataset completeness based on date criteria—Minimum and maximum dates on critical date fields conform to a defined range or rule such as a reasonability check based on known parameters for loading data (i.e., data loaded in February as part of a monthly process would contain records largely from January); can include additional tests, for example, data should not contain future dates

---

[2] As a category of measurement, understanding the level of duplicate records is simple. It means counting them. However, it depends on having rules for identifying duplicate (or triplicate, etc.) records, and de-duplication rules are not usually simple. To remove multiple instances of the same record requires a clear definition of one instance of a record. Requirements around what equals a record differ greatly depending on what kind of data you are managing. For example, managing master data requires identifying one record (the "golden record") that represents an individual instance of an entity. In contrast, transactional data may have many records associated with the different states of one transaction (corrections, reversals, multiple billings, and payments). See Talburt (2011) and McGilvray (2008).

The presence of a higher ratio of duplicate records may indicate a change in processing in a source system, as could a change in the population level of critical fields. Like other reasonability checks, these apply where there is an expectation that data would have relatively consistent content each time it is processed.

Assessing the Results of Data Processing

Data processing jobs should be thoroughly tested before they are put into a production database. However, processing data can produce unexpected results if untested conditions appear in the data or if changes made in one area of a database adversely affect another area. Controls and measurements can be put in place to detect such situations. For example,

- Dataset completeness through a process—Balance record counts throughout a process, account for rejected records, including duplicates, for exact balance situations
- Dataset completeness through a process— Reasonability check comparing size of input to size of output, to create a ratio of input to output; ratio would be consistent each time the data is processed
- Dataset content completeness—Balance Summing—Balance amount fields throughout a process, account for rejected records, including duplicates, for exact balance situations
- Field content completeness—Number and percentage of records dropped due to being incomplete based on defined conditions, such as missing identifiers, during data processing; compare with a defined threshold or historical number and percentage
- Field content completeness—Amount field reasonability check—Ratio of summed amount field at start and completion of a process, for nonexact balance situations where ratio is expected to be consistent each time the data is processed
- Field content completeness—Number and percentage of records defaulted in a derived field compared with defined threshold or historical number and percentage
- Timely delivery of datasets for processing—Actual time of data delivery versus scheduled data delivery
- Timing of data processing—Reasonability check of process duration comparing the duration of any instance of the process to historical duration; for processes expected to have a consistent duration
- Timely availability of data—Actual data availability versus scheduled data availability

Each of these assessments can provide a level of assurance about the condition of the data. Determining the ones that will work best within a particular system requires knowledge of the system, the data content, and the data model.

Assessing the Validity of Data Content

While many measures of completeness and timeliness are interwoven with data processing, measures of validity are based on comparisons to a standard or rule that defines the domain of valid values. Most fields for which validity can be measured are populated with codes or other shorthand signifiers of meaning. Codes may be defined in a reference table or as part of a range of values or based on an algorithm. Conceptually, a validity measure is just a test of membership in a domain. From a technical point of view, ways of measuring validity depend on how the data that defines the domain is stored. Validity checks can be understood in terms of the way their domains are defined.

- Basic validity check—Comparison between incoming values and valid values as defined in a code table or listing.
- Basic range of values check—Comparison of incoming data values to values defined within a stated range (with potential for a dynamic range) including a date range.
- Validity check based on a checksum or other algorithm—for example, to test the validity of Social Security numbers, National Provider Identifiers, or other numbers generated through an algorithm.

The question most people want to answer in relation to validity is: How much of this data is invalid? In some cases, domains contain a small set of values, and validity measures at the level of the individual value are comprehensible. For example, in most systems, the gender code consists of representations of male, female, and unknown. While the concept of gender in our culture is changing (so that some systems will have values to signify transgender or changes in gender), the set of codes values used to represent gender is still relatively small. On the other hand, codes representing medical procedures (CPT codes, HCPCS codes, ICD procedure codes) number in the tens of thousands. To make measurement of validity comprehensible (especially for high cardinality code sets), it is helpful to have both detail of the individual codes and a measure of the overall level of valid and invalid codes.

When we first defined the DQAF, we included pairs of validity measures: a detail measure at the level of the value and a summary accounting for the roll-up of counts and percentages of valid and invalid codes. However, it quickly became clear that the validity summary measure looked pretty much the same (and thus could be represented the same way) regardless of the basis of the detailed validity measure. So, we created one type to describe all validity roll-ups.

- Roll-up counts and percentage of valid/invalid from a detailed validity measurement.

Validity checks against code tables or ranges of values focus on one field at a time. More complex forms of validity involve the relationship between fields or across tables. These can be more challenging to measure because they often require documentation of complex rules in a form that can be used to make the comparisons.

- Validity of values in related columns on the same table; for example ZIP codes to State Abbreviation Codes.
- Validity of values based on a business rule; for example, Death Date should be populated only when Patient Status equals "deceased".
- Validity of values across tables; for example, ZIP Code to State Code on two different tables.

As with the single-column measures of validity, each of these validity measurement types should include a roll-up of valid-to-invalid results (see Figure 6.2). In many cases, because of differences in the timing of data delivery and the nature of the data content, cross-table relationships cannot be measured effectively through in-line measures. These are better thought of as measures of integrity that can be taken as part of periodic measurement of data.

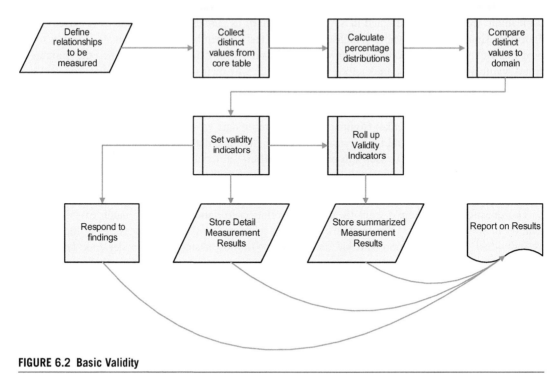

FIGURE 6.2 Basic Validity

The process to confirm data validity is similar regardless of how the domain of valid values is defined (set of valid values, range of values, or rule). First, the data that will be validated must be identified and its domain defined. Next, record counts for the distinct value set must be collected from the core data. Then the distinct values can be compared to the domain and validity indicators can be assigned. The results of the comparisons constitute the detailed measurements. For reporting purposes, these results can be rolled up to an overall percentage of valid and invalid values.

Assessing the Consistency of Data Content

Like validity measures, consistency measures focus on data content. Assessing consistency in any manner requires an expectation that data elements or datasets will be similar to each other in definable ways. Consistency can be understood in several ways depending on data content and the activities related to collecting and storing it.

Medical claim data, for example, represents the activities of medical providers interacting with patients. In a large set of claim data, such as the millions of records that might be loaded to a data warehouse for a health insurance company, there will be repeated patterns in the data. For a given week, month, or quarter, many features of this data will be similar to data representing these activities for any other week, month, or quarter. There will be a similar proportion of claims related to office visits, inpatient hospital stays, and outpatient events. In any large set of such data, there will also be a consistent ratio between the number of individual patients receiving care and the number of medical providers giving care. Significant changes in these patterns or ratios can alert data managers to potential data quality problems. Such changes can also reflect genuine changes in medical practices.

Such real-world changes, however, tend to happen more slowly over time and often as the result of known causes. Monitoring data quality provides a level of knowledge about expected consistency of practices the data represents. This knowledge, in turn, can be used to help detect actual problems with the data when those arise.

The first set of consistency measures applies data profiling-like activities to single fields or to related fields, in increasingly more complex ways.

- Consistent content of an individual field—Measured through a record count distribution of values (or column profile). For example, run-over-run or per load column distribution analysis, including row counts and percentage of row counts (ideally with a validity check).
- Consistent dataset level content—Reasonability check based on distinct counts of important fields or entities represented in those fields compared. For example, a count of the distinct number of customers represented in sales data or the distinct number of insured persons (members) represented in medical claim data.
- Consistent dataset level content—Reasonability based on ratio between distinct counts of important fields/entities (e.g., customers/sales office, claims/insured person).
- Consistent content across fields—Relationship profile of values in two or more data elements within a table/dataset (multicolumn relationship), ideally with qualifiers that enable precise definition of expectations and rules.

In each case, consistency of the data is determined through comparisons with previous instances of the same specific measurements.

Consistency can be measured in ways in addition to record counts. Data in amount fields may also have patterns that are expected to stay reasonably stable if business conditions and processes are stable. For example, in any large set of medical claims not only would there be a similar proportion of claims related to office visits, inpatient stays, and outpatient events, but the costs associated with these types of medical events would have consistent relationship to each other. Consistency measures related to amount fields include, for example,

- Consistent content—Reasonability check based on total amount calculations (sum [total amount]) across a secondary field or fields.
- Consistent content— Reasonability check based on average amount calculations across a secondary field or fields.
- Consistent content— Reasonability check based on ratio between two amount fields, potentially across a secondary field or fields.

From a business perspective, expenses and revenue are often associated with specific time periods, such as a month, quarter, or year. For this reason, it is helpful to measure consistency patterns based on aggregated dates. Whether or not these measures can be taken in-line depends on how a particular database processes its data. For example, it would not make sense to take aggregated date measures in-line in databases that process incremental loads. Such checks could be run against whole tables as part of processing that takes place after incremental data has been loaded. However, in a database that reprocesses an entire dataset, aggregated measures could be taken as part of data processing. Such measurement types include

- Consistent content—Record count and percentage reasonability based on an aggregated date, such as a month, quarter, or year.

- Consistent content within a table—Total amount reasonability based on aggregated dates; distinct counts against an aggregated date, such as a month, quarter, or year.
- Consistent content across tables—Total amount reasonability based on aggregated dates; distinct counts against an aggregated date, such as a month, quarter, or year between two tables within the same database. This concept can be extended to data from two systems.

Date fields also often play an important part in business rules and relationships. Most business processes have a logical order that should be reflected in data representing process steps. A customer must place an order before products can be shipped, for example. Some of these relationships can be understood through measures of data consistency, such as,

- Consistent relationship between important date fields, based on chronological business rules in one table. For example, in medical claims, date of service must come before adjudication date.
- Consistent relationship between important date fields, calculated as a difference between dates, expressed as days elapsed. For example, the number of days elapsed between when an order is placed and when a product is shipped is expected to be consistent. Can also be applied to dates associated with data delivery and processing.
- Roll-up of consistent relationship between important date fields, calculated as the difference between dates, expressed as days elapsed.
- Timeliness—Lag time between business processes—Measured by date fields representing the process points (e.g., for medical claims, date of service, and adjudication date).

Measuring consistency between date fields is a little tricky. Unlike other kinds of data (code sets, for example), the specific values found in date data are not expected to correspond exactly with each load of a database. While we may expect a similar number of records to be processed in April and June, we would not expect the same date values (because time would be marching on and new specific dates would be populated in new data). However it may be reasonable to expect a consistent duration of time to pass between events. For example, you may expect at least 80% of your orders to ship within two days of being placed. Such a measure of days elapsed may be both a data quality and service quality measure. If you are monitoring the consistency of days elapsed between two critical fields and you see a change in results, you will need to investigate whether the change is caused by a problem in your data or a change in business processes. From a data management point of view, dataset delivery and processing dates can be used to measure the efficiency of a system in making data available, as well as adherence to service-level agreements (See Figure 6.3).

Comments on the Placement of In-line Measurements

As noted earlier, in order to identify ways to measure data, we asked some basic questions about dimensions of quality and data processing. Once we had identified a set of measurement types, it became clear that they aligned with a basic data flow. Types designed to ensure the correct receipt of data or confirm the condition of data upon receipt should be executed before data is processed. Data should be measured at the earliest point in any process, so if something is wrong with it, that fact can be detected and costly re-running of data processes can be avoided. For example, validity checks and some consistency checks on source data can be taken before data is processed. Additional consistency and completeness checks can be taken as in-line measurements. If the results of data transformation

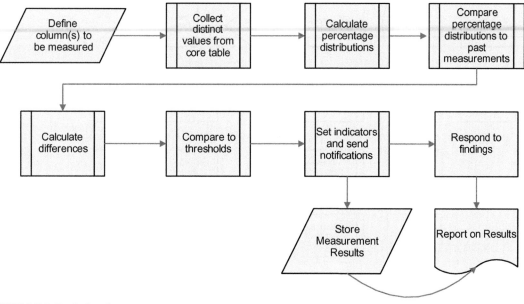

FIGURE 6.3 Basic Consistency

The process of measuring consistency compared with past instances of the same dataset follows a pattern. First, the data that will be measured must be identified. Next record counts for the distinct value set must be collected from the core data, so that the percentage of records associated with each value or set can be calculated. Then the percentage of each distinct value set can be compared to the percentage in past instances of the dataset, and a difference can be calculated. If this difference is significant, notifications should be sent so that analysts can review the data and determine whether the difference indicates a problem with the data. The results of the comparisons constitute the detailed measurements.

are being measured, measurements should be taken immediately after the transformation process to ensure that the results meet expectations. Process duration measurements may pertain to the overall process or to any subprocess.

Where the DQAF measures are applied therefore depends on both the type of measure and the specifics of the data flow. Some—such as checks on the timing of files delivered for a process—are easy to place. By definition and logically, they need to come at the beginning of a data flow; everything that follows depends on them. Other measures, such as consistency checks on amount fields or dates, do not have one set place. Placing them requires not only a plan for how to build them, but also an assessment of risks related to late detection, the process for notification when thresholds are crossed (see Figure 6.4).

A few basic principles can be applied to determine placement of measures:

- Data quality should be measured at the earliest possible point in the data flow (as far upstream, as close to the source, as possible) to confirm data meets business expectations before time is invested in processing it.

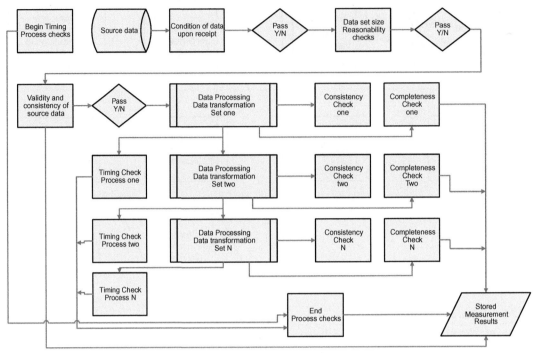

FIGURE 6.4 DQAF Measurement Types in a Generic Data Flow

In-line measurement types include both content and process measures. Types related to ensuring the correct receipt of data for processing and understanding the condition of data upon receipt should be executed before data is processed. Validity, consistency, and additional completeness checks can be taken as in-line measurements. Process duration measurements may pertain to the overall process or to any sub-process.

- Direct-moved fields can be measured at the beginning of a data flow (i.e., before processing begins.
- If they cannot be measured in the ideal position, either type of field can be measured from a load file. In situations where distributions are being taken for multiple fields on one file, measuring from the load file simplifies the data collection.
- Lower risk data—data that is not transformed during processing—can be measured once and then monitored in a simpler manner as it flows downstream. Monitoring ensures that its quality does not deteriorate. (Even data that is not supposed to be transformed can be changed—truncated, misaligned—if it is unexpectedly impacted by other changes in the data flow).
- Data transformations and derivations are the points of highest risk to data. Therefore data should be measured in conjunction with transformation processes to ensure the transformations have produced expected results. It should be measured as soon as possible after the transformation or derivation has taken place.

Periodic Measurement of Cross-table Content Integrity

While relationships within a table can represent measurable rules, many of the benefits of large databases come from relationships between tables. If these relationships do not adhere as expected, data will be difficult to use. One of the most basic expectations of quality within a database is the expectation of referential integrity between related tables. Measuring referential integrity requires identifying instances where this relationship does not hold. The concept of referential integrity is often expressed in terms of "parent" and "child" tables. A child table inherits values from its parent table. Therefore all values on a child table are expected to be present on the parent table. In some cases, there is an expectation that all parent records will have at least one child record. Referential integrity can also be described in terms of header and detail records. Header/detail is a useful way of discussing the concept because it emphasizes the relation between records, whereas discussions of parent/child referential integrity often focus on reference data and therefore on specific values, rather than records. Whichever way it is expressed, the two basic ways of measuring referential integrity are:

- Parent/child referential integrity between tables to identify parentless child (i.e., "orphan") records or values.
- Child/parent referential integrity between fact tables to identify "childless" parent records or values.

Referential integrity can be described through several dimensions of quality. As the name implies, referential integrity is a form of data integrity representing the degree to which data conform to data relationship defined in a data model. Integrity itself can be thought of as the internal consistency of a dataset. And a referential relation between two tables can be understood as a form of data completeness. We chose to associate these measures with the dimension of integrity because DQAF integrity measurement types emphasize cross-table relationships. Other cross-table consistency measures extend concepts associated with fields in one table.

- Consistent relationships within the data—Relationship profile of two or more data elements within a set of tables or between files (multicolumn relationship across tables); with or qualifiers that enable precise definitions of expectations and rules.
- Consistent content—Consistency between summed amount fields across tables.
- Consistent content—Consistent ratio of amount fields across tables.
- Consistent relationship between important date fields across tables, based on business rules for chronology (e.g., birth date must be before death date, even if records for these events are stored in different tables).

These more complex measures refer to more complex rules. When the kinds of relationships implied by these measures do not meet expectations, data consumers often report quality problems. Because cross-table relationships are critical, it is tempting to try to measure them as a starting point for improving data quality. But there is a point of diminishing returns in relation to metrics intended for monitoring data quality. Measures that are overly complex are less likely to identify specific problems than are simpler measurements, since a complex process of measuring may mask the relationships that speak to the quality of the data. The key to measurement is to measure the right relationships in the right way. From a practical point of view and in terms of problem analysis, it is necessary to measure basic data characteristics before tackling complex relationships. If the basic characteristics are not sound, the more complex relationships cannot be. Basic characteristics are important in and of themselves, and they are also the raw material of more complex measures. The basics can often be monitored on an ongoing basis as part of regular data processing, while more complex relationships require periodic measurement apart from database loads.

Assessing Overall Database Content

Knowledge of the data model is critical to assessing overall database content. The model provides a picture of the data content and is the foundation for understanding whether content is suitable and sufficient for defined purposes. Data consumers can use the model, along with requirements for specific purposes (defined based on objective criteria, such as sample size) to make an initial determination of the data's suitability. The quality of data overall can also be compared to a standard dataset that has been assessed based on defined criteria. Two measurement type candidates address these options:

- Sufficiency and suitability of the data for a specific purpose based on a defined rule, such as record count, date range, time frame, or presence of a particular record type or represented entity.
- Consistency of data in relation to a benchmark or set of benchmarks, such as external industry or nationally established measurements for similar data.

Measures of overall content are less about the quality of individual data elements or rules than they are about whether the set of data present in a database aligns with the fundamental requirements of any specific purpose for which data consumers intend to use it. And they introduce two new concepts that we did not originally call out as dimensions: sufficiency and suitability.

Sufficiency is a variation on completeness; it refers to "the condition of being adequate" (*NOAD*). If you have a sufficient amount of something, then you have enough. With respect to data quality, sufficiency can be measured against the requirements of a particular use of data. So, for example, an analysis of demographic data may require that a certain percentage of a population be represented in the data for the data to be sufficient for statistical uses. *Suitability* also pertains to how well data meets requirements; it refers to "being right or appropriate for a person, purpose, or situation." A data sample might be sufficient (of the right size, representing a sufficient percentage of a population) but still not be suitable. For example, it might contain records related only to people over the age of 62 and therefore would not have the kind of demographic spread needed to study a wider population. Or the dataset might differ significantly from an established benchmark, such as a set of measurements produced by a standards organization. In the health care industry, there are many such benchmarks; for example, HEDIS measurements of quality.[3] To the degree that their requirements can be defined objectively, in terms of number of record, dates, or other attributes, sufficiency and suitability can be measured. Both of these concepts can be extended to a wide set of requirements that might be defined by the community of data consumers who use a particular data store.

---

[3]The Healthcare Effectiveness Data and Information Set (HEDIS) is a tool used by more than 90% of America's health plans to measure performance on important dimensions of care and service.

Assessing Controls and Measurements

While developing the listing of measurement types, it became clear that measuring would produce both metadata for the measurements (in the form of metric definitions) and metadata related to the data store's core data (in the form of measurement results) and that this data would need to be managed. One of the temptations associated with automating measurement is that you might try to measure everything. Doing so is counterproductive. The goal of in-line data quality measurement should be to establish an optimal set of measurements to provide quality assurance and to minimize risk.

Successful measurement absolutely requires having people in place to review and use the results. Very few organizations have the resources needed to manage results related to all the measurements they could possibly take.

These conditions of successful measurement mean that it is important periodically to review the specific metrics you establish in order to determine whether they are helping you understand, speak to, and improve the quality of your data. Our final measurement type refers to this need:

- Assess the effectiveness of measurements and controls

The Measurement Types: Consolidated Listing

The comprehensive set of DQAF measurement types contained a mix of possibilities: content measures and process measures; simple controls and complex in-line measurements; attribute-focused validity measures and comprehensive assessments; widely applicable consistency measures and measures focused on particular data types.

While we began our project with the hope of establishing repeatable processes for in-line measurements, ultimately we produced a set of measurement types that can be applied at different points in the general process of data assessment: initial assessments that establish the baseline condition of the data, the data model, and the metadata; process controls that assure the integrity of data as it moves between or within systems; in-line measurements taken as part of data processing; periodic measurements that test the integrity of data relationships within a database; and periodic assessments that analyze the sufficiency of database content to meet the ongoing needs of the organization.

Having established the listing, we removed some of the redundancy and tightened the descriptions to include 48 individual measurement types (see Table 6.1). Each type is numbered, associated with a dimension of data quality, named, and briefly described. Each is also associated with an object of measurement so that you can understand what aspect of data structure, content, or process is being measured; and with an assessment category that indicates the frequency as well as the kind of assessment represented by the measurement type.

In reviewing the set of measurement types, it is helpful to remember that the DQAF's original purpose was descriptive: It was intended to build a common vocabulary around data quality measurement. While the framework is comprehensive, implementing the entire thing should not be a goal in and of itself. Organizations should look to implement an optimal set of metrics for managing risks associated with their particular data. The range of options should aid in making decisions about where to begin.

Table 6.1 The Measurement Types: Consolidated Listing

Number	Dimension of Quality	Measurement Type	Measurement Type Description	Object of Measurement	Assessment Category
1	Completeness	Dataset completeness—sufficiency of meta and reference data	Assess sufficiency of metadata and reference data	Overall database content	Initial one-time assessment
2	Consistency	Consistent formatting within a field	Assess column properties and data for consistent formatting of data within a field	Data model	Initial one-time assessment
3	Integrity/Consistency	Consistent formatting cross-table	Assess column properties and data for consistent formatting of data within fields of the same type across a data base	Data model	Initial one-time assessment
4	Consistency	Consistent use of default values for a field	Assess column properties and data for default value(s) assigned for each field that can be defaulted	Data model	Initial one-time assessment
5	Integrity/Consistency	Consistent defaults cross-table	Assess column properties and data for consistent default value for fields of the same data type	Data model	Initial one-time assessment
6	Timeliness	Timely delivery of data for processing	Compare actual time of data delivery to scheduled data delivery	Process/Adherence to schedule	In-line measurement
7	Completeness	Dataset completeness—availability for processing	For files, confirm all files are available for processing (with version check if possible).	Receipt of data	Process control
8	Completeness	Dataset completeness—record counts	For files, compare record counts in a file to record counts documented in a control record	Receipt of data	Process control
9	Completeness	Dataset completeness—summarized amount field data	For files, compare summarized data in amount fields to summarized amount provided in a control record	Receipt of data	Process control

(Continued)

Table 6.1 The Measurement Types: Consolidated Listing (*Continued*)

Number	Dimension of Quality	Measurement Type	Measurement Type Description	Object of Measurement	Assessment Category
10	Completeness	Dataset completeness— size compared to past sizes	Reasonability check, compare size of input to size of past input for previous runs of the same process; record count for files, number or rate of messages, summarized data, etc.	Receipt of data	In-line measurement
11	Completeness	Record completeness— length	Ensure length of records matches a defined expectation	Condition of data upon receipt	Process control
12	Completeness	Field completeness— non-nullable fields	Ensure all non-nullable fields are populated	Condition of data upon receipt	Process control
13	Integrity/ Completeness	Dataset integrity— de-duping	Identify and remove duplicate records	Condition of data upon receipt	Process control
14	Integrity/ Completeness	Dataset integrity— duplicate record reasonability check	Reasonability check, compare ratio of duplicate records to total records in a dataset to the ratio in previous instances of dataset	Condition of data upon receipt	In-line measurement
15	Completeness	Field content completeness— defaults from source	Reasonability check, compare the number and percentage of records defaulted for source-provided critical fields to a defined threshold or historical number and percentage	Condition of data upon receipt	In-line measurement
16	Completeness	Dataset completeness based on date criteria	Ensure minimum and maximum dates on critical dates fields conform to a defined range identified parameters for loading data	Condition of data upon receipt	Process control
17	Completeness	Dataset reasonability based on date criteria	Ensure minimum and maximum dates on critical dates fields conform to a reasonability rule	Condition of data upon receipt	In-line measurement

(Continued)

Table 6.1 The Measurement Types: Consolidated Listing (*Continued*)

Number	Dimension of Quality	Measurement Type	Measurement Type Description	Object of Measurement	Assessment Category
18	Completeness	Field content completeness— received data is missing fields critical to processing	Inspect population of critical fields before processing records	Condition of data upon receipt	Process control
19	Completeness	Dataset completeness— balance record counts through a process	Balance record counts throughout data processing, account for rejected records, including duplicates; for exact balance situations	Data processing	Process control
20	Completeness	Dataset completeness— reasons for rejecting records	Reasonability check, compare number and percentage of records dropped for specific reasons with a defined threshold or historical number and percentage	Data processing	In-line measurement
21	Completeness	Dataset completeness through a process—ratio of input to output	Reasonability check, compare the ratio of process input/output to the ratio in previous instances of dataset	Data processing	In-line measurement
22	Completeness	Dataset completeness through a process—balance amount fields	Balance amount field content throughout a process, for exact balance situations	Data processing	Process control
23	Completeness	Field content completeness— ratio of summed amount fields	Amount field reasonability check, compare ratio of summed amount field input and output to ratio of previous instances of a dataset, for nonexact balance situations	Content/ amount fields	In-line measurement
24	Completeness	Field content completeness— defaults from derivation (subtype of #33 multicolumn profile)	Reasonability check, compare the number and percentage of records defaulted for derived fields to a defined threshold or historical number and percentage	Data processing	In-line measurement

Table 6.1 The Measurement Types: Consolidated Listing (*Continued*)

Number	Dimension of Quality	Measurement Type	Measurement Type Description	Object of Measurement	Assessment Category
25	Timeliness	Data processing duration	Reasonability check, compare process duration to historical process duration or to a defined time limit	Data processing	In-line measurement
26	Timeliness	Timely availability of data for access	Compare actual time data is available for data consumers access to scheduled time of data availability	Process/ Adherence to schedule	In-line measurement
27	Validity	Validity check, single field, detailed results	Compare values on incoming data to valid values in a defined domain (reference table, range, or mathematical rule)	Content/row counts	In-line measurement
28	Validity	Validity check, roll-up	Summarize results of detailed validity check; compare roll-up counts and percentage of valid/ invalid values to historical levels	Content summary	In-line measurement
29	Integrity/ Validity	Validity check, multiple columns within a table, detailed results	Compare values in related columns on the same table to values in a mapped relationship or business rule	Content/row counts	In-line measurement
30	Consistency	Consistent column profile	Reasonability check, compare record count distribution of values (column profile) to past instances of data populating the same field.	Content/row counts	In-line measurement
31	Consistency	Consistent dataset content, distinct count of represented entity, with ratios to record counts	Reasonability check, compare distinct counts of entities represented within a dataset (e.g., the distinct number of customers represented in sales data) to threshold, historical counts, or total records	Content summary	In-line measurement

(*Continued*)

Table 6.1 The Measurement Types: Consolidated Listing (*Continued*)

Number	Dimension of Quality	Measurement Type	Measurement Type Description	Object of Measurement	Assessment Category
32	Consistency	Consistent dataset content, ratio of distinct counts of two represented entities	Reasonability check, compare ratio between distinct counts of important fields/entities (e.g., customers/sales office, claims/insured person) to threshold or historical ratio	Content summary	In-line measurement
33	Consistency	Consistent multicolumn profile	Reasonability check, compare record count distribution of values across multiple fields to historical percentages, in order to test business rules (multicolumn profile with qualifiers)	Content/row counts	In-line measurement
34	Consistency	Chronology consistent with business rules within a table (subtype of #33 multicolumn profile)	Reasonability check, compare date values to business rule for chronology	Content/date content	In-line measurement
35	Consistency	Consistent time elapsed (hours, days, months, etc.)	Reasonability check, compare consistency of time elapsed to past instances of data populating the same fields	Content/date content	In-line measurement
36	Consistency	Consistent amount field calculations across secondary fields	Reasonability check, compare amount column calculations, sum (total) amount, percentage of total amount, and average amount across a secondary field or fields to historical counts and percentages, with qualifiers to narrow results.	Content/ amount fields	In-line measurement

(*Continued*)

Table 6.1 The Measurement Types: Consolidated Listing (*Continued*)

Number	Dimension of Quality	Measurement Type	Measurement Type Description	Object of Measurement	Assessment Category
37	Consistency	Consistent record counts by aggregated date	Reasonability check, compare record counts and percentage of record counts associated an aggregated date, such as a month, quarter, or year, to historical counts and percentages	Content/ aggregated date	Periodic measurement
38	Consistency	Consistent amount field data by aggregated date	Reasonability check, compare amount field data (total amount, percentage of total amount) aggregated by date (month, quarter, or year) to historical total and percentage	Content/ aggregated date	Periodic measurement
39	Integrity/ Completeness	Parent/child referential integrity	Confirm referential integrity between parent/child tables to identify parentless child (i.e., "orphan") records and values	Cross-table content	Periodic measurement
40	Integrity/ Completeness	Child/parent referential integrity	Confirm referential integrity between child/parent tables to identify childless parent records and values	Cross-table content	Periodic measurement
41	Integrity/ Validity	Validity check, cross table, detailed results	Compare values in a mapped or business rule relationship across tables to ensure data is associated consistently	Cross-table content	Periodic measurement
42	Integrity/ Consistency	Consistent cross-table multicolumn profile	Cross-table reasonability check, compare record count distribution of values across fields on related tables to historical percentages, in order to test adherence to business rules (multicolumn profile with qualifiers)	Cross-table content	Periodic measurement

(*Continued*)

Table 6.1 The Measurement Types: Consolidated Listing (*Continued*)

Number	Dimension of Quality	Measurement Type	Measurement Type Description	Object of Measurement	Assessment Category
43	Integrity/ Consistency	Chronology consistent with business rules across-tables	Cross-table reasonability, compare date values to business rule for chronology	Content/ chronology/ cross-table	Periodic measurement
44	Integrity/ Consistency	Consistent cross-table amount column calculations	Cross-table reasonability check, compare summed amount calculations (total, percentage of total, average or ratios between these) on related tables	Cross-table content/ amount fields	Periodic measurement
45	Integrity/ Consistency	Consistent cross-table amounts columns by aggregated dates	Cross-table reasonability check, compare amount field data (total amount, percentage of total amount) associated with an aggregated date (month, quarter, or year) on related tables	Cross-table content/ aggregated date	Periodic measurement
46	Consistency	Consistency compared to external benchmarks	Compare data quality measurement results to a set of benchmarks, such external industry or nationally established measurements for similar data	Overall database content	Periodic measurement
47	Completeness	Dataset completeness —overall sufficiency for defined purposes	Compare macro database content (e.g., data domains, sources, number of records, historical breadth of data, represented entities) to requirements for specific uses of the data	Overall database content	Periodic measurement
48	Completeness	Dataset completeness— overall sufficiency of measures and controls	Assess effectiveness of measurements and controls	Overall database content	Periodic assessment

Concluding Thoughts

This chapter has presented the DQAF measurement types at the level of initial definition to enable you to see how they fit together. Section Six fleshes out the framework in significantly more depth, describing how a system might be implemented to comprehensively execute data quality measurement. It includes detail on measurement definition, business concerns, measurement methodology (including calculations common to the measurement types), programming, support processes and skills, and the measurement logical data model. Readers who want to understand this detail may want to read Section Six at this point. Sections Three, Four, and Five, meanwhile, will describe (respectively) assessment scenarios, establishing data quality measurement requirements, and the role of measurement in data quality strategy.

Concluding Thoughts

Data Assessment Scenarios

"We can start measuring only when we know what to measure: qualitative observation has to precede quantitative measurement, and by making experimental arrangements for quantitative measurements we may even eliminate the possibility of new phenomena appearing."
—Heinrich Casimir, Dutch Physicist (1909–2000)

Purpose

The DQAF was originally developed to describe in-line data quality measurements, those that can be taken as part of data processing, in a data warehouse or other large system on an ongoing basis. In-line measurements can be used for monitoring because they can detect changes to patterns in data. Such measurements can also be used to identify opportunities to improve that quality. The DQAF describes a range of ways to take in-line measurements that assess data completeness, timeliness, validity, consistency, and integrity. Having read through the options presented by the framework, you may be ready to set up your in-line processes. Before doing so, it is important to understand which data you should measure so that you can determine which measurement types will serve your organization best.

In-line measurement is more effective if it is part of an overall approach to data assessment that takes place at different points in the information life cycle. This approach has four components (see Table: Assessment Scenarios Summary):

- *Initial assessment of data for purposes of data discovery and to formulate or clarify data quality expectations*
- *Assessment within projects specifically focused on data quality improvement*
- *Ongoing assessment through in-line measurement, monitoring, and control*
- *Periodic reassessment for purposes of sustaining data quality*

Table Assessment Scenarios Summary

Assessment Scenario	Goals	Deliverables
Initial Assessment: Comprehensive, across a dataset or related datasets	• Build overall knowledge of data and the processes that produce it • Identify and measure baseline condition of: 　• critical data 　• high-risk data 　• data that does not meet expectations (candidate data for improvement projects) • Identify data to be measured on an ongoing basis	• Measurement results • Improved data definitions • Documented business processes • Documented understanding of technical processes • Documentation of data properties with evaluation of criticality, risk, and suitability, as well as improvement opportunities • Recommendations for ongoing measurement
Improvement Projects: Narrowly focused on specific data fields or relationships that limit data's suitability	• Implement changes in data capture or processing that show measureable improvement over previous state	• Documented process changes • Measurement results showing improvement in data quality
In-Line Measurement: Focused on critical and high risk data	• Ensure data continues to meet expectations • Detect and investigate changes in data patterns • Identify opportunities for improvement of data quality	• Measurement results • Reports on the condition of existing data, including identification of changes in data patterns • Root cause analysis for data issues • Recommendations for remediation and improvement
Periodic Measurement: Focused on data that cannot be measured in-line and on less critical, less-risk-prone data	• Ensure data continues to meet expectations • Detect and investigate changes in data patterns • Identify opportunities for improvement of data quality	• Reports on the condition of existing data, including identification of changes in data patterns • Action plans for further improvement

The purpose of Section Three is to describe this wider context. Chapter 7: Initial Data Assessment *describes goals associated and input for an initial understanding of data. It discusses data profiling and describes deliverables to be produced from an initial assessment. One of the significant benefits of initial data assessment is the metadata it produces about the content, structure, and condition of the data being assessed.* Chapter 8: Assessment in Data Quality Improvement Projects *describes the relation of measurement to data quality improvement projects.* Chapter 9: Ongoing Measurement *presents guidelines related to the effective use of in-line measurements, controls, and periodic assessments.*

Data quality measurement is not an end in itself. It must be purposeful. In the most general sense, measurement is necessary to managing data. When applied to data about which not much is known, its purpose is discovery and definition. When applied to data with known issues, its purpose is to provide a basis for improvement. When applied to data that is stable, its purpose is sustaining quality. Measurement can also be extended to data that has not had problems in order to manage the potential risks associated with that data.

Assessment Scenarios

As noted in Chapter 4, to assess means to "evaluate or estimate the nature, ability, or quality" of a thing. Data quality can be assessed to different degrees using tools and techniques, ranging from simple qualitative assessment to detailed quantitative measurement. Assessments can be made based on general knowledge, guiding principles, or specific standards. They can be executed against data about which little is known or about which there is significant knowledge. The general purpose of data quality assessment remains the same: to understand the condition of data and to draw a conclusion about its impact in relation to expectations or particular purposes or both.

Whether they are generated as part of initial discovery, in-line measurement, or periodic review, assessment results can be used to formulate or confirm expectations related to the quality of data. The assessment scenarios are interwoven. Initial assessment that identifies critical and at-risk elements and rules influences which data requires improvement, as well as which data to measure in-line. Once improvements are made, sustaining them requires a level of ongoing monitoring. And even data that is meeting expectations initially needs to be reviewed periodically to understand whether and how it may have changed.

The principles can be applied to assessing data for a large project, such as setting up a data warehouse, in an existing data asset or, at a micro level, to understanding the impact of an individual data quality issue.

Metadata: Knowledge before Assessment

Many people find data quality measurement challenging. Measurement itself is not the biggest challenge. There are plenty of ways to measure data. The bigger challenge comes in making measurements purposeful. Doing so requires knowing what data consumers expect from the data. Without knowledge of expectations, you can still measure, but you do not have a basis from which to draw conclusions about a consumer's estimate of quality. Effective measurement of data depends on the same thing that effective use of data requires: reliable metadata that accurately describes data content and structure and clear expectations related to data uses. Metadata is explicit knowledge documented to enable a common understanding of an organization's data, including what the data is intended to represent, how it effects this representation, the limits of that representation, what happens to it in systems, how data is used and can be used, and how it should not be used. Metadata is not a technical problem—although, clearly, technology is necessary to store and provide access to such information. The condition of metadata depends on having processes in place to ensure its quality and to manage its currency.

Assessment requires some level of metadata describing the data to be assessed. However, because few organizations manage their metadata well, it should be used with caution. In Data Quality: The Accuracy Dimension, *Jack Olson describes metadata as both an input to and output from data profiling. Metadata is needed in order to establish initial understanding of data, but it must be updated based on actual findings from the discovery process (p. 123). In* Data Quality Assessment, *Arkady Maydanchik issues a similar warning: Metadata should be used with caution, he says; the cure for metadata maladies is data profiling, "a combination of techniques aimed at examining the data and understanding its actual content, rather than that described theoretically in the data models and data dictionaries" (2007, pp. 64–65). Metadata also results from assessment and measurement. David Loshin's* Enterprise Knowledge Management: The Data Quality Approach *demonstrates how institutional knowledge (rules, assumptions, relationships) is embedded in data.*[1] *Data analysis and assessment are means of mining for this knowledge, which is frequently undocumented.*

There is a challenging circularity to the role of metadata in data quality assessment. Reliable metadata is necessary input to the profiling process as well as to automated in-line measurement. Without reliable metadata, you will be making guesses about the meaning of data and therefore about expectations for it. With reliable metadata, measurement can be focused on critical data, and measurement results will show the degree to which data meets expectations. But you cannot know how reliable (or unreliable) your metadata is until you compare it to your data. In each of the scenarios described, improved metadata is a deliverable. Assessment builds knowledge of data. This knowledge should be explicitly captured and made available to the organization.

---

[1] Loshin makes a similar point about the role of metadata in relation to master data management: "[T]o be able to manage the master data, one must first be able to manage the master metadata" (2008, p. 95).

Initial Data Assessment

7

"There are two possible outcomes: If the result confirms the hypothesis, then you've made a measurement. If the result is contrary to the hypothesis, then you've made a discovery."
—Enrico Fermi, Italian Physicist (1901–1954)

Purpose

This chapter discusses the process of initial data assessment. It describes goals associated with and input to such an assessment and delves into the details of profiling data (column profiling, structure profiling). It also describes deliverables to be produced from an initial assessment. Initial data assessment produces valuable metadata (including specific baseline measurements) about the content, structure, and condition of the data being assessed. One goal of an initial assessment is to produce a set of recommendations for data quality improvement and for ongoing measurement and control (see Figure 7.1).

Initial Assessment

Initial assessment or data discovery is conducted in order to understand the structure and content of data, usually about which little is known. Such assessment can be used to formulate or confirm expectations for the quality of the data. Initial assessment can be conducted against an existing data store or against candidate data for a project. It can be focused on multiple sources and the relation between them, on a single data source, or even on an individual dataset.

Input to Initial Assessments

You will get more out of the assessment if you plan and prepare for it before beginning detailed analysis of data. Planning includes identifying and reviewing any documented knowledge about the data you need to assess, ensuring that you have tools to document your findings, and identifying resources who will be able to answer your questions. Preparing for an assessment includes gaining an understanding of

- Business processes represented by the data.
- Completeness, consistency, and integrity of the data model (if one is available).
- Data processing in source and target systems.
- Data standards (to the extent that they exist).
- Data producer expectations and assumptions.
- Data consumer expectations and assumptions.

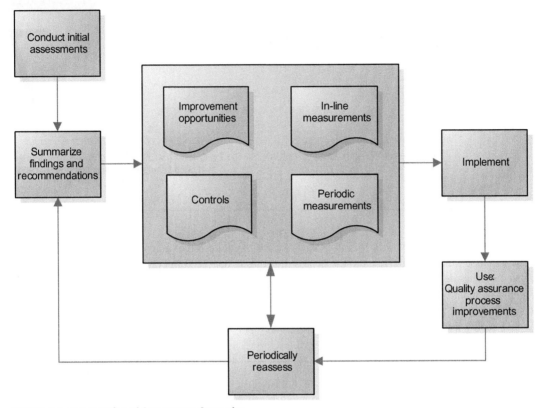

FIGURE 7.1 The Relation of Assessment Scenarios

The primary goal of initial assessment is to understand the condition of the data and identify improvement opportunities. From initial findings, a program of measurement can be established which includes controls, in-line measurement, and periodic measurement. Data quality measurement is not an end in itself. It should be applied to find improvement opportunities. Measurements should be periodically reviewed to assess their effectiveness.

As part of the analysis, you should also identify which data elements and rules appear to be most critical and most at risk. As you investigate questions raised by the assessment, you should actively seek input from business users about data criticality. This input is needed to prioritize any improvement projects and to formulate a plan for in-line measurements. Initial assessment provides metadata that is the foundation for other assessments. To ensure this foundation is firm, you should plan from the beginning to systematically and consistently capture findings (see Figure 7.2).

Data Expectations

The assessment itself will focus on the condition of the data in relation to the expectations of both data producers and data consumers. As was described in Section One, an *expectation* is "a strong

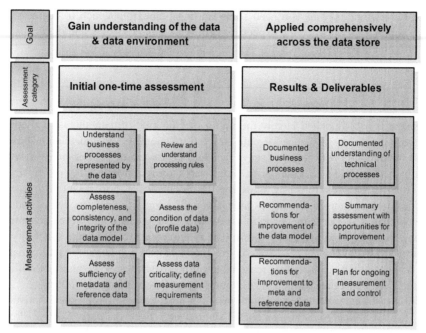

FIGURE 7.2 Initial One-Time Assessment

The goal of initial one-time assessment is to gain an understanding of the data and its environment and to characterize the condition of the data. Preparing for an assessment includes gaining an understanding of business processes represented by the data, the completeness, consistency, and integrity of the data model, and data processing in source and target systems. The assessment itself will focus on the condition of the data. As part of the analysis, you should also identify which data elements and rules appear to be most critical and most at risk. From input gathered during the process, you should have a clear understanding of which data is most critical to your organization. Output from the process will include valuable metadata, for example, documented business processes and documented understanding of technical processes. The two primary deliverables from an initial assessment are a summary of assessment results, including identified opportunities for improvement, and recommendations for ongoing measurement and control.

belief that something will happen or be the case in the future" (*NOAD*). Expectations related to data quality include assumptions related to the condition of the data. These may be based on limited or extensive knowledge of the data. They may bear directly on the intended uses of the data or on what the data is intended to represent. Expectations are usually connected with requirements or standards, or both. Data standards are formalized expectations that can pertain to any level of data (column, table, database). *Data quality standards* are assertions that relate directly to quality dimensions. Standards for a given system should cohere. One of the outcomes of an assessment might be to identify contradictory standards. Standards should also be measurable. Another outcome of an assessment might be to associate specific measurements with data that is expected to conform to standards. But expectations play an even simpler role in assessment: In asserting that one must assess data against expectations, I am simply saying you need some starting point from which to begin to learn about the data. It is important to identify the expectations of both data producers and data consumers since these likely differ and identifying such differences is necessary to resolving them.

Data Profiling

Initial assessment is accomplished largely through a specific kind of data analysis called data profiling. Data profiling provides a picture of data structure, content, rules, and relationships by applying statistical methodologies to return a set of standard characteristics about data—data types, field lengths, cardinality of columns, granularity, value sets, format patterns, implied rules, and cross-column and cross-file data relationships, as well as the cardinality of those relationships.

Profiling results can be used directly as metadata and as input for data modeling and processing. They can be compared to source metadata to assess how closely data conforms to documented specifications. They can also be compared to known data requirements to assess the suitability of data for particular purposes. In cases where profiling is executed against completely unfamiliar data, profiling results may be needed simply to define reasonable initial (baseline) expectations. Profiling findings can help identify candidate data for data quality improvement or ongoing monitoring.

Data profiling is often executed using data-profiling tools designed to produce statistical analysis of data sets. Data-profiling tools have matured significantly since the early 2000s.[1] Profiling tools have robust functionality for identifying patterns and data relationships, and they can find characteristics that analysts may not be looking for. Tools simplify the process of understanding data. But do not confuse the tool with the process of assessing data. A tool can tell you what the data looks like and draw your attention to facets of the data that you should investigate. It cannot draw conclusions about whether the data meets expectations.

Column Property Profiling

Column property profiling includes identification of data type, length, and format associated with data in a column. It also includes the calculation of a percentage distribution of distinct values. Distribution analysis entails counting all the records associated with each value (the numerator for each calculation) and dividing these by the total number of records (the denominator for all the calculations), so that you can see what portion of the data is associated with any specific value, as well as how the proportions of the different values compare to each other. Percentage calculations are helpful in enabling you to comprehend the relative proportion of individual values, especially when you are looking at a large number of records or of distinct values. Percentage calculations also help in identifying other relationships within the data. Columns that have similar distributions may have a dependent relationship on each other, for example.

---

[1] In a 2004 design tip (#59), Ralph Kimball wrote about the "surprising" value of data profiling. It seems surprising that anyone should be startled that we need to understand the facts about data before we can process it. Kimball's point is that data should to be profiled at the beginning of projects in order to understand the data, in addition to being profiled near the end of projects, as part of ensuring that ETL has been correctly implemented.

Distribution analysis provides a set of distinct values whose validity can be confirmed. Each column should have a defined domain of values; these may be a distinct set, a defined range, or a range established by a rule. Profiling will help identify any values that do not fit the domain constraints. It is just as important that profiling results for each column be reviewed to ensure that the content makes sense in relation to the definition of column and the overall content of the table or file. To answer the question of whether results make sense, the first place to look, after confirming the domain, is at the values with the highest frequencies and those with the lowest frequencies.

High-Frequency Values

If high-frequency values follow expected patterns, they can provide a level of assurance that business is operating as expected. They can also point to unexpected conditions in the data. Take medical claim data, for example. It would be expected that a larger portion of claim records are associated with office visits than with hospital stays. More people make visits to their doctors than are hospitalized. A claim dataset with a large proportion of hospital claims would be unusual and a cause for investigation—unless you could identify conditions in data collection or processing that would result in a distribution different from this general expectation.

High frequencies may also draw your attention to unexpected patterns. For example, in doing an analysis of death dates on health plan membership data, a colleague of mine found that an unusual number of death dates were recorded at the first of the month (January 1, February 1, etc.). It seemed unlikely that more people died on the first of any given month than on any other day. Analysis showed that the dates were entered based on when our company received data and the form in which data was received. We were able to record the fact that a member had passed away, but we did not always have the exact date, so the data was entered on the first of the month in which the fact was known.

Low-Frequency Values

Low-frequency values often appear as outliers in percentage distributions. It is easy to jump to the conclusion that such records represent errors. However, sometimes having only a few records associated with a value is expected, given real-world conditions. For example, medical claim data related to in-patient hospitalizations is often organized by the Diagnostic Related Group (DRG). Within a large set of medical claim records there will be very few with DRGs representing organ transplants and many with DRGs representing maternity stays. An example from retail sales makes a similar point. Most of the customer base for brick-and-mortar businesses will live within the same geographic area as the business itself. Finding customer records with ZIP codes from distant states would be unexpected but not necessarily incorrect. It would require investigation to determine whether such outliers are errors or explainable anomalies.

Date Data

The distribution of date data can provide useful insight into data reasonability. It is often possible to make common-sense hypotheses about date content based on even minimal knowledge of data. For example, you can make reasonable guesses about what to expect from birth date data related to college students, as opposed to birth date data related to employees at a large company. Date data can help you understand relationships between other fields. For example, you would expect a ship date to come after an order date, rather than the other way around. And date data is often critical in understanding whether recorded sequences of events make sense. In medical claim data, for example, a hospital admission date must always come before a discharge date (because common sense says you cannot leave the hospital before you are admitted to the hospital). Being out of sequence, these dates would indicate a problem with the data. It is usually possible to spot outliers or questionable values in date data by looking at the sequence of events represented by the dates using a rule that identifies all records where the relationship is the opposite of what is expected; as in the example above, one would identify records with admission dates after discharge dates.

Expectations related to reasonability can also be established by considering the amount of time between events. Not only would a ship date be expected to come after an order date, but most companies who rely on shipping their product try to do so within established time frames, such as a day, a week, or a month. Identifying records where there is an unexpectedly long or short duration between dates could indicate a problem with the data or an anomaly within the business process represented by the data.

Observations about Column Population

Distribution analysis provides information related to the population density of all data columns (how frequently a column is populated with values that are not defaulted), as well as the cardinality of the column (distinct number of values), the specific percentage of defaulted records, and the number of data format patterns for each column. As with other aspects of profiling, you will understand the results of column property analysis better if you have reliable metadata to support the process. Ideally, source metadata should be used as part of the profiling process to establish baseline expectations (Olson, 2003). Source metadata should include listings of valid values, valid ranges, or other rules about what constitutes the domain for any column. If this metadata is not available, then you will start your assessment with very limited knowledge. You will need to rely on common sense and the willingness iteratively to confirm both your actual findings and your assessment of their implications.

The following conditions warrant further investigation of a column because they imply problems with validity, completeness, and consistency:

- The presence of values that are not identified as valid values.
- Cardinality different from expected (high cardinality where low is expected or low cardinality where high is expected).
- Less-than-complete population of a column where you expect complete population.
- The presence of multiple data patterns in one column.

The Presence of Invalid Values

Validity and domain rules are a form of data expectation. If you know nothing about a column except its valid values, you can still draw some conclusions about the quality of the data based on a distribution analysis of those values. For example, if values are present in the data that are not in the valid value listing, then the data does not meet the simple expectation of validity. The difference may be easy to explain. The values may, in fact, be valid, and the listing may simply be missing them. Or the data with invalid values may itself be old or out of date. Whatever the cause, the initial assessment can identify that the data does not meet the expectation. If none of the values in the data correspond to the validity test, then you have a different situation. The data or the listing may be mislabeled; one or the other may be incorrectly formatted; or data may have been populated incorrectly. You may also find values that are clearly invalid; for example, the presence of values such as DO NOT USE or TEST RECORD or even BABYGIRL in a first name field. Each of these represents an unexpected situation. The name field has been populated with a value other than a first name. The values that are populated provide clues to the reasons they are present. These clues do not solve the quality problem, but they may help in root cause analysis.

The Absence of Valid Values

A trickier situation to assess than the presence of invalid values is the absence of some valid values. In some situations, having no records associated with a specific value may be a good thing. For example, if the concept of gender is represented by three values, M, F, U, for male, female, unknown, and your data contains only M and F, the absence of U may indicate that you have high-quality data in the gender field. In other situations, the absence of a specific value may indicate a problem. For example, in a medical claim file that is expected to contain original claims, as well as adjustments, the absence of records with a claim type of "original" would be an indication that you may not have a complete set of data. Finally, there are situations in which you can conclude that the absence of records associated with a particular value is not a problem For example, if you have customers from across the United States, your data will contain a large number of valid ZIP codes, but very few organizations would expect to have at least one record associated with every ZIP code in the United States.

Columns with the Cardinality of One

Cardinality is a term from mathematics that refers to "the number of elements in a set or other grouping as a property of that grouping" (*NOAD*). By definition, a column with a cardinality of one is populated with only one value. If all records in a table contain the same value, it is difficult to understand what the purpose would be in capturing the data at all. Common sense may tell you that you do not have a problem. For example, if the column represents the date on which the data was processed and you are profiling a sample that was processed on only one date, then cardinality of one would be expected for a field like system processing date. Common sense will also tell you when you do have a problem. For example, if you are profiling employee data from an HR system and the column employee birth date has a cardinality of one, you probably have a problem. You would not expect all employees to have the same birth date.

A specific instance of a column with a cardinality of one is a column that is not populated at all—for example, one that has all NULLs or another default value. Not being populated at all is an unexpected condition. If a column is present, we usually expect it is there for a reason. Again, there may be a reason it is not populated. The column may be new and therefore not yet populated. Or it may be old and therefore no longer populated. Or it may have been included but not used and therefore never populated. Either way, you should investigate its status in order to understand why it contains no data.

Columns with High Cardinality Where Low Cardinality is Expected

High cardinality means that there is a large number of distinct values in a field. High cardinality is not a problem in and of itself—unless you expect only a few distinct values. High and low are, of course, relative. For example, it would be questionable to find a column representing a concept such as gender, for which three values are valid, being populated with dozens of distinct values. Columns that have many distinct values where you expect only a few distinct values may be mislabeled or populated incorrectly when they are brought into a data store, or they may be populated incorrectly at the source. The column is perhaps being used for more than one purpose, or perhaps it is being used for a purpose other than what its name reflects. It may be populated by two different sources, each of which has a different set of values to represent the same concept. As part of initial assessment, you first want to identify that there is a difference between the expectation and the actual data. Then you will want to investigate what has caused the difference.

Columns with Low Cardinality Where High Cardinality is Expected

Having low cardinality where high cardinality is expected means that you have fewer values than you expect. Take employee birth date as an example. At a large company it would be reasonable to expect a large set of distinct values to be present in the employee birth date field. Even at a company that employs fewer than 100 people, it would be rare for many individuals to share exactly the same birth date (day, month, and year). If you find only a few distinct values in a column for which you expect a large set of distinct values, then, again, the column may be mislabeled, data may have been entered incorrectly, or the values may be populated incorrectly at the source. When two fields have the same exact cardinality, they should be compared. They may contain redundant data.

Columns with Less-Than-Complete Population

When you observe the degree to which a column is populated, you are trying to understand if the data is as complete as expected. All columns should be reviewed to identify the specific values that represent defaulted records. Some fields are optional and expected to be sparsely populated. For example, health care eligibility records often have a field called Death Date. Most of the people to whom these records refer (members in a health plan) are still alive. So Death Date is rarely populated. If, based on data content, a column appears to have a high level of defaulted values and the reason is not clear, research the business processes that drive source system transactions. Under what conditions is the column expected to be populated, and under what conditions is it not expected to be populated? Knowing and documenting these conditions can also help in the investigation of dependency rules and other data relationships.

When reviewing column population, it is important to recognize not only the degree to which a column is populated but also the nature of that population. Look for both the defined default (the value that source metadata identifies as the default) and functional defaults (a value or values that appear to be used as a substitute for a meaningful value). For example, some records may be populated with a value of SPACE, while others contain a value of UNKNOWN. Both of these values serve the same function of telling you that the data is not available. Even if they are valid (present and defined within a set of valid values), the fact that there are two values representing essentially the same idea should be investigated.

Multiple Data Format Patterns in One Column

One of the central principles of relational data is that each distinct data element should be stored as a separate attribute and in a consistent manner. In most cases, this principle means that all the data in a given field fits a specific pattern and that it can be formatted in the same way. Nevertheless, there are cases where fields are used (or misused) to capture data related to more than one concept. The presence of different format patterns within one field can indicate that the field is being populated in unexpected ways. At the very least, it implies that format constraints are not enforced consistently somewhere in the data chain. It may imply that the system from which you are sourcing data itself receives data from multiple sources, or that rules are enforced differently depending on transaction types or other factors.

Formatting differences have different implications for data use. Depending on the tools used to access data, differences may prevent joins between tables, putting data consumers at risk of having incomplete data. Format differences can also cause data to look wrong, as, for example, when some data values are in ALL CAPS and others are in Mixed Case.

Structure Profiling

Data profiling can be used to identify the characteristics of data structure required for data modeling and processing. For example, profiling can identify candidate primary keys within a table or relationships between columns or between tables and the rules that govern those relationships. These relationships will imply referential (parent/child or foreign key) rules, as well as dependency rules (which can often be expressed in "if … then" statements). Structure profiling will enable you to understand aspects of data integrity by showing whether the data coheres in expected ways. Such relationships imply expectations about the quality of data that can be asserted as data quality rules.

Initial assessment of data may be conducted in order to gather information for the modeling process, or it can be conducted with a conceptual data model already in hand. Structural profiling can thus help formulate or refine a data model. One purpose of having a data model is to illustrate relationships between entities. (A model is a visual representation of data content and relationships.) Profiling can test assumptions about these relationships, as well as uncover those that you have not assumed or identified as part of modeling.

Some characteristics of structure profiling that warrant further investigation include incomplete referential integrity relationships, missing or unanticipated dependency rules, differences in representations of the same concept in different datasets, and differences from expected cardinality of relationships.

Incomplete Referential Relationships

The term *referential integrity* is used to describe a specific relationship between tables. Each table in a database must have a primary key, the set of columns that define what constitutes a unique row of data. In relational databases, tables often also contain foreign keys. A foreign key represents data in another table, for which it is the primary key. For example, medical claims records should always contain a diagnosis code. The meaning associated with standard diagnosis codes will be defined on a separate reference or dimension table. On the claim table the diagnosis code column is a foreign key. On the diagnosis code table, diagnosis is the primary key. In this situation, the diagnosis code table is said to be a *parent* to the medical claim table that is a *child* of the diagnosis code table. Records in a child table that do not have corresponding references in the parent table are called *orphan* records. If all records on the child table do have references on the parent table, then referential integrity exists between the two tables. This relationship is sometimes called an inheritance rule.

Foreign key relationships always represent an expectation about the data. It is expected that any value present in the foreign key column (diagnosis code column on the claim table) will be present in the table for which it is the primary key (the diagnosis code reference table). If the value is not present on the parent table, then the expectation has not been met. The cause of the problem may be simple. Reference data may be incomplete or the relationship may be mislabeled or the column may be populated with an invalid value. Whatever the cause of a particular problem, profiling allows you to observe that there is a difference between what is expected and what is present in the data.

Referential relationships have been implied in the preceding discussion about validity, and to a large degree, the two concepts overlap. There is one difference between them, however: referential integrity is usually described as a specific relationship between tables in a database, whereas validity as a concept is not dependent on particular data structures. Valid domains are not always defined within a table. They can be represented as ranges, as well as through listings that do not exist in table form. Another difference is that we usually think of validity in relation to codified data. Referential integrity governs relationships in addition to those between reference and core (or dimension and fact) data. So in the medical claims example above, in addition to the relationship between the claim data and the diagnosis code reference table, there is a relationship between tables referring to other details of the claim process: specifically, between a claim header record and the associated service records, as well as between claim data and medical provider data, member data, policy holder data, and health plan data.

Referential relationships speak first to data completeness. The presence or absence of orphan records can be used as a measure of completeness. These relationships also depend on data consistency. For them to work at all depends on representing the same information in the same form across tables.

When profiling data, you should be looking for instances where references are missing from parent tables (*orphan records*). Such a situation goes against the expectation defined by the foreign key relationship and indicates that you are missing data. You should also look for *childless parents*. Such a situation is more difficult to read and does not always indicate a problem. Its meaning depends on the expectations specific to the data. It may indicate that you do not have a complete set of child records. The expected, generic relationship between products and sales illustrates these relationships. Sales data is a child of product data. No products should be represented in sales data that do not exist on a product table. There should be no orphan product references on sales records. However, it is possible to have products that never actually get sold. There may be some childless parents among the product records.

During initial assessment, it can be challenging to characterize these relationships, especially if you are working with a limited set of sample data. Sample data may imply you have a problem when you do not have one in your production data (Parent records may be missing from the sample but present in the production data). Or it may not contain evidence of a problem that exists in production data. (The sample may have full referential integrity while production data does not.) It is still critical to assess these relationships and to bring findings and questions to the data source. The results may tell you that the sample itself is not adequate for the work you need to do. Or they may show you that these relationships do not inhere in the data in the way they should based on known rules.

Missing or Unexpected Dependency Relationships and Rules

Dependency rules describe expected relationships between tables (entity relationship dependency) or between columns (attribute dependency) (Wells & Duncan, 1999; Adelman et Al., 2005; Maydanchik, 2007). Such rules may be defined in terms of the existence of two datasets and can be either negative or positive. In a positive or mutually dependent relationship, existence of one data relationship requires that another data relationship also exists. As just described, to record the fact that a product has been purchased requires that the product exist within a product table. Or in health care, the fact that a member is enrolled in a health plan that requires a primary care physician means that that a primary care physician may be associated with the member within the eligibility data. Alternatively, in a negative or mutually exclusive relationship, the existence of one relationship prohibits the existence of another. For example, in most countries, a person who is married to one person cannot be legally married to another person at the same time.

Entity-relationship dependencies can also be based on particular conditions or states. Again, using health care as an example, the services a person is eligible for depend on the health care products to which he or she subscribes. Some health care plans include dental or vision coverage; others do not. Conditional relationships can be challenging to describe because doing so can require a significant amount of detail about each of the conditions. They can also be more challenging to detect, even with a profiling tool. Understanding them fully often requires first knowing that they exist and then using data to identify and test scenarios involving variations on rules.

Attribute dependency rules are similar to entity-relationship dependency rules. One attribute value may require the existence of another attribute value. For example, a ZIP code of 06085 requires a state code of CT. One attribute value may prohibit the existence of another attribute value. For example, any product that is listed as "unavailable" or with a stock quantity of zero cannot be shipped. Or an attribute value may be constrained based on the value in another attribute. In our discussion about dates, for example, we pointed out that there may rules inherent in business processes, such as the idea that a product cannot be shipped before it is ordered.

Like validity rules, dependency rules imply data quality expectations. Identifying these as part of the initial assessment process enables testing of the degree to which they are fulfilled. The two conditions to look for during initial assessment are the absence of a dependency relationship where you expect to find one or the presence of such a relationship where you do not expect to find one. If, for example, you find a set of records in which the relationship between ZIP code and state code does not correspond to the published USPS relationship, then you will need to understand why this dependency is not manifest in the data. A situation in which you find a relationship between two attributes where you do not expect a relationship also requires investigation. It may be that the attributes represent something different from what the metadata indicates they do. Or that analysis has identified a business rule that no one had explicitly described before. Discovery of such rules and relationships is one of the benefits of profiling data. It is critical to document such discoveries so that this knowledge can be shared.

Because they define details about the real-world entities they represent and the data used to represent them, dependency rules provide insight into data consistency, as well as validity and completeness.

Differences in Granularity and Precision

Initial assessment of data will provide insight into the different ways that data can be structured to represent objects and events. The purpose of integration projects, such as those that build data warehouses, is to combine data from source systems built for different purposes. Across such systems, it is not unusual that data representing the same concept is presented at different levels of grain or different levels of precision.

Granularity refers to the degree to which information is represented by constituent parts. A simple illustration can be made with phone numbers. In the United States, telephone numbers include three parts: the area code, the exchange, and the individual phone number. A phone number can be stored in one field, or each of its parts can be stored. A system that stored the parts separately would have finer grain data than a system that stored the telephone number as a whole. If two such systems were integrated, then the process of integration would need to combine the data of finer grain to correspond to the data of coarser grain or separate the data of coarser grain into its elemental parts. The phone number example is simple because the rules are clear about how we represent telephone numbers and what each of the parts means. We can take telephone numbers apart and fit them back together again and still understand them as telephone numbers.

The challenge of data granularity comes with how more complex concepts are represented. For example, one system designed to identify records related to an individual person might require a set of four attributes: first name, last name, birth date, and ZIP code. In another system, identifying records related to an individual person might require six attributes: first name, last name, Social Security number, birthplace, highest level of education achieved, and blood type. The same people (real-world objects) might be represented in both systems, but the details available about any given person and the way each system distinguishes a unique record for a person differ from each other in granularity.

The concept of precision is sometimes confused with granularity, but the two are not the same. Precision refers to how fine the data is in a given field. For example, the concept of marital status might be represented in one system as a simple binary: married/not married. In another system marital status might include a set of values such as married, widowed, divorced, in a domestic partnership, remarried. Both systems would have the same data granularity (one attribute to represent marital status), but within that attribute, the sets of valid values offer different degrees of precision. Precision is more easily understood in terms of fineness of measurement. For example, a measurement expressed to the nearest millimeter would be more precise than one expressed to the nearest centimeter.

Profiling can be used to understand data granularity and precision. The ways in which these can differ between systems serves as a reminder of the constructedness of data. You do not want to make the mistake of assuming that representations of the same concept are structured with the same level of grain or precision in different systems. Instead, as part of the initial assessment of data, you should identify the fact that data representations differ, and then you should define the specific ways they differ from each other. These differences represent risk because they break the expectation for similarity between data representing the same concept and because integrating data of different granularity requires developing a data model that can appropriately accommodate the differences. In many cases, it is possible to roll-up data to a coarser granularity. Creating a finer level of grain can be significantly more difficult, and between some datasets, it may not be achievable.

Relationship Cardinality Different from Expectations

Relationship cardinality describes the ways in which entities can be related to each other. A simple expectation for data is that the data will reflect the ways real-world entities are related. There are three basic cardinality relationships (Wells & Duncan, 1999; Adelman et al., 2005):

- *One-to-one*: An entity is related to another entity once and only once. The one-to-one relationship necessarily goes in both directions. A wife can have only one husband at a time, and a husband can have only one wife at a time.
- *One-to-many:* An entity is related to many instances of a second entity, but any instance of the second entity can only be related to one of the first entity. A woman can have many children, but each child has only one mother.
- *Many-to-many:* An entity can be related to another entity many times in both directions. Aunts can have many nieces and nephews. Nieces and nephews can have many aunts.

Cardinality is also understood in terms of optionality. Two entities may have a mandatory relationship (they must be related at least once) or an optional relationship (they do not have to be related at all). There are three optionality relationships (Adelman et al., 2005):

- *One-to-one*: Each entity has a mandatory relationship with the other. If an entity exists, it must be related to a second entity. If a person is a parent, then he or she must have a child.
- *One-to-zero*: The first entity has a mandatory relationship with the second, but the second entity has an optional relationship with the first. For an example here, we must step outside the realm of family. A car owner must own a car, but a car does not have to have an owner.
- *Zero-to-zero*: Two entities have a completely optional relationship. Zero-to-zero is the equivalent of two people walking down the street without knowing each other and not even looking at each other.

Within relational databases the concept of optionality is also applied to referential relationships. There is a mandatory relationship if every instance of an entity referenced in another entity (a foreign key) must exist in that other entity (where it is the primary key). There is an optional relationship if the foreign key can be null.

Assertions about the cardinality of relationships are a form of expectation about data. If there are differences between the cardinality you expect and the cardinality that exists in the data (for example, you are expecting a one-to-many relationship between two entities and you find a one-to-one relationship; or if you are expecting to find a mandatory relationship and you discover an optional one), then you should determine the reasons for the differences and their impact on uses of the data.

Profiling an Existing Data Asset

The discussion on initial assessment has focused on discovery work for data that has not yet been brought into a data warehouse. In such a situation, assessment focuses on aspects of data structure that influence the development of a data model.

Comprehensive assessment is also sometimes required for a data asset whose quality is not known, either because information about data quality was never captured or because data has not been assessed within a reasonable time frame and therefore data consumers have no reason for confidence in the data. Profiling data in an existing data asset follows much the same process as data discovery. It includes assessment of column and structural properties, and the integrity of relationships. However, usually initial input is better. If you are working with an existing asset, you are likely to have a documented data model and an accompanying data dictionary. A best case scenario for profiling an existing asset is that it confirms what is documented. As most people who work in data management know, few data stores will have metadata that perfectly reflects the condition of the data. A more likely scenario is that profiling will result in the detection of unexpected conditions in the data and gaps or inaccuracies in the metadata or both.

From Profiling to Assessment

Profiling will produce a set of facts about data, but it does not, in and of itself, constitute assessment. To be meaningful, assessment requires comparison. To characterize the quality of data, you need to compare the facts you have discovered up against expectations about the data and draw conclusions about how well the data meets those expectations. If you find a column that is populated for 50% of records, you need to determine whether or not this percentage makes business sense based on data content. If you discover a data relationship that implies a rule between two columns, you can identify the degree of adherence to the rule, you may even find additional subrules that explain where the relationship might be different from expected. And then, again, you need to determine whether the degree of adherence makes sense. Doing so requires asking the people who produce or use the data what they expect from the specific column or rule. If they do not know—if they have no expectations—that is itself a finding and should be documented. At the very least, the absence of expectations tells you that the data appears not to be critical to the people from whom you have solicited input.

Deliverables from Initial Assessment

The primary goal of initial assessment is to characterize the condition of the data you are assessing. From input gathered during the process, you should also have a clear understanding of which data is most critical to your organization. Usually, assessment is directly connected to a project. Projects may include building a data store, integrating new data into an existing one, or, analyzing the condition of existing data for purposes of identifying improvement opportunities. Some criteria for quality should be associated with project goals.

The primary deliverables from an initial assessment are a summary of assessment results: the measurements that were taken against the data and the degree to which the data conform to expectations (whether those expectations are general or in the form of requirements or standards). The results summary should also identify opportunities for improvement, recommendations for data standardization, and recommendations for ongoing measurement and control. Opportunities for improvement and standardization can be identified for individual data elements, data rules, the data model, or metadata and references data (see Figure 7.3). Recommendations for ongoing measurement should not only describe how data should be measured; they should also include an assessment of the criticality

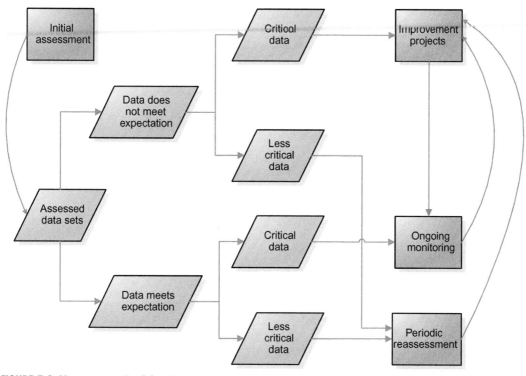

FIGURE 7.3 Measurement Decision Tree

One of the deliverables from an initial data assessment is a plan for ongoing data quality measurement and control. This plan depends on the initial condition of the data and on the criticality of particular data elements and rules. Critical data that does not meet expectations based on the initial assessment should be prioritized for improvement projects. Critical data that does meet expectations should be prioritized for ongoing measurement. Ongoing monitoring and periodic measurement may result in finding other opportunities for improvement to data or the processes that create data.

of any data elements or rules to be measured. Recommendations for controls should describe how to reduce risks associated with source data or data processing.

Output from the initial assessment will also include valuable metadata; for example, improved definitions of data elements, documented business processes, and documented understanding of technical processes. This metadata is also required as input for ongoing measurement and control.

Concluding Thoughts

Initial data assessment should provide a comprehensive picture of a dataset. The assessment is referred to as a "one-time, initial" assessment because it is not likely you will execute it as comprehensively more than once. Deliverables from the process provide the foundation for ongoing measurement, whether that is in-line or periodic.

Assessment in Data Quality Improvement Projects

8

"I hope my recordings of my own works won't inhibit other people's performances. The brutal fact is that one doesn't always get the exact tempo one wants, although one improves with experience."

—Aaron Copland, American Composer (1900–1990)

Purpose

The process of initial assessment enables you to identify which data is critical and to characterize its condition. In doing so, it points to opportunities for data quality improvement. The process provides baseline measurements against which to observe subsequent changes to data. Change may be positive (improvements to the condition of the data) or negative (deterioration of the condition of data) or neutral (changes in the data caused by changes in business processes). When data content evolves along with business practices, metadata related to quality expectations should be updated. Changes may also be deliberately brought about through data quality improvement projects. The purpose of this chapter is to describe the relation of measurement to data quality improvement projects. It is not the purpose of this chapter to show how to perform process analysis or root cause analysis, nor does it describe how to execute an improvement project. For these things I would recommend Danette McGilvray's book, *Executing Data Quality Projects: Ten Steps to Quality Data and Trusted Information.*™

Data Quality Improvement Efforts

Data quality improvement efforts are just what the name implies: work whose goal is to make data better suited to serve organizational purposes. Improvement projects may bring data into closer alignment with expectations, or they may enable data consumers to make decisions about whether to use data for particular purposes, or both. Projects can be large or small, including numerous data elements or just one. They can focus on process improvement, system improvement, or a combination. Other times, such work is part of a larger project or part of ongoing operational improvement efforts. Whatever the approach to improvement, it is important to have specific, measurable improvement goals.

113

Measurement in Improvement Projects

Measurement is critical to data quality improvement efforts for one simple reason: If you cannot measure the quality of your data, you cannot characterize the problem you are trying to solve. Some form of measurement—at least a basic comparison against an assumption or expectation—is needed just to recognize the need for improvement. And if you make changes without measuring before and after, you cannot tell whether or not you have improved your data. Measurement is important for another reason, too. While people can often recognize that there is a problem with their data and they may be able to describe it in general terms, measurement is required to assess the impact and to provide facts needed to make decisions about when and how to remediate the problem.[1]

The approach to measurement in data quality improvement efforts is similar to that of initial assessment. Indeed, in many organizations, initial assessment is used to identify opportunities for improvement, and the same measurements that identified candidate data are repeated to show that improvement has indeed taken place. Both kinds of measurement require establishing expectations and measuring the degree to which data does or does not meet them. As part of initial assessment, those expectations may be very general or incompletely formulated. Measurement is needed to solidify expectations. As part of improvement efforts, expectations are formulated in terms of improvement goals.

Not all improvement projects grow out of formal initial assessment of data. Some originate when issues are discovered within existing data assets. In order to be addressed, such problems require a definition and quantification. These processes follow the same path as initial assessment. An issue indicates that an expectation has not been met. Both the expectation and the difference from it must be defined, and the impact must be assessed in order to move forward with remediation.

Improvement projects also go further than initial assessment in their goals and depth of their analysis. Initial assessment merely shows that data does not meet an expectation. Improvement projects include root cause analysis to determine why data doesn't meet expectations and remediation of root causes to bring about desired changes (see Table 8.1). If, for example, assessment reveals that data from different systems cannot be integrated because it is collected at different levels of grain, improvements might include changes to one or both of the originating systems, as well as changes in the data model for the target system. Once root causes have been remediated, results need to be measured to see if the changes have had the desired effects. The specific measurements applied to data that has been improved will have as their starting point measurements used to identify the problem in the first place. If, for example, you discover through distribution analysis that a field is not populated as fully as expected, then as part of an improvement project, you would want to re-measure the full distribution of values to test that it is populating as required. However, as you make decisions about ongoing monitoring, measurements can often be honed and refined. You may focus the measurement only on the default value, on a set of highly critical values, or on the highest or lowest frequency values. The choices you make depend on the overall context of the data you are measuring: the objects or events it represents, the processes that move it from system to system, its uses, and risks associated with any of these.

---

[1] The need for data quality measurement and impact analysis is described in steps three and four of McGilvray's Ten Steps to Quality Data and Trusted Information™. See McGilvray (2008).

Table 8.1 Root Causes and Improvement Opportunities

Root Cause	Origin	Improvements and Opportunities
Errors or unexpected data coming into an organization from external vendors, partners, or customers	Point of entry	• Clarify rules, requirements, or expectations • Provide training for vendors, partners, or customers • Assess and adjust programming to receive data • Reject data that does not meet expectations
Errors in internal business process that provides input to source system	Business process	• Evaluate process • Clarify rules, requirements, or expectations
Errors in data from source system internal to the organization	Source system	• Remediate causes of errors in source system processes • Implement source system-based controls to prevent future errors • Make source systems more fully aware of the impact of these errors and costs of downstream remediation • Increase awareness by source system of the uses of their data in downstream systems; solicit their input on process improvements
Source system changes have unintended effects on the data they provide to downstream systems; downstream systems are not aware or not prepared for the effects	Source system	• Document data lineage to enable understanding of data origins and potential changes to data as it passes from system to system • Incorporate into project processes risk assessment based on data lineage • Increase awareness by source system of the uses of their data in downstream systems • Add target system test scenarios to source system regression testing plans • Implement source system-based controls
Incomplete/incorrect assumptions about source data results in logic that does not meet requirements	Project teams from the data store (target system)	• During the project process, profile data to confirm assumptions about data • Document cases where data differs from assumptions • Ensure data consumers and source system Subject Matter Experts (SMEs) are engaged as part of target system projects • Change assumptions and assess implications to project • Address revised requirements with the source
Projects do not have clear requirements or requirements are not implemented in such a way that they meet customer needs	Project teams from the data store (target system) and data consumers	• Improve requirements definition process and standards • Ensure business data consumers are fully engaged in projects • Account for additional project time to clarify requirements • Profile data as part of project analysis • Improve testing practices to identify when data does not meet expectations

(Continued)

Table 8.1 Root Causes and Improvement Opportunities (*Continued*)

Root Cause	Origin	Improvements and Opportunities
Implementation of logic in one area of a downstream system that unexpectedly affects data in another	Data store (target system)	• Assess risks based on technical metadata that enables understanding the relation between parts of the target system • Improve regression testing practices • Improve intra-team communications practices, especially for implementations
Data changes over time (data evolution/data drift), but downstream consumers are not aware of changes	Data producers	• Document data lineage • Document initial expectations • Establish ongoing measurement to identify evolutionary change • Improve communication between systems to understand and respond to changes
Business needs change over time	Data consumers	• Plan for evolution (e.g., create flexible data structures to reduce the costs of system change) • Create a feedback loop so that new requirements can be defined and acted upon in a timely manner
Business needs conflict	Data producers and data consumers	• Enact governance that can prioritize requirements • Plan for multiple needs (e.g., create flexible data structures)
Data consumers misunderstand the data or do not know how to use it	Data consumers	• Improve training for end users • Document data lineage, data transformation details, and other metadata
An issue is identified but not communicated sufficiently and is "rediscovered"	Data store managers	• Systematically track and communicate about issues • Ensure data consumers have access to information about known issues (e.g., metadata related to known issues)

While improvement efforts focus on specific data, as part of an improvement projects, it also is important to assess all the associated data that are potentially impacted by changes to ensure that the improvements have not had any negative effects. Once again, initial assessment pays off, since it provides a baseline against which to understand subsequent changes to associated data. The main goal of improvement projects is to ensure that the quality of data actually gets better. To sustain improvements, an additional deliverable from an improvement project should be a set of recommendations related to ongoing or periodic measurement of the data that was the subject of the improvement efforts.

Ongoing Measurement

"The use of force alone is but temporary. It may subdue for a moment; but it does not remove the necessity of subduing again: and a nation is not governed, which is perpetually to be conquered."
—Edmund Burke (1729–1797)

Purpose

This chapter presents general principles related to ongoing measurement in its three forms: in-line data quality measurement, controls, and periodic measurement. To do so, we will look at the reasons for establishing ongoing measurement and explore each of its forms in more depth. The chapter discusses the input needed for ongoing measurement (an understanding of data's critical and risk), the need for automation of such measurement, and the deliverables associated with the process of ongoing measurement.

Initial data assessment is wide-ranging. It includes profiling the condition of each attribution in a dataset and the relations between them. It requires and produces knowledge about the business and technical processes that create and utilize data. Data quality improvement projects are narrowly focused on a subset of data that requires improvement. But such projects also produce in-depth analysis of business and technical processes that produce data. The focus of in-line measurement and control is neither as wide and comprehensive as initial assessment nor as narrow and in-depth as improvement projects. The focus is on critical or at risk data, even if assessment indicates that the data is meeting expectations. In-line measurement and control have three closely connected goals: (1) to monitor the condition of data and provide a level of assurance about the degree to which data is meeting expectations; (2) to detect changes in the data that might indicate a data quality issue or other change in data production; and (3) to identify opportunities for improvement. Combined, these functions help to support and sustain data quality. Periodic measurement has similar goals. It is executed against less critical data or data that cannot be measured in-line.

The Case for Ongoing Measurement

Some people may hesitate to invest in ongoing measurement, especially if data is meeting expectations. But there are two strong arguments in favor of such investment. The first is based in best practices for quality control. The second recognizes that measurement mitigates risks associated with our complex and rapidly changing data environments.

The first argument for ongoing measurement is based on best practices in quality control. Most experts in data and information quality recognize the desirability of some form of ongoing data quality monitoring.[1] Quality control through inspection is firmly rooted in manufacturing practices that provide the foundation for much data quality practice. The idea of in-line data monitoring to sustain data quality is the logical extension of the manufacturing paradigm. Still, relatively few organizations actually do automate in-line data quality measurement. This tendency is a result of two things: first, the project-oriented character of most IT organizations and with them data quality management teams (IT tends to think in terms of development projects, even though most IT organizations are responsible for a significant number of operational processes); and second, the connection of the project paradigm to business process improvement projects rather than to the kind of ongoing quality control that we associate with manufacturing.

That paradigm looks like this: Identify a data quality pain point; assess the data and the data chain to identify the root cause of the problem; set up a project to address the root cause; ensure that the project has successfully remediated root cause; then measure the data to ensure that it stays in control. Or don't do that last part because the root cause has already been addressed and the data should be okay, and we don't have enough people to monitor the data if it is not having a problem. Go on to the next project.

In fairness, it is necessary to address data issues, and the best way to do so is to remediate root causes. In a few cases where there is an identifiable, remediable root cause, and that cause is effectively remediated, and there is little risk that it will raise its ugly head again, this approach works. But problems often have multiple causes. And new and different problems can also raise their ugly heads. What can be done to prepare for problems we don't know about yet? When deployed effectively, in-line measurement can mitigate such risks.

The first challenge to establishing effective in-line measuring is figuring out which data to measure and how to measure it. Initial assessment should be used to determine which data is most critical and most at risk. The DQAF measurement types can be used to determine how to measure.

The second argument for ongoing measurement is based on the role of data and information in our world today and on the complexity of our ways of managing these things. Beginning in the early 2000s, published articles started referring to a concept called the data ecosystem.[2] This concept acknowledged that data appear to have "organic" characteristics. They seem to grow and evolve on their own. Data "evolution" happens because our ability to store massive amounts of data enables us also to manipulate, share, move, and repurpose data almost at will. In the constantly evolving data ecosystem, data is subject to two basic influences: changes in business processes that impact its meaning or uses and changes in technical processes that can impact its format, accessibility, or

---

[1] Redman refers to this as "hold the gains" (1996). English (1999), Loshin (2001), and McGilvray (2008) all assert the need to impose a level of control to sustain data quality.

[2] This metaphor is intended to draw attention to the idea that data are not simply static, residing in tables. Instead, people use them. And with social media and electronic interaction, data about us are everywhere. In business, data are all over the place—in the "white space" of organizations (Redman, 2008). However the metaphor has had an interesting consequence of expanding the notion of what data are. In her blog on philanthropy, Lucy Bernholz writes: "Data are the most basic organic matter for the ecosystem of social good. They provide fodder for how we identify 'the problem,' which then plays a huge role in 'the solutions' that we build." She goes on to call data a "'nutrient' in a healthy, diverse ecosystem of social solutions."

transportability. These two forces can change data intentionally or accidentally. Even intentional changes can have unintended consequences.

This metaphor is a little dangerous. Data does not evolve organically. But the term speaks to our perception that data and systems have speeded up and seem to have taken on a life of their own. Almost any enterprise's data storage systems can be thought of as a data ecosystem, fed by and feeding a multitude of business processes that touch and change data. Even if they do this mechanically, rather than organically, there are so many rules and so much activity that data seems to be growing. The data most at risk of being changed is data that is most often used. In other words, the most critical data is also the most at risk data. While an isolated system may be insulated from some of the change, not all of its input will be. Monitoring data through quality measurements is one way of detecting unexpected changes in data received by a system, whatever the cause, business or technical, in upstream processes.

Some data expectations are related directly to the way the data is instantiated within a particular system. So, as systems are changed to meet evolving business needs, their ability to produce data that meets expectations also changes. And very few systems are insulated from change. As organizations evolve, they upgrade and develop their systems to meet emerging organizational needs. But data storage systems are themselves complex. A change in one part of a data store can have unintended consequences in another area. Monitoring data can enable detection of changes caused by the technical processes within a data store.

Measurement allows us to name levels of quality and to identify factors that diminish quality. Ideally, it also allows for implementation of improvements, the impact of which must be assessed via measurement. To maintain or continuously improve quality, one needs to monitor and assess the effects of process improvements and also be able to detect the impact of other changes, some of which data consumers may not otherwise be aware of. In short, to improve data quality and to sustain improvements, one must apply the basic principles of quality improvement to data—and central to these is measurement.

Example: Health Care Data

The use of data within the health care system illustrates some of the reasons why data storage systems should have appropriate measurements and controls to prevent data in an unacceptable condition from being allowed in. The business of health care is data driven (see Figure 9.1). The health care system is also, ideally, driven by continuous improvement. Stakeholders in the system (providers, insurance companies [known as payers], policy holders, and consumers) have two goals: to improve health outcomes and to ensure business success.

Even simple health care events are complex, producing a lot of data. A visit to the doctor's office for an annual physical produces data to represent the patient, the provider, the patient's condition, and the patient's treatment. Data related to the patient's insurance and the provider's contracts is required to pay claims. This data is stored in systems owned by the health care provider, the payer (insurance company), the policy holder, and outside vendors who provide data to support the overall process of paying claims. All of these systems are subject to legal and regulatory requirements (see Figure 9.2).

Before data arrives in an analytic data store, it is fully enmeshed in a complex data chain. At any point in this environment, changes may have been introduced that cause unexpected effects within the

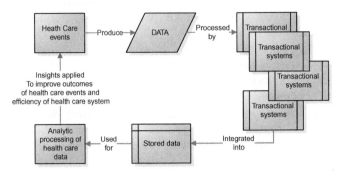

FIGURE 9.1 The Role of Data in Improving the Health Care System

The figure illustrates the role of data in enabling improvement of the health care system. Health care events produce data that is processed by transactional systems. This data enables health care entities to take care of the business aspects of health care. Stored data is used to assess the effectiveness of treatment plans on health care outcomes, as well as the efficiencies of administration. Results of these analyses are used in subsequent health care events.

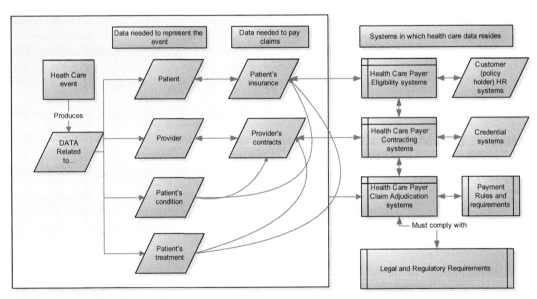

FIGURE 9.2 Data within the Health Care Environment

Data in the health care environment is complex and comprehensive. To represent a health care event, data is needed to represent the patient, the provider, the patient's condition and treatment, as well as to pay claims. This data resides in numerous systems owned by providers, payers, policy holders, and vendors.
The processes that govern the use of health care data are subject to legal and regulatory requirements.

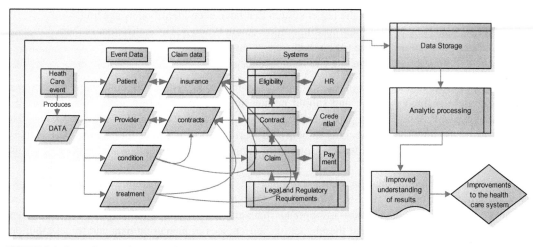

FIGURE 9.3 Analytic data in Health Care

Seen in the light of how the data gets to analytic processing, the environment is suddenly more complex (even in this very simplified schematic). Because changes to how data is collected and processed can take place in any of the systems that ultimately provide data to a data storage system, it is important for the storage system to implement measurements and controls to prevent data from being allowed to enter the system if it is in an unacceptable condition.

data store (see Figure 9.3). There is always risk associated with data being collected, processed, and moved, especially in a complex system. This complexity is one of the primary reasons data storage systems should implement measurements and controls to prevent data from being allowed to enter if it is in an unacceptable condition and for measuring the results of their own processing to detect changes to data before they have an impact on data consumers. Even in a complex system, measurement provides a way to characterize the condition of the data.

Inputs for Ongoing Measurement

As is the case with initial assessment, so too with ongoing measurement: You will get more out of the process if you plan for it. While the capture of measurement results should be automated, the analysis, documentation, and communication of findings require people with skills to accomplish these tasks.

Deliverables from initial data assessment provide input to planning for in-line measurement, controls, and periodic measurement. These include not only the recommendations that pertain directly to measurement, but also the metadata and documentation produced or improved through the assessment:

- Documented understanding of the business processes that produce data
- Documented understanding of technical processes in source and target systems
- Data definitions and data lineage

- Data elements and rules within the target system that have been identified as needing improvement and reasons for their needing improvement (known issues, differences from expectations, level of adherence to standards, etc.)
- Documented limitations in metadata and reference data

Along with the data analysis from the initial assessment, an analyst should understand the options for measurement—which data can and should be measured in-line, where controls are appropriate, and which data will be measured periodically. Successful measurement implies knowing what you are measuring and how (or having tools to help you learn how) to interpret the results. Deliverables from in-line measurement will include summaries of results and recommendations for improvements (see Figure 9.4).

Preparation for ongoing measurement should include a plan to share results with data consumers. Data consumers can provide valuable input about data criticality and the priority of improvements. An equally important consideration is ongoing interaction with data producers. This interaction allows data producers to understand the impact of their choices in managing data and to get input on

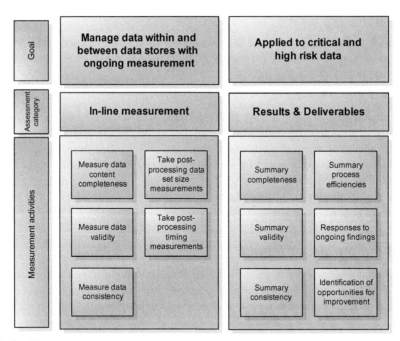

FIGURE 9.4 In-line Measurement

The goals of in-line measurement are directed at sustaining data quality. In-line measurement should monitor the condition of data and provide a level of assurance about the degree to which data is meeting expectations. It should be used to detect changes in the data that might indicate a data quality issue or other change in data production. In-line measurement is generally directed at high-criticality or high-risk data. It should also help identify opportunities for improvement. Deliverables from in-line measurement include summary reports and recommendations for improvement.

those choices. It thus reduces the risk of surprises in the data chain and facilitates the process of doing things in the best way the first time.

Criticality and Risk

In-line measurement should be purposeful and actionable. Proposed measurements should be assessed for business criticality and for potential risks. If they are not and you have a system in which you can measure just about anything you want, then you may be tempted to set up a lot of specific metrics without thinking through their purpose and meaning and without establishing protocols for responding to findings. It is not a good thing to be taking lots of measurements that people do not understand: These won't be used and therefore will not return any value.

Critical data includes data that is necessary to run an enterprise, is the subject of reporting, or is essential input for other business processes. Criticality is relative and must be defined in the context of particular uses. Data that is critical for one process may not be critical for another. Still, many organizations can identify data that is critical to multiple processes (Loshin, 2011). At risk data includes data that has had problems in the past (known risks), data or processes similar to those that have had problems in the past (potential risks), and new critical data whose behavior is not yet known.

Risks can be associated with either business or technical processes. Any process in which data is created, collected, transformed, stored, or used will have risk points—places where things can go wrong. The combination of content expectations based on business processes and knowledge of data movement through technical processes helps identify risk points. Some risk points—those associated with known problems—are obvious. Assessing these points and identifying their characteristics can also help you predict where you might have problems in the future. Identifying these kinds of measures depends on being able to see the pattern of known problems in order to identify potential problems.[3]

Automation

To measure and monitor data in a complex environment requires automation. Without automation, the speed and volume of data will quickly overwhelm even the most dedicated efforts to measure. Automation is another reason why the focus for ongoing measurement should be on critical and high-risk data. It is neither possible nor cost effective to measure the quality of every piece of data. While measurement and the detection of anomalies can be automated to a large degree, analysis of findings is resource-intensive.

Automation includes not only the capture of measurement results, but also the execution of first-level analysis of those results. First-level analysis includes comparisons to data quality thresholds that indicate whether data quality is within acceptable limits. The ability to detect unexpected conditions before data is loaded mitigates the risk that bad data will be loaded to a data store. The ability to

---

[3]Chapter 10 presents some examples that flesh out this concept.

capture the results of measures surfaces opportunities for improvement. Measurement data can be used for trend analysis which identifies changes over time.

In-line measurement should be automated in such a way that it is extensible. (Extensibility is one of the advantages of the DQAF, which describes measurement in generic terms.) If you build a set of measurements related to known risks, you can also identify data and processes that are likely to be at risk. Identifying this data and measuring it proactively enables you to quickly detect if the data's quality has deteriorated.

Many DQAF measurement types depend on an assumption that data within a given system will be consistent in terms of volume or content. This assumption of consistency may not always be valid, especially as data production and uses change. However, data should always reflect a relationship with organizational processes, so even knowledge of inconsistencies is valuable. Having measurement in place on critical data provides a means of continuous knowledge about the data's condition, however consistent or inconsistent that condition may be. Measurement provides the vocabulary for understanding the condition of data.

Controls

As described in Chapter 4, a control is a form of feedback built into a system to keep it stable. A control can detect conditions that indicate a lack of stability (most often in the form of a measurement) and initiate action based on this observation. Actions may include stopping the system, adjusting the system, or reporting on the condition of the system. Putting in place a set of data quality controls requires knowledge of both data processing and data content. General process controls should be comprehensive and built into the system for obtaining, staging, and processing data. They include things like ensuring correspondence between the number of records sent and the number of records received.

Implementing controls based on content requires a significant amount of analysis, especially if one of the actions the controls may take is to stop the system from processing data. Generally speaking, systems engineers and database administrators (DBAs) are loath to stop data processing, especially for data quality problems. Their stance makes a certain amount of sense. Stopping processing introduces risk to the system and may cause more or different data quality problems. The benefits of stopping the system must outweigh the risks.

When we implemented a set of data quality measurements in our warehouse in 2004, I was informed by our technical teams that they would never stop a data load for a data quality problem. Nevertheless, they built a feature of the measurement process called an emergency threshold designed to do just that. All emergency thresholds were initially set at 100%, essentially shutting off the functionality. They also built a notification process so that I received an e-mail when our basic data quality threshold was exceeded. One day, for an attribute that normally defaulted at about a tenth of a percent, I received a notification that records were defaulting at 90%. The technical teams brought processing to a halt, identified the root cause of the problem (a missing index), and remediated it. Then they agreed that in some cases, the emergency threshold made sense. In this situation, the benefits of taking action on an identified problem far outweighed the cost of that action.

Content controls are measurements of content characteristics that can be directly compared to a standard for performance. If that comparison indicates that content does not meet the standard, the control includes a response (an action by the system or people) to the fact of the difference. Some content measurements—likely the most critical ones—can also be used as controls.

Periodic Measurement

While it is not cost effective to apply in-line measurement to all data, less critical data should not be completely neglected. Like in-line measurement, periodic reassessment provides a level of assurance that data is in the condition it is expected to be in. Periodic reassessment of data ensures that reference data stays current, relationships remain sound, and business and technical evolution does not cause unexpected changes to data. Periodic reassessment will usually not have as broad a scope as initial assessment, in part because in-line measurement will already be delivering information about a set of columns and relationships that were part of initial assessment and in part because some data will be of very low priority and very low risk (see Figure 9.5).

Reassessment can use the initial profiling data as a point of comparison; indeed, this data is essential, since one task of such an assessment is to determine whether anything has changed from the

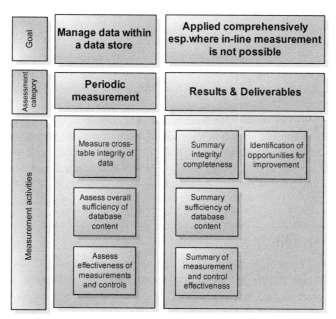

FIGURE 9.5 Periodic Measurement

Like in-line measurement, periodic measurement is directed at sustaining data quality. It is applied to less critical data or data that cannot be measurement in-line—for example, certain kinds of referential relationships. Deliverables include summarized results of findings and recommendations for improvement. Periodic measurement should also include a review of the effectiveness of existing measurements.

initial assessment. If the initial assessment determined that the data met expectations and the data has remained stable, then reassessment can be a simple confirmation of this condition. Of course, since systems evolve, reassessment should also ask whether or not the data is expected to remain stable.

Another reason for periodic assessment is that some data relationships (certain kinds of referential integrity) do not lend themselves to in-line measurement. In medical claim data, for example, every claim is expected to be associated with a health care provider. But sometimes claims can be processed before provider contract data is available in the warehouse. A similar situation can take place between claim and membership data. Even when member data is available, records related to a specific member may not be part of the same processing cycle as claim records. Measuring the referential integrity in such cases is better accomplished through a full comparison of the core tables, rather than through a comparison of a subset of records to another subset of records.

Periodic reassessment can also take place at the macro level. It can ask whether the data store continues to meet requirements and be used to identify gaps in data content. Importantly, periodic assessment should also include assessment of the set of in-line data quality measurements to determine whether they are providing effective feedback to data consumers.

Deliverables from Ongoing Measurement

Ongoing measurement is directed at sustaining data quality. Measuring and monitoring the condition of data provides assurance about the degree to which data meets expectations. In-line measurement can also detect changes in the data that might indicate a data quality issue. And observation of the data, whether in-line or through periodic measurement, can surface opportunities for improvement.

Deliverables from ongoing measurement include summary reports on data quality (completeness, consistency, validity) and on process efficiency; responses to any data quality issues identified through the measurements; and identification of opportunities for improvement. Periodic assessment should also include evaluation of the effectiveness of measurements themselves and recommendations for improvements in specific measurements and the use of measurements for keeping data consumers and producers informed about the condition of data. Both in-line and periodic measurement produce knowledge about the data. This knowledge should be captured and made available to data consumers, not only in the form of reports, but also through augmentation of existing metadata.

In-Line versus Periodic Measurement

The measurement method you choose will affect what the measurements tell you about the data. The examples in Figure 9.6 and Figure 9.7 illustrate one potential risk of periodic measurements: They can hide characteristics of the data that you want to detect. Figure 9.6 represents measurements taken once a quarter against an entire table. For several years, the overall percentage of defaulted data holds steady at about 12.5%. It climbs late in 2011 and appears to spike in 2012. The "spike" itself appears as a relatively small increase of just 0.15% when the measurement is taken across the whole table.

Figure 9.7 shows measurements of the same data taken as part of an incremental load. When measured this way, the increase in the level of defaulted data is apparent sooner. From mid-2009 to mid-2011, the data appears stable (defaulting at approximately 12.5%), as it does in the periodic measure.

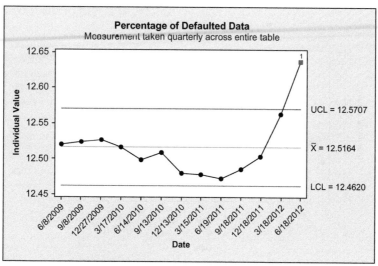

FIGURE 9.6 Periodic Measure of Defaulted Data

The graph represents measurements taken once a quarter against an entire table. From mid-2009 to late 2011, the overall percentage of defaulted data holds steady at about 12.5%; it even decreases starting in mid-2010. It begins to climb in the last two quarters of 2011 and seems to spike in 2012. Note that the "spike" itself (at around 12.65%) is only 0.15% greater than the mean measurement (12.50%), when the measurement is taken across the whole table.

The percentage of records that default with each load begins to climb in the second half of 2011. By mid-2012, the attribute is defaulting at approximately over 14%. The rate at which records default has increased by 1.5% (from 12.5 to 14%).

Both measurements detect change in the data, but in this case, the in-line measure detects it sooner. The other obvious factor here is that the first measurements (Figure 9.6) are taken against an entire table. For databases that load incrementally, periodic measurements can be refined to look at trends between data loads.

Concluding Thoughts

In discussing data assessment, we have been talking largely in terms of a data storage system that already exists and that receives data from pre-existing transactional systems. If you were to approach the problem with a completely blank slate, the options for building quality become clearer. While few, if any, blank slates exist, measurement nevertheless provides an opportunity to be proactive about quality by expanding our vocabulary about the condition of data. It gives us words to describe how to build the "product" right in the first place. In manufacturing, if you can define tolerances before you begin to machine your parts, you can prepare your machines to meet the tolerances. And, if defined beforehand, measurement can be embedded in the data chain (Redman, 1996, p. 284).

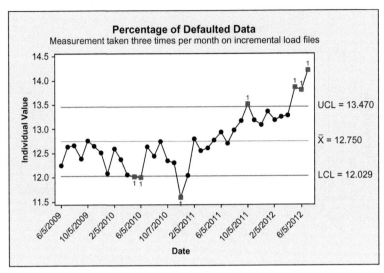

FIGURE 9.7 In-line Measure of Defaulted Data

This graph shows measurements taken of the same table and attribute as in Figure 9.6, but taken with each incremental load of the database rather than across the entire table. In this graph, the increase in the level of defaulted data is apparent sooner than in Figure 9.6. From mid-2009 to mid-2011, the data is stable (defaulting at approximately 12.5%), with one data point as an outlier on the side of the lower control limit. However, the percentage of records defaulting with each load begins to climb in the second half of 2011, and by mid-2012, the attribute is defaulting at approximately over 14%. The rate at which records default has increased by 1.5% (from 12.5 to 14%).

Those who are familiar with the Shewhart cycle of Plan-Do-Check-Act and its Six Sigma descendant, the DMAIC—Define, Measure, Analyze, Improve, Control—methodology for process improvement, have probably recognized a similar contour to this discussion of assessment scenarios. I started by emphasizing the importance of knowing your data, not only its content, but the processes that created it and the systems in which it resides. Initial assessment provides an understanding of current state. It is necessary for defining the problems you need to address and planning to address them. Initial assessment paves the way for improvement. Control is usually seen as the capstone to any improvement project. Once the root cause is eliminated, all you need to do is put a control measure in place and everything should be smooth sailing. But it does not always work that way, especially in an environment of rapid change. The process of ongoing measurement (in-line, controls, and periodic measurement) serves as a form of overall control. These processes can detect situations where data is not aligned with expectations so that you can take action on them.

Data monitoring is necessitated not only by the complexity of systems, but also by the speed at which business needs evolve. In order to understand whether data is fit for new uses, businesspeople need to have better ways of understanding what the data represents, what it looks like, and how it changes as business practices change. The complexity of many business systems necessitates that a level of control and detection be built in to data processing. In order to be good stewards of data, IT should have in place both process controls and data content measurement.

Applying the DQAF to Data Requirements

"Whether you can observe a thing or not depends on the theory which you use. It is the theory which decides what can be observed."
—Albert Einstein, 1879–1955

Data quality measurement requires defining the characteristics of high-quality data and assessing data against these characteristics. The process of defining specific quality metrics involves understanding data content, including the relative criticality of different data elements and rules, identifying business expectations related to data use, and assessing processes for risks to data. DQAF measurement types describe different ways to measure data completeness, timeliness, validity, consistency, and integrity. The assessment scenarios in Section Three describe contexts in which the quality of data can be understood, from initial assessment and improvement projects to in-line measurement and periodic reassessment. The purpose of Section Four is to demonstrate how DQAF categories can be used to formulate data quality requirements so that in-line data quality measurements, controls, and periodic measurements can be specified. Chapter 10: Requirements, Risk, Criticality *defines requirements related to the quality of data content in the general context of business requirements. Chapter 11:* Asking Questions *discusses a set of techniques that can be used to define characteristics about the expected condition of data in relation to completeness, validity, consistency, and integrity. Assertions formulated through this process can then be associated with DQAF measurement types to define specific data quality metrics.*

In-line measurement serves three primary goals that need to be accounted for when specifying measurement requirements: to monitor the condition of data and provide a level of assurance about the degree to which data is meeting expectations; to detect changes in the data that might indicate a data quality issue or other change in data production; and to identify opportunities for improvement. Because of these functions, measurement is essential to establishing and sustaining data quality. Because it is automated, in-line measurement can be widely applied. However, for in-line measurement to be effective requires that analysts be assigned to review and respond to measurement results. Therefore it is important to establish criteria for determining which data to measure in-line. These criteria should be based on a combination of how critical data is to the organization and what risks are associated with data production, storage, and consumption.

Context

In presenting this information, I am assuming a particular context, namely, that of a large project that moves data from a set of transactional source systems to a large data store, such as a data warehouse (see Figure 10.0). Such a project will have multiple development iterations, all of which include requirements definition, modeling, programming, and testing of the database before data is made available to data consumers.

For such projects, data itself originates through processes needed to transact business and through systems based on requirements for transacting business. Such systems are rarely designed to produce data for downstream uses. People wishing to use this data will have expectations about its content and condition. Expectations of data consumers influence their perceptions of the systems and the data contained in them. These expectations may be based on direct experience with the data and knowledge of the processes that produce it. Or they may be based solely on the intended uses data consumers have for the data. Many of these expectations can be articulated as requirements—needs that are defined and documented. Most data consumers will also have assumptions about the condition of data, some of which they may not even be aware of until they see the data and perceive it as different from what they expected. Requirements and assumptions may pertain to the content of source data (what the data represents and how it represents), the relationship between data from different sources (how data from different parts of an organization should fit together), and the ways the warehouse will integrate data.

Data quality experts agree that data should be managed like a product. To have high-quality data requires that you understand and manage the processes through which it is created and, especially, that when you find problems, you remediate their root causes. Managing data as a product requires managing the supply chain. Unfortunately, few organizations actually manage their data in this way. There are many reasons why they don't. The complexity of organizations, information systems, and the amount of data they

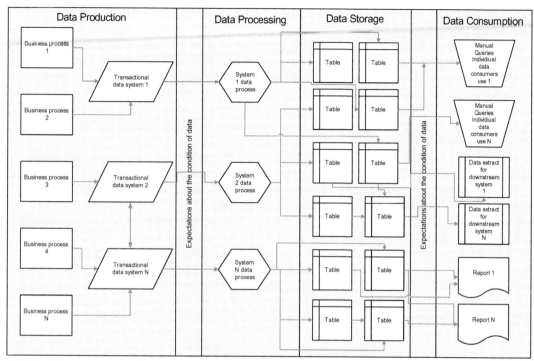

FIGURE 10.0 Context of Requirements Definition and Measurement Specification

The figure depicts the context for the formulation of expectations related to the quality of data. Data is produced through multiple business processes using transactional systems. It is moved from these systems into a data warehouse where it is stored for access by data consumers. Consumption can take different forms, for example, queries by individual users, canned reports, and extracts for downstream systems. Expectations of data consumers influence their perceptions of the systems and the data they contain. Ideally, expectations related to data use should be identified as part of transactional system design, so that initial business processes can ensure that the data collected supports the needs of downstream users. In most organizations, however, transactional systems have been designed to conduct immediate business and have not taken into consideration the downstream uses of the data they produce. Designers of downstream systems must do considerable analysis and processing to ensure that the data is suitable to meet the needs of their data consumers.

produce are among the biggest challenges to data management. Added to these is the fact that people who use data frequently come up with new ways to use it. Since few of us have the luxury of starting with a blank slate, how do we counteract the potential for chaos? One step is to have as clear a picture as possible about what data you are responsible for, what characteristics data consumers expect it to have, and how closely it adheres to those characteristics. Such a picture can be drawn through a combination of direct input from data consumers about their expectations and a set of measurements related to those expectations. Such input is not always gathered as part of requirements definition. I am advocating that it should be.

Once you know what you have and what condition it is in, the next step is to get it into the condition it needs to be in for your purposes. Doing so requires knowledge of the data chain and the ability to influence source systems (in other words, managing the supply chain). Here again, measurement is critical. Most organizations have more data quality issues than they will ever be able to address. Issues are of different sizes, and they differ in their impact on organizational success. To improve data quality, you will need to prioritize which issues to address.

The techniques described in this section assume the existence of a process to define business requirements related to data content. Their purpose is to extend the usual edges of the requirements definition process to include an articulation of quality characteristics. This work is most likely to be carried out by business analysts from IT teams who are charged with helping businesspeople articulate their needs. Its success depends on bringing together both technical and business knowledge.

A working assumption is that current practices do not often ask enough questions about expectations for data. One of the goals of defining quality requirements is to make explicit any assumptions pertaining to the quality of data. When assumptions are understood, they can be used to assess the condition and suitability of data. If they are not made explicit as part of project analysis, they can frequently become the cause of project failure.

Requirements, Risk, Criticality

10

"A wise man sets requirements only for himself; an unwise man makes requirements for others."
—Leo Tolstoy, *A Calendar of Wisdom* (1908)

Purpose

This chapter reviews the concept of data quality requirements in the context of business requirements and for the purpose of identifying characteristics of data that can be measured in-line. It describes how risk and criticality can be assessed to identify specific data and rules to be monitored on an ongoing basis through in-line measurements, controls, and periodic measurement.

Business Requirements

To require a thing means to need it for a particular purpose or to depend on it for success or survival. A required thing is specified as compulsory to a purpose. Requirements define things or actions that are necessary to fulfill a purpose. *Require* shares its Latin root, *quaerere, to seek,* with *requisite*, "made necessary by particular circumstances or regulations" (*NOAD*). In its simplest definition, a requirement is a thing that is needed for a particular purpose. A *business requirement* is thus a synonym for a *business need* that contributes to a business goal. Business needs come in all shapes and sizes. They can range from the broad ("We need a system that will process claim data") to the very specific ("The system must be able to validate the relationship between diagnosis and procedure codes"). Often such assertions are packed with unarticulated assumptions about what it means to meet such needs. When these assumptions are not articulated, there is a risk that they will not be met. When they are not met, data consumers will perceive a problem with the quality of data delivered through a data store or application.

Business requirements define the things that people who run the business side of an enterprise must have to do their jobs and thus accomplish the goals of an enterprise. They include assertions about what a system must do (functional requirements) and characteristics that a system must possess (nonfunctional requirements, also referred to as quality or service requirements). Business requirements are defined at the beginning of IT projects that develop technical solutions to business problems. Requirements provide the basis for the work accomplished by software engineers and other technical personnel. Business requirements take the form of statements describing what a system must have or what a system must do. They are usually articulated first in general terms. Through the requirements definition process, which is, ideally, a dialog between the customer requesting the application and the business analyst documenting the needs, they are articulated in more detail.

For example, a general requirement might read like this: We need a way to get consistent feedback from our customers about their satisfaction with our services. Through the requirements definition process, additional characteristics of the system can be defined.

> The system must be accessible to our customers via their personal computers.
> The system must enable users to select from a set of options for standard questions.
> The system must allow users to add comments.

The combination of general and detailed requirements provides input into the process of designing a system to meet them.

Even though they are the driving force behind IT projects, business requirements are often a source of contention in these projects. When projects do not go well, or when the end users of the system are dissatisfied with results, fingers are quickly pointed at the business requirements process or at the requirements themselves.[1] The requirements are not clear, or they are not fully defined, or they are too detailed and presuppose only one solution.

Projects are supposed to fulfill requirements. So why is there contention about them? In many organizations, the long answer is related to the relationship between IT and businesspeople and the different ways that they communicate with each other. In many organizations, conversations about requirements do not involve much dialog. Businesspeople are supposed to "have" requirements, and IT is supposed to "meet" requirements. The short answer is simpler: People do not always know what they need. Even when they do, it is not always easy for people to define what they need. It is often even harder get other people to understand what is needed. In addition, there are almost always differences of opinion about how a set of needs might be met.[2]

Business people and IT people make assumptions about business requirements that are similar to the assumptions that they make about data. One assumption, implicit in the phrase "requirements gathering," is that requirements are just out there waiting to be picked up off the ground or plucked off a tree, like so much fruit. The Wikipedia article titled "Business Requirements" claims, "Business requirements *exist* within the business environment and must be *discovered*, whereas product requirements are *human-defined* (specified)" (emphasis added).[3] I do not agree with this perspective on business requirements. They do not simply exist within the business environment to be *"discovered."* Requirements are, fundamentally, ideas, and they must be defined and developed. The process of definition itself enables clarification of both the business needs and the options for addressing those needs. There are various methodologies for defining business requirements. Each uses particular tools

---

[1] Ellis (2012) cites several other sources that identify the financial impacts of poorly defined requirements.

[2] When asked about how he responded to the needs of his customers, Henry Ford reputedly said "If I had asked my customers what they wanted, they would have said a faster horse" (http://quoteinvestigator.com/2011/07/28/ford-faster-horse/ accessed 10/3/2012). IT people are often driven by the desire to innovate, while businesspeople are generally more concerned about meeting current needs. With some individuals, this tension between innovation and meeting current needs can be productive. It can lead to forward-looking solutions. With others, it can be an obstacle to communication, leading to a dissatisfying solution or no solution at all.

[3] Business Requirements, Wikipedia (2012). To be fair, the Business Requirements article presents a relatively messy discussion on requirements. The article entitled "Requirements Analysis" is more rigorous and informative.

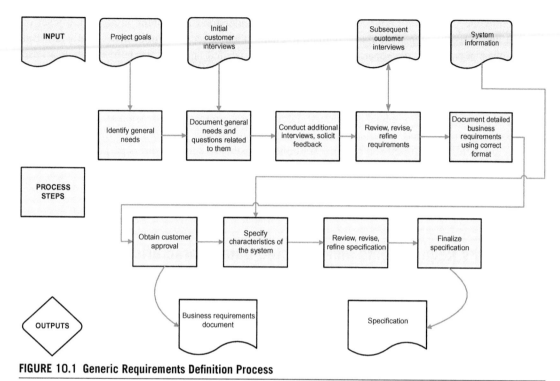

FIGURE 10.1 Generic Requirements Definition Process

The process of defining requirements and specifications is one of the iterative conversations about what a customer needs. Requirements can start at very different levels of detail. Ultimately, they need to be translated into technical specifications so that a solution can be developed.

and templates. But all of them entail asking a set of questions that unfold facets of the needs that are to be addressed (see Figure 10.1). It is important to keep in mind that the goal in defining requirements is to enable solutions to be developed that meet business needs. More harshly put, the goal is not simply to execute the requirements methodology; it is to understand the needs in relation to business goals and to find the best way to meet them. The process of defining requirements can become a semantic battle if people lose sight of its primary purpose.

Another common assertion about business requirements is that they can and should be clearly distinguished from system design itself. This idea usually is often expressed (mostly by systems designers) like this: Business requirements must state the *what*. Design will take care of the *how*. To a degree, this assertion is correct. Requirements, the things that a system must supply or functionality that it must provide, can be fulfilled through different designs. Just look at the differences between cars, buses, and trains. All meet the requirement of being able to transport people from place to place, but they look and act quite differently from each other. Their design differences exist, in part, because each meets a full set of other requirements, in addition to the central requirement of being able to transport people from place to place.

Much of the contention about requirements can be understood as contention about the level of detail at which requirements should be defined to enable their successful fulfillment. That's fair. But from another perspective, the separation between what is needed and how the need is met is a false distinction. Many people describe what they need in terms of how they will use it. People charged with writing requirements need to understand this tendency if they are to help stakeholders articulate the *what*. System design choices are the means of meeting requirements. We should not pretend that the two can or should be completely separated. Because they are mutually dependent, they have to be understood together. [4] Their mutual dependency stems from the fact that both exist to serve the same end: Requirements are fulfilled and systems are built ostensibly to serve business purposes carried out through business processes. Often the fulfillment of requirements in a system does not fully account for business processes. Thomas Redman has observed: "Failure to design processes and systems in concert has contributed to poor data quality" (Redman, 1996, p. 150).

Data Quality Requirements and Expected Data Characteristics

The definition of data quality we have been using asserts that the concept of quality is integral to purpose: The level of quality of data represents the degree to which data meets the expectations of data consumers, based on their intended use of the data. Data quality is thus directly related to the perceived or established purpose of the data. High-quality data meets expectations to a greater degree than does low-quality data. Inherent in this definition is the idea that data will effectively represent the objects, events, and concepts it is intended to represent.

Data quality requirements are a specific kind of business requirement. They define expectations related to data characteristics that ensure the suitability of data for particular purposes. Just as there can be general or detailed business requirements, data quality requirements can be general or detailed. They can focus on the overall environment in which data is used and accessed, the suitability of a dataset for particular uses, or the quality of content in individual fields. In a system that collects data for a particular function, for example, business requirements will focus on what data content is needed, while quality requirements may further articulate the level of detail of data collected or define constraints on validity. These requirements will result in data content of a particular granularity and precision—data that looks like it is supposed to. If quality requirements can be translated into characteristics associated with data, they can be measured.

There are different techniques for making this kind of translation. Thomas Redman describes defining data quality requirements using the Quality Functional Deployment (QFD) or "house of quality" method (Redman, 1996, pp. 139–154). This method begins with input about what the customer wants and builds out a set of matrices related to the quality attributes of the product or service that might fulfill the requirements (Tague, 2005, pp. 305–314). The matrices are both a visual and an analytic tool. They allow for correlations to be made among requirements. And they can be used to translate customer requirements into technical specifications.

---

[4]This idea seems to have been recognized early on in the Information Age. See Ackoff (1967) and Ivanov (1972), both of whom recognize that choices system design have a direct influence on the quality of the information that a system can produce.

The general process steps for the house of quality include:

- Understanding and documenting the customer's requirements.
- Documenting the associated characteristics of the product or service.
- Identifying and characterizing the relationships between the requirements and the desired characteristics.
- Defining the technical requirement to fulfill the customer's business requirement at the level of quality desired.
- Associating the characteristics with performance expectations or other measurements.

Redman's use of this method focuses on building quality expectations into the processes that create data. The result of the requirements matrix is a set of performance specifications that can be measured. These can be related to dimensions of data quality, such as timeliness, accuracy, and consistency. Ultimately, the requirements are fulfilled if the performance metrics are achieved.

David Loshin's approach to defining data quality requirements uses the use case model. Use cases depend on understanding the actors in a system, the information chain that produces data, and the effects of low-quality data. Those effects can be associated with costs or other relevant impacts to the use of the data and can also be translated into data quality dimensions. The data quality requirements become the threshold measurement levels associated with selected data quality dimensions for particular data elements and rules (Loshin, 2001, p. 248).

DQAF categories can be used to translate in a similar way. Doing so, they can be used to identify expectations about the degree to which fields should be populated (is the field required or optional?), how they will be populated (what values comprise the domain? what values are valid or invalid?), as well as the consistency and integrity of that population (how are fields related? what rules govern the relationships?). In executing the data quality requirements process for a large data store, we used a tool similar to the QFD matrix. Our requirements (rows in the matrix) included all the data elements from the model of the data store. Our columns were the data quality dimensions associated with the DQAF. Our process included asking data consumers their expectations for the data elements in relation to the dimensions, as well as their assessment of the criticality of individual data elements or rules. From this information we were able to associate critical data with ways to measure it (see Figure 10.2). We will explore the measurement requirements definition process in more depth in Chapter 11.

If such requirements are identified as part of system development for transactional systems, they may be met through functions such as system edits, which require input on particular fields or place constraints on field content—for example, Web forms that not only require you to supply an e-mail address but also check the format of input to the e-mail address field to ensure it has the @ symbol and a valid domain suffix (.com, .net, .gov, etc.). If quality requirements are not identified, then there is a risk that the data will not be in the condition that data consumers expect it to be in when it is sent downstream to a data store.

When data stores are built, project teams tend to emphasize content requirements ("This is the data our customers need"). Few focus on the condition or quality of that data. Data consumers always have expectations about data quality, but these are not always articulated. The most fundamental expectation is that the data they want already exists in some system. Next, when the data store is built, they expect data to be accessible and usable (organized, complete, valid, and correct) when they need it. People can make the mistake of assuming that because the data is present in a source system,

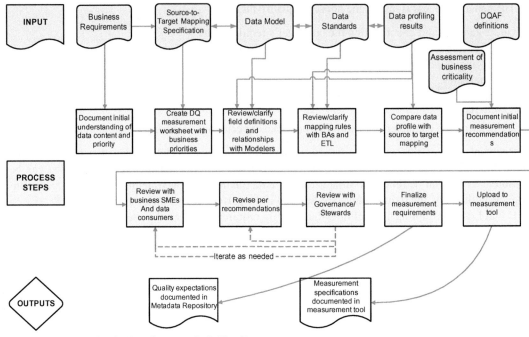

FIGURE 10.2 Data Quality Requirements Definition Process

The process of defining data quality requirements and specifications is also one of iterative conversations about what a data consumer expects about the condition of the data. The goal is to define which measurements should be taken and what the results of those measurements are expected to be. This figure depicts the analysis process for measurement requirements for a data store that has been modeled. Metadata from the model is part of the input to the measurement requirements process.

it is also in a condition that meets the needs of the target system. Unfortunately, existence and suitability are not the same things. Data may be of a different granularity or precision than required, it may contain fewer attributes, or the desired amount of historical data may not be available from the source system.

In both transactional and data storage systems, quality requirements can be understood in relation to dimensions of data quality, such as completeness, consistency, validity, timeliness, and integrity. The difference is that a data store cannot always impose constraints on source data to ensure it meets quality requirements. Nor can most data stores demand that sources change the precision or granularity of source data to meet the needs of data consumers. For situations in which a data store must accept source data as is, staff can at least measure the degree to which data does or does not meet requirements of data consumers. Even when a store cleanses data, it is important to understand the degree of change that data goes through. This knowledge also comes from measurement.

Data quality requirements differ from other business requirements in that they are meta requirements. They represent characteristics about the data content needed to meet *other* business requirements. They build additional meaning into business requirements. While in this sense they may be perceived as added on to what we traditionally understand as business requirements, they are not secondary. Most data quality requirements are implicit in data content requirements. Precisely because they are implicit, they can also remain unmet. Failure to meet data quality requirements undermines the ability to meet data content requirements. Data consumers will get the data they asked for, but it may not be in usable condition. If it does not meet their quality expectations, they will perceive it as poor quality data. This perception will undermine their trust in the surrounding data.

Data Quality Requirements and Risks to Data

Risks are the dark underbelly of quality requirements. Every business expectation for data implies a risk. Risks can be expressed by stating what will happen if an expectation is not met. For example, say you expect that every transaction should be associated with one-and-only-one customer. What happens if a transaction can be associated with more than one customer? Or what if it cannot be associated with any customer? In the transactional system, the immediate risk will be that you cannot complete the transaction. A second risk is that you will have duplicate records for the same customer. The longer term risk for stored data is that you will not have reliable data about customer activity with which to make decisions.

Risks are connected with undesirable conditions of data and undesirable events that can happen to data or that can happen as a result of using data that is in an undesirable condition. Data producers should be able to identify risk inherent in business or technical processes through which data is created. Business processes that are overly complex or poorly defined present risks because complexity and poor definition make it difficult for people to understand what they are expected to do. People are more likely to make mistakes collecting or entering data when they are not sure exactly what is expected. Data consumers should be able to define the business risks associated with poor quality data. That is, people using data should be able to identify data conditions that may have a negative impact on their uses of data. These conditions can be understood in the context of business processes that produce data. Reducing risks in business processes that produce data requires that data producers understand their own processes and the downstream uses of their data. Of course, very few business processes, especially those that produce data, exist independently from the technology that supports them. So, often, improvements in applications—sometimes simple ones, such as system edits described previously—can help business processes create cleaner data.

Technical risks are associated with the movement of data from one system to another or with the transformation of data within a system. As is the case with business processes, overly complex or poorly defined technical processes present greater risk than simpler, better defined processes. Technical risks include obstacles or delays in the data delivery channel, unusual files sizes, failure of complex rules due to unexpected conditions in the data, or coding errors introduced to the data processing flow. Technical risks can be measured at points in the data flow where adverse events are most likely to happen or where changes can be detected. For example, data input and output can be measured where rules are executed. Understanding of technological risks comes largely from technology staff and from documentation about the data flow.

Risks are related to how data is created or moved, and criticality is related to how data is used. But discussion about risks frequently reveals which data is critical because it forces data consumers to articulate the implications to their uses of data if data is incomplete, invalid, or processed incorrectly. Exploring risks not only enables you to understand assumptions about data; it also allows you to define the relative criticality of data elements and rules. The relative criticality of data provides input into decisions about which data to measure and how frequently to measure it.

Factors Influencing Data Criticality

The best way to identify which data is most critical is to ask data consumers. They can tell you which data they use and how they use it. They can also probably share stories about what has happened when critical data has been unavailable or of poor quality. But most of us are faced with hundreds of data elements and dozens of data consumer groups. Data that is critical to one part of an organization may be of less importance to another part. Customer phone numbers that are critical to a sales team that needs to be in direct contact with customers are not important to analysts studying aggregated customer behavior. If your data store has a large and diverse consumer base and you need to understand the relative importance of different data elements, you should identify consistent criteria through which to define criticality. These can include:

- The number of data consumers or teams who use the data.
- Whether the data is used in reporting.
- The type of reporting it is used in (internal or externally facing, for example).
- Whether the data is used as input to a downstream system.
- Whether the data is used as input to other business processes.

The criticality of data can also be understood from its uses within a data store. A simple count of the occurrence or the number of joins associated with a field is an indication of how integral the data is to relationships within the data store.

David Loshin (2011) defines critical data elements as "those on which the success of business processes and corresponding business applications rely." He recognizes that different facets of the business (analytics, operations, etc.) will rely on different specific data elements, and he points out several general criteria that can be applied to identify critical data elements. In addition to being used in reporting, critical elements may be used to support

- Business policies
- Regulatory compliance
- Business intelligence applications
- Operational decision making
- Scorecard performance

Or they could contain critical information related to employees, suppliers, or products.

Danette McGilvray (2008) describes a process to rank and prioritize data elements that are candidates for improvement projects. The same approach can be used to assign criticality ratings to data elements. The approach includes the following:

- Identify the business processes that use the data that needs to be prioritized.
- Engage a range of people who represent various interests within the organization and ensure they have the information they need to contribute.

- Get agreement on the processes and information to be ranked, as well as the scale to be used in ranking.
- For each data element, ask a standard set of questions to identify potential business impacts of poor data quality.
- Allow participants to rank the criticality of the data based on their knowledge of the process.
- Assign an overall ranking, document, and analyze the results

This approach can also be used to identify candidate data and metrics for in-line measurement (as will be discussed in Chapter 11).

Specifying Data Quality Metrics

Defining data quality requirements involves asking questions that enable data consumers to explicitly state their assumptions about the condition they expect data to be in for it to be usable. Implicit in data content requirements will be a set of characteristics data consumers expect data to have. In many cases, data consumers will not have thought about the condition of data. They will be able to tell you after the fact that data is not right, but they may not be able to tell you ahead of the fact all the details about what constitutes "right."

Defining data quality metrics starts with documenting known business expectations and then prompting data consumers to further articulate their assumptions. Most expectations can then be formulated as rules. For example, there can be a simple rule that a field should always be populated or a more complex rule that it should be populated only under specific conditions. Complex rules can then be broken into a series of simpler clauses. In other cases, expectations have to be formulated in terms of reasonability tests. For example, in most cases, it is reasonable to expect that a dataset drawn from a large group of the general population will share demographic characteristics, such as the distribution of ages or the relative proportion of men to women, with the general population. Reasonability assertions themselves can often be examined in greater detail to define specific, more concrete rules.[5]

Once you have documented expectations, the next step is to understand how to measure the degree to which data meets those expectations. This step involves associating expectations with a DQAF measurement type. These steps will result in two levels of detail: data quality content requirements that define characteristics data should have, and data quality metrics that define how a particular characteristic can be measured.

Data quality metrics cannot be created in a vacuum. To formulate them, you must first have not only content requirements but also a data model that defines how those content requirements will be met. Ideally, you should also have documented knowledge of the processes that have contributed to the production of data in transactional source systems, so that you understand the risks associated with the data even before you receive it. Unfortunately, often you will not have an ideal situation. You may just have the content requirements themselves, and you may need to work backwards and forwards to research data process flows and build out your understanding of risks and criticality.

---

[5] Sometimes the number of rules implied in data structure can be surprising. Wells and Duncan (1999) use a simple data model of five tables from a human resources system to identify a set of 32 specific rules.

Subscriber Birth Date Example

Each data quality content requirement should clearly state an expectation related to a dimension of quality. Data quality measurement requirements should state how this expectation will be measured. Let's look at an example of a relatively simple attribute: birth date on subscriber records related to a large health care policy holder. In commercial health insurance, policies are held by the companies that provide a health insurance benefit to their employees. Subscribers are employees who take advantage of this benefit. Members include subscribers and their dependents. This example focuses on subscribers only. Since subscribers are all individual human beings and all employed at a large company, common sense tells us we have the following data quality requirements, all of which are instances of assumptions made explicit:

- *Completeness*: Each subscriber should have a birth date because every person is born. No records should have a blank or NULL birth date.
- *Timeliness*: Birth date should be provided by the subscriber as part of the on-boarding process as a requirement for employment, as well as for taking advantage of a health care benefit, so birth date should be populated on all subscriber records and no records should be processed with a defaulted birth date.
- *Validity*: Birth date should be a valid date (e.g., February 30 is not a valid date).
- *Consistency*: Each subscriber should have only one birth date.
- *Integrity*: Therefore, for any individual subscriber, all records should have the same birth date.
- *Reasonability*: Birth date should reflect a reasonable age for an employee. That is, we would not expect a large company to have employees who are under the age of 18 or over the age of, probably, 70 but in almost all cases, 80.

Reasonability tests are harder to establish than the other rules. There may be a firm rule at one end of the scale—in this case, the youngest age at which a person can be hired. This rule can be checked by comparing birth date to hire date and calculating the age of any employee at the time he or she was hired. At the far end of the scale, a reasonable age for the oldest employees, there may be more flexibility. While it is unusual to have employees older than 80, it is not usually illegal. The key thing for any reasonability check is to set criteria that make sense in the specific situation and then look at real data to see if these criteria are met. From there, you can refine the rules. In a case like subscriber age or birth date, you can use common sense to establish your working hypothesis. For some other data attributes, reasonable starting points may not be as clear.

Once the assertions are made, the options for assessing them become clearer. If you are reviewing data in a single table, all but one rule (the assertion about integrity) can be addressed through a simple distribution of values, a common calculation in profiling. To take a distribution of values, count the number of times a distinct value appears in a field and then calculate the percentage of records associated with each value, using the distinct count as the numerator and the count of total records as the denominator.

As an example, let's look at the distribution of subscriber birth date. The company has approximately 79,000 employees, and data was collected over ten years. The range of ages in a large company is bound to be wide, since there will be employees who have just entered the workforce, as well as those who are near retirement. The 45- to 50-year age difference between the youngest and oldest employees means there are potentially more than 18,000 birth dates associated with employees (365 days/year *50 years). Indeed, pulling a full distribution of data resulted in more than 16,000 distinct dates. However, we have no assertions related to distinct dates. The main criterion for reasonability is employee age. So for ease of understanding, and because it makes the data more suitable to the purpose of initial assessment, the data is aggregated by year (see Table 10.1) The aggregation results in 69 distinct years, a few more than the 50 or so that were expected, and the first sign that we will have some details to look at.

Table 10.1 Counts and Percentages of Employees by Birth Year

Year	Count	Percentage	Year	Count	Percentage
1882	1	0.0013	1964	2206	2.7992
1930	1	0.0013	1965	2218	2.8144
1931	2	0.0025	1966	2266	2.8753
1932	2	0.0025	1967	2271	2.8817
1933	1	0.0013	1968	2317	2.9401
1934	4	0.0051	1969	2530	3.2103
1935	8	0.0102	1970	2634	3.3423
1936	4	0.0051	1971	2594	3.2915
1937	16	0.0203	1972	2331	2.9578
1938	17	0.0216	1973	2385	3.0263
1939	21	0.0266	1974	2287	2.9020
1940	34	0.0431	1975	2345	2.9756
1941	52	0.0660	1976	2307	2.9274
1942	103	0.1307	1977	2292	2.9083
1943	132	0.1675	1978	2132	2.7053
1944	161	0.2043	1979	2147	2.7243
1945	230	0.2918	1980	2222	2.8195
1946	415	0.5266	1981	2192	2.7814
1947	580	0.7360	1982	1955	2.4807
1948	677	0.8590	1983	1851	2.3487
1949	820	1.0405	1984	1736	2.2028
1950	855	1.0849	1985	1625	2.0620
1951	1076	1.3653	1986	1390	1.7638
1952	1193	1.5138	1987	1118	1.4186
1953	1282	1.6267	1988	787	0.9986
1954	1408	1.7866	1989	429	0.5444
1955	1511	1.9173	1990	190	0.2411
1956	1535	1.9478	1991	86	0.1091
1957	1760	2.2333	1992	22	0.0279
1958	1818	2.3069	1993	6	0.0076
1959	1794	2.2764	1994	2	0.0025
1960	1986	2.5200	1995	2	0.0025
1961	2085	2.6457	1997	1	0.0013
1962	2139	2.7142	1998	2	0.0025
1963	2207	2.8005			

FIGURE 10.3 Percentage of Subscriber Birth Dates by Year

The figure shows the percentage of subscriber birth dates by year for employees at a large company of approximately 79,000 employees. The graph enables an analyst to assess the reasonability of the data. It is reasonable that the largest portion of employees was born between 1960 and 1980, since (as of 2012) very few people from this group will have retired. What is unexpected are the values at either end of the graph. The records with birth years indicating that subscribers are very old or very young represent errors in the data. While the graph helps an analyst understand the condition of the data, it does not in itself point to the root causes of the errors. From the data and the graph, it is reasonable to assume that there are not systematic errors in the collection of birth date data.

The first rule to review is the assertion about completeness. It states that every subscriber should have a birth date. This rule is confirmed. All records are populated with a date. There are no NULL or blank records. Our second rule, for timeliness, requires essentially the same test. All records have a birth date, and no records have a default birth date of 1/1/1900. The data was also tested for validity, by joining the birth date field to the valid date table. No records were dropped, indicating that all individual dates are valid.

Things get more interesting when we come to the question of reasonability. The first thing that stands out from both the data table and the graph shown in Figure 10.3 itself is that the data for employee birth year resembles a normal distribution, a bell curve in which most values land in the center and only a few reside at the ends. The left side of the curve shows that one record has an employee birth year of 1882, indicating an employee who is about 130 years old. Clearly this date is unreasonable and represents some kind of error. Determining the error requires looking at other details on the record. The error could be a simple typo; for example, someone may have mistakenly entered 1882 instead of 1982. Inspection of the record itself, or, if they are available, any additional records associated with the employee, may give clues as to the nature of the error. Next, there are several records for employees with birth years in the 1930s, indicating a small set of people working well into their 70s. From the distribution alone, there is no way to tell whether or not these records are correct. At first glance, however, they are not unreasonable in the way the 1882 date is. Finally, there is a set of five records for people who are under 18 years of age (those born after 1994). These records do seem unreasonable, since it is unlikely that a large corporation would employ people who are not yet 18. Again, the distribution cannot answer the question of correctness; it can only identify suspicious or clearly incorrect records.

The initial assessment indicates there are only six unreasonable records in a set of 78,808. From the perspective of reasonability, the data appears sound. Well over 99.99% of it meets the criteria for reasonability. The six records that do not meet the criteria amount to 0.0076% of the total set. Nothing in the data indicates a systematic problem. So, while the six records require additional investigation, the initial data quality content requirements for completeness, validity, and reasonability have been met. The next step is to define requirements for ongoing measurement.

In the birth date example, several choices present themselves. If new subscriber data is loaded to a data warehouse once a week, the first option is to take a full distribution of values each time new data is loaded. The second is to measure the distribution by year, as was done in the example. Neither measurement is likely to tell you much about the data that you do not already know. While it is important to ensure the birth date field is populated, there is no expectation of consistency between sets of data representing existing employees and new hires. In fact, we would expect differences. It is very likely that over time, most new hires would be younger people entering the workforce. The third option is to focus on data that do not meet the criteria for reasonability. This option entails setting up a rule to identify what percentage of records represents employees under the age of 18 or over the age of 80.

The data quality content requirement could look like this:

We do not expect to have employees over the age of 80 or under the age of 18.

Or like this:

We expect the age of employees to be between 18 and 80 years.

Expressing the requirement in both positive and negative terms may seem redundant. But stating the requirement both ways can help to ensure that it is fully understood by stakeholders. People see things in different ways, and providing two perspectives on the same condition can help communicate its meaning.

Age is a rolling figure. You would most likely not have a field on a record to capture employee age. Instead you are more likely to capture birth date, from which age can be calculated. The data quality rule that assesses the reasonability of subscriber age would need to do so in relation to another date on the record. This date could be the hire date, the enrolled date, or the current date, depending on the structure of the data.

The data quality metrics corresponding to the content requirement for employee age could look like this:

With each load of commercial subscriber records, count and calculate the percentage of records where birth date is before current date minus 80 years or where birth date is after current date minus 18 years.

A metric like this one can be taken using measurement type #30 Consistent Column Profile with qualifiers. Or if there were a need to take it at the policy-holder level, it could be taken through #33 Multi-Column Profile with qualifiers.

In addition to defining the metric itself, you should also track the purpose for the measure. State specifically what the measurement will show and identify actionable items and response scenarios, as well as business and system contacts.

> In the past, birth date data outside this range has indicated a problem with data entry. When the measure indicates a finding, identify the specific records, contact the policy holder's HR department, and request that they review and update records appropriately.

The results would be reflected in subsequent measurements. This kind of measurement can be used to provide feedback to the policy holder's Human Resources Department to improve its process for providing data to the health insurance company.

Analysis Summary

The subscriber birth year example explained how to think through quality requirements related to subscriber age. This process helps articulate assumptions about the expected condition of the data. The principles can be applied to any date data for which you can make common-sense assertions about a range of date values. For example, within an educational setting, you may have expectations related to the ages of students. Within a club or other organization, you may have expectations related to members' ages or to the duration of membership.

The initial findings greatly influence the choices for ongoing measurement. From the assumptions about the expected condition of the data, you can determine what characteristics of the data to measure. From there you can associate requirements for measurement with a measurement type. What the process does not identify, in and of itself, is the tolerance for data that does not meet expectations. If data consumers cannot use the data at all if it contains unreasonable birth dates, then you may want to have a control in place that rejects records based on the criteria for reasonability. If data consumers have an idea of how much unreasonable data they can tolerate, then you can put in place a threshold to alert you when that level is passed. If data consumers do not know how much unreasonable data they can tolerate, then (as described in Section Six) you can automate the establishment of the threshold at three standard deviations from the mean of past measurements. Notifications of measurement results at that level will be a trigger to investigate the condition of the data.

But the choices for ongoing measurement also need to be understood in relation to both criticality and risk. For example, if the initial assessment had revealed a high level of defaulted data where defaults were not expected, it would be necessary to understand the root cause of that condition. If root cause analysis revealed that the data was at risk because the processes that captured it allowed room for error, you have a case for ongoing monitoring. Ongoing monitoring of the level of defaults would be warranted at least until the root cause was remediated and, if the data were considered critical enough, also after remediation to ensure the problem does not reemerge (see Figure 10.4).

Additional Examples

The example of the subscriber birth date illustrates the process of establishing the basic expectations and defining rules to measure them. For health care data, birth dates are important. Not only

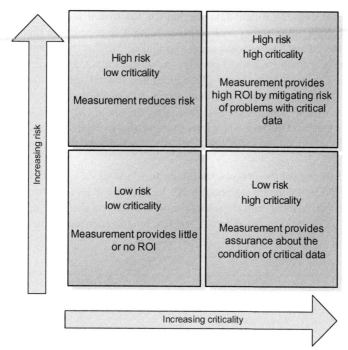

FIGURE 10.4 Measurement Return on Investment (ROI)

Determining which data to measure on an ongoing basis requires understanding both how important the data is to organizational processes (criticality) and the potential for data not to meet expectations (risk). The primary focus of in-line measurement should be data that is both critical and associated with risk. Measurement of low-criticality, low-risk data is unlikely to provide return on investment.

do they provide a means of identifying individuals (your doctor's receptionist will almost always ask for your birth date), but also they are a critical piece of demographic data for analyses of treatments and trends. Two other examples illustrate the decision-making process for establishing specific measurements.

A primary purpose of most data warehouses is to integrate data from disparate systems. Integration is usually thought of in terms of datasets with similar conceptual content (e.g., claim data from several systems). Also of significance is the ability to associate records from one data domain with those from another. In the case of health care data, for example, there is a need to associate records from eligibility systems that process membership data with records from claim processing systems in order to populate a member identifier on the claim tables. In one warehouse where I worked, this match process worked inconsistently and the data was perceived to be unreliable. Every few months, a data consumer would contact the help desk and report a problem with defaulted member identifiers on claim records.

Root cause analysis turned up different factors each time. In one case, problems arose with the source membership data; in another, processing of that membership data within the warehouse was incomplete. In a third case, customer data needed for the match process was missing. And in a fourth, there was a technical problem with implementing a change in the claim process (an index was missing from the table). The process used to populate the member identifier was complicated and high risk. It was a warehouse-owned process, but it used input data from several different systems. The measurement process we put in place measured the percentage of records for which the match failed (a variation on Measurement Type #s 24 & 33). We took this measurement from the load file so that if the result was above its data quality threshold, we could investigate root causes before the data was loaded. On three occasions in eight years, we held the data because loading it would have caused significant remediation work in the warehouse as well as in downstream systems (see Figure 10.5).

Because we had automated the process for taking this kind of measurement, we put it in place to measure all match processes in the warehouse. All had a similar level of business criticality: They populated attributes that enabled data consumers to join data from different data domains. They had different levels of risk; most were less complex and had not experienced problems.

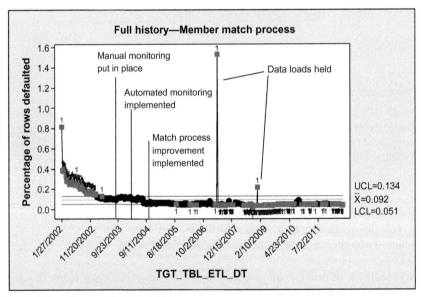

FIGURE 10.5 Full History Member-to-Claim Match

The graph shows as full a history as is available on the member match process on a claim table. The data before September 2003 was fixed several times when remediation was required. The data points associated with those incidents are not included. In addition, the graph does not contain a data point from 2004 when data processing resulted in nonmatches for more than 25% of data—the emergency threshold control level to stop data processing for this kind of measure. The in-line measurement detected that problem, the load was stopped, and data was reprocessed. As of 2012, the mean percentage of nonmatch records per load was 0.05%. The process is stable, and minor fluctuations can be investigated immediately to determine causes.

We also extended this type of measurement to attributes that were critical but for which we thought there was very little risk: source-supplied attributes that were directly moved to warehouse load files without any derivations. In fact, in one instance—the population of the primary diagnosis code on claims—we measured for several years (2005–2008) and, out of the millions of claims stored in the warehouse, only a few dozen records were not populated. Then the measurement detected a change in the quality of the data. Suddenly several hundred records were defaulting with each load. Still this was not a high overall percentage, but it marked a definite change and was not an expected condition of this attribute. Every claim should have at least one diagnosis code, and that code populates the primary diagnosis code field. Root cause analysis showed that there had been a change in the claim adjudication system, and, in some cases, the way claim processors saved updated records resulted in the diagnosis code being dropped. The source was not aware of this effect but our measurement process detected it.

In determining which data to measure, both criticality and risk should be taken into account. You cannot predict everything that might go wrong in your warehouse or your source systems, but you can identify risk points and you can establish which data is critical. As noted earlier, in-line measurement serves three primary goals: monitoring the condition of data and providing a level of assurance about the degree to which data is meeting expectations; detecting changes in the data that might indicate a data quality issue or other change in data production; and identifying opportunities for improvement. Measuring the condition of critical data enables you both to gain a level of confidence that it is meeting expectations and to identify changes that might indicate a problem.

Concluding Thoughts

I have emphasized that a primary challenge of defining quality is getting data consumers to articulate their expectations. As big a challenge is ensuring that both businesspeople and technical people have concrete knowledge about the condition of data. Neither of these challenges will magically be resolved. Meeting them requires data inspection, assessment, and analysis that enable data consumers to understand their own expectations and the reality of the data. This work requires a positive partnership between IT and businesspeople so that both can understand how to improve the quality of data in their organizations.

Is it realistic that businesspeople should describe the details of their quality requirements to the point were they essentially specify measurements? That depends on the organization. But there are a couple of things to keep in mind if you do not take the time to define quality requirements. First, for IT people, there is a pay-me-now-or-pay-me-later element to requirements definition. If you do not work with data consumers to define quality characteristics at the beginning of a project, you will have to take the time addressing problems related to them once your data store is up and running. Second, while IT people still habitually say they do not know the business and businesspeople often profess that they do not understand technology, in this day and age, with the dependence most organizations have on data and technology simply to do their jobs, both sides need to come closer to the middle. I have argued that IT has stewardship responsibilities. Stewards manage the property of other people. IT staff manage data. IT should take this responsibility seriously and use its tools and knowledge to propose common-sense approaches to measuring quality. It is not necessary to be an actuary to understand which data is critical for insurance companies. Rather, it is necessary to know what insurance companies do, how data enables their business, and how they measure success. Employees in all roles should know this basic information and understand how their jobs contribute to organizational success.

Until a conversation about quality characteristics is initiated and unless it is focused on real obstacles to business success, a productive dialog about data quality will not be possible. In the case of most data warehouses, if you are on the IT side, your customer is also most likely your colleague. If you are on the business side, your programmer or database administrator (DBA) is probably also a stockholder. There is a need for people within any organization to work together to make the data in that organization as good as it can be and to ensure that it is produced and managed for the benefit of the organization as a whole.

Asking Questions

11

"It is common sense to take a method and try it: If it fails, admit it frankly and try another.
But above all, try something."
—Franklin Delano Roosevelt (1882–1945)

Purpose

Defining business requirements for data projects entails asking questions that unfold facets of the needs that are to be addressed. One of the challenges with some approaches to requirements definition is that they do not encourage analysts to ask directly about quality expectations. The previous chapter presented an example of applying business knowledge and common sense to define measurements related to a specific attribute, birth date. This chapter presents a set of questions that can help data consumers articulate their assumptions and expectations about data quality characteristics, critical data and process risks. Their answers can be used to determine how to measure particular data elements and rules. From the exchange, analysts have input for the definition of specific data quality metrics to be taken in-line, as well as those that might be taken periodically. The chapter includes a set of examples describing the requirements that result from the process of applying the DQAF dimensions and measurement types.

Asking Questions

Some people work best by starting with large concepts and working to the details; others work best by starting with the details and working back to the larger concepts. Data analysis and requirements definition require understanding both the details and the larger concepts of which they are a part. Very little analysis is linear. In many instances, successful data analysis depends on working from both ends to find a problem in the middle. In describing the process of helping data consumers articulate their expectations and data producers articulate their insights on risk, I will start with questions about the big stuff (project goals, data domains, source systems) and work toward the detail of expectations for specific data elements and rules. Collecting information about these topics is not a linear process, but I'll describe it in a linear fashion. As noted in the section introduction, the context I am assuming is that of a large project that moves data from a set of transactional source systems to a relational database, such as a data warehouse. The overall process, however, can also be used to assess measurement options for data in an existing database.

At a high level, the process steps include:

- Gain a thorough understanding of the project's overall goals, including the data domains it will set up, the sources it will include, and the data consumers it will serve. This information will help you understand the context in which data will be used. It provides a foundation for identifying the critical data that is likely to be measured in-line.

- Ensure you build a knowledge base about the project's source systems: their business functions, the data they produce, the business processes they interact with, and their data consumers. You should gain an understanding of the relative complexity of source processes and data in order to identify data that may be at risk. And you should research which data elements are most critical to the functions the source performs. If data elements that are critical to your project are not critical to the source systems, it can be difficult to get the source to address concerns about them.
- Ensure you understand the business requirements of the data consumers of the database you are building. These provide the starting point for data quality requirements and an ongoing touch point for data quality measurements.
- Draw on profiling results and other analyses from initial assessments of data to identify any known limitations, anomalies, or concerns about the data from each source.
- Ensure that you understand the data structure (model) and the transformation rules applied to data coming into the system you are building. And be familiar with the system architecture. Basic knowledge of the system's design can help you identify the best places to take in-line measurements within a data flow.

It is quite possible that at the initial stage of a project, the answer to all the questions you could ask will be, "I don't know." That's okay. You can and should come back to the questions multiple times to develop your knowledge of the data your project is charged with making available. And, of course, you won't be asking these questions all by yourself. You will be part of a team that is interacting with data consumers to define the overall set of business requirements.

Understanding the Project

The first thing you should make sure you understand is your own project. Some projects can roll along regardless of whether team members are aware of goals. In order to establish quality requirements, however, you need to clarify the purposes for making data available in the first place. Without this information, the project may make available the data your customers say they want, but it may not be in the condition they need it to be in. If it is not in the expected condition, they will not trust it and will not use it, or they will use it only with reservations. Such a situation thwarts the short-term and long-term goals of making data available.

The following questions allow the project team to capture high-level information about the business context of the project and known requirements about the ongoing use of the data. These questions should be answered initially by project team business analysts (BAs), and they should be updated via conversations with data consumers and source system subject matter experts (SMEs).

- What are the project's goals?
- What high-level business requirements will the project fulfill?
- What data domains will the project make available or extend?

For most projects, the answers to these questions are already defined as part of a Project Charter, Statement of Work, or other document used in high-level project definition. The important thing in preparation for developing quality requirements is to read these materials and ensure you ask any clarifying questions you need to have answered in order to understand what the project is trying to accomplish.

If your project is large and complex, such as a warehouse project addressing multiple requirements across data domains, then you should address the next set of questions at the data domain level:

- Who will use the data made available through the project? (i.e., who are the data consumers?)
- How will the data be used once it is made available?
- What business processes will it support?
- How do these processes currently obtain the data they need?
- What are the limitations of the current data?
- What are the greatest risks to the data? What could go wrong with the data that would prevent the project from meeting business goals?
- Try to identify at least three risks, which can serve as examples to prompt data consumers to identify additional concerns.

Answers to these questions will flesh out the context of the project and contribute to the identification of potential gaps in or risks to the data.

Learning about Source Systems

Once you understand the purposes for which data will be used, you need to understand the options for sourcing it. In some cases, options will be obvious or they will already have been decided as part of project initiation. For example, if you need data to manage your company's sales, you will have to obtain current sales data from internal transactional systems. In other cases, sourcing may be more challenging. If you want data against which to benchmark your company's performance, you may need to research options for purchasing it. No matter what the reason for using a particular data source, you should review documentation related to data sources so that you understand any known limitations or risks.

- From what sources will the project obtain data? (i.e., who are the data producers?)
- Are the sources familiar to the project's data consumers, or are they new?
- Do the sources have documentation describing their data content, processes, and known issues or limitations of the data?

With draft answers to these questions, the project team can establish a plan of action to gather information from source systems and follow up with data consumers. The goals and requirements also provide touch points for data assessment. If it appears that data will not meet requirements, this finding will need to be addressed as soon as possible.

To avoid surprises and to make good decisions about how to structure data, you should understand important features about data sources. Obviously, you will want to know what data the sources contain. It is also important to understand how a source processes its data. In systems that execute complex transactions (such as paying medical claims) there are often significant differences between data input and data output. If consumers of downstream data systems are not aware of how a transactional source modifies input data, there is likely to be a larger gap between their expectations and the data available from the source.

Ideally, you will be able to obtain data process flow diagrams that will enable you to understand data origin and lineage and identify risks. If such documentation is not available, you should develop it yourself. The following questions allow you to capture high-level information about data sources as well as to document how data is processed in transactional systems, and capture important features related to data lineage. They should be answered for each dataset for each source by the BA, based on discussions with source system SMEs. The questions are divided into three sets: those used to understand the source's goals in producing data for its data consumers; those focused on the processing of data; and those focused on individual data attributes and rules.

I have described a simple version of a data "source." To prepare to store the data, you will need to have a documented understanding of what happens to data within the system from which you will receive it. If that system is not the system of origin, then you will need to trace its lineage back further, using an information product map or other process flow diagram, to its system of origin or to the point where it enters your organization's systems. For the sake of simplicity in organizing the questions, we will assume that the direct source is also the system of origin.

Source Goals and Source Data Consumers

In order to understand the condition of source data, you should know why the source system exists in the first place. Its data will have been structured to support a set of business processes that may or may not align with downstream uses of data. Such can be the case with health care data. Claim adjudication systems are in place to determine how to pay claims, not specifically to provide data that can be used to understand trends within the health care system. They may bundle claims, split them, or pay one portion and not another. These complicated transactions on the claim processing side may change data that health care analysts require to analyze trends.

- What type of data content does the system store or process?
- What business processes does the system enable?
- Who is the business owner of the system and its data?
- How is the system used?
- How is data entered into the system?
- What are the roles of people responsible for the data in the system?
- Who can answer questions about data content?
- Who can answer technical questions about data processing?
- Where is the system's metadata located?
- Are there published references materials describing the data?
- Who currently uses data from this system? (i.e., who are the system's customers?)
- How is the data used? What processes does it support?
- How does the system track data quality concerns?
- What are the known quality concerns related to the system's data?
- How often are technical changes made to the system?
- What is the process for informing downstream data consumers about system changes?
- What risks are associated with the system?
- Define these risks in terms of rules that might be measured.

Answers to these questions should provide an overview of the system's goals, support mechanisms, and risks. Knowing who the system's customers are will provide you with contacts who can speak to the content and limitations of the system.

Source Data Processing

Most people have a limited view of data within a transactional system. They know either what goes in or what comes out, and they base their expectations on one or the other. In order to understand output from a system, it is important to know both the input and how the system processes data input. The more complex the work of the system, the greater the risk that something unexpected can happen to data.

- How complex is data processing within the system?
- What systems provide data to the system?
- To what systems does it supply data?
- What kinds of transactions does it process?
- What data is critical to the processing of each type of transaction?
- Under what conditions does the system reject a transaction?
- What are the data characteristics of each type of transaction?
- Which transactions are the most complex? What makes them complex?
- What measurements are in place in the system to understand data quality?
- What controls are in place to monitor data processing?
- How much is the data input changed as part of processing within the system?
- What kinds of changes are made?
- What controls are in place to ensure the quality of the data set within the transactional system?
- How are the functions of the system documented? Is documentation available?
- If the system is a database, how complex is its data process? For example, what types of transformations are executed and how many are there?
- What volume of data (records, bytes, transactions) is expected from the system per day, week, or month?
- What factors can influence volume?
- What will a complete set of data from this system look like?
- How does the system show that data might be missing?
- What validation rules are in place in the system?
- What integrity rules are in place in the system?

The purpose of these questions is to gain knowledge of ways in which a system changes input data to execute business transactions. Answers can be used to assess the suitability of the source to meet the needs of your system's data consumers.

Individual Data Attributes and Rules

Once you understand the overall content and general complexity of the data you will bring into your storage system, you are ready to dig into the details of individual attributes and the rules that govern them. Remember that your questions at this point are still being asked about the transactional source system.

- Which attributes are the most critical for processing transactions?
- Why are they critical?
- Which attributes are associated with simple processing?
- Which attributes are associated with complex processing?
- What types of transformations are executed against these attributes?

- What attributes are associated with business rules?
- How are rules enforced? (Are they enforced by the intake interface, for example?)
- What controls are in place to detect data that does not adhere to rules?
- Which attributes are expected to be populated 100% of the time? (i.e., which are mandatory?) Why? What is the business reason they are mandatory?
- Which are expected to be populated less than 100% of the time? (i.e., which ones are optional?) Why? Under what conditions should they be populated? Under what conditions should they not be populated?

This overall set of questions should allow you to gain considerable knowledge about the candidate source data. In order to determine whether any given source will meet requirements, this information needs to be aligned with the expectations of data consumers of the database your project is building.

Your Data Consumers' Requirements

Data consumers' requirements will be articulated at a variety of levels and to a lesser or greater degree of detail, depending on their knowledge of existing data and the maturity of the processes for which they require the data. Data consumers will not be able to answer all of the questions outlined here at first pass. Quite a few will take multiple passes and may require other input, such as profiling results. The important thing is to begin asking the questions so that consumers can begin to articulate expectations. The process of documenting expectations may lead data consumers to articulate assumptions that they were previously unaware of.

- How will you use this data? (For what processes is it used as input?)
- Identify the most critical data associated with this project.
- Why is the data critical?
- What business questions will this data be used to answer?
- Will this data be used (or is it already used) in reporting? If so, what kind?
- What are the known business rules connected with the data?
- What are the known or potential risks associated with the data?
- What are the known issues with the data?
- What are the most important individual data elements in the dataset?
- What are the most important data relationships in the dataset?
- What are the potential issues with the data?
- How/why would these issues arise?
- What is the impact if there is an issue with the data?
- What can go wrong with this data?
- What types of problems have you had with similar data in the past?

Since the purpose of asking questions is to understand assumptions about quality, sometimes the best approach is to ask directly about quality characteristics. The questions below can be asked about attributes, rules, records or the dataset itself.

- What does the data look like or act like if it is incorrect? Invalid? Incomplete?
- What are the business implications if the data is incorrect? Invalid? Incomplete? Not available on time? Inconsistent?

- What does the data look like or act like if it is of high quality?
- What does the data look like or act like if it is it is *not* of high quality?
- How would you measure the quality of this data?

These questions get to the heart of data consumers' quality expectations. Responses will surface previously unarticulated assumptions about the data. They will also enable you to identify the relative criticality of specific data elements. Responses thus provide input to measurement specifications. If an attribute is critical and if there are negative implications to its being invalid, then a measurement of basic validity should be specified.

In a recent project, we used the data model and the transformation rules as the input to this kind of assessment. Business analysts did a preliminary assessment of assumptions about the validity, completeness, consistency, and integrity of each attribute. They identified rules that were at high risk due to their complexity. They reviewed this information with business SMEs and asked SMEs to categorize the attributes in terms of criticality. The result was a comprehensive set of options for how to measure the data content, prioritized based on business criticality and technical risk.

The Condition of the Data

The expectations of data consumers drive quality requirements. Both must be understood in relation to the reality of the data you will be bringing into your system. As described in Chapter 7: Initial Assessment, the best way to understand data you are not familiar with is by profiling it. Profiling can be used to document basic facts about the data. These facts, when compared with data consumers' expectations, provide the basis for assessing the data's suitability for a given purpose.

Data that has not been profiled represents a high risk, simply because you do not know about it. Basic data profiling reduces risk because it reduces uncertainty (Hubbard, 2010). Profiling findings should be shared with data consumers, not only to confirm whether data meets expectations and to document differences from expectations, but also to further clarify those expectations. In many cases, seeing "real" data will enable data consumers to make additional observations about data suitability. As part of the requirements development process, you should capture the following information.

- Has the data been profiled?
- When was it profiled?
- How was it profiled? (e.g., was a specific tool used to profile it?)
- What data has actually been profiled? (e.g., test data, production file?)
- How much data was profiled?
- Summary of findings or issues
- Summary of rules discovered
- Summary of known issues
- Identify known risk points
- Define how these rules or risk points might be measured.
- Date that findings were reviewed with customers
- Summary of customer responses to profiling results
- Did the review identify additional requirements?
- Did the review identify any data quality issues?

The Data Model, Transformation Rules, and System Design

Having developed an understanding of source data and of data consumers' needs, you will begin to get a picture of what the data will look like coming into a data store. To measure the quality of data, you will need to know how data is structured in the data store. Different types of models serve different purposes. Conceptual data models represent entities so that they can be understood in relation to each other. Logical models flesh out these concepts with detailed attribution. Physical models focus on enabling access and ensuring that the database performs well. But all data models are intended to show the relationship between business concepts.

How these relationships are modeled depends on the processes and data being modeled, the modeling approach and standards, the system being built, and the individual modeler. Some models correspond very closely to the structure of source data. Others may differ significantly from source data; for example, those that are highly normalized. Models are valuable for many reasons, not the least of which is that they condense complex information into a consumable form. Models have rules embedded in them. Knowing how to read these rules allows you to confirm rules that are candidate measurements.

- For each table, which data comprises the primary key? By definition, this data is critical data.
- Which attributes are foreign keys? To what other data structures do they relate? Foreign key relationships establish the basis for many validity measures.
- Does the model represent data from one source or multiple sources?
- How closely does the model correspond to source data structure?
- In what ways does it differ?

The model is also the key to how data will be transformed as it is brought into the storage system. It provides the target structure to which source data will be mapped. Source-to-target mapping can help you assess data criticality and risk. Derived data is almost always both critical and at risk. Mapping rules themselves can be used as the basis of measurement.

- How many mapping rules are simple (direct moves from the source)?
- How many and which ones are complex? (these represent risks points)
- Which data is input to derivations or other complex transformations? (more risk points)
- Which data is output from these processes? (its quality should be tested)

Measurement Specification Process

As noted in the introduction to Section Four, when it is automated, in-line measurement can be widely applied. In-line measurement will be effective only if analysts are able to use measurement results. You don't want to measure everything you can measure because doing so may produce more results than you can respond to. You should aim at establishing an optimal set of metrics. Criteria for determining which data to measure in-line should be based on a combination of data criticality and risk.

The comprehensive set of questions described in this chapter aim at helping you acquire the knowledge and background you need to make assertions about data quality measurement within the system you are developing. The goal of the measurement specification process is to translate this knowledge into measurements at the field or rule level.

Direct input to the measurement specification process includes

- Documented business requirements.
- Source-to-target mapping specifications.
- The data model and any data standards.
- Data profiling results.
- Initial assessment of which data is critical to the business (gleaned from interviews and process documentation).
- DQAF definitions.

The following process can be executed by a business analyst, who then reviews results with a larger group that includes business and technical SMEs. Or the work can be done in a group setting. Or it can be divided in other ways. For example, a business analyst can obtain criticality ratings from business SMEs before specifying the measurements. How to approach the analysis depends in part on the number of entities and attributes to be included in the review and on the capacity of the organization to provide resources.

To do the analysis

- Prepare a spreadsheet includes the entities and attributes being developed in the target system, along with the mapping and transformation rules.
- Set up columns to rate attribute criticality and risk, to collect notes about business expectations, and to document known issues
- Set up columns for each dimension of quality (completeness, timeliness, validity, consistency, integrity)
- Set up a column to capture recommendations for what to measure
- Based on input from interviews with data consumers, assign a criticality rating to each of the attributes in order to accomplish two goals: (1) to identify the most critical attributes so that they can be given the attention they need; and (2) to identify attributes that are of very low criticality so that you do not expend effort on them.
- Review all high-criticality attributes and document why they are of high criticality. This documentation does not need to be detailed. Instead it should simply indicate the basic driver of criticality, such as use in reporting.
- Based on transformation rules and knowledge of source system processes, assign a risk rating to each of the other attributes. As with the assignment of criticality, here you want to identify the attributes that are at highest risk and those that are associated with very little risk.
- Review all high-risk attributes and document why they are at high risk. As with criticality, keep this documentation focused on primary drivers, such as complex derivations, or a lack of controls in place at the source.
- At this point, you will be able to identify all high-criticality/high-risk attributes. These are candidates for in-line measurement.
- Review each attribute in relation to the dimensions of quality. Revisit information provided by data consumers (and apply common sense and your own knowledge of the data).
- What does the data look like or act like if it is incorrect? Invalid? Incomplete?
- What are the business implications if the data is incorrect? Invalid? Incomplete? Not available on time? Inconsistent?

- What does the data look like or act like if it is of high quality?
- What does the data look like or act like if it is it is *not* of high quality?
- How would you measure the quality of this data?
- For each attribute and each dimension of quality, determine whether any of the information you have gathered implies an assertion about quality.
- Associate this with a measurement type.

This process will result in a detailed set of assertions about expected quality characteristics. If the initial analysis has been executed by a business analyst, the next step is to review the document with business SMEs to get their confirmation about the recommendations. If programming is in place to support DQAF measurements types, then any measurements you specify through the process can be instantiated in the DQAF tables. (See Figure 10.2, Data Quality Requirements Definition Process).

The tables in this chapter provide examples of specified measurements. They all come from the same requirements definition process, but have been broken apart for explanatory purposes. Table 11.1 shows the four example data elements. The first, Market Segment Code, is critical to the business processes related to customer data. From its definition, we see that its purpose is to categorize customers based on their size. This categorization has a direct effect on how the business interacts with these customers. But this element has low risk. It is moved directly from the transactional systems that store customer data. The second data element, Customer Group Plan ID, is also high criticality, although its definition does not convey this information as well as the definition of Market Segment Code does. The Customer Group Plan ID is the data store's identifier for a unique customer. It is the key to the customer table and the foreign key in other tables. In the table from which this example is pulled, it is populated using a match process. This process is associated with risk. It is technically complex and requires more than a dozen data elements as input. Therefore there are a dozen chances that the match will fail. The next element, Insert Batch ID, is a technical attribute (the batch number

Table 11.1 Data Elements Associated with Criticality and Risk

Data Element Name	Data Element Definition	Criticality	Risk
Market Segment Code	Code that categorizes customers based on number of employees. Segment size determines the marketing and account administration area that handles the organization as a potential and existing customer.	High	Low—Direct move
Customer Group Plan ID	Warehouse assigned surrogate key of the Customer Group Plan.	High	High—Complex transformation
Insert Batch ID	The ETL Batch Id associated with the Insert of the row into the table.	Low	Low—Direct move
County Code	Code (FIPS 6-4) that uniquely identifies counties and county equivalents in the United States, certain U.S. possessions, and certain freely associated states. Populated only for government business.	Medium	Low—Direct move

Table 11.2 Data Elements Associated with Dimensions of Quality

Data Element Name	Completeness	Validity	Consistency
Market Segment Code	Expect complete population. Every customer should be associated with a market segment	Only valid market segment codes should be populated in the source. Validity based on Market Segment Table.	A customer's market segment may change, but very rarely.
Customer Group Plan ID	Expect complete population, but there may be situations where a match is not made.	N/A system-generated key.	Expect a consistent level of nonmatched records
Insert Batch ID	Expect complete population; system generated.	N/A system-generated key.	N/A system-generated key
County Code	Populated only for Medicare and Medicaid	Expect only valid county codes (based on County Code Table).	Expect a consistent level of membership in individual counties over time.

associated with the arrival of the data) that is populated by the system to enable data processing to take place. The Batch ID is significant for data processing, but it is a low-risk element and has no quality criteria from a data consumer's point of view. The final element, County Code, can be used to associate individuals with a geographic area, a county. This element is populated only for lines of business associated with government insurance (Medicare and Medicaid). As you can see, the data definitions themselves can provide (or not provide) a significant amount of information.

Table 11.2 contains expectations related to the data content of the four examples, based on the quality dimensions of completeness, validity, and consistency. Market Segment Code is expected to be populated 100% of the time with only valid values. There is little risk that it will not be, since the data is direct-moved from a source system. Customer Group Plan ID is also expected to be populated 100% of the time, but there is a high risk that it will not be, due to the complexity of the match process. This attribute has no expectations of validity, since the ID is a system-generated number.[1] Insert Batch ID is expected to be completely populated, but there are not any expectations related to validity or consistency. Finally, County Code is expected to be populated completely on records related

---

[1] There are two expectations of integrity between the customer table and any record populated with a Customer Group Plan ID. The first is that all populated Group Plan IDs should exist on the Customer table. It is impossible that they would not exist at the time the Group Plan ID is populated in another table, since this population depends on a match to retrieve the number. However, if data were to be dropped from the Customer table for some reason, it is possible that this referential relationship would be broken. The second expectation is that no two customers would share the same Group Plan ID. Because it is the key to the Customer table, it is not possible for two records to share the same ID at the same time. However, if something goes wrong with the generation of IDs and if data is dropped from the Customer table, it is possible that the same ID could be associated with two customers on other tables in the database. Detecting these conditions requires measurements taken periodically rather than in-line.

Table 11.3 Data Elements Associated with Measurement Types

Data Element Name	Recommended Measurement Type	Reasoning
Market Segment Code	#27 Validity check, single field, detailed results & #28—Validity check, roll-up (In-line).	Enables identification of invalid values. Also enables tracking of level of customer records without a market segment code.
Customer Group Plan ID	#33 Consistent multicolumn profile (In-line).	Can be specified to measure level of records defaulted in the match process. Has control to stop data processing if threshold is exceeded.
Insert Batch ID	None	No criteria for quality.
County Code	#27 Validity check, single field, detailed results & #28—Validity check, roll-up (Periodic).	This measure should be executed as part of periodic measurement, not in-line. Very little risk and high cardinality results.

to Medicare and Medicaid business, but not on other records. County Codes are expected to be valid (they should exist on the County Code table).

Table 11.3 provides the reasoning for the choices. Market Segment, critical but low risk, can be measured in-line using a basic validity check. This measurement will also produce a distribution of values that will enable assessment of the consistency with which the segments are populated. Such a measure may or may not be valuable for data quality purposes. It is not clear whether there is an expectation of consistent population with each load of the database. The population of defaulted Customer Group Plan ID can be measured using a consistency measure. This measurement can be used first to assess the stability and predictability of the match process and then to detect changes to that process. If it is determined to be unstable to start with, it is a good candidate for an improvement project. Insert Batch ID is not associated with any measurement. County Code, medium criticality but low risk, is associated with a periodic validity check.

Concluding Thoughts

As described earlier in this section, the process of defining requirements is one of iterative dialog with a customer or customers. The questions outlined in this chapter are aimed at enabling that dialog. The DQAF dimensions and measurement types provide a vocabulary through which to assert expectations related to the condition of data. Once these are identified, actual data can be tested against them to determine its quality.

A Strategic Approach to Data Quality

5

The purpose of this section is to describe the relationship between organizational strategy, strategies for improving quality, and data quality strategy. It provides an approach to strategic organizational readiness for data quality improvement.

Chapter 12: Data Quality Strategy describes strategy as a plan for accomplishing the organization's mission. It discusses the relation between data quality strategy, data strategy, systems strategy, and data governance. It then provides a set of general considerations to account for in data quality strategy.

Based on the concept of strategy, and the work of data quality thought leaders, Chapter 13: Directives for Data Quality Strategy synthesizes a set of 12 directives that can drive data quality strategy. The directives focus on the importance of data within an enterprise, the need to manage data as knowledge, recognition of the similarity between manufacturing physical goods and creating data, and the need to build a culture of quality in order to respond to the fluid nature of data and meet the ongoing challenges of strategic management. To help you use the 12 Directives, the chapter also includes a set of questions and tactics to assess organizational readiness for data quality strategy. The purpose of such an assessment is to surface priorities for strategic action and to formulate a long-term approach to an organization's data quality improvement.

Any organization that wants to sustain high-quality data needs to recognize that data and data uses will change over time. Because data touches all aspects of an enterprise and because the uses of data evolve, sustaining high-quality data requires an overall orientation toward producing good data. Data quality goes beyond the data itself to the enterprise's culture.

Details about the tactics to implement these strategic directives will differ between organizations, but all 12 should be considered when defining the overall data strategy.

Data Quality Strategy

12

"I tell this story to illustrate the truth of the statement I heard long ago in the Army: Plans are worthless, but planning is everything. There is a very great distinction because when you are planning for an emergency you must start with this one thing: the very definition of 'emergency' is that it is unexpected, therefore it is not going to happen the way you are planning."

—President Dwight D. Eisenhower (1957)

Purpose

This chapter defines the concept of data quality strategy so that it can be understood in relation to an organization's overall strategy and to other functions (data governance, systems strategy) that also contribute to the effort to produce better data. These efforts go by different names in different organizations. To the degree possible, within any given organization, they should be harmonized since they serve a single purpose: to enable the organization to make better decisions about its data so that it can achieve long-term success.

The Concept of Strategy

The word *strategy*, derived from *strategia*, the Greek word for generalship, was first used to describe military operations and movements. A strategy is a plan of action or policy designed to achieve a major or overall aim. It is worth exploring the military origins of the concept of strategy and strategic planning for how these inform other uses of the terms. Strategy is both the art of planning and directing overall military operations and movements in a war or battle and the plan itself. Strategy is often contrasted with tactics, as in the assertion, "Strategy focuses on long-term aims; tactics on short-term gains." But in the military sense, strategy and tactics are not opposites. They are different levels of engagement. Strategy is planning for a set of engagements (battles and other military interventions) that will achieve the overall goal of a war. Tactics describe how each of these engagements will be carried out. Tactical success that does not contribute to strategy—of the "we won the battle, but lost the war" kind—can be detrimental to an organization. Between these two levels is the concept of operations, which deals with size, scale, and scope, as well as the placement of military forces and equipment.

Strategy has two contrasting characteristics: It needs to be focused on the overall aim (winning the war), but it also needs to be flexible in its plan to meet that aim, adapting to new battle conditions, to the evolution of factors influencing a war, and to the strategy and tactics of the other side. Overall strategic aims provide criteria for making decisions about tactics and operations, especially in situations where the results of tactical efforts are different from what was anticipated. Strategy is future-focused. Strategic decisions contribute to the success of the end game.

The purpose of a business or an organizational strategy is to align work efforts with long-term goals and to plan for achieving overall interests. Organizational strategy begins with a vision, mission, and goals for the enterprise. The vision represents what an organization aspires to be. The mission represents how the organization will achieve its vision, and the goals represent steps contributing to the organization's mission. A strategy then identifies the tactics required to accomplish goals and establishes teams to execute tactics. A strategy must also assess the current state for gaps and obstacles to reaching goals. Tactics must address gaps and overcome obstacles that would otherwise prevent the organization from achieving its mission. The strategy provides the criteria needed to set priorities and to make decisions when conflicting needs arise between or within teams.

Systems Strategy, Data Strategy, and Data Quality Strategy

Most often we think about vision, mission, and strategy at the enterprise level. And indeed, most successful organizations have clear vision and mission statements that address their enterprise goals. However, strategic thinking can be applied at all levels of an organization. And it should be because aligning work efforts with long-term goals is a constant struggle (and because strategic thinking is a form of problem solving focused on moving an organization forward). So it is possible to have a systems strategy, a data strategy, a data management strategy, and a data quality strategy all at the same time, and these should be highly dependent on each other. An organization might define these separately because different teams are charged with executing them, or in order to understand the relation between them, or to determine the work required to advance these facets of the organization's overall strategy. The critical thing is to ensure that the strategic goals of any part of the organization support the overall vision and mission of the organization and that they do not contradict or inhibit each other. Aligned, they enable each other's success.

The difference between a data strategy and a data quality strategy can also be purely semantic. Adelman, Abai, and Moss (2005) begin their discussion on data strategy by pointing out the effects of a lack of strategy for data: "Rarely do organizations work from the big picture, and as a result they suboptimize solutions, introduce programs which may have a deleterious effect on the overall enterprise, cause inconsistencies that result in major efforts for interfacing, or develop systems that cannot be easily integrated" (2005). They further point out that most organizations do not have a data strategy because they do not understand the value of their data and they do not view it as an organizational asset; instead data is seen as the province of the department that created it. To the extent that strategic questions about data are addressed, they are addressed piecemeal. Adelman and colleagues compare working without a data strategy to allowing each department in a company to establish its own chart of accounts. Lack of a data strategy results in "dirty data, redundant data, inconsistent data, inability to integrate, poor performance, terrible availability, little accountability, users increasingly dissatisfied with the performance of IT, and the general feeling that things are out of control" (2005). Not surprisingly given their recognition of the problems caused by the lack of a strategy, they define data strategy as encompassing a range of functions related to data management, such as data integration, data quality, metadata, data modeling, security and privacy, performance and measurement, tool selection, and business intelligence.

I agree with their characterization of how a lot of organizations approach the problems associated with data management. But what they call *data strategy* might also be called a *data management strategy* or a *data quality strategy*. The International Association of Information and Data Quality's (IAIDQ) certification program identifies six performance domains, 29 tasks, and hundreds of skills required to be an information quality professional. The performance domains include:

- Information Quality Strategy and Governance.
- Information Quality Environment and Culture.
- Information Quality Value and Business Impact.
- Information Architecture Quality.
- Information Quality Measurement and Improvement.
- Sustaining Information Quality.

The skills required to carry out these functions range from technical understanding of data quality measurement and information management to strategic planning (IAIDQ, 2011).

An organization's data or data management strategy must also be a data quality strategy, since the purpose of data management overall should be to ensure the existence and availability of high-quality data for the organization. The discussion that follows refers specifically to *data quality strategy* in order to highlight activities related to assessment, measurement, and improvement of data.

System strategy (or IT strategy or technology strategy) is often seen as separate from data strategy because its primary focus is hardware, software, and the technical environment, rather than data. Hardware, software, and the technical environment are associated with hard budget numbers. However, system strategy has direct effects on the quality of data. In her discussion about a strategy to reduce system complexity, Nancy Couture (2012) presents observations about systems strategy that echo those of Adelman, Abai, and Moss on data strategy. She states: "Most companies are not strategic about systems development. They lack a system domain road map strategy along with appropriate governance. The end result is a spider web of systems, system dependencies, data feeds, and so on. The longer this situation continues, the more complicated the system dependencies become and the more difficult it is to address them" (Couture, 2012, p. 32). Factors contributing to complexity include the lack of an overall plan, the pressures of continuous systems development, the lack of coordination between IT groups charged with systems development, and the failure to decommission legacy data assets.

Couture's strategic approach to the problem of system complexity is to create an overall roadmap for systems development; simplify the technical environment by eliminating redundancy and reducing the number of technologies used by the enterprise; decommission older assets; and establish an enterprise system sourcing strategy (ESSS) that identifies enterprise systems of record to source a central data warehouse and makes those systems accountable for the data they produce (Couture, 2012, p. 33). Data quality practitioners are very familiar with the concept in which an ESSS makes source systems aware of how their data is used downstream and makes them responsible for the quality of the data they provide. This concept is called managing the data supply chain.[1] By approaching

---

[1] Redman (2001) states that data supplier management "effectively moves responsibility for quality back to the supplier. In doing so it integrates … customer needs analysis, measurement, quality control, quality improvement and planning … into a step-by-step procedure. In addition, data supplier management helps an organization define its most important suppliers. Finally, supplier management enables an organization to simultaneously strengthen its suppliers and reduce its supplier base" (p. 153).

the question of data quality from the perspective of systems strategy, Couture not only points to the benefits of systems strategy for data quality, but also reminds us (once again) that improving data quality demands a multifaceted approach that, in addition to direct improvement to the data itself, includes process improvements, system improvements, and strategic thinking.[2]

Data Quality Strategy and Data Governance

The IAIDQ data quality knowledge domains recognize data governance as a facet of the overall approach to data quality management. But some people would say that data quality strategy must be part of a data governance strategy. The Data Management Association (DAMA) recognizes data governance as a critical function of data management, at the center of a set of 10 data management activities, including data quality management, security, operations, business intelligence, and metadata management. DAMA defines data governance as "the exercise of authority and control (planning, monitoring, and enforcement) over the management of data assets. Data governance is high-level planning and control over data management" (Mosely, Early, & Henderson, 2009, p. 19). DAMA's definition draws on the formulation by Gwen Thomas of the Data Governance Institute: "Data Governance is a system of decision rights and accountabilities for information-related processes, executed according to agreed-upon models which describe who can take what actions with what information, and when, under what circumstances, using what methods" (Thomas, 2011). Thomas points out that, based simply on its definition, data governance has a wide reach. It touches on organizational relationships, rules, policies, standards, guidelines, accountabilities and enforcement methods not only for people, but also for information systems. She asserts that data governance programs will differ depending on their focus, but they all do three things in the effort to support data stakeholders: make, collect and align rules; resolve issues; and enforce compliance.

Clearly, data quality strategy and data governance are interrelated. Like data quality efforts, data management, and system planning, data governance efforts should be ultimately directed at ensuring the production, availability, and use of high-quality data within an organization. These goals cannot be achieved by one team alone. They require overall commitment of an organization to execute key functions in a strategic way. Key functions include those often associated with governance (e.g., decision making, consensus-building, enforcement of policies), as well as those associated squarely with data quality (e.g., quality measurement, process improvement projects). These concepts are so closely intertwined that sorting them out can become largely a semantic exercise. And it is not a goal of this book to do such sorting. Organizations must think through their own uses of these terms based on its strategic needs. That kind of thinking is a way of learning and owning the concepts. I will use the term *data quality strategy* to discuss a set of concepts and practices that relate to how an organization can position itself to get the most value out of its data over the long term.

---

[2] In *The Quality Toolbox*, Nancy Tague (2005) observes that the need for a comprehensive approach is not limited to data quality. "Sometimes the label 'quality' is considered separate from day-to-day activities, but quality improvement extends into many areas that are not labeled 'quality.' Anyone planning strategy, solving a problem, developing a project plan, seeking ideas or agreement from other people, or trying to understand the customer better can use [the tools of quality improvement] to produce higher quality outcomes more easily" (xxi).

Decision Points in the Information Life Cycle

Data governance and data quality strategy both involve decision making at different points in the information life cycle—that is, in Danette McGilvray's formulation, in relation to planning for, obtaining, storing and sharing, maintaining, applying, and disposing of data (POSMAD) (McGilvray, 2008, pp. 19, 23–24). The POSMAD steps enable us to better understand what happens to data and information as it moves horizontally through an organization. Like all models, POSMAD is a simplification. McGilvray warns that the information life cycle is not linear; it is iterative and multifaceted. Data can be stored in multiple systems, shared in different ways, and applied for different purposes. McGilvray advocates "life-cycle thinking" as a way to analyze the relationship between activities within the information life cycle, in order to make decisions about what is working and not working and to identify improvement opportunities (p. 27).

McGilvray's POSMAD matrix identifies sets of questions related to each phase of the life cycle that organizations should be able to answer to fully understand the life cycle of their data. These questions are associated with the data itself, the processes that affect data, people, and organizations who manage, support, or use data, and the technology that stores, manages, or enables use of the data (McGilvray, 2008, p. 21). This approach provides a framework to support strategic, tactical, and operational decisions about data. Answers to these questions may differ depending on whether they pertain to data strategy, tactics, or operations.

In the planning phase, executive leadership makes decisions about what purposes data should serve in the organization, as well as what investments the organization will make in technology to meet long-term goals. Ideally, they plan for the evolution of both data and the systems that store it. Project teams plan the tactical execution of strategic goals. If an organization decides to implement a data warehouse in order to support its long-term goal of improved analytics, a project team will be responsible for planning the project and for decisions that may affect how data is obtained, stored, shared, and maintained, as well as for how it will ultimately be archived or disposed of. Project teams should include both business and technical people. Operational teams are by and large IT teams. They need to plan how they will support any given application. They may need to drive discussions about maintenance requirements, including scheduling, and will need to plan for ongoing support and establish protocols for issue management. In most situations, the results of such planning would be formalized in a service-level agreement. Such an agreement is between data consumers, largely from the business, and data stewards from the IT side. In the planning phase, strategic goals provide the primary criteria for tactical and operational decisions.

In the obtain phase, when data is acquired or created, executive leadership may need to make decisions about strategic sourcing, but most decisions will be tactical and will fall to project teams. Data assessment and profiling may uncover unexpected characteristics in the data. Such findings need to be shared with businesspeople in order to determine how they impact a project's ability to meet requirements. If findings represent obstacles to the use of the data, they will need to be remediated. Other unexpected characteristics, for example differences in granularity or precision, may simply add to an understanding of the data and may be accounted for in the data model. If there is a clear data strategy, the number of tactical decisions that need to be made can be reduced because, again, the primary criteria for making them will be the strategy itself. Situations that may require teams to diverge from the strategic path will need to be escalated to executive management. Once data delivery and processing are made operational, operational teams will need to enact protocols if data is not delivered on time or in the condition required for processing.

When data is being stored and maintained, many decisions involve ongoing operations teams. Ideally, protocols can be established for situations that might recur or for situations resulting from similar conditions. If operational teams establish protocols—that is, if they plan for certain decisions—then the decisions themselves are less contentious because they are really not decisions anymore; they are processes that can be shared and agreed to before they need to be invoked.

Once information is shared or applied, new uses for it will evolve. These uses may be ad hoc, or they may present new strategic opportunities that will require changes to or evolution of the data itself—for example, through the acquisition of additional data elements or the development of data enhancements. Changes in database structure or processing require a set of tactical decisions designed to enable the strategic opportunities.

The data disposal phase should be simple, based on time frames for required data, regulatory requirements regarding data retention and disposal, or other clearly defined criteria. However, because data is shared and applied and because new uses for it evolve, it is more difficult to archive or otherwise dispose of. As with other aspects of data, there is always the possibility that new requirements for data retention will be defined. For many organizations, decisions regarding disposal need to account for both the legal implications of retaining or not retaining data with the costs and risks of maintenance.

General Considerations for Data Quality Strategy

An enterprise data quality strategy should be similar to other strategies. It should

- Be aligned with the organization's vision and mission.
- Be integrated into the organization's overall strategy.
- Include a current state assessment in order to set priorities and measure success.
- Describe tactics for reaching goals.
- Specify accountabilities for teams.
- Establish criteria for decision making.
- Communicate its contributions.

Ultimately, the goal of any data quality strategy is to ensure that an organization has and can use the data it needs to be successful. Unfortunately, no data quality program starts with a blank slate. All parts of the strategy should contribute to the overall aim of improving the creation, maintenance, and use of data throughout the organization. The strategy must be focused on continuous improvement of data quality, but also it also must not disrupt the day-to-day operations of managing data.

The ability to measure data quality is critical to data quality strategy. Initial assessment of an organization's data provides the starting point for improvement. Data quality goals should be aligned with the organization's overall mission and should include being able to show measurable improvement in the condition of data.

Managing data and improving the quality of data in a complex organization require striking a balance between the comprehensive vision that a strategy provides and the ability to execute tactically and show results. Ideally, a data quality program should define and implement a plan for process improvement covering the entire information life cycle, from the initial creation of data to cross-system integration, archiving, and destruction. It should identify the major obstacles to improving data quality and the major risks associated with poor quality data. In reality, no program can do everything at once, so those leading the program will need to prioritize which data to focus on and which processes to improve.[3] In other words, the DQ program's tactics for overcoming obstacles and mitigating risks should be clear, specific, and driven by agree-to priorities. Priorities should be established through a common understanding of which data and processes are most critical to the enterprise, combined with consensus on which process improvements are likely to deliver the highest return on investment.

One goal of the data quality program is to establish common processes to support the production and use of high-quality data. These include data definition and metadata management, initial data assessment, ongoing data quality measurement, issue management, and communications with stakeholders. In a complex enterprise, the DQ program team will need to work with a range of teams to implement common processes and methodologies. Depending on how the enterprise organizes its approach to data quality, the data quality program may exist on its own or as part of a wider governance structure.

A data quality strategy should always be understood as a strategy for improvement. It should help teams responsible for individual data assets to develop their data quality practices in relation to the overall enterprise business and data strategy. Supporting this kind of improvement and ensuring that processes are implemented consistently (so that all teams execute them in the same way) and effectively (so that they produce measurable benefit) will require that the DQ program team develop policies to articulate and enforce the overall strategy.

Concluding Thoughts

While a data quality team may drive tactical implementation of the strategy, neither the team nor the strategy will be successful without engagement from the wider organization. Quality improvement does not happen without a wide recognition of its necessity and enforcement of the policies that support it. The data quality strategy should be understood by people playing different roles, business and technical, across the enterprise: managers and staff of transactional systems; managers and staff of data assets; operational teams responsible for measuring and monitoring the data quality of specific data assets; and project teams charged with integrating or transforming data in or for critical business processes.

Data consumers are critical to an organization's overall ability to improve its data. They should help define the data quality strategy and supporting policies. Because data quality should be measured in comparison to data consumer expectations, their input is required to assess the condition of data, define its criticality, and measure its quality. Ideally, the data quality team can facilitate the interaction between data producers and data consumers that is necessary to clarify the expectations that form the basis of data quality requirements.

Implementation of any strategy requires a degree of flexibility. Because specific applications and data stores serve different consumers, the managers and stewards of those data assets will need to

---

[3]"[D]ata quality strategy requires governance, policies, practices, technology and operational solutions that are all-encompassing yet present themselves to all participants as pragmatic and practical" (Loshin, 2007).

adapt the proposed strategy, policies, and processes to the business goals with which they are most closely associated. The overall strategy should be formulated to provide criteria for resolving conflicting demands between assets. These criteria include consensus on the relative criticality of specific processes and the data they require. The strategy should enable business process owners and data asset owners to make decisions about their links in the data chain while having in mind the organization's need to create, maintain, and use high-quality data.

Because data presents similar kinds of problems in different organizations, most data quality strategies will share certain broad features. In the next chapter, we will explore these principles in more depth and discuss how to assess an organization's readiness for strategic data quality improvement.

Directives for Data Quality Strategy

13

"In real life, strategy is actually very straightforward. You pick a general direction and implement like hell."
—**Jack Welch**, *Winning* (2005)

Purpose

This chapter presents a set of 12 directives for establishing an organization's data quality strategy and describes how to assess organizational readiness for such a strategy.

Thought leaders in the product quality movement recognized that the manufacture of quality products depends on many factors, including cultural and environmental ones. They introduced some of the key tools and methods for assessing and maintaining quality—the control chart, the Plan-Do-Study-Act approach, the Pareto diagram, and the Ishikawa (fishbone) diagram. More important than the tools themselves, pioneers in product quality demonstrated how organizations work. They recognized that producing quality products requires the commitment of an enterprise to a quality result. This commitment must come first from the top of the organization. Its goal must be to foster a culture of quality in which all members of the organization are engaged. (The companion web site includes additional background on the origins of product quality.)

Data use, however, also requires knowledge of what the data represents and how it effects this representation. Managing data and ensuring that it is of high quality therefore requires an understanding of knowledge management. Organizations that want to get the most out of their data must be learning organizations. They must capture, make explicit, and actively manage knowledge about their data, as well as the data itself.

Data quality improvement is built on the same foundation as manufacturing quality improvement, but also recognizes the need to manage data knowledge. Thought leaders in data quality recognize a set of directives necessary to the success of any organization's efforts to improve and sustain data quality. This chapter will summarize those directives and how to assess an organization's strategic readiness for data quality management and improvement.[1]

The directives break down into three sets. The first set focuses on the importance of data within an enterprise and needs to be driven by senior management. The second applies concepts related to manufacturing physical goods to data and should be driven by a data quality program team. The third focuses on building a culture of quality in order to respond to the fluid nature of data and meet the

---

[1] This discussion draws on the work of leading thinkers in data quality (Chisholm, English, Loshin, McGilvray, Redman, Wang and his colleagues, and collaborators at the MIT Information Quality program), as well as on the many papers I have heard on Data Governance at MIT, IDQ, and DGIQ conferences from 2004 to 2012.

ongoing challenges of strategic management. A mature organization will plan for its own evolution and the ongoing health of its cultural orientation toward quality.

The directives are numbered and presented in these sets so that they can be better understood. (see Table 13.1). However, they are not sequential in the sense that process steps are. Each is important in and of itself, and they are interrelated. (Will you be able to obtain management commitment without recognizing the value of data?) So your strategic plan should account for all of them. However, which ones you focus on first tactically will depend on your organization's starting point and its receptivity to data quality improvement.

Table 13.1 Twelve Directives for Data Quality Strategy

Directive	Actions	Drivers
Directive 1: Obtain Management Commitment to Data Quality	Associate data with the organization's vision and mission. Orient the organization toward quality.	Recognize the importance of data to the organization's mission. Driven by senior management
Directive 2: Treat Data as an Asset	Define the value of data to the organization. Determine the willingness of the organization to invest in data quality. Recognize data as a knowledge asset.	Recognize the importance of data to the organization's mission. Driven by senior management
Directive 3: Apply Resources to Focus on Quality	Commission a data quality program team to support the achievement of strategic goals related to data quality improvement. Improve processes by which data is managed; put in place measurements to maintain data quality.	Recognize the importance of data to the organization's mission. Driven by senior management
Directive 4: Build Explicit Knowledge of Data	Recognize that data quality management is a problem of knowledge management, as well as product management. Build knowledge of the data chain and ensure processes are in place to use that knowledge.	Recognize the importance of data to the organization's mission. Driven by senior management
Directive 5: Treat Data as a Product of Processes That Can Be Measured and Improved	Establish a realistic orientation toward data. It is something people create. Measure its quality. Apply quality and process improvement methodology to improve its production.	Apply concepts related to manufacturing physical goods to data. Driven by the data quality program team
Directive 6: Recognize Quality Is Defined by Data Consumers	Build a vocabulary around data quality. Ensure that data consumers articulate their data quality requirements.	Apply concepts related to manufacturing physical goods to data. Driven by the data quality program team

(Continued)

Table 13.1 Twelve Directives for Data Quality Strategy   (*Continued*)

Directive	Actions	Drivers
Directive 7: Address the Root Causes of Data Problems	Apply knowledge of data processes and root cause analysis to understand issues and problems. Invest in remediating root causes rather than symptoms.	Apply concepts related to manufacturing physical goods to data. Driven by the data quality program team
Directive 8: Measure Data Quality, Monitor Critical Data	Broadly assess overall data quality. Regularly monitor critical data.	Apply concepts related to manufacturing physical goods to data. Driven by the data quality program team
Directive 9: Hold Data Producers Accountable for the Quality of Their Data (and Knowledge about That Data)	Engage data producers to prevent data problems. Improve communications between producers and consumers. Ensure producers have the tools and input they need to deliver high-quality data.	Build a culture of quality that can respond to ongoing challenges of strategic data management. Partnership between senior management, the data quality program team, and other governance structures
Directive 10: Provide Data Consumers with the Knowledge They Require for Data Use	Ensure data consumers have the tools they need to understand the data they use. Build data consumers' knowledge of the data chain and its risks.	Build a culture of quality that can respond to ongoing challenges of strategic data management.
Directive 11: Data Use Will Continue to Evolve— Plan for Evolution	Recognize the environment is evolving. Plan for constant change.	Build a culture of quality that can respond to ongoing challenges of strategic data management.
Directive 12: Data Quality Goes Beyond the Data— Build a Culture Focused on Data Quality	Recognize high-quality data does not produce itself. Put in place the governance and support structures needed to enable the production and use of high-quality data.	Build a culture of quality that can respond to ongoing challenges of strategic data management.

Articulating a strategy can be very clarifying: It helps people understand how pieces of an organization work together. Because clarification is energizing, it is also tempting to try and implement an overall strategy immediately. However, it is very difficult to do so. A successful approach to reaching long-term goals depends on many small steps. It also depends on knowing your starting point.

Assessing the current state for the implementation of strategy is separate from assessing the current state of data (as described in Section Three). Like any assessment, assessing strategic readiness consists of asking the right questions and understanding options presented by the answers. A primary goal of the assessment is to help you determine which directives to prioritize and to associate them with measurable actions that support the overall strategy.[2]

Directive 1: Obtain Management Commitment to Data Quality

Improving the quality of data in an enterprise requires the commitment of senior management to creating better data through a culture focused on quality.[3] In any enterprise, a lot of good can be and is done by individual staff people striving to make things better. However, very little change can take place in most enterprises without the engagement, endorsement, and ongoing support of senior management. Sustained improvement of data quality requires that the overall organization be oriented toward the goals of knowing its data better and producing better data.

Creating a corporate culture focused on quality can only be achieved if senior leaders recognize its importance and endorse and reward the efforts to achieve it. Senior management should sponsor the enterprise data quality strategy. That said, getting management commitment means more than getting funding for a data quality program. It means that management recognizes the value of high-quality data and is willing to invest in improvements and reward behavior that contributes to this end. And while it is critically important, management commitment is not an end in itself. It is a necessary step to orient an entire organization toward quality.

Assessing Management Commitment

Assessing management commitment requires an understanding of management priorities and of the role data plays in your organization. It also requires understanding your organization's characteristic ways of responding to change.

- Does your organization have a shared vision and mission?
- What is it?
- How does data support it?
- What is the current attitude of management toward data quality?
- Why does management hold this attitude?
- What are the obstacles to change within your organization?
- What are the obstacles to knowledge-sharing?
- How effective is your organization at solving its own problems?
- What strategies has it adopted in the past to improve its performance?
- How effective have they been?
- What organizational strengths can contribute to improved quality?
- Identify examples that show the positive effects a commitment to quality has had on the organization.

---

[2] There are models that can help in the assessment process. Baskarada (2009) has documented a full *Information Quality Management Capability Maturity Model*. See also Loshin (2011), Chapter 3: Data Quality Maturity and Jim Harris's (2012) *Five Stages of Data Quality*.

[3] Redman (1996), pp. 37–39, 62, 66, Chapter 14, p. 274. English (1999), p. 308; relation to Deming's 14 points, p. 339. Loshin (2001), pp. 464–465. McGilvray (2008), pp. 12–13.

These are big questions, and they are central to organizational change. Strategy must always look forward. If your organization does not have a clear vision and mission, then it is hard to generate commitment to strategic direction of any kind. Assessing management commitment to data quality requires knowing not only management's current attitudes but the origins of those attitudes, which may reveal opportunities or obstacles. In other words, it means understanding your organization's current culture. If your organization is not already oriented toward quality, then it will require work to turn it in that direction. This work will include understanding the benefits and costs of investing in improved data quality, as well as the risks of choosing not to make the investment.

Tactics include:

- Surveying management directly.
- Reviewing past business plans and other documentation related to data decisions.
- SWOT—strengths, weaknesses, opportunities, threats analysis.
- Making formal recommendations based on cost-benefit analysis.

Information gathered through the assessment of Directive 2: Treat Data as an Asset can be leveraged as part of the process of educating management.

Directive 2: Treat Data as an Asset

An *asset* is defined as "a useful or valuable thing, person or quality" or as "property … regarded as having value and available to meet debts, commitments or legacies" (*NOAD*). It has become commonplace to say that data is an asset.[4] In most enterprises today, people understand that data can be a strategic differentiator, though very few organizations actually treat it this way. To get long-term value out of data, an organization must recognize and manage it as a strategic asset, one that can help the organization achieve its mission. Management of an asset requires knowledge of how the asset is used, how its value is measured, how it retains or generates value, and how it may lose value. Managing data's value also requires understanding both the benefits of high-quality data and the costs of poor-quality data. (See the companion web site for a summary of how data quality experts recommend assessing the value of data).

An enterprise data quality strategy should propose ways to understand data as a strategic asset by explicitly connecting it to the enterprise's mission and by recognizing the role data plays in strategic business initiatives. The data quality strategy must assess and measure the value of high quality data.

In today's organizations, where so much work is data-driven, it is not difficult to relate data directly to the enterprise's strategic goals. The mission of the workers' compensation firm where I worked was "We save life and limb." The firm's claim data was used to identify ways of improving safety so as to prevent injuries in the workplace. There was a direct relation between the mission and the data. UnitedHealth Group's mission is "to help people live healthier lives." The claim data used

---

[4]Mosely, Brackett, Early & Henderson, [DAMA-BOK] (2009), p. 1. Redman (2008), pp. 3–5. Costs of poor data quality: Redman (1996), Chapter 1; English (1999), Chapters 1 and 7, p. 426; Loshin (2001), Chapter 4; McGilvray (2008), Business impact key concept, pp. 35–39, discusses both the costs and benefits of addressing data issues. Benefits of good data quality: Redman (1996), p. 12; English (1999), p. xvi, 13, 456–457, and throughout. Managing information costs/assets: English (1999), p. 208; McGilvray (2008) p. 6, emphasis on information life cycle, pp. 23–30.

for outreach to members with chronic conditions, the analytic data used to assess the efficacy of treatment protocols, and the company's numerous other uses of data directly support this mission. In both these examples, data is a knowledge asset. Data collected by the organization enables insight that is not available elsewhere into the behavior of customers, the health of populations, and the effectiveness of the organization's responses to meeting needs.

Characterizing an Organization's Data Assets

Understanding data as an asset requires the ability to connect data to your organization's mission and business goals. It further requires analysis of the costs of poor quality.

- What is your organization's mission?
- How does data contribute to that mission?
- How can poor-quality data undermine the organization's mission?
- What would ideal data do for the organization?
- How much money does the organization currently invest in managing data?
- What costs are associated with data problems?

These questions aim at two things: first, understanding the value of data in relation to what the organization does and what it wants to accomplish, and second, understanding how data is currently managed in order to get as much value as possible out of the existing investment in data. Data exists in all organizations. It costs money to maintain it as well as to use it. What differentiates organizations is their ability to use their data to meet their goals. That ability requires knowledge and focus.

Tactics include:

- Identifying business uses of data and relating these uses directly to the organization's mission statement and strategic goals.
- Surveying management and staff about the value of data for specific functions.
- Reviewing operational and project budgets for an understanding of current investment in data management.
- Identifying potential improvements and their benefits.

Directive 3: Apply Resources to Focus on Quality

Every enterprise has competing internal needs. Resources are applied to those needs that are prioritized and staffed. The DQ strategy needs an executive champion, but it will not be executed unless there is a team to execute it. The team will need expertise in a range of areas related to data quality, including:

- Defining information and data quality strategy and governance.
- Building a data quality culture and measuring the value of information (both the costs of poor-quality data and benefits of high-quality information).
- Supporting efforts to implement reliable, flexible information architecture, including clear data definitions, and other critical metadata.

- Assessing and measuring the quality of data for purposes of improvement, including
  - Measuring critical data,
  - Identifying data improvement opportunities.
  - Addressing root causes of poor quality data.
- Establishing data quality monitoring and reporting to sustain information quality.[5]

Assessing Readiness to Commission a Data Quality Team

To remove obstacles to commissioning a data quality team, you need to understand how your organization currently responds to data quality issues and how effective these responses are.

- How does the organization currently assess and communicate about data quality?
- Who is responsible for the content and consistency of assessments and communications?
- How successful are they?
- What activities are integrated into the project development life cycle that contribute to the creation of high-quality data?
- What activities could be integrated?
- What operational activities support an ongoing assessment of the quality of data?
- Are any activities in place directed at sustaining data quality?

These questions are aimed at identifying what operational and tactical processes are in place to support data quality functions.

Data quality does not happen by itself. Producing high-quality data requires people who are focused on that goal. Commissioning a team is also an outward sign of management commitment to the improvement of data quality. The data quality program team will perform many functions. The specifics will depend on the nature and complexity of the organization and on where they sit within it. One of the most important of these will be to function as a central point of contact for sharing knowledge about the quality of data as well as for prioritizing data quality improvement projects.

Tactics include:

- Reviewing documentation (such as help desk tickets or break-fix project information) about data quality issues.
- Surveying different teams to get an understanding of what activities they engage in to assess or ensure data quality.
- Surveying teams to understand whether they feel they have the tools to successfully respond to data issues.
- Surveying customers to understand their perceptions of the quality of the organization's data.

---

[5]These six domains were formulated by the IAIDQ as part of their work in defining the profession of Information and Data Quality. The domains comprise the areas of focus for the Information Quality Certified Professional designation (IQCP[sm]) (IAIDQ 2011). (See IAIDQ.org.) English (1999) does not discuss roles, but does address the capability/maturity model of the information quality status of the enterprise (p. 433) and suggests that organizations identify and empower an information quality leader (p. 438). See organizing for information quality (pp. 450–454) and improvement does not just happen— someone must take the initiative (p. 455). McGilvray (2008) addresses projects. She does not come out and say, "You need to have someone responsible for data quality." But she points out that without some degree of data governance, data quality improvements are not sustainable (p. 54).

Existing responses to data issues will have differing degrees of success. Depending on the communication between teams, there may be a significant amount of redundancy in these activities. Consolidating and streamlining this kind of work can provide the basis for a business case to establish a data quality program team.

Directive 4: Build Explicit Knowledge of Data

Data is valuable not only for how it is used, but also for what it contains: knowledge about an organization, its customers, its rules, and it past actions. Producing high-quality data and getting value out of data both require knowing what the data represents, how it represents, and how it changes as it moves through systems. Knowledge of risks associated with data production reduces risks associated with data consumption.

Data quality can be improved for all data consumers if those responsible for producing data have a clear understanding of the downstream uses (including potential future uses) of the data they produce, and if they design input and production processes with those uses in mind. These links in the data chain—from data producers in source systems to data consumers of downstream applications— need to be connected in order to create better data across the data chain.

Delivering quality data requires not only communication, but also a focus on building explicit knowledge about how data is produced and consumed. Explicit knowledge is documented so that it can be shared among stakeholders. It includes metadata, training materials, and system documentation. It also includes measurements of data and process quality.

Building explicit knowledge requires integrating its development into the project development life cycle and managing it as uses of data evolve. Building explicit knowledge has the added benefit of reminding people who use data that data does not simply exist in the world. It is created by people and systems. Therefore, its quality can be improved through decisions about how it is created, stored, and shared.

The enterprise data quality strategy should include building a close working relationship between data producers and data consumers. These teams must share the common goal of improved data quality, and they should define, as specifically as possible, what "improved data quality" means. When conflicting needs arise, they will need to resolve or escalate these for the benefit of strategic progress. The Data Quality program team should facilitate these relationships to resolve cross-system data questions.

Assessing the Condition of Explicit Knowledge and Knowledge Sharing

To assess your organization's knowledge sharing practices, you need to identify the structures that capture explicit knowledge and determine how comprehensive and current they are. Assessment also requires understanding how people solve problems in the absence of such structures. In the very likely event that your organization relies on the tacit knowledge of SMEs, rather than explicit knowledge, your data quality strategy should include working with SMEs to document what they know. It should also put in place ongoing processes to capture and manage knowledge.

- Where do metadata, training materials, and system documentation originate?
- Who is responsible for creating and maintaining them?
- Are there specific standards for their creation and maintenance?

- Where (or to whom) do people go when they have questions about data?
- How do people learn about the origins of their data and processes it goes through before they use it?
- Is documentation on the data chain and information life cycle available and maintained? If so, to what extent, and who is responsible for it? For whom is it produced for (technical people, businesspeople, or both)?

These questions aim at discovering the level of documentation that exists to support the use and maintenance of the information chain. The better people understand the data they use, the better able they will be to make decisions about when and how to use it. In most organizations many people will use the same data for different purposes. Information about data's origins and transformations should be explicitly captured and shared with all data consumers, so that there is a common understanding of the data. While having this metadata available does not completely guarantee that data will be well understood, not having it is an open invitation to misunderstanding.

Tactics include:

- Surveying teams about how they find answers to data questions.
- Reviewing existing data dictionaries, training materials, and system documentation for currency and comprehensiveness.
- Reviewing results of assessment of data quality readiness, especially those questions related to issue management to characterize the use of documentation or the effects of the absence of documentation.
- Producing an inventory that describes available documentation, its intended audience(s) and its currency.

Directive 5: Treat Data as a Product of Processes that can be Measured and Improved

Data is produced through business and system processes that influence its quality.[6] The collection of processes through which data is created is usually referred to as the data chain. As is the case with the quality of physical products, data quality can be improved through knowledge of and management of the processes through which it is manufactured. Improving data quality requires at least three steps:

- Assess data in relation to expectations to identify improvement opportunities.
- Remediate the root causes of data issues (including gaps) and measure improvement.
- Maintain quality through ongoing assessment and monitoring.

Measurement is central to process and quality improvement. If you do not measure, you cannot tell whether or not you have improved. But many organizations measure neither the processes

---

[6] Redman (1996), Chapter 12. Redman does not come right out and say data is a product. He says data is produced through processes. Redman (2001) makes the product analogy more explicit, especially with the use of the customer-supplier model (Chapter 16) and data supplier management (Chapter 26) and management of the information chain (Chapter 24). English (1999), 19, Chapter 3, p. 52, knowledge workers are dependent on information products from other employees (71) and Chapter 9 Build quality in (286—Quoting Crosby, *Quality Is Free*). Loshin (2001), p. 26, and throughout Chapter 2, discussion of the "information factory" delineates a series of roles and processes related to the production and use of data. McGilvray (2008), p. 4, and the overall discussion of the information life cycle, pp. 23–30, 102–104, 258–263.

through which data is produced nor the quality of the result. The data quality strategy should advocate the application of the directives of continuous improvement (define, measure, analyze, improve, control) to the production and use of data. The DQ program team should work with management and data consumers to prioritize which processes to address and which data to focus on. To do so, requires knowledge of the processes (directive 4). Priorities should be based on an understanding of the ways data contributes to the organization's mission, the value of data (directives 1 and 2), and the expectations of data consumers (directive 6).

Assessing Organizational Understanding of Data as a Product

To assess how your organization views the production of data, look for places where data is managed and measured and where such practices are not in place. Identify potential obstacles to measuring processes and their results.

- What is the current attitude of IT and businesspeople toward the processes and systems through which data is created, maintained, and stored?
- What is the attitude of businesspeople toward data quality improvement?
- What is the attitude of IT toward data quality improvement?
- Which (if any) processes are measured?
- Which (if any) data is measured?
- Who is responsible for the measurements?
- How are the measurements used, and with whom are they shared?
- How comprehensive and effective are the measurements?
- What degree of confidence do people have in the measurement processes? In the results?
- Do people have a common understanding of the meaning of measurements?
- What opportunities do teams responsible for these processes see for improvement?

These questions are aimed at uncovering the perspective of both IT and businesspeople. Improvement requires knowledge of the processes that produce data. The teams responsible for these processes usually understand where they work well and where they do not. The magic wand question (if you had a magic wand, what's the first thing you would do to make this data better?) is very helpful in getting people to be frank about how to make a process better.

Tactics include:

- Surveying IT and business stakeholders involved with data production.
- Reviewing operational logs and other instruments that collect process data.

Directive 6: Recognize Quality is Defined by Data Consumers

As with the quality of any product, the quality of data is defined by how well it meets the needs and expectations of its consumers.[7] Perception of the quality of specific data depends largely on how data

---

[7] Meeting customer expectations: English (1999), pp. 24–27 and throughout. Redman (2001), Chapter 17. Fitness for use: Loshin (2001), p. 47. English (1999) objects to the definition of "fitness for use" and instead proposes "fitness for all purposes" (pp. 16, 151). Wang and Strong (1996) recognize that fitness for use is directly related to customer expectations.

consumers intend to use the data and on whether the data is fit for these uses. What is considered good-quality data in one area may be considered poor-quality data in another; just as what is critical data for one function may be irrelevant for another. Perception is also tied to the expertise of data consumers. People who are very knowledgeable about a dataset or the processes that produce it are more likely to identify errors and anomalies in the data. They are also better able to work around these. The perception of quality is also connected to the technical means by which data is stored and accessed.

Different facets of quality are usually understood through dimensions of quality, such as completeness, validity, and accuracy. (See the companion web site for several comprehensive definitions of data quality dimensions).[8] The data quality strategy should enable consumers with different needs and different levels of expertise to contribute to the goal of better data within the enterprise. To do so, the strategy needs to establish a common vocabulary around data quality dimensions. Quality dimensions can be used to define consumer expectations and ways to measure those expectations. The strategy will require that stakeholders be directly involved in defining quality measurements. Effective channels of communication will need to be established between data producers and data consumers to ensure that data meets expectations.

Assessing How Data Consumers Define Data Quality

Assessing how your organization's data consumers define quality requires understanding who the consumers are, how they use data, and how well the processes for which they require data are working for them.

- Who are the sets of data consumers in your organization?
- How do they use data? What processes is it used in?
- What data is most important to them? Why is it important?
- What can go wrong with the data they use? (Or what has gone wrong in the past?)
- How do they define quality?
- What is their current perception of the quality of the data they use?
- What data is meeting expectations?
- What data problems cause them pain?

These questions focus on understanding the effects of poor data quality on business success, from the point of view of people who use data. Data consumers will be the starting and ending point of efforts to improve data quality. It helps to recognize which current state data is considered high quality as well as which is recognized as having low quality. Since improvement projects will need to be prioritized, it is also important to know the relative criticality of different data elements and datasets. Some information about data criticality should emerge in your analysis of the asset value of data (directive 2), and some of the information you collect from data consumers will inform your assessment of asset value.[9]

---

[8]In addition to the approaches to quality dimensions summarized on the companion web site, the approach of McGilvray (2008) to dimensions provides a starting point for such a process (pp. 30–37) and Chapter 3, Step 3, Assess Data Quality.
[9]McGilvray (2008), Step 3.10, Perception, Relevance, and Trust, can provide a jump start (pp. 155–158).

Tactics include:

- Surveying data consumers about their needs, perceptions, and concerns.
- Reviewing documentation on known data problems (help desk tickets, problem reports, remediation projects, etc.) in order to identify recurrent problems or other patterns that cause problems for data consumers.
- Reviewing what data is accessed most frequently. (Using a query monitoring tool, for example)
- Reviewing reports to identify which data elements and sets are incorporated in them.

Directive 7: Address the Root Causes of Data Problems

Sustaining long-term data quality depends on addressing the root causes of data problems. Failure to do so is an invitation for issues to recur. When data does not meet expectations, the first step is to understand why. If there are genuine issues with the way data is defined, collected, processed, or stored, the root causes of issues should be identified and remediated. If root causes are not addressed, the costs associated with data issues will increase, sometimes exponentially (See Figures 13.1 and 13.2).[10] A range of tools, including the fishbone diagram, are available to conduct root cause analysis.

While we often think of "remediating root causes" as implementing a technical solution to a data issue, not all problems are technical. Root causes often reflect a lack of understanding on the part of data producers, data consumers, or both, about what the data represents or how

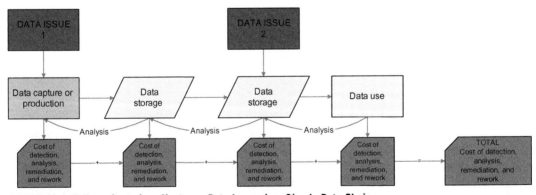

FIGURE 13.1 Fall-out Costs from Upstream Data Issues in a Simple Data Chain

Using a simple data chain, the figure illustrates the costs associated with data issues introduced at different points in the data chain. Fall-out from Data issue 1 will create detection, analysis, and remediation costs in all downstream systems. Data issue 2 will impose these costs on data uses. However, in order to determine the root cause of data issue 2, there may also be analysis costs imposed on upstream systems.

[10] English (1999), pp. 294 and 332. Redman (2001), Chapter 22. Loshin (2001), Chapter 15. McGilvray (2008), Chapter 3, Step 5, Identify Root Causes.

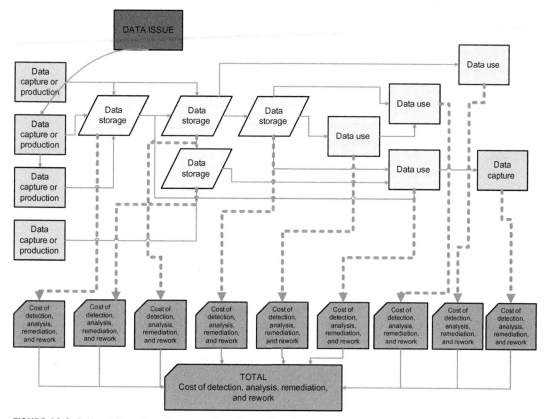

FIGURE 13.2 Fall-out Costs from Upstream Data Issues in a Complex Data Chain

In a complex data chain, the costs of data issues increase significantly. Not only is the impact of the issue felt more widely, but significantly more collective time is needed to get to the root causes.

it represents. There can be confusion about data precision or granularity, data processing rules, or how concepts are represented in the data model. Remediation can therefore include business process changes, training, or other "soft" solutions. In many such cases, a technical solution may mask the root of the problem and cause further misunderstanding. Documented knowledge of the data (directive 4) can help reduce the incidence of data questions and help identify the presence of genuine issues.

The enterprise data quality strategy should support the process of root cause analysis and should advocate for remediation of data problems at their sources. Doing so will require active engagement of representatives of all systems in the overall data quality effort. In the area of issue resolution, it is extremely important to have senior management's commitment (directive 1), since resolving issues costs time and money and requires that teams work together.

Assessing Organizational Ability to Address Root Causes

Understanding organizational readiness to address the root causes of problems means understanding the organization's cultural habits toward any kind of problem solving. If the organization is disciplined in its approach to problem solving and is capable of working across teams, it will have a strong foundation for tackling data quality problems. (Information gathered under directives 4, 5, and 6 can also contribute to this understanding).

* What are the current approaches to analysis and quantification of data problems?
* How well adapted is the organization to working across and between systems?
* How are change requests prioritized and funded?
* Identify examples of problems rooted in one system that impact other systems.

These questions aim at understanding how an organization responds to data issues as well as whether the organizational structures are in place to resolve them at their root causes.

The tools of root cause analysis are well known. But executing a root cause analysis is still challenging. Despite the fact that many people understand the concept of the "Five Whys" and can use the Ishikawa diagram, many people stop at the symptoms, rather than digging into the underlying causes of data problems. Many times, the cause of a data problem may be rooted in the original data collection (data collected at a different level of grain or precision than current use requires), or in an understanding of what happens to the data in the information chain, rather than in a technical problem that has somehow damaged the data.

Analyzing the root causes of problems takes knowledge of the processes that produce data (hence the need for explicit knowledge, directive 4), skill at tracing those processes and seeing their effects, and courage to name the problems once they are identified and quantified. Addressing them takes knowledge of the organization and the ability to get teams to work together—one person's root cause of a problem could be another person's "that's working just fine from my point of view." Making decisions about root causes takes common sense. Remediation always carries a cost as well as a benefit. Not all problems are worth the cost of fixing them.

Tactics include:

* Understanding and documenting how different parts of the organization work.
* Identifying opportunities for them to work together more effectively.
* Finding a good example of a problem to illustrate both root cause analysis and the benefits of resolving a problem at its root cause.

Directive 8: Measure Data Quality, Monitor Critical Data

Measurement enables consistent characterization of data quality. Measurement is also necessary to determine the degree to which efforts to improve data quality have been successful (directive 5). Sustaining long-term data quality depends on ongoing assessment of the quality of critical data. The directives of process improvement include instituting a level of monitoring and control to ensure that processes continue to function as expected. To *monitor* a thing is "to observe or check its progress or quality ... over a period of time; to keep under systematic review" (*NOAD*). A *control* means both "a place where an item can be verified" and "a means of limiting or regulating something" (*NOAD*).

A control on data measures actual data against a standard and stipulates actions based on the result.[11] For example, a control may be put in place to detect a specific data condition, and if that condition is met, data processing may stop.

Ongoing data quality measurement, monitoring, and control are about managing risk. While not all problems are worth fixing, some are definitely worth preventing. Most organizations know or can determine which data is critical to their processes. This data should be cared for on an ongoing basis. Without scrutiny, data can go wrong and create costly problems for an organization.

Like physical manufacture, data production includes input, processes, and outputs. The condition of inputs and outputs can be influenced by business and technical processes for creating, storing, and using data. Input can change because business processes evolve or because they are executed in an unexpected way. Technical data processing can change through use of new tools. Change can be introduced accidentally, when processes influence each other in unanticipated ways; or purposefully in order to improve the quality of the data. When unexpected changes take place, it is best to be able to detect them, understand (i.e., measure) their impact, and communicate their existence before they surprise data consumers.

Monitoring can involve repeated measurement (as is described for in-line DQAF measurements) or the establishment of a condition, which if met, serves as a process control, or both. While data monitoring can be automated to a large degree, it still requires resources, human beings who can respond to findings. Most large organizations have dozens of official databases with thousands of data elements and millions or billions of records. It is not cost efficient to monitor all data. Therefore, it is important to understand which data is the most critical, define what it means for this data to be of high quality, understand the risks associated with it, and put controls and measurements in place to mitigate against those risks. Monitoring should focus on critical data and critical processes. Findings from monitoring should be actionable: They should help prevent errors or reveal opportunities for improvement.

The data quality strategy should establish criteria for identifying critical and high-risk data for ongoing monitoring.[12] It should also include an approach to conducting this measurement. The in-line measurement types described in the DQAF are intended to aid in this process.

Assessing Organizational Readiness for Ongoing Measurement and Monitoring

Assessing readiness for ongoing measurement requires knowledge of the organization's culture and data, including its disposition toward a sustained commitment to quality. It requires consensus on which data is most critical (directive 2) and most at risk (directives 4 and 7).

- What data is most important to the organization?
- What does it mean for this data to be of high quality?
- How much risk is this data subjected to within the data chain or information life cycle? (i.e., how complex are the business and technical processes associated with it? And what could happen to it that might adversely affect its quality?)

---

[11] Thanks to Tom Redman for this definition, which derives from Juran's work.
[12] Loshin (2001), Chapter 4. Loshin (2011), Chapters 5 and 12, see especially pp. 211–212. McGilvray (2008), Step 4, "Assess Business Impact," pp. 163–197.

- How much discipline does the organization have for operational activities related to quality?
- Are there resources already engaged in monitoring?
- How successful have they been at detecting problems?
- What current operational practices can be applied to data quality monitoring?

These questions aim at identifying the organization's most important data and understanding the benefits of monitoring it, as well as identifying who might be prepared to execute monitoring.
Tactics include

- Surveying key data consumers to understand what data is critical to them.
- Reviewing problem reports and help desk tickets to understand what problems have occurred in the past.
- Reviewing the data chain for critical data to identify potential risks.
- Identifying critical data to use in a pilot for monitoring.

From these findings, you can propose ways to monitor data using DQAF measurement types.

Directive 9: Hold Data Producers Accountable for the Quality of their Data (and Knowledge about that Data)

Data chains can be long and complex. Untangling them when data issues are discovered is time-consuming and therefore costly. It is far better to prevent problems from happening than it is to sort them out after they have had negative effects on data consumers. Knowledge of the data chain (directive 4) is necessary but not sufficient for preventing problems. Data producers, especially owners of processes that create data, need to supply data of high quality. They cannot do so alone. Producing high-quality data requires input from data consumers about their needs and expectations. However, once these needs and expectations are defined, management must ensure that data producers are accountable for their links in the data chain. Producing high-quality data also requires knowledge, and that knowledge, like the data itself, must be shared and managed. Producers must know their own systems well, have a solid understanding of downstream systems, and put in place mechanisms to ensure they communicate about any changes in their systems that might impact downstream consumers.

Assessing Options for Accountability

Understanding how receptive an organization is to holding data producers accountable requires exploration of organizational culture, including existing mechanisms for accountability. If accountability consists largely of finger-pointing, then holding people accountable will probably not result in process improvements or measurable gains in quality. However, if accountability means enabling people to take responsibility for their own success, then there is a lot of potential for improvement. Data producers must have the tools and input they need to be successful in preparing data for downstream uses. Input includes knowledge of the data chain and a means of engaging in ongoing dialog with data consumers. Assessment includes understanding the following:

- What is the organization's cultural attitude toward accountability?
- What mechanisms exist within the organization for ensuring communication takes place up and down the data chain?

- What obstacles may prevent data producers from responding to requests from data consumers?
- What structures are in place to encourage teams to work together on data improvements?

Tactics include:

- Sharing explicit knowledge of the data chain (process flows, SIPOC analyses, fishbone diagrams) with data producers to build their understanding of their role in the data chain.
- Seeking input from data producers as to how they can improve their processes.
- Establishing a pilot improvement project with a key measurement.
- Incorporating data quality goals into performance evaluations.

Directive 10: Provide Data Consumers with the Knowledge they Require for Data Use

In an ideal world, data producers know their data well and measure it to ensure it meets requirements. Even in such a world, data consumers have responsibility for data use and therefore for data knowledge. They must know what the data they use represents and how it represents. They should also have an understanding of the processes by which data is created and the risks associated with those processes. New data consumers will appear more often than data producers. They, too, need tools to be successful. These include access to explicit knowledge about data, such as training on what data is available and how to use it (directive 4). Ideally, data consumers should actively learn about the data they use, rather than passively accepting it. The enterprise data quality strategy must identify ways in which data consumers can develop their knowledge of the data chain and any risks within it.

Assessing the receptivity of data consumers within an organization relies on many of the same questions and tactics outlined in Directive 6. In addition, it requires asking them directly what they would do to improve their ability to understand and use data.

Directive 11: Data Needs and Uses will Evolve—Plan for Evolution

Data is critical to most business processes and the way business processes evolve.[13] Because processes need to respond with agility to new business opportunities and demands, the data produced through them will also continue to evolve. Not only that, but data consumers will come up with new requirements and new ways of using existing data—ways that may not align with those for which data was originally produced and stored.

The most realistic approach to managing evolution is to recognize the fact that it is not possible to predict all the specifics. One should instead plan for the general condition of constant change. The enterprise data quality strategy must recognize that the uses of data will change over time. It must advocate for managing data in ways that enable this evolution, including the production of robust metadata and other forms of explicit knowledge.

---

[13] In *Data Driven* (2008), Redman revisits the properties of data he described in his earlier writings and points to additional qualities related to their movement and evolution. Not so much a stream, data and information are more like birds that "zip around, they change and grow to meet the needs of people, departments and companies that use them" (p. 23).

Developing a Plan for Evolution

Assessment of the potential for evolution involves knowing your organization's current data assets. It also requires thinking forward about potential changes in your industry and emerging opportunities related to technology.[14]

- What data assets and applications are most critical to the organization?
- How old are they?
- What technology do they use?
- How are they supported?
- Does management have plans for future development, retirement, or replacement?
- How might changing technology impact critical data?
- What are the major trends within your industry?
- In what ways might these affect your organization's data needs?
- What business needs are likely to emerge in the next five years? Ten years?
- Does the organization have a long-term technology plan to respond to emerging business needs and technical developments?
- How agile are your system development processes?
- How capable are your business and technical teams at working together?

This set of questions focuses on evolving technology (the technical side of data production within systems) and evolving business needs. As evolution speeds up, good working relationships between business and technical teams will enable a swifter, more effective response to business needs.

There is a tendency to depict data quality work as consisting of either performing initial assessments of data to determine its suitability for a particular purpose or of solving big data problems through root cause analysis and remediation. There is a tendency to depict all IT work in a similar manner. IT work is seen as very project-oriented, despite the amount of time and talent invested in ongoing operations. Very few organizations these days build applications or warehouses on virgin soil. Most are continually balancing the need to support current business processes with the need to advance technologically. This balance is influenced by numerous factors and is not completely predictable. However, some parts of it can be predicted and planned for. The smartest organizations are those that take the time to scan the horizon and understand and plan for likely changes in their environments—both business and technical. Staying ahead of trends requires a significant amount of forward-thinking data governance. The Data Quality program team may lead the way in data governance or be part of an overall data governance initiative.

Tactics include

- Assessing risks associated with current systems.
- Understanding the relation between business and technical opportunities
- Engaging in an ongoing discussion about strategy. Many organizations do not take the time to review and reassess strategy on an ongoing basis. Such activity is necessary if an organization truly intends to act strategically.

---

[14] The best book I know on this kind of thinking is Peter Senge's *The Fifth Discipline* (1990 and 2006).

Directive 12: Data Quality Goes beyond the Data—Build a Culture Focused on Quality

Data is critical to organizational success because it provides the foundation for business decisions and because it reflects the realities of the organization (its customers, products, transactions, etc.) in a manner that nothing else does (Redman, 1996). Successful execution of data quality processes requires a governance structure (data stewardship, accountability for data quality, advocacy of improvement projects). Effective use of data requires a support structure (capture and management of explicit knowledge, employee training, metadata management, master data management), and processes for managing and resolving data issues (escalation and prioritization, consistent communication between data producers and data consumers). Support structures and processes must be matured to ensure that the enterprise continues to derive value from its data assets. Such activities serve as another reminder that producing high-quality data requires enterprise-wide commitment.

The data quality strategy should support effective improvement of the overall information life cycle. This support includes ensuring that data producers in transactional systems are aware of the downstream uses of the data they produce; that data storage teams have means of measuring and monitoring the quality of the data they are responsible for; that data consumers have the training, metadata, and other support structures they need to use the data effectively; and that data consumers can provide input and feedback related to their uses of the data so that those responsible for the storage and access of the data are able to improve its quality for evolving business uses. The DQ program team will need to work with all these groups and other governance structures to facilitate the maturity of these support functions. While launching the process of improvement requires management commitment, long-term success depends on the overall organization's commitment to its own data needs and priorities.

Building a Culture Focused on Data Quality

Results from all the previous directives can be used as input to assess the overall commitment of the organization to improving its data quality. In addition, you should determine:

- What structures are currently in place to encourage the production of high-quality data?
- What is the level of organizational awareness of how data is produced and shared?
- Are there enterprise-endorsed ways of reporting and remediating data issues and questions?
- How well-known and well-used are the channels of communication related to data decisions?
- Are decision-making accountabilities clear and communicated?
- Are they functioning as intended (to reduce risk, enable compromise, and ensure that decision criteria are applied fairly and consistently)?

These questions are aimed at understanding the overall support of the organization for producing high-quality data. Most of them are centered on governance structure, but they also bring us back to Directive 1: Data quality depends on management commitment to a culture of quality.

Tactics include

- Assessing the organization's governance structures.
- Understanding their goals and effectiveness.
- Proposing how to improve them to support the improvement of critical data and critical processes.

Concluding Thoughts: Using the Current State Assessment

Producing high-quality data involves the overall commitment of an organization. This commitment requires that different parts of the organization see themselves in relation to the whole. It also requires the organization to balance competing needs and priorities between its parts.

The purpose the current state assessment is to surface priorities for strategic action and to formulate a long-term approach to an organization's data quality improvement. Findings from the current state assessment provide the input needed to develop a data quality strategy. This input should be recognized as data and analyzed as data. (Recognizing it as such is another reason to try to ask some questions that people can actually quantify, for example, how many data issues they have addressed in a given time period.) From it, you will need to identify patterns related to particular processes, problems, datasets, or data elements. These present opportunities for the direct improvement of the condition of data and the processes that create, maintain, and store data.

Other patterns from the current state assessment will point to the strengths, weaknesses, opportunities, and threats facing your organization. Some of these will provide you with insights about your organizational culture, such as what kinds of projects get support, the best ways to communicate about problems, and the ways that teams work together. Keeping these cultural ideas in mind as you plan for quality improvement can help you avoid obstacles and build the wider engagement of the teams you need to work with.

Most importantly, the current state assessment should also include a vision of future state. Strategy looks forward. It is driven by vision and mission. With a picture of current state and a vision of future state, you can make decisions about which opportunities to act on to move your organization forward on the road to higher quality data.

The DQAF in Depth

"They are structures that embody special kinds of perceptions and awareness. Each is a kind of example or anecdote. Each is a kind of little world that has to be apprehended in depth."
—**Marshall McLuhan, *The Book of Probes***

The Data Quality Assessment Framework measurement types describe generic ways to measure data quality. A DQAF measurement type is a category within a dimension of data quality that allows for a repeatable pattern of measurement to be executed against any data that fits the criteria required by the type, regardless of specific data content. In developing the listing presented in Section Two, we recognized the need to flesh out these concepts with additional information such as how each type could confirm expectations, detect unexpected changes, or reduce risks associated with data processing. We also recognized the need to describe how the measurement process needed to be executed and how measurement results would be captured and stored. Section Six addresses in detail these aspects of the framework in order to describe how a system might be implemented to comprehensively execute data quality measurement.

The original purpose of the DQAF was descriptive and educational. The team wanted to build a common vocabulary around data quality measurement. A goal of the framework is to allow each type to be understood independently (as well as in relation to each other). The framework is comprehensive. However it should not be a goal to implement the entire thing. Instead, the goal is to implement the set of measurement types that will provide the optimal set of specific metrics for your system or organization. Understanding the range of options should aid in making decisions about where to begin. Presenting the DQAF measurement types in depth provides a fuller level of specificity for people who plan to implement them.

The section consists of three chapters. The first describes functions in the measurement process (collect, calculate, compare), detailing a set of calculations that are used throughout the framework. The second describes common features of the DQAF measurement logical model. The third provides a detailed description of each measurement type, using the six facets of the DQAF: definition, business concerns, measurement methodology, engineering and programming, support processes and skills, and measurement logical data model.

Functions for Measurement: Collect, Calculate, Compare

Chapter 14: Functions of Measurement: Collection, Calculation, Comparison *describes the process of taking the in-line measurements, including what raw measurement data needs to be collected, what calculations need to be made with it (i.e., how raw measurement data needs to be processed), and what comparisons need to be made to produce measurement results. Calculations and comparisons are intended to identify measurement results that may indicate a problem. Related sets of measurement types use similar calculations. For example, most of the consistency measurements depend on calculating a distribution of values. The purpose in describing these common functions first is to reduce redundancy in the detailed descriptions of the measurement types.*

Features of the DQAF Measurement Logical Data Model

Similarly, Chapter 15: Features of the DQAF Measurement Logical Data Model *describes features in the DQAF measurement logical data model (LDM) that are common to many of the measurement types. The measurement LDM consists largely of two types of tables: those that define specific metrics and those that store measurement results. (Several measurement types also require additional data structures to store summarized results.) These tables have many common features. The purpose in presenting these before going into detail on the measurement types is to clarify in one place information that pertains widely to the system, thereby reducing redundancy.*

Facets of the DQAF Measurement Types

Chapter 16: Facets of the DQAF Measurement Types *describes DQAF measurement types in detail. As outlined in Section Two, the team that developed the types began by asking basic* questions about what it would mean to measure the completeness, timeliness, consistency, validity, and integrity of data. In doing so, we defined a set of generic patterns of measurement related to dimensions of quality. To build out the framework and ensure other people understood it, we approached the measurement types from several different angles. How would businesspeople best understand the types? How much could the detection of anomalies be automated? What programming would they require? What skills and processes would be needed to use them? And, very importantly, what would the measurement results themselves look like?

Using this approach, we developed additional categories to describe six facets of each measurement type:

- **Definition:** Includes the dimension of quality that the measurement type is part of, its name and description, and its relation to other measurement types.
- **Business Concerns:** Describes why measurement type is important, the risks it addresses, the benefits it provides, and the situations in which it can be used.
- **Measurement Methodology:** Describes how the measurement will be taken, what data needs to be collected, what calculations comparisons are required to detect changes and make results meaningful.
- **Programming:** Describes the functions that need to be built to take the measurement and process the results.
- **Support Processes and Skills:** Describes the processes and skills required to use the measurement results and respond to findings.
- **Measurement Logical Model:** Describes the logical attributes required to define specific metrics, collect measurement data, and store results.

In Chapter 16, the measurement types will be cross-referenced to highlight related types. However, because one goal of the framework is to allow each type to be understood independently, in some cases, similar information is repeated for similar measurement types.

Functions of Measurement: Collection, Calculation, Comparison

14

"It is by the art of statistics that law in the social sphere can be ascertained and codified, and certain aspects of the character of God thereby revealed. The study of statistics is thus a religious service."
— **Florence Nightingale**[1] **(1820 – 1910)**

Purpose

This chapter describes the high-level process of taking the in-line measurements in terms of a set of functions common to many of the Data Quality Assessment Framework measurement types. Measurement types (generic patterns for taking specific measurements) begin with the collection of raw measurement data. They process that data through calculations that make the measurements comprehensible and through comparisons that make the results meaningful. These calculations and comparisons are intended to detect changes in data patterns that may indicate quality problems. The chapter presents relatively dense, technically oriented material. It should be read in conjunction with Chapters 15 and 16.

DQAF calculations and comparisons are based on statistical techniques. In order to understand how the DQAF measurement types work and how to apply them to particular data and to interpret results, it is important to know what these techniques are and the concepts behind them. There are software programs that can execute the calculations themselves. The chapter presents high-level definitions of statistical concepts that are necessary for the general context of measurement and to the DQAF's automation of data quality thresholds.

Functions in Measurement: Collect, Calculate, Compare

The DQAF describes the measurement of data quality in generic terms at the level of the measurement type. A measurement type is a category within a dimension of data quality that allows for a repeatable pattern of measurement to be executed against any data that fits the criteria required by the type, regardless of specific data content. Measurement types occupy a middle ground between abstract dimensions of data quality and measurements of specific data. Validity is a dimension of data quality. The percentage of records containing invalid diagnosis codes is a metric related to specific

---

[1] Attributed by F. N. David.

data. An example of a measurement type is the capability of measuring the validity of any designated data field based on a defined domain of values and calculating the percentage of records where values are invalid. (These relationships are illustrated in Figure 4.1 in Chapter 4.)

Automating DQAF measurement requires building functions to collect raw measurement data, execute appropriate calculations against that data, and compare against thresholds or past history to make the data meaningful so that data's quality can be assessed. The ways of collecting raw measurement data can be understood largely in terms of what features of the data need to be counted (file sizes, process duration, record counts, group-bys, etc.). Making measurements meaningful can be understood through the kinds of calculations (percentages, averages, etc.) that put results from large datasets into comprehensible terms and set up a means of making useful comparisons. The comparisons utilize statistical methods to understand results in relation to an established threshold or to determine how similar any instance of a measurement is to previous instances of the same measurement (see Figure 14.1).

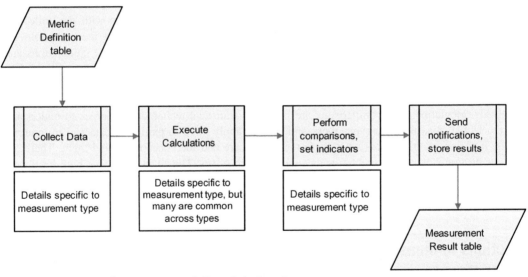

FIGURE 14.1 Functions in Measurement: Collect, Calculate, Compare

Definitions of specific metrics are stored in metric definition tables. These drive the collection of measurement data. Once this data is collected, calculations are executed against it. While each measurement type requires a specific set of calculations, there are many commonalities between them. For example, many of the consistency measurement types require the calculation of a percentage distribution of values. The results of the initial calculations provide input to comparisons. Comparisons are made either against quality thresholds defined by subject matter experts or based on the results of past measurements of the same dataset. The comparison process assigns indicators against these thresholds. If the measurements produce unexpected results, notifications will be sent and response protocols initiated. Results are stored in the measurement result tables, where they can be used for trend analysis and reporting.

Collecting Raw Measurement Data

Even in a complex dataset, there is a limited number of ways to collect basic input for quality measurement. These include:

- Capture the start and stop times of a process.
- Count total records in a dataset.
- Count records grouped by values in a field.
- Count records grouped by values across fields.
- Count and group records based on filters or qualifying criteria.

Data are abstract representations of real-world objects, concepts, or events, often referred to as entities. An entity may have numerous references (records) in a dataset. A distinct count of entities represented in a dataset determines how many individual entities the data contains references to, regardless of how many references there are. For example, a library may have 10 books (records) by Mark Twain, but Mark Twain is only one entity (author). Or it may have 10 copies of *Tom Sawyer*, but *Tom Sawyer* is only one entity (one novel, printed in numerous editions). Basic input related to distinct entities includes:

- Count the distinct number of a represented entity within a dataset.
- Count the distinct number of a represented entity within a dataset based on qualifying criteria

Date fields can help confirm expectations related to data content completeness and consistency and to assess the reasonableness of other data. However, the specific values of dates are not directly comparable in transactional data. Meaningful comparisons related to date data often require data be aggregated at the weekly, monthly, quarterly, or annual level. Basic aggregations based on date fields can make comparisons between datasets more meaningful.

- Count total records per aggregated date.
- Count records associated with two date fields.

Amount fields contain data in numeric form representing the number of objects associated with a record (such as number of products ordered) or representing currency amounts (such as net sales amount). For such fields, even the collection of "raw" data requires basic calculations that can be used as input for quality measures.

- Calculate the total value in an amount field within a dataset.
- Calculate the total value in an amount field based on filters or qualifying criteria.
- Calculate the value in an amount field grouped by values in another field or fields.
- Calculate the value in an amount field grouped by values in another field or fields based on filters or qualifying criteria.

Calculating Measurement Data

Raw counts, calculations, and even aggregations are of limited use by themselves. They can be made meaningful through calculations that enable people to see the relation of data within the set. Some basic calculations that make raw counts more meaningful include:

- The percentage of records associated with each distinct value in a field (percentage distribution of values).
- The ratio of total records to represented entity (the average number of records per represented entity).
- The percentage of total records associated with each distinct represented entity.
- The percentage of total amount associated with each distinct value in a field.
- The average amount associated with each distinct value in a field.
- The ratio of two related amount fields.
- The percentage of total records per aggregated date.
- The summed amount per aggregated date.
- The percentage of total amount per aggregated date.

Percentages and averages enable people to understand raw measurement data better, especially if raw measurements involve very large numbers or large sets of numbers. In some data warehouses, tables may contain billions of rows, and any given update may contain millions of rows. Some code sets, such as ICD diagnosis and procedure codes, include thousands of distinct values. Percentages and averages situate the data within a comprehensible context and enable assessment of quality. These calculations are summarized in Table 14.1.

Table 14.1 Summary of Calculation Types for Processing Measurement Data

Description	Equation	Example
Percentage of records associated with each distinct value in a field	(Record count of distinct value/Total record count)*100	Percentage of records associated with each Place of Service Code
Ratio of total records to represented entity (average number of records per represented entity)	Total record count/Distinct number of represented entities	Average number of claims per member
Percentage of total records associated with a represented entity	(Record count of distinct entity/Total record count)*100	Percentage of claims per provider
Percentage of total amount associated with distinct values in a field	(Amount per distinct value/Total amount)*100	Percentage of net paid dollars by Place of Service Code
Average amount associated with distinct values in a field	Amount per distinct value/Record count for distinct value	Average net paid dollars for each Place of Service Code
Ratio of two related amount fields	Total amount field #1/Total amount field # 2	Total billed amount/Total net paid amount
Records per aggregated date	Records/Aggregated date	Claims per month-year
Percentage of total records per aggregated date	(Records per aggregated date/Total records)*100	Percentage of claims per month-year
Amount per aggregated date	Amount/Aggregated date	Total Net Paid per month-year
Percentage of total amount per aggregated date	(Amount per aggregated date/Total amount)*100	Percentage Total Net Paid per month-year

Comparing Measurements to Past History

Understanding very large numbers or large sets of numbers is even more complex if measurements are taken over time. A primary goal of the DQAF is to describe in-line data quality measurement that enables analysis of trends in data quality. DQAF measurement types include not only basic calculations to make raw measurements meaningful within the context of one instance of measurement, but also additional comparisons to past measurements. These comparisons include:

- Comparison to the historical mean percentage of row counts.
- Comparison to the historical mean total amount.
- Comparison to the historical percentage of total amount.
- Comparison to the historical average amount.
- Comparison to the historical median duration.

For a stable process that is producing data that meets data consumers' expectations, comparisons to historical data can confirm that facets of data content are consistent. Historical data measurement data can provide the basis for automation of an initial level for data quality thresholds. To understand how such a process can work, we will discuss some basic concepts in statistics.

Statistics

Statistics is "the practice or science of collecting and analyzing numerical data in large quantities, especially for the purpose of inferring proportions in a whole from those in a representative sample" (*NOAD*). Statistics use mathematical procedures to describe data—that is, to create data about data so that large datasets can be described in more comprehensible terms and so that comparisons can be made between datasets.

The general practice of measuring involves assigning quantities (numeric values) to qualities of the thing being measured in order to understand those qualities (Kircher, 1962, p. 72). Measuring data quality is the process of assigning quantities to qualities of data that we want to understand. Statistics provides critical tools for data quality, and statistical methods allow the creation of comprehensible measurements of data quality.

Many books on statistics begin by acknowledging that most people find statistics difficult (Rumsey, 2011; Salkind, 2011). Most studies also acknowledge that we live in a world described through statistics—the Dow Jones average, the gross domestic product, the unemployment rate, the Scholastic Aptitude Test score, the batting average, and so on.

Measuring data quality does not require mastery of statistics. But the use of statistical tools to measure data quality depends on applying the appropriate tool to the situation. To take basic measurements and interpret them, it is important to know the basic concepts. As with all data quality measurement, effective use of statistical tools depends on understanding expectations for the data.

Statistics includes a large set of methods for understanding data. I will focus on a small set of descriptive statistics that has a direct bearing on basic measures of quality: measures of central tendency (mean, median, mode) and measures of variability around a central tendency (range, variance, standard deviation).[2] Measures of central tendency (also called measures of location) enable you to understand one value that can be understood as "typical" for the set. They describe "the tendency of quantitative data to cluster around some random value. The position of the central variable is usually determined by one of the measures of location, such as mean, median, or mode. The closeness with which the values cluster around the central value is measured by one of the measures of dispersion, such as the mean deviation or standard deviation" (Dodge, 2006, p. 60). While measures of central tendency quantify how data cluster around a value, measures of variability (also called measures of dispersion) describe how "spread out" the data in a set are from such a value.

Measures of Central Tendency

Common measures of central tendency include the mean, median, and mode. At its simplest, the *mean* refers to what most people understand as the mathematical average.[3] The mean is calculated by adding a set of numbers and dividing by the number of numbers in the set. The *median* of a dataset is the value that occupies the middle position of a dataset. When the data points are ranked in ascending order, an equal number of values are above and below the median. The median value does not have to exist as a value in the dataset. (If a dataset contains an even number of values, the average of the two middle numbers is the median.) The *mode* is the value that occurs most frequently in a dataset.

Each of these measures has advantages and disadvantages as a measure of central tendency. The mean is useful because many people understand it. But it can be influenced significantly by extreme values (lows, highs, outliers). It may also be misleading for nonsymmetrical data (data that has extreme values at one end of its set). This problem can be mitigated by calculating a *trimmed mean*, which is based on discarding extreme values in a distribution. The median is less influenced by extremes and can therefore be a better way to understand the central tendency of nonsymmetrical data (Boslaugh & Watters, 2008).

Measures of Variability

Measures of variability provide an understanding of how spread out data is. These measures include the range, variance, and standard deviation. The *range* is the difference between the largest and the smallest number in the dataset. Variance and standard deviation need to be understood in relation to each other and to a measure of central tendency, usually the mean. *Variance* is a measure of "the fluctuation of observations around the mean" (Mitra, 1993). Technically, *variance*, or *mean squared*, is the average of the squared deviations from the mean. A deviation is the difference from a standard value. The *standard deviation* is the square root of the variance.

While *range* describes the extreme values of the dataset, *variance* uses information associated with each observation. A larger value for the variance indicates a greater dispersion of data points (Mitra,

---

[2]The discussion on statistics draws from Boslaugh and Watters (2008), Mitra (1993), Ott and Schilling (1990), and Dodge (2006). I am grateful for feedback from Dick Janzig and Kent Rissman on the use of specific terms.

[3]Technically, the term *average* refers to the set of measures of central tendency (Salkind, 2011; Dodge, 2006). Practically, *average* and *mean* are synonyms. I will use the term *mean* in this discussion, except when I describe average amount as part of the individual measurements that can be taken on amount fields. I choose to use *average amount* to distinguish from *mean*, as I hope will be clear in the detailed definitions included later in the chapter.

1990). Statisticians look at the standard deviation as a measure of variance because it can be related to the distribution of data. Most of us are familiar with standard deviation because of its role in the bell curve. Roughly 68% of data fall within one standard deviation, 95% is within two standard deviations, and 99.7% is within three standard deviations of the mean on a bell curve (see Figure 14.2).

Understanding both the central tendency and the variation in a dataset is necessary to interpret data quality measurement results. Two datasets can have the same mean but have different ranges and different deviations from the mean, as is illustrated in Table 14.2. New values added to each set need to be assessed within the context of that set. Figures 14.3 and 14.4 illustrate the impact of the measures of dispersion on our understanding of the numbers.

Knowledge of the basic concepts of these measures of central tendency and variation helps in identifying outliers. Unfortunately, there is not an agreed-to definition of *outlier*. Conceptually, *outliers* are data points with values recognizably different from others in the dataset being analyzed. They may imply a different pattern, appear to come from a different population, or represent an error (Boslaugh & Watters, 2008).

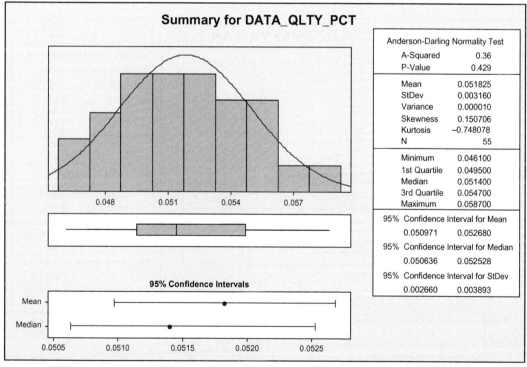

FIGURE 14.2 Summary Statistics for a Data Quality Metric

The figure, produced by the software package Minitab, includes summary statistics for a data quality measurement. The chart depicts a bell curve from the results. It is not completely symmetrical. I have defined only a few basics (the mean, standard deviation, and variance). Minitab generates a range of detail which you may want to take advantage of in analyzing your results.

Table 14.2 Value Sets with the Same Mean but Different Standard Deviations

Value Set 1	Value Set 2
12	20
12	23
14	23
14	25
15	25
15	25
16	27
44	31
50	32
74	35
Total = 266	Total = 266
Mean = 26.6	Mean = 26.6
Range = 62 (74–12)	Range = 15 (35–20)
Standard Deviation = 21.7	Standard Deviation = 4.8
Variance = 469	Variance = 21.8

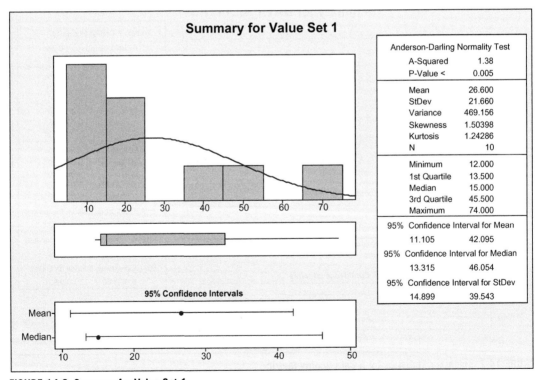

FIGURE 14.3 Summary for Value Set 1

The mean of the values in set 1 is 26.6. But the set has a range of 62 and a standard deviation of 21.7. So, while its measures of central tendency make it look similar to value set 2, its measures of dispersion are quite different.

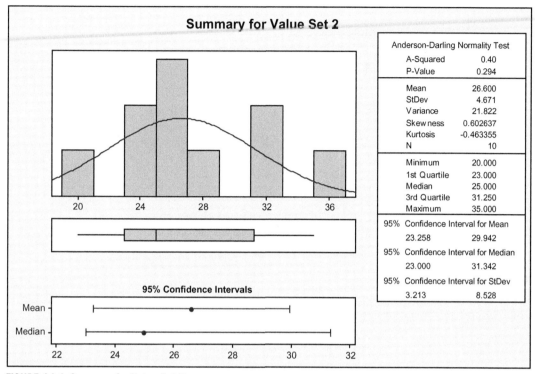

FIGURE 14.4 Summary for Value Set 2

The mean of the values in set 2 is the same as in set 1, 26.6. But set 2 has a much narrower range (15 as opposed to 62) and a smaller standard deviation (4.8 as opposed to 21.7) and variance (21.8 as opposed to 469). While measures of central tendency are similar between the two sets, measures of dispersion differ greatly.

The Control Chart: A Primary Tool for Statistical Process Control

Statistical process control (SPC), a method for measuring the consistency and helping ensure the predictability of manufacturing processes, was pioneered by Walter Shewhart in the first half of the twentieth century. A primary tool for SPC is the control chart, a time series plot or run chart that includes a representation of the mean of the measurements and of the upper and lower control limits (three standard deviations from the mean of the measurements). (See Figure 14.5 Sample Control Chart.) One of the biggest benefits of the control chart is its visual nature. From the chart, one can see the range of measurements (the difference between the maximum and minimum Y values) as well as the consistency of the measurements (how much up and down there is between the measurements and across the set) to gain an understanding of the stability of the overall process.

Shewhart used control charts to measure levels of product defects. From his analysis he discerned that two kinds of variation contributed to differences in the degree to which products

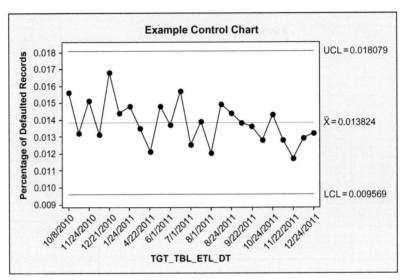

FIGURE 14.5 Sample Control Chart

The figure shows results from a process that is stable (in statistical control). All the measurement points are within the upper and lower control limits (UCL and LCL on the chart) around the mean.

conformed to specification: normal or common cause variation that is inherent in the process; and special cause or assignable variation that is the result of elements outside the process. Process measurement aims first to detect and remediate the root causes of special cause variation. Once a process is stable and predictable, efforts to improve it are directed at reducing the effects of common cause variation.

For a process that is in statistical control (special cause variation has been eliminated), 99.7% of all measurements fall within the upper and lower control limits (because 99.7% of all measurements should be within three standard deviations from the mean of the set of measurements). The question of whether a process is statistically under control is separate from the question of whether the end product of the process meets requirements. A process can be under control (exhibiting only common cause variation), but the quality of the end product still might not meet customer expectations.

The DQAF and Statistical Process Control

As discussed in Section Five, most approaches to data quality improvement start with a comparison between the production of data and the production of manufactured goods and recognize the value of treating data like a product. Much thinking about data quality is directly rooted in methods for process quality. Statistical process control methods have been successfully applied to the measurement of data quality both for initial analysis which identifies special causes and for ongoing measurement to confirm whether a process remains in control.[4] The DQAF draws directly on this body of work, especially for its approach to automating measurement.

The third basic step in making quality measurements meaningful is to explicitly compare any new measurement to a standard for quality. The DQAF describes how to collect the raw data of measurement (record counts, amounts, etc.) and how to process this data to make it comprehensible and meaningful through the calculation of percentages, ratios, and averages. Most measurement types compare new measurements to the history of past measurements. These comparisons include:

- Comparison to the historical mean percentage of row counts.
- Comparison to the historical mean total amount.
- Comparison to the historical percentage of total amount.
- Comparison to the historical average amount.
- Comparison to the historical median duration.

Comparisons to historical data can be used to measure the consistency of data content for processes where content is expected to be consistent. For example, tests of reasonability based on the distribution of values can be automated to identify instances where changes in distribution fall outside of three standard deviations from the mean of past measurements. These comparisons can identify changes in data distribution that are statistically unusual (those that are outside of the 99.7% of all measurements). Not every measurement that falls outside of three standard deviations from the mean of past measurements represents a problem. Such measurements point to data that needs to be reviewed. Because thresholds based on three standard deviations from the mean of past measurements provide a test for potential problems, historical data can be used as the basis for automation of an initial level for data quality thresholds. Keep in mind that there is risk involved in using historical data as the standard. For this data to provide an effective standard, the data must come from a process that is both under control (stable, not influenced by special causes) and meeting expectations. If it does not meet both of these conditions, then it can be used to gauge consistency, but review of results requires significant skepticism (in the pure sense of that word, "doubt and questioning").

Concluding Thoughts

One of the goals of the DQAF is to describe in-line measures—those taken as part of data processing, especially processes that prepare data to be loaded to a database. In-line measures enable measurement of large amounts of complex data in an automated manner. To effectively monitor data quality, they need to be designed to detect unexpected conditions or unexpected changes to data. Guidance for what is unexpected comes from the fundamentals of statistical process control.

An understanding of basic statistical concepts is needed to see how the DQAF measurement types work and how to apply them to particular data. Fortunately, most tools for managing large data stores include software that can execute the calculations themselves. Measurement types that are based on distribution of values (these include most of the consistency measurement types) rely largely on

---

[4]My initial exposure to the concept of applying SPC to data quality measurement comes from Redman (2001). Loshin's description of SPC for data quality (2011, pp. 99–113) is the clearest, most succinct I have read.

comparisons to the historical mean. Such measures are based on an assumption about consistency of content. If this assumption is not reasonable (if there are good reasons to expect content to be inconsistent), then the measurement type will not produce useful results. If the assumption is reasonable, then historical measurements can surface unusual individual measurement results and increase the chances of discovering potential problems.

Knowledge of the options can help you make better choices. For example, because it is less influenced by extremes, the median may be more effective than the mean for measuring file sizes and process duration. If you have an understanding of your data and the processes that manage it, assumptions about the best options can be tested before measurements are implemented.

Ultimately, the goal of implementing data quality measurement within an organization is to ensure that the organization knows the quality of its data and can take actions to improve and maintain data quality. To achieve these goals requires that you understand measurements of specific data (the data critical to your organization) in relation to the processes that comprise the data chain within your organization. It is said that statistics is as much art as it is science. Because measurements must be interpreted, it important to understand how they are generated and what their limitations are.

Features of the DQAF
Measurement Logical Model

15

Purpose

This chapter describes features in the DQAF measurement logical data model (LDM) that are common to many of the measurement types. It provides general information related to the structure of tables that define specific measurements and store measurement results. The logical models for the individual measurement types are presented in the next chapter, which contains the details of the framework.

This chapter discusses optional fields that might be included in these tables and describes additional features of a system to automate in-line data quality measurement. One goal in presenting these first is to answer some general questions in one place. The chapter provides relatively dense, technically oriented material. It should be read in conjunction with Chapters 14 and 16.

Metric Definition and Measurement Result Tables

With a few exceptions noted in the text, the in-line measurement type logical models include two kinds of tables:

* Metric Definition tables in which to store the definition of specific metrics to be taken using the type. Metrics define the particular data that is being measured and what is being measured about it. In this sense, they function as reference tables. Most measurement types can be understood as asking a question. Metric Definition table structure (the columns) contains the basic pieces needed to ask the generic question. The individual rows contain the specific detail with which to construct an SQL query to ask the question of a database.
* Measurement Results tables that house the measurements taken. Measurement results record individual instances of measurements of particular data. In this sense, they are the "fact" tables of the measurement process. The rows contain the answers to the questions asked by the dimension table. Results tables are structured based on the requirements of the measurement type.

Included here are two samples. Tables 15.1 and 15.2 are Metric Definition and Measurement Results table for Measurement Type #6, Timely Delivery of Data for Processing. Each contains standard fields required for most measurement types and additional fields particular to Type #6.

Depending on the design of the system in which they are implemented, building DQAF components may also require other tables. For example, for measures that include comparisons to the historical mean or historical median, it makes sense to build tables to store these details. In many instances, it will also be helpful to create tables through which results can be annotated. Tables supporting this kind of additional functionality are not included in the models presented with the LDM.

Table 15.1 Metric Definition Table for Timely Delivery of Data for Processing (Measurement Type #6)	
Attribute Name	**Attribute Definition**
Measurement Type Number	This field identifies the DQAF measurement type. Measurement type influences rules for defining specific metrics and defines how results will be captured and calculated.
Specific Metric Number	This field contains a unique number that serves as a key between the definition table that houses the specific metric and results table that captures individual instances of measurements of that metric.
Dataset Name	This field contains the name of the dataset being measured. The name will usually be a target table, but it may also be a file. For process measures, the job name may be used.
Dataset Source	This field contains the name of the source system from which the warehouse received the data, or it indicates that the data originates within the warehouse itself.
Dataset Type	This field refers to the form the dataset takes. For example, a dataset can be a file, a set of messages, or a table. Some measurement types apply to only one type of dataset, and measurements may be taken differently depending on the type of dataset being measured.
Range Minimum	For any measurement based on a range of values, this field represents the lowest value in that range. For data delivery measurement, it represents the earliest time at which scheduled data is expected to arrive. For dates, it represents the earliest date considered valid for the data. For numeric values, it represents the lowest number in the range. Ranges are not usually used for alphabetic values, but they can be expressed as AAA-ZZZ. In the case measurement type #6, this field contains the earliest expected delivery time for scheduled data.
Range Maximum	For any measurement based on a range of values, this field represents the highest value in that range. For data delivery measurement, it represents the latest time at which scheduled data is expected to arrive. For dates, it represents the latest (most recent) date considered valid for the data. For numeric values, it represents the highest number in the range. Ranges are not usually used for alphabetic values, but they can be expressed as AAA-ZZZ. In the case of measurement type #6, this field contains the latest expected delivery time for scheduled data.
Data Quality Threshold Type	A data quality threshold is a numeric representation of the acceptable limit of a measurement. Thresholds may be established in several different ways. For example, for measurements that return only one row of results data, they may be set manually. They may also be automated based on a calculation of a measure of statistical variation, such as the historical mean, median, or average. The working standard for DQAF thresholds is three standard deviations from the historical measure of variation. Valid values for Data Quality Threshold Type are: manual, automated based on mean, automated based on median, automated based on average.
Data Quality Threshold (if threshold is set manually)	This field contains the data quality threshold number for thresholds that are set manually. This field is populated only if the type is manual.

The tables in the model are described at the logical level. Logical data models include both entities (tables) and attributes (fields) needed to represent concepts and characteristics of concepts.

Some systems and some data content may require additional attributes. For example, in health care data, attributes that can be used to individually identify a person (such as name, birth date, and

Table 15.2 Measurement Results Table for Timely Delivery of Data for Processing

Attribute Name	Attribute Definition
Measurement Type Number	This field identifies the DQAF measurement type. Measurement type influences rules for defining specific metrics and defines how results will be captured and calculated.
Specific Metric Number	This field contains a unique number that serves as a key between the definition table that houses the specific metric and results table that captures individual instances of measurements of that metric.
Measurement Date	Date the measurement is taken.
Dataset Arrival Time	This field records the actual time that data is made available for access.
Difference from Expected Delivery Time	This field records the difference between the range minimum for data delivery and dataset arrival time.
Threshold exceeded indicator	This field records whether or not a specific measurement has been greater than the established data quality threshold. Y = Yes, the threshold was exceeded. N = No, the threshold was not exceeded. The different types of threshold indicators are based on which threshold is being evaluated. Some measurement types include more than one threshold check.
Notification Sent Indicator	This field captures data about the measurements for which notifications have been sent. Y = a notification was sent. N = a notification was not sent.

Social Security Number) are considered personal health information (PHI) require a special level of protection. If you are measuring the quality of health-related data, you may need to identify which fields contain PHI and ensure that they are properly secured. This identification can be accomplished through the Metric Definition table for the type of measurement you are taking.

The purpose of a logical data model is to define data relationships. An LDM cannot be implemented without additional work. Some naming conventions are adopted here in order to show the similarities between attributes used in taking measurements. For example, in tables that define measurements of particular fields, the term *Target Column* refers to any field whose contents are being measured. When multiple fields are included in a measurement, they are named sequentially: Target Column 1, Target Column 2, Target Column N. In some cases, attribute names are relatively long and descriptive rather than generic. These are included in order to help people understand what is being represented. A data modeler might choose to further normalize these relationships. This model is a sketch, not an oil painting.

Common Key Fields

A set of fields in the model will appear on almost all Metric Definition tables. These include:

- Measurement Type Number—Identifies the DQAF measurement type. Measurement type influences rules for defining specific metrics and defines how results will be captured and calculated.

- Specific Metric Number—A unique number that serves as a key between the definition table that houses the specific metric and results table that captures individual instances of measurements of that metric.
- Dataset Name—Identifies the dataset being measured. The name will usually be a target table, but it may also be a file. For process measures, the job name may be used.
- Dataset Source—Contains the name of the source system from which the warehouse received the data or indicates that the data originates within the warehouse itself.
- Dataset Type—Refers to the form the dataset takes. For example, a dataset can be a file, a set of messages, or a table. Some measurement types apply to only one type of dataset, and measurements may be taken differently depending on the type of dataset being measured.

These are key fields (needed to define a unique row) in nearly all Metric Definition tables. Because they are critical to structure, they are referenced in representations of the logical model. In some systems, it may be possible to replace them with a similar field. For example, a Dataset Number could replace the Dataset Name.

Similarly, nearly all Measurement Results tables include the following fields:

- Measurement Type Number
- Specific Metric Number
- Measurement Date

Optional Fields

The tables presented include all attributes essential to taking the measurements. Additional attributes may be desirable, but do not pertain to all measurement types or to all implementations. For example, each Metric Definition table can include any of the following set of attributes:

- Metric Name—Provides a name that enables people to understand what data is being measured.
- Metric Description—Provides additional information needed to understand what data is being measured.
- Metric Criticality—Records a level of criticality for the metric; for example, high, medium, low.
- Business Contact/Steward—Provides the name of a businessperson who needs to be informed if the metric generates an unusual result.
- Date the measurement was established—Records the Effective Date or Start Date for the metric.
- Date the measurement was made inactive—Records the End Date or Expiration Date for the metric.
- Active Indicator—Shows whether the metric is active; prevents the collection of additional results if there is a need to turn the metric off.
- Frequency at which measurement should be executed—Describes how often the metric should be run. While in-line measurements are intended to be executed with each ETL process, periodic measurements can be based on another schedule, such as monthly, quarterly, or annually.
- Notification indicator—Records whether a notification should be sent if a metric produces an unusual result. Ideally, notifications should be automated. If they cannot be, this field still records the fact that action is required when a metric produces an unusual result.
- Notification contact person—Records the name of the person who should be contacted if the measurement produces an unusual result. Ideally, notifications should be automated. However, if they are not, it is also helpful to have a contact name as part of the metadata for the metric.

- Notification contact information—For automated notifications, the contact information is likely to be an e-mail address. For non-automated notifications, this field is likely to contain a phone number.

While these fields are not part of the key structure, they contain metadata that can be useful in understanding and managing the specific metrics. These attributes are not included on the Metric Definition tables described in the next chapter for two reasons: First, because including them would create unnecessary redundancy in the text; and second, because some implementations may choose not to include them. For example, if the only metrics that are implemented are critical, then there is no need to include Metric Criticality for each one. Or if business stewards are assigned at the data domain level, then it is not necessary to assign an individual steward to each specific metric. The way that metrics are constructed (based on type) and associated with columns that will be measured may preclude the necessity of naming or describing them.

Denominator Fields

In their simplest forms, many of the measurement types that create a distribution of values use record counts as the denominator in calculations of percentages of row counts. Counts of records associated with individual values serve as the numerators. Similarly, those that measure the consistency of amount field data use the calculation of total amount for a column as the denominator for percentage calculations and the amount associated with a value in a secondary field as the numerator.

While basic distributions of values can confirm the consistency of the data with each incremental load of a database, they do not often serve as a means of measuring business rules. When qualifications or filters are added to queries collecting the measurement data, measurements can be refined to focus on specific aspects of business rules to produce measurement results that are more useful in confirming expectations or identifying problems. In some cases, additional refinement is needed to ensure that results are at the appropriate level of grain. Such refinement can be achieved by designating fields to serve as the denominator for percentage calculations.

The ability to refine the construction of the denominator is especially important for tables fed by multiple sources. Take, for example, a table that includes data from two sources that have different rules for the population of a specific field. For the first source, the field is mandatory; for the second it is optional. A distribution of values that does not account for this difference may result in distorted results. Tables 15.3, 15.4, and 15.5 provide an illustration of a situation where an additional attribute needs to serve as the denominator in analysis of a distribution of values. They also illustrate the value of using percentage calculations to make measurement results comprehensible. Simply looking at the data (yes, the counts are from an actual query) reveals how challenging it is to detect the differences in proportion because the numbers are so large.

Table 15.3 contains data from a simple distribution of values in a single field. It does not account for differences in the way individual sources populate the field. The value 999 appears to be a default. It is numeric while other values are expressed in characters. It also accounts for almost three quarters of the data when the total record set is used as the denominator for percentage calculations.

Table 15.4 includes a source system code that enables an understanding of the different ways the field is populated. Records from Sources 1 and 2 are populated with the default value, 999. To assess quality, research should confirm whether or not this condition is expected. If it is, measurement should focus on distribution related only to Source 3. Records related to other sources should not be part of the distribution, and percentages should be recalculated based on the total number of records associated with Source 3.

Table 15.3 Distribution of Values

Value	Count	Percentage
999	27841906	74%
ABC	126759	0%
DEF	1492674	4%
HIJ	1388023	4%
KLM	724408	2%
NOM	806392	2%
PQR	778572	2%
STU	4220971	11%
TOTAL	37379705	

Table 15.4 Distribution of Values Including Source System Signifier

Value	Count	Source System Code	Percentage
999	2907062	Source 1	8%
999	24934844	Source 2	67%
ABC	126759	Source 3	0%
DEF	1492674	Source 3	4%
HIJ	1388023	Source 3	4%
KLM	724408	Source 3	2%
NOM	806392	Source 3	2%
PQR	778572	Source 3	2%
STU	4220971	Source 3	11%
TOTAL	37379705		

Table 15.5 Distribution of Values for One Source

Value	Count	Source	Percentage
ABC	126759	Source 3	1%
DEF	1492674	Source 3	16%
HIJ	1388023	Source 3	15%
KLM	724408	Source 3	8%
NOM	806392	Source 3	8%
PQR	778572	Source 3	8%
STU	4220971	Source 3	44%
TOTAL	9537799		

Table 15.5 contains results from the focused metric. The total number of records associated with Source 3 provides the denominator for percentage calculations. These calculations enable analysts to see the relative proportion of each value in the set for the source. Determining whether these are reasonable is the next step. That analysis requires knowledge of the concepts and processes represented by the data.

A more complex example would be a table with multiple sources that provide significantly different proportions of data. Say a table with 10 sources, one of which supplies 80% of the data. Unless there is a means of separating measurement results by source, there is a high risk that results from the source that supplies 80% of the data will mask changes in the sources that supply the other 20%. As importantly, data from those sources might also be an obstacle to understanding results from the larger source.

As has been emphasized throughout successful measurement depends on understanding what you are measuring and why. The flexibility to designate a denominator field or fields is important for this simple reason: If you are measuring two different things at the same time, such as the population of one field by two different sources with two different rules, then you are not actually measuring either one of them. For many organizations implementing in-line data quality measurement, it will be necessary to build in the flexibility of designating a field or set of fields to refine the denominator for measurement of some business rules. Achieving this level of refinement requires including table fields in the Metric Definition for this purpose.

Incorporating this flexibility into the model can be done in at least two ways: either by having fields called Target Denominator 1, Target Denominator 2, and so on; or by associating an indicator with Target Column fields (so, Target Column 1 Denominator Indicator), where a Yes shows that the field should be used as a denominator and a No indicates it should not be.

Automated Thresholds

A *data quality threshold* is a numeric representation of the acceptable limit of a measurement. Most of the DQAF measurement types assume the use of automated thresholds. Measurement Results tables include threshold exceeded indicators and notification sent indicators. As described in Chapter 14, it is possible to automate the establishment of thresholds based on the calculation of three standard deviations from the mean or median of past measurements. This kind of automated threshold will identify unusual measurement results—those that are outside of the 99.7% of measurements that would be within three standard deviations of the mean for a stable process.

Automating the calculation of thresholds may seem risky or counterintuitive. If thresholds are automated, how does one know if they mask a problem or a change? Shouldn't data consumers make a decision about what threshold is appropriate, rather than have the threshold generated through calculation?

There are at least two reasons for automating thresholds. First, having one threshold defined at the level of the metric would be inappropriate for many of the measurement types. Many of the measurements return a distribution of values; this means they return more than one row of data. A single threshold will not be applicable to all the rows returned. Second, if you are investing time and energy to automate the measurement of data quality, chances are you have a lot of data to measure. To the degree that you can automate the identification of anomalies, you will be more successful in benefiting from the measurement results.

Thresholds often measure what is incorrect about the data. For example, if there is a business expectation that a field will be populated 100% of the time, measurement can determine which percentage of records are not populated. Distributions of values work differently. They answer the question: What percentage of records is associated with each value? Comparisons between iterative distributions can then determine whether what the data looks like has changed. They answer the question: What is the difference between the percentage of records in this update to the database and the percentage in previous updates?

Automated thresholds can be applied both to metrics that return only one row of data, such as a row that measures the level of incorrect records, and to those metrics that return multiple rows. In either case, their purpose is to detect changes in the data. The math determines whether those changes are large or small. An analyst must determine whether they reflect and improvement in or deterioration of the quality of data.

The key to using thresholds of any kind is to recognize them for what they are: little red flags telling you that a measurement result is different from past measurement results and therefore needs to be looked at by a human being. Thresholds identify statistically unusual situations; they do not solve problems. Problems are solved by people who can understand measurement results and perform root cause analysis to determine whether or not they have a data quality problem.

In order to calculate statistical thresholds based on past data, you may need to design your implementation so that it includes additional tables from which calculations can be made or in which the results from such calculations can be stored.

Manual Thresholds

Despite the option for automating the calculation of quality thresholds, some of the Metric Definition tables include a field called "Data Quality Threshold (if threshold is set manually)." This field applies in situations that meet specific conditions. The first condition is that the result set for a metric will consist of one row. Measuring the level of defaulted data in a particular field, or measuring a condition, such as a level of unexpected birth dates will return one row of data. Second, this field applies when the automated threshold is not fine enough—that is, when the business-acceptable level of data quality is outside of three standard deviations from the mean of past measurements.

Emergency Thresholds

Another set of attributes can be added to Metric Definition tables where appropriate. These are emergency thresholds that may be put in place to stop data processing if they are crossed. They are not included in the representation of the logical model in the next chapter because many implementations will choose not to include them and because the model sketched there is intended to be an understandable beginning point (rather than a specification) for anyone choosing to implement component pieces of the DQAF.

Here is how such a feature works. The purpose of an emergency threshold is to prevent data from being loaded to a database, when a measurement result shows that the data is clearly wrong. As with a manual threshold, an emergency threshold can be applied to specific metrics that will return only one row in their result set. An example will help illustrate. Say you are measuring the level of defaulted data in a critical field populated through a derivation. The business rule states that the field should always be populated with a valid result (100% population). However, experience shows that if input data is missing, the field will not populate fully. If business conditions tolerate a small portion of defaulted data, the programming logic can include an "else" clause to cover the contingency of processing data despite some missing input. Past history has shown that the mean level of defaulted data is 0.5% (the mean population of the field is 99.5%). The statistical threshold for defaults would be set at 0.5% +/− three standard deviations from the mean of past measurements. If three standard deviations amount to 0.25%, then the statistically established threshold would be 0.75%. If this threshold were exceeded—if more than 0.75% of records defaulted—a notification would be sent so that the data could be investigated.

Half a percentage is a small portion of data. If the process being measured is stable and if the data is critical, an emergency threshold could be set at a significantly higher percentage of defaulted records, say 5% or even 10% (10 and 20 times the mean). If this threshold were exceeded, then data processing would stop, preventing data from being loaded to the database.

In order to incorporate emergency thresholds into Metric Definition tables, the following logical fields would be required:

- Emergency Threshold Indicator—Indicates whether or not emergency threshold functionality should be invoked for a specific metric. Y = it should be invoked. N = it should not be invoked.
- Emergency Threshold Percentage—Contains a percentage of records that must meet the condition of the metric which, if reached, should bring a technical process to a stop.

Manual or Emergency Thresholds and Results Tables

If a manual threshold is part of the Metric Definition, then Measurement Results tables need to account for actions based on these thresholds. In addition to recording the result that exceeded the threshold, the tables should also include two fields that are noted on the representations of the logical model in the next chapter. They are:

- Threshold Exceeded Indicator.
- Notification Sent Indicator.

  If an emergency threshold is also included, then additional fields will be required.

- Emergency Threshold Exceeded Indicator.
- Emergency Notification Sent Indicator.

Additional System Requirements

The primary functionality of the DQAF in-line measurements includes collecting measurement data, processing that data to make it understandable, and comparing these results to previous measurements to draw conclusions about the degree of change in the data. Results must be stored in database tables that can be queried.

Enabling the use of such a measurement system has additional requirements. For example:

- The system may include ancillary tables required for the calculations.
- The system may include tables for management of outliers. These tables may be the same as those used for calculations. They would include functionality to identify outliers so that these can be removed from future calculations.

- The system must include functionality to manage content in the Metric Definition tables. Establishing the metrics may be a one-time event, but maintaining contact data, and, where applicable, managing manual and emergency threshold information require a means for business-oriented staff to update the tables.
- The system may include auxiliary tables that enable tracking any findings associated with measurement results and functionality to manage the content of these tables.
- The system must be able to generate notifications when thresholds are exceeded.

Support Requirements

The assertions made here about support requirements are very similar for all the measurement types. They include the following:

- Staff in the target system must be in place to respond to alerts that a threshold has been exceeded.
- Staff must be able to perform analysis of records to detect any patterns that might indicate a problem or an unexpected condition.
- Source system staff must also be available to contribute to analysis.

These assertions amount to one thing: The ability to measure does not solve problems. People solve problems. Unless there are people in place to analyze and act on measurement results, the organization will not benefit from them.

Concluding Thoughts

This chapter has presented a set of considerations for the implementation of a system based on the measurement types described in the DQAF. These are presented before the detail of the framework so that a set of obvious questions are answered ahead of time. Once you have read through the details and determined how to approach your organization's measurement needs, it will be helpful to return to this chapter and review its implications for your approach.

Facets of the DQAF Measurement Types

16

"The progress of science requires the growth of understanding in both directions, downward from the whole to the parts and upward from the parts to the whole."
—**Freeman Dyson, English-born American Physicist (1995)**

Purpose

The purpose of this chapter is to describe each of the DQAF's 48 measurement types in relation to the six facets of the DQAF: definition, business concerns, measurement methodology, programming, support processes and skills, and the measurement logical data model (See Figure 16.1). The LDM is fully detailed on the companion web site.

Facets of the DQAF

Each definition section includes the measurement type's name, description, dimension of quality, and cross references to other measurement types. The definition also associates each type with an assessment category and with an object of measurement. These two groupings provide a means, in addition to the dimensions of quality, of understanding similarities between measurement types. *Assessment categories* pertain to both the frequency of the measurement (periodic or in-line) and the type of assessment involved (control, measurement, assessment). Assessment categories include initial assessment, process controls, in-line measurement, and periodic measurement. *Objects of measurement* categorize the measurement types in terms of whether they focus process or content, or on a particular part of a process (e.g., receipt of data) or kind of content (e.g., amount fields, the data model). Objects of measurement include the data model, receipt of data, condition of data upon receipt, data processing, content/row counts, content/amount fields, content/date content, content/aggregated date, content summary, cross-table content, cross-table content/aggregated date, cross-table content/amount fields, content/chronology/cross-table, and overall database content.

The business concerns describe why a measurement type is important, the risks it addresses, the benefits it provides, and the situations in which it can be used. While the definitional information describes what the measurement types are, the business concerns explain the purposes they serve. Since many types are variations on a theme, the business concerns will be fully discussed in relation to the basic type and simply referenced in descriptions of the more complex types.

The type's measurement methodology describes how the measurement will be taken, what data needs to be collected, and what calculations and comparisons are required to detect changes and make results meaningful. (Refer to Chapter 14 for additional information.)

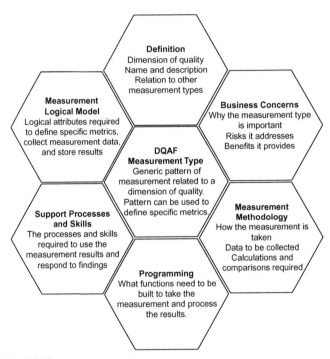

Figure 16.1 Facets of the DQAF

Each measurement type is defined by six facets: definition, business concerns, measurement methodology, engineering and programming, support processes and skills, and measurement logical data model.

The programming sections describe the functions that need to be built to take the measurement and to process the results. These functions are based on the measurement methodology, but they provide a greater level of detail. Common functions and calculations have been described in Chapter 14. This chapter will make general assertions about the programming needed for measurement types for which data collection can be automated.

The support processes and skills section describes how to use the measurement results and respond to findings. These skills are very similar. The basic requirement is to have knowledgeable people in place from both the target data store and the source systems to respond to findings. In some cases, there are more particular assertions about responses. Each organization will also need to establish specific response protocols for critical data. These may be general approaches, such as which documentation to review or what analysis to perform first when looking for root causes. They may also include very specific instructions, such as notifications to particular individuals. Response protocols should be built out over time as more knowledge is gained about the data.

The measurement logical model describes the logical attributes required to define specific metrics, collect measurement data, and store results. Common features of the measurement models have been described in Chapter 15. The present chapter will include table and attribute descriptions for in-line and other measurement types for which data collection can be automated, so that a model can be built for metric definitions and measurement results. (Only in-line measurement types and a subset of periodic measurement types will include a measurement logical model.) The measurement logical data model should not be confused with the target data store model.

Organization of the Chapter

Because the DQAF contains a complex set of information, several options are available for organizing it—for example, by the dimensions of quality, the objects of measurement, and the assessment categories. The order of the measurement types as finalized in the framework is governed by two factors: chronology and increasing complexity. The first measurement types (1–5) focus on the data environment, data model, and standards related to data structure. The next set (6–18) focuses on the receipt of data and the condition of data as it is received from a source system by a target data store. These are followed by types that focus largely on data processing (19–22, 24–26). The majority of the remaining measurement types focus on data content. These are organized in terms of the type of content they address and the way they measure: simple row counts (27, 29, 30, 33) amount fields, including aggregated amounts (23, 36, 44), date content, including aggregated dates and chronological rules (34, 35, 37, 38, 43), and combinations of these concepts (45). The last set focuses on the overall database content and the data environment (46–48). (The system is not perfect, but it does try to be comprehensive within defined limits.) Table 16.1, DQAF Cross Reference, summarizes the measurement types and the relationships between them. As noted in the introduction to Section Six, one goal of the framework is to allow each type to be understood independently. So, in some of the descriptions that follow, similar information is repeated for similar measurement types.

Table 16.1 DQAF Cross Reference

Number	Measurement Type	Object of Measurement	Assessment Category	Cross Reference
1	Dataset completeness—sufficiency of meta and reference data	Data environment	Initial assessment	Potentially all
2	Consistent formatting in one field	Data model	Initial assessment	1, 3
3	Consistent formatting cross-table	Data model	Initial assessment	1, 2
4	Consistent use of default value in one field	Data model	Initial assessment	1, 2, 3, 5, 15, 23
5	Consistent use of default values, cross-table	Data model	Initial assessment	1, 2, 3, 4, 15
6	Timely delivery of data for processing	Process/Adherence to schedule	In-line measurement	7, 25, 26
7	Dataset completeness—availability for processing	Receipt of data	Process control	6, 10
8	Dataset completeness—record counts to control record	Receipt of data	Process control	7, 9, 10
9	Dataset completeness— summarized amount field data	Receipt of data	Process control	7, 8
10	Dataset completeness—size compared to past sizes	Receipt of data	In-line measurement	7, 8

(Continued)

Table 16.1 DQAF Cross Reference   (*Continued*)

Number	Measurement Type	Object of Measurement	Assessment Category	Cross Reference
11	Record completeness—length	Condition of data upon receipt	Process control	1, 12
12	Field completeness—non-nullable fields	Condition of data upon receipt	Process control	1, 11
13	Dataset integrity—de-duping	Condition of data upon receipt	Process control	1, 14, 19
14	Dataset integrity—duplicate record reasonability check	Condition of data upon receipt	In-line measurement	1, 13, 19
15	Field content completeness—defaults from source	Condition of data upon receipt	In-line measurement	1, 4, 5, 33
16	Dataset completeness based on date criteria	Condition of data upon receipt	Process control	1, 17
17	Dataset reasonability based on date criteria	Condition of data upon receipt	In-line measurement	1, 16
18	Field content completeness—received data is missing fields critical to processing	Condition of data upon receipt	Process control	1, 11, 12, 14, 20, 30
19	Dataset completeness—balance record counts through a process	Data processing	Process control	8, 21
20	Dataset completeness—reasons for rejecting records	Data processing	In-line measurement	1, 11, 12, 14, 18, 24, 27, 30
21	Dataset completeness through a process—ratio of input to output	Data processing	In-line measurement	8, 19
22	Dataset completeness through a process—balance amount fields	Data processing	Process control	9, 23
23	Field content completeness—ratio of summed amount fields	Content/Amount fields	In-line measurement	9, 22
24	Field content completeness—defaults from derivation (subtype of #33 multicolumn profile)	Data processing	In-line measurement	1, 15, 33
25	Data processing duration	Data processing	In-line measurement	6, 35
26	Timely availability of data for access	Data Processing	In-line measurement	6, 25
27	Validity check, single field, detailed results	Content/Row counts	In-line measurement	1, 20, 28, 29, 31, 39
28	Validity check, roll-up	Content summary	In-line measurement	1, 27, 29, 30, 41
29	Validity check, multiple columns within a table, detailed results	Content/Row counts	In-line measurement	1, 27, 28, 41

(*Continued*)

Table 16.1 DQAF Cross Reference   (*Continued*)

Number	Measurement Type	Object of Measurement	Assessment Category	Cross Reference
30	Consistent column profile	Content/Row counts	In-line measurement	27
31	Consistent dataset content, distinct count of represented entity, with ratios to record counts	Content summary	In-line measurement	1, 32
32	Consistent dataset content, ratio of distinct counts of two represented entities	Content summary	In-line measurement	1, 31
33	Consistent multicolumn profile	Content/Row counts	In-line measurement	24, 27, 30, 34
34	Chronology consistent with business rules within a table (subtype of #33 multicolumn profile)	Content/date content	In-line measurement	1, 16, 17, 33, 35
35	Consistent time elapsed (hours, days, months, etc.)	Content/Date content	In-line measurement	1, 16, 17, 25, 34
36	Consistent amount field calculations across secondary fields	Content/Amount fields	In-line measurement	1, 23, 33
37	Consistent record counts by aggregated date	Content/Aggregated date	Periodic measurement	30
38	Consistent amount field data by aggregated date	Content/Aggregated date	Periodic measurement	36, 37
39	Parent/child referential integrity	Cross-table content	Periodic measurement	1, 27, 28, 40
40	Child/parent referential integrity	Cross-table content	Periodic measurement	1, 27, 28, 39, 41
41	Validity check, cross-table, detailed results	Cross-table content	Periodic measurement	1, 27, 28, 29
42	Consistent cross-table multicolumn profile	Cross-table content	Periodic measurement	33
43	Chronology consistent with business rules, cross-table	Content/Chronology/ Cross-table	Periodic measurement	34
44	Consistent cross-table amount column calculations	Cross-table content/ Amount fields	Periodic measurement	36
45	Consistent cross-table amounts columns by aggregated dates	Cross-table content/ Aggregated date	Periodic measurement	38
46	Consistency compared to external benchmarks	Overall database content	Periodic measurement	Potentially all
47	Dataset completeness—overall sufficiency for defined purposes	Overall database content	Periodic assessment	Potentially all
48	Dataset completeness—overall sufficiency of measures and controls	Overall database content	Periodic assessment	Potentially all

Measurement Type #1: Dataset Completeness—Sufficiency of Metadata and Reference Data

Definition

Description: Assess the completeness, sufficiency, and quality of metadata and reference data.
Object of Measurement: Data environment
Assessment Category: Initial Assessment (with periodic review)
Cross Reference: Potentially all

Business Concerns

Data is not meaningful without context. In a database, metadata and reference data provide the context needed to support the use of core data. Without business metadata, there is a risk that data can be misunderstood and misused. Basic business metadata includes definitions of entities and attributes represented in a database, along with their valid domains and details about their storage characteristics, such as data type and field length. More complex business metadata can include details about business uses, risks, rules, and limitations. Technical and operational metadata provide information about the structure and operations of an information system, as well as about movement of data within such a system.

Business metadata is necessary input for quality assessments and measurements. An initial assessment of metadata and reference data should be conducted as part of planning for a program of data quality measurement.[1]

Over the life of a database, opportunity costs are associated with insufficient metadata. Redundant data may be stored because people are not aware of what data an organization already possesses and in what form. Data consumers may use data inappropriate to their purpose because they make incorrect assumptions about it. Or different consumers may use different data for the same kind of analysis, generating inconsistent results.

Metadata assessment tests first for existence and completeness (percentage of tables defined, percentage of columns defined; percentage of code fields supported by references data, etc.) and next for the clarity and quality of definitions (clear, comprehensible, unambiguous, grammatically correct, etc.), and consistency of representation (the same field content defined in the same way). Reference data plays a role similar to metadata. It provides context and enables the appropriate and consistent use of core data. It should also be assessed for existence and completeness, as well as for the clarity and quality of definitions.[2] Metadata and reference data should be periodically reassessed to ensure that it is maintained in conjunction with the growth and evolution of the database.

Measurement Methodology

This periodic assessment confirms the existence, completeness, and quality of metadata and reference data. It compares existing metadata and reference data to a set of requirements as defined in the data

---

[1] English (1999), Loshin (2001), Olson (2003), McGilvray (2008).
[2] See Section Three and ISO/IEC 11179-4.

model. It reviews individual definitions for consistency, comprehensibility, level of detail, and accuracy in representing concepts.

Assessing metadata can also include assessing its comprehensiveness. Comprehensiveness is a form of completeness. It refers to how broad the metadata is; for example, in addition to the basic necessities (definitions, domains, data types), metadata can include data lineage, business usage notes, and other details that can better enable use of core data. Part of assessment can include identification of metadata gaps and their impact.

Input for the metadata assessment depends in part on how metadata is managed. If business metadata is stored in a metadata repository, then initial actions related to its quality will be similar to those of other data. It can be profiled for completeness and consistency of population, for example. However, standard profiling will only open the door to metadata assessment, as understanding whether metadata is usable requires review of actual meaning.

Programming

This assessment requires output from a metadata repository, a modeling tool, or a data dictionary in a usable form, such as a spreadsheet or a database that can be queried so that comparisons can be made. But it does not require programming per se.

Support Processes and Skills

Staff need a high degree of business knowledge and access to business SMEs who can confirm definitions and clarify other metadata elements. The process should be executed by individuals with excellent writing and editing skills. The tools that store metadata should enable efficient updates and revisions.

One of the primary goals of metadata management is to document organizational understanding of terms and usage (Mosley, Bracket, Early, Henderson, 2009 [DAMA BOK], p. 260). Metadata management is recognized as a fundamental need for data governance efforts (Mosley, Bracket, Early, Henderson, 2009 [DAMA BOK], p. 42). Failure to capture metadata sufficiently and clearly and to maintain it as the data environment evolves usually means a lot of work needs to be invested in rediscovering business rules and assumptions (Loshin, 2001; Olson, 2003; Maydanchik, 2007).

In order to make decisions about data, it is necessary to know what the data represents and how it is used. The governance process can hardly begin without clarifying terminology. In most organizations, the process of defining terms is continual and itself must operate based on a consensus-driven model. Periodic or ongoing review of metadata can enable other facets of a data quality program, such as the determination of data's criticality (which is needed as input for decisions about how to measure the data) and the prioritization of data quality issues.

Measurement Type #2: Consistent Formatting in One Field
Definition

> **Description**: Assess column properties and data for consistent formatting of data within a field.
> **Object of Measurement**: Data model
> **Assessment Category**: Initial assessment
> **Cross Reference**: 1, 3

Business Concerns

Data consumers rightly expect a degree of consistency within a database—especially regarding details of data presentation, such as how fields are formatted and defaulted. Formatting is a basic component of technical data definition. Inconsistent formatting makes data difficult to use. Setting and enforcing standards for formatting and defaulting can prevent minor inconsistencies that will otherwise diminish confidence in the data. Standards also make life easier for modelers, database administrators, and programmers. If there are clear standards for such details, modelers can focus on the more important work of ensuring that the model is comprehensive and usable and represents business processes and relationships accurately and at a sufficient level of detail.

The format of each field should be defined in the data model. Each column will be defined with a data type that governs its format. But formatting is actually accomplished as part of data processing. Inconsistencies in format result from inconsistent application of rules when integrating data from different sources or different job streams, for example, trimming leading spaces for one source and failing to do so for another.

Precision, a specific kind of formatting, refers to how fine numeric data are—for example, whether they extend to tenths, hundredths, or thousandths. Formatting includes ensuring there is a consistent representation of precision within a field.

Formatting rules should be included within the metadata, so that data consumers are aware of them, especially since format can have a direct effect on queries.

Measurement Methodology

Assessment of formatting consistency should be conducted in conjunction with other column-level assessments. This assessment uses metadata from the model to identify data types and from specifications that define formatting rules. The rules themselves must be inspected for consistency. Then data must be profiled in order for results to be compared to the rules. Where differences are found, inspection of programming code is required to determine where the discrepancies were introduced.

Programming

This assessment can be executed using a profiling tool or through ad hoc queries. Most profiling tools can identify data format patterns, thus simplifying the analysis needed for the assessment.

Support Processes and Skills

Ongoing support requires that standards and definitions of data types are clearly documented and that standards are applied consistently, especially as new data is brought into the data store. Consistent application of standards requires that they be published, systematically enforced, and periodically reviewed so that changes to them are managed. For employees that will need to use and enforce these and other data standards, on-boarding processes should include training on what the standards are and how they are enforced.

Measurement Type #3: Consistent Formatting, Cross-table
Definition

Description: Assess column properties and data for consistent formatting of data within fields of the same type across a database.
Object of Measurement: Data model
Assessment Category: Initial assessment
Cross Reference: 1, 2

Business Concerns

As noted under Measurement Type #2: Consistent Formatting in One Field, formatting is a basic component of data definition that makes data easier to understand and to use. Consistent formatting starts with applying the same format to all columns of the same data type and includes applying the same trimming rules and the same degree of precision to similar fields. Inconsistent formatting of fields representing the same or similar data usually results from the absence of data standards or the inconsistent enforcement of existing standards.

Measurement Methodology

This assessment uses as input the results of Measurement Type #2, metadata from the model, and findings from assessment of the data model to identify differences in how formats are defined. Results should identify gaps in data standards or in the application of those standards.

Programming

This one-time assessment requires column profiling of data to confirm differences. It should be conducted in conjunction with other column profiling assessments. It can be executed using a profiling tool or through ad hoc queries.

Support Processes and Skills

See Measurement Type #2.

Measurement Type #4: Consistent Use of Default Value in One Field
Definition

Description: Assess column properties and data for default value(s) assigned for each field that can be defaulted.
Object of Measurement: Data model
Assessment Category: Initial assessment
Cross Reference: 1, 2, 3, 5, 15, 23

Business Concerns

A field may be defaulted for one of three reasons: A field may not apply for a particular record, the data may not be available, or the data may be recognizably incorrect and a default is assigned to signify this condition. In some systems, one default value may be used to signify all three conditions. In others, different values will be used to signify these different conditions. Some systems will have several functional defaults (e.g., UNKNOWN and Blank or Space could all signify that data is not available). Defaults can convey significant information. But if rules related to their assignment are not enforced, this information can be confusing.

Default values should be clearly identified and defined as such. The fewer specific values used to signify defaults, the easier it is to understand the data. Consistency in defaults serves purposes similar to consistency in formatting. Ideally, each data element should have one-and-only-one default value (for example, all columns that contain ZIP code should have the same default value) and each data type should have one-and-only-one default (all character fields of the same size should have the same default value; all numeric fields of the same size should have the same default value). When there are differences in meaning (e.g., data is missing vs. the field is not applicable to a particular record type), those differences should be clearly defined.

Measurement Methodology

This assessment uses source and target system metadata to identify documented default values. It requires column profiling to detect the presence of more than one functional default value and to determine the level (percentage of total records) of defaulted records. Profiling may also be used to detect business rules associated with the assignment of defaults.

Programming

This one-time assessment can be executed using a profiling tool or through ad hoc queries.

Support Processes and Skills

All default values should be documented so that data consumers know what they are and what they represent. New values may be detected as part of in-line validity measurements or periodic reassessment. While they often appear minor in and of themselves, such changes should be investigated to determine whether they reflect changes in business processes.

Measurement Type #5: Consistent Use of Default Values, Cross-table Definition

Description: Assess column properties and data for consistent default value for fields of the same data type across the database.
Object of Measurement: Data model
Assessment Category: Initial assessment
Cross Reference: 1, 2, 3, 4

Business Concerns

As noted under Measurement Type #4: Consistent Use of Default Value in One Field, because default values convey important information, they should be used consistently within a database. If different default values are used to convey the same information (for example, using both 00000 and 99999 to signify an invalid ZIP code), data consumers may be confused. As importantly, the presence of different defaults creates unnecessary complications for those working with data.

Measurement Methodology

This assessment uses as input the results of Measurement Type #4, metadata from the model, and findings from assessment of the data model to identify differences in how standard defaults are defined. Results should identify gaps in data standards or in the application of those standards.

Programming

This one-time assessment requires column profiling of data to confirm differences. It should be conducted in conjunction with other column-profiling assessments. It can be executed using a profiling tool or through ad hoc queries.

Support Processes and Skills

Differences between default values should be resolved with help from business and source system SMEs. Ideally, the use of standard defaults should be enforced systematically in transactional systems. This assessment can provide feedback to such systems.

Measurement Type #6: Timely Delivery of Data for Processing
Definition

> **Description**: Compare actual time of data delivery to scheduled data delivery.
> **Object of Measurement**: Process/Adherence to schedule. The measurement type intended to assure that a process has the inputs it needs to run on schedule and to identify instances when data is not delivered on time.
> **Assessment Category**: In-line measurement
> **Cross Reference**: 7, 25, 26

Business Concerns

In order for stored data to be used, it must first be delivered to a data storage application for processing. In most organizations, data is obtained from source systems according to a set schedule. Schedules are usually negotiated based on the ability of the source system to send data and the ability of the data store to receive data. If schedules are not maintained and there are dependencies between datasets, then there is a risk that data will not be correctly associated between tables (see Measurement

Type #24). Data timeliness includes not only delivery from a source but also processing within a warehouse or other application (see Measurement Type #25). At the time it is updated, data is expected to contain all the updates available from its originating source per its update schedule. Meeting a schedule for making data available directly affects data consumers' expectations about the reliability of the data store. This perception will often translate to the data itself. If data is not available, data consumers will not trust the data or the data store.

Source systems sometimes do not deliver data on time because they experience problems preparing files or transmitting data. Data processing within a data store can be pulled off schedule by unexpected events. Timely delivery is a sign that the data chain overall is functioning as expected, while not adhering to schedules is a sign that it may not be. The purpose of this measurement type is, first, to determine whether schedules are being met and, second, to detect patterns that can help to ensure that schedules continue to be met. This measurement type can also be used to manage service level agreements with data suppliers.

Measurement Methodology

This in-line measurement records the actual arrival time for a dataset (usually expressed as a time frame as in "the file is expected to arrive between midnight and 1:00 A.M. each Monday"); compares it to scheduled arrival times; and calculates the difference. It can include a comparison of any instance of a measurement to the historical difference between actual and scheduled for that dataset and schedule. Such data can be used for analysis of data delivery patterns.

Measuring how late a file is will not be very useful if the file never arrives. To process data at all, it is necessary to know that an expected file has not yet arrived—especially if its absence prevents jobs from being run on schedule. Measurement Type #7: Dataset Completeness—Availability for Processing describes the need to have a process control in place to ensure that files have arrived.

Programming

As input, the measurement requires metadata describing the scheduled delivery of source data, along with data collected on the actual arrival time and historical data on delivery times. It compares the actual delivery time to the expected delivery time and calculates the difference. It compares the result to the median of past differences and calculates the difference from the median. It calculates whether this difference is more than three standard deviations from the median and sets an indicator.

The result of this calculation can be used to establish an automated threshold based on the difference from the expected delivery times. Or a threshold can be established based on SME recommendations.

Support Processes and Skills

Taking this measure allows for an understanding of data delivery patterns. Staff must have time and ability to assess those patterns and identify changes that indicate risks or problems.

Measurement Logical Data Model

Table 16.2 Metric Definition for Measurement Type #6

Attribute Name	Attribute Definition
Measurement Type Number	This field identifies the DQAF measurement type. Measurement type influences rules for defining specific metrics and defines how results will be captured and calculated.
Specific Metric Number	This field contains a unique number that enables a join between the definition table that houses the specific metric and the results table that captures individual instances of measurements of that metric.
Dataset Name	This field contains the name of the dataset being measured. The name will usually be a target table, but it may also be a file. For process measures, the job name may be used.
Dataset Source	This field contains the name of the source system from which the warehouse received the data, or it indicates that the data originates within the warehouse itself.
Dataset Type	This field refers to the form the dataset takes. For example, a dataset can be a file, a set of messages, or a table. Some measurement types apply to only one type of dataset, and measurements may be taken differently depending on the type of dataset being measured.
Range Minimum	For any measurement based on a range of values, this field represents the lowest value in that range. For data delivery measurement, it represents the earliest time at which scheduled data is expected to arrive. For dates, it represents the earliest date considered valid for the data. For numeric values, it represents the lowest number in the range. Ranges are not usually used for alphabetic values, but they can be expressed as AAA-ZZZ. In the case measurement type #6, this field contains the earliest expected delivery time for scheduled data.
Range Maximum	For any measurement based on a range of values, this field represents the highest value in that range. For data delivery measurement, it represents the latest time at which scheduled data is expected to arrive. For dates, it represents the latest (most recent) date considered valid for the data. For numeric values, it represents the highest number in the range. Ranges are not usually used for alphabetic values, but they can be expressed as AAA-ZZZ. In the case measurement type #6, this field contains the latest expected delivery time for scheduled data.
Data Quality Threshold Type	A data quality threshold is a numeric representation of the acceptable limit of a measurement. Thresholds may be established in several different ways. For measurements that return only one row of results data, they may be set manually, and the definition table must also contain the threshold percentage. They may also be automated based on a calculation of a measure of statistical variation, such as the historical mean, median, or average. The working standard for DQAF thresholds is three standard deviations from the historical measure of variation. Valid values for Data Quality Threshold Type are: manual, automated based on mean, automated based on median, and automated based on average.
Data Quality Threshold (if threshold is set manually)	This field contains the data quality threshold number for thresholds that are set manually. This field is populated only if the type is manual.

Table 16.3 Measurement Results for Measurement Type #6

Attribute Name	Attribute Definition
Measurement Type Number	DQAF measurement type (see #6 Definition table)
Specific Metric Number	Unique key to definition table; enables a join between the definition and results tables. (see #6 Definition)
Measurement Date	Date the measurement is taken
Dataset Arrival Time	This field records the actual time that data is made available for processing.
Difference from expected delivery time	This field records the difference between the range minimum for data delivery and dataset arrival time.
Threshold Exceeded Indicator	This field records whether or not a specific measurement is greater than the established data quality threshold. Y = Yes, the threshold was exceeded. N = No, the threshold was not exceeded. The different types of threshold indicators are based on which threshold has been evaluated. Some measurement types include more than one threshold check. Automated thresholds are calculated at three standard deviations from the mean or median of historical measurements.
Notification Sent Indicator	This field captures data about the measurements for which notifications have been sent. Y = a notification was sent. N = a notification was not sent

Measurement Type #7: Dataset Completeness—Availability for Processing

Definition

Description: For files, confirm all files are available for processing (with version check if possible).
Object of Measurement: Receipt of data
Assessment Category: Process control
Cross Reference: 6, 10

Note

- This control does not require capture of results as many of the other measures do does. But if it is being used to manage the data supply chain or to ensure that service level agreements are enforced, then it will be useful to collect trend information to identify opportunities to improve data delivery.

Business Concerns

Most data processing requires multiple files as input. Unless controls are in place, however, some processes can be executed even if all required data is not available. If files are missing or empty, data may not process completely. Or technical processes may abort, introducing risk to the system.

If technical processes are complete despite not having all the expected data, then incomplete data will be made available to data consumers and they will probably not be aware that it is incomplete. Use of an incomplete set of data can lead to faulty analysis or incorrect conclusions being drawn from the data. When the problem is discovered, in addition to the costs of re-running data, there will be costs related to reworking analysis.

The purpose of this control is to confirm that the target data store has received all the required data from source systems and to prevent further processing if a discrepancy is detected. This control can be put in place for any process that receives datasets. At its simplest it entails confirmation of receipt of one dataset. But it will be most valuable for complex processes involving multiple datasets. Combined with timeliness measures, this measure can be used to help manage the data supply chain by quantifying adherence to service level agreements. It can identify which suppliers deliver data as expected and which do not. If data is extracted, rather than delivered, the controls can be used to confirm that the extraction has produced the expected results.

Measurement Methodology

This process control is intended to assure that a data process has all necessary inputs so as to prevent it from either failing midprocess or producing incomplete results if it finishes despite missing data. It compares data delivered for processing to specifications for data required for processing in order to determine whether or not data processing can move forward. It detects differences, alerts staff to the fact of differences, and prevents data processing from being initiated.

Programming

As input, this control requires metadata naming the files that are expected for the process being measured. It must collect data describing the files received and compare the two sets in order to identify discrepancies. If discrepancies are found, the process must notify staff that data is not available and prevent additional jobs from executing.

Support Processes and Skills

This control depends on having accurate and complete metadata about datasets required and for specific data processing. Staff must be in place to respond to alerts when data is detected as missing.

Measurement Type #8: Dataset Completeness—Record Counts to Control Records
Definition

Description: For files, compare record counts in a file to record counts documented in a control record.
Object of Measurement: Receipt of data
Assessment Category: Process control
Cross Reference: 7, 9, 10

Business Concerns

When data is moved from one system to another, there is a risk that data will be lost in transit and therefore be incomplete. In some cases, there is also a risk that it may be duplicated in transit. The purpose of this control is to confirm that the target data store has received the same number of records that the source system says it has sent and to prevent further processing if a discrepancy is detected.

Measurement Methodology

When a data file is sent from a transactional system to a target data store, it should be accompanied by a control record that identifies how many records it contains. This process control includes counting the number of records actually received and comparing the result to the number documented in the control file.

Programming

This control requires the presence of a control record from a source system, the ability to count records received, and the ability to compare the two numbers. The process must include notifications to staff if the two datasets are not reconciled.

Support Processes and Skills

Staff in the target data store must be in place to respond to alerts when data does not reconcile. Staff must be able to perform analysis of the data chain to identify where records may have been dropped or duplicated. Source system staff must be available to contribute to this analysis in the event that the problem originates in the source system.

Measurement Type #9: Dataset Completeness—Summarized Amount Field Data

Definition

> **Description**: For files, compare summarized data in amount fields to summarized amount provided in a control record.
> **Object of Measurement**: Receipt of data
> **Assessment Category**: Process control
> **Cross Reference**: 7, 8

Business Concerns

As noted under Measurement Type #8: Dataset Completeness—Record Counts to Control Records, when data is moved from one system to another, there is a risk that data will be lost or duplicated in transit. Such conditions can be detected through record counts, or by summarizing columns that contain numeric data such as currency amount fields in financial data. The purpose of this control is to confirm that the target data store has received records representing the same summarized data as the source system says it has sent and to prevent further processing if a discrepancy is detected.

Measurement Methodology

When data files are sent from transactional sources to target data assets, they may be accompanied by a control record that, in addition to record counts, includes summarizes data from critical numeric columns. This number should be compared to the number actually received.

Programming

This control requires the presence of summarized data on control records from a source system, the ability to summarize the data received following the same criteria that the source used, and the ability to compare the two numbers. The process must include notifications to staff if the two datasets are not reconciled.

Support Processes and Skills

See Measurement Type #8.

Measurement Type #10: Dataset Completeness—Size Compared to Past Sizes
Definition

Description: Reasonability check, compare size of input to size of past input for previous runs of the same process; record count for files, number or rate of messages, summarized data, etc.
Object of Measurement: Receipt of data
Assessment Category: In-line measurement
Cross Reference: 7, 8, 9

Business Concerns

Data sent from a source may include all files needed, and each file may reconcile to a control record. Yet the data can still be incomplete if it does not include all the records that would be reasonably expected. For example, if a process that usually receives a million records receives only 100,000 records, it is likely that data is missing. Similarly, if one that usually receives 100,000 records suddenly includes a million, data may have been duplicated or additional data may have been sent.

The purpose of this in-line measurement is to test the reasonability of the size of a dataset by comparing it to the size of past instances of the same dataset. This measurement works for processes where there is an expectation of consistency. It does not work well to detect anomalies where file sizes are expected to vary to a large degree.

Even in those cases where variation is expected, there is value in capturing the raw data related to file size. Those measurement results can provide input for analysis of data delivery patterns that may themselves provide other means of detecting anomalies. For example, while incremental updates are not expected to be consistent, patterns discernible over the course of a year may be used to analyze reasonability.

Measurement Methodology

This measurement type compares the size of an individual dataset to past instances of the same dataset in order to detect significant differences in size. How a dataset is measured depends on its delivery mechanism. For example, file size can be measured in record counts, whereas messages can be measured based on the rate at which they are received.

The measurement compares data on the size of the incoming dataset to the median of past sizes and calculates difference from the median. It uses a threshold based on past measurement results or otherwise defined by SMEs to determine whether the proportion is unexpectedly large or small.

Programming

As input, this measurement type requires rules for defining the size of a dataset, along with measurements of past dataset sizes. It must calculate the median of those sets. Once the size of the given set is determined and the median is calculated, the process must calculate the difference between them (historical median minus the most recent measure). Additional calculations can also be executed. For example, calculating the given set as a percentage of the historical median (most recent measure divided by the historical median multiplied by 100); or calculating the standard deviation from the historical median and identifying instances where a given measure is greater than three standard deviations from the historical median. The process must include notifications to staff if the measurements exceed expected thresholds.

Support Processes and Skills

Taking this measure allows for an understanding of data delivery patterns. Staff must be able to assess those patterns and identify changes that indicate risks or problems. As with other data delivery measures and controls, staff in the target data store must be able to respond to alerts and perform analysis of the data chain to identify where records may have been dropped or duplicated or not sent in the first place. Source system staff must also be available to contribute to this analysis in the event that the problem originates in the source system.

Measurement Logical Data Model

The metric definition table for Measurement Type #10 contains the following attributes (as defined under #6): Measurement Type Number, Specific Metric Number, Dataset Name, Dataset Source, Dataset Type, Data Quality Threshold type, Data Quality Threshold (if threshold is set manually).

The Results table for Measurement Type #10 contains Measurement Type Number, Specific Metric Number, Measurement Date, and Notification Sent Indicator, Threshold Exceeded Indicator (as defined in #6), and the attributes listed in Table 16.4.

Table 16.4 Measurement Results for Measurement Type #10

Attribute Name	Attribute Definition
Dataset Total Record Count	This field contains the number of records present in the dataset being measured. It serves as the denominator in percentage calculations. For some measurement types, it may also contribute in other ways as a measurement of consistency.
Historical Median of Dataset Size	Calculated historical median. The median is a statistical measure of variation. It represents the middle measurement when a set of measurements are collected in ascending order. 50% of the measurements are above the median and 50% are below it.
Difference from Historical Median of Dataset Size	Historical median minus current measurement (In #10, current measurement = Dataset Total Record Count)
Percentage of Historical Median of Dataset Size	Current measurement divided by historical median multiplied by 100.

Measurement Type #11: Record Completeness—Length
Definition

Description: Ensure length of records matches a defined expectation.
Object of Measurement: Condition of data upon receipt
Assessment Category: Process control
Cross Reference: 1, 8, 12

Business Concerns

As noted under Measurement Type #8: Dataset Completeness—Record Counts to Control Record, in addition to the possibility that records may be lost in transit from one system to another, there is also the possibility that records will be truncated or that fields will be duplicated. Truncation results in missing data. In some cases, missing data can cause downstream data processing to fail. Such failures increase costs because data must be re-obtained and reprocessed. Any re-running of data implies a delay in data availability. Files can also be corrupted so that data is duplicated. Duplication can cause technical process failures and business process complications. The purpose of this control is to ensure that incoming records are of expected length and to prevent further processing if a discrepancy is detected.

Measurement Methodology

This control compares the length of incoming records to documented expectations for record length to determine whether the incoming records match the expected length or fit within a defined range.

Programming

This control requires metadata documenting expected record lengths and the ability to measure the length of incoming records. The two inputs can then be compared to determine whether the incoming records match the expected length or fit within a defined range. In cases where record length does not meet expectations, individual records can be rejected or a data processing job can be stopped. The process must include notifications to staff if this situation transpires.

Support Processes and Skills

Staff in the target data store must be in place to respond to alerts that a process has been stopped. Staff must be able to perform analysis of the data chain to determine why the records are not in the expected condition. Source system staff must also be available to contribute to analysis.

Measurement Type #12: Field Completeness—Non-Nullable Fields
Definition

> **Description**: Ensure that all non-nullable fields are populated.
> **Object of Measurement**: Condition of data upon receipt
> **Assessment Category**: Process control
> **Cross Reference**: 1, 11. See Measurement Type #7, 9, and 10 for the risks associated with incomplete data.

Business Concerns

A basic expectation of completeness can be understood at the field-level. Some fields are mandatory and others are optional. Some columns allow NULL; others do not. The purpose of this control is to interrogate a dataset upon receipt to ensure that all non-nullable fields are populated and to prevent further processing if they are not. Having it in place can detect instances where the source is not populating data as expected and reduces the risk that incomplete data will be processed.

Measurement Methodology

This process control compares rules related to field population against the actual population in order to identify instances where non-nullable (mandatory) fields contain NULL.

Programming

This control requires metadata documenting which fields are mandatory and which are optional. It requires programming to interrogate mandatory fields and detect any instances where they contain NULL. Depending on data processing requirements, the control may also stop a job or prevent further processing. If so, the process must notify staff about the condition of the data.

Support Processes and Skills

Staff in the target data store must be in place to respond to alerts that a process has been stopped. Staff must be able to perform analysis of the data chain to identify fields that are not populated as expected. Source system staff must also be available to contribute to analysis.

Measurement Type #13: Dataset Integrity—De-Duplication
Definition

Description: Identify and remove duplicate records.
Object of Measurement: Condition of data upon receipt
Assessment Category: Process control
Cross Reference: 1, 14

Business Concerns

A fundamental function of data management is to define what constitutes a unique record in order to have one-and-only-one record of any given fact stored in a database. Because transactional systems do a different kind of work than databases do, a transactional source system may present multiple instances of a record that are duplicates (or triplicates) from the point of view of the data store. The data store must define what constitutes a unique record as well as what constitutes a duplicate record. Multiple records representing the same fact can cause confusion for data consumers. Their presence introduces the risk that data will be misunderstood and counts of objects represented within a dataset will be incorrect. The data store must contain logic to identify unique records and to remove other instances of those records. If duplicate records are not removed, then data processing will fail.

The purpose of this control is to remove multiple instances of records in order to prepare the dataset for additional processing.

Measurement Methodology

This control applies logic associated with a database table's definition of a unique record in order to remove multiple instances of the same record from an incoming dataset.

Programming

This control requires metadata documenting the definition of a unique record. It also requires logic or criteria to choose the expected record from a set of multiple instances of the record—for example, the most current version of the record based on a time stamp. It needs a means of disposing of unselected records, either by storing them in a reject table or placing them in a file. The process can also include notifications to staff if the level of rejected records exceeds expected thresholds (see Measurement Type #14).

Support Processes and Skills

The de-duplication process is based on rules that are fundamental to the structure of data in a table. These rules should not change unless there is a change in the structure of the data. So once the de-duplication process is developed, tested, and productionalized, additional support processes should not be necessary.

Measurement Type #14: Dataset Integrity—Duplicate Record Reasonability Check
Definition

> **Description**: Reasonability check, compare ratio of duplicate records to total records in a dataset to the ratio in previous instances of dataset.
> **Object of Measurement**: Condition of data upon receipt
> **Assessment Category**: In-line measurement
> **Cross Reference**: 1, 13

Business Concerns

De-duplication of records is fundamental to managing data (see Measurement Type #13). Under similar conditions, a source system may be expected to present a similar proportion of duplicate records within instances of the same dataset. Significant changes in the proportion of duplicate records to total records can indicate changes in business processes, source system data, or other factors that might put data at risk.

The purpose of this in-line measurement is to test the reasonability of the level of duplicate records in an incoming dataset and take action if it is not reasonable. The measure works for processes where there is a reasonable expectation of consistency in the source data.

Measurement Methodology

This measurement type compares the proportion of duplicate records (expressed as a ratio between records rejected and total records) in an instance of an individual dataset to past instances of the same dataset. It uses a threshold based on past measurement results (past ratios) or otherwise defined by SMEs (a given percentage of records) to determine whether the proportion is unexpectedly large or small.

Programming

This measurement uses output from the de-duplication process to calculate the percentage of the original records that are duplicates (records rejected/total records multiplied by 100). It compares the result of this calculation to the historical mean of past measurements and calculates a difference. It then compares the difference to a threshold based on three standard deviations from the mean or a business established threshold to determine whether the difference is significant, sets an indicator, and notifies staff if the threshold is exceeded.

Support Processes and Skills

Staff in the target data store must be in place to respond to alerts that a threshold has been exceeded. Staff must be able to perform analysis of the duplicate records to detect any patterns that might indicate a problem or an unexpected condition. Source system staff must also be available to contribute to analysis.

Measurement Logical Data Model

The metric definition table for Measurement Type #14 contains the following attributes (as defined under #6): Measurement Type Number, Specific Metric Number, Dataset Name, Dataset Source, Dataset Type, Data Quality Threshold Type, Data Quality Threshold (if threshold is set manually).

The Results table for Measurement Type #14 contains Measurement Type Number, Specific Metric Number, Measurement Date, and Notification Sent Indicator, Threshold Exceeded Indicator (as defined in #6), and the attributes listed in Table 16.5.

Table 16.5 Measurement Results for Measurement Type #14

Attribute Name	Attribute Definition
Dataset Total Record Count	This field contains the number of records present in the dataset being measured (see #10).
Measurement Record Count	This field contains the number of records that meet the condition being measured and serves as the numerator in percentage calculations (in this case, it contains the number identified as duplicate for a dataset).
Record Count Percentage	This field includes the calculated percentage of the measurement record count [(Measurement record count/Dataset total record count)*100].
Historical Mean Record Count Percentage	Calculated historical mean. The mean is a statistical measure of variation. It is most easily understood as the mathematical average. It is calculated by summing the value of a set of measurements and dividing by the number of measurements taken. The historical mean of record count percentages sums the value of the previous measurements for a specific metric and divides by the number of measurements to establish the mean.
Difference from the Historical Mean Percentage of Duplicate Records	Historical mean percentage minus the percentage of the current measurement

Measurement Type #15: Field Content Completeness—Defaults from Source
Definition

Description: Reasonability check, compare the number and percentage of records defaulted for source-provided critical fields to a defined threshold or historical number and percentage.

Object of Measurement: Condition of data upon receipt

Assessment Category: In-line measurement

Cross Reference: 1, 4, 5, 33

Business Concerns

As noted under Measurement Type #5 Consistent Use of Default Values for a Column and Cross-table, a field may be defaulted on incoming source data because the data does not apply for a particular record, the data is not available, or a default has been assigned to signify that the data is recognizably incorrect. Default values therefore convey significant information. When other conditions are similar, fields in source data can be expected to contain defaults in a consistent proportion of records for individual instances of the same dataset. Significant changes in the levels of defaults may indicate data is missing or that there have been changes to business processes or source system data processing that have an effect on downstream data storage.

The purpose of this in-line measurement is to confirm that a field is being populated as expected and to detect unexpected changes in population. Once detected, changes can be analyzed for root causes. If the changes are undesirable, the root causes can be remediated. If the root causes reflect changes in business processes or in how the source collects, processes or stores data, information about these process changes can be shared in metadata. Even if they are business-expected, such changes require explanation because they can impact uses of the data. Changes in trend are hard to detect without monitoring. Because this measurement detects change, it can also be used to show improvement in the population of a field.

Not all defaults are bad or incorrect because not all fields are expected to be populated 100% of the time. Some fields are optional. Others are populated only under specific conditions. Getting value out of this measurement depends on defining a clear expectation for the fields measured so that the comparisons to actual population are meaningful. This measurement works best when applied to critical fields where few defaults are expected and where missing or defaulted data can cause problems with downstream uses of the data. Critical fields include those that are used in downstream derivations or transformation or those that are direct input to reports or other analyses. The condition of the data it measures (the level of a default value) will not necessarily be picked up with the data inspection processes because defaults are valid values.

Measurement Methodology

This measurement type compares the proportion of defaulted records in a single column in an instance of a dataset to the proportion in past instances of the same dataset in order to detect changes in the level of population. It uses a threshold based on past measurement results or one defined by SMEs to determine whether the proportion is unexpectedly large or small. It can also be used for trend analysis.

Programming

As input, this measurement type requires metadata identifying the fields and values to be measured. This measurement type counts the total number of records in the dataset and the number of records for which the specified column contains the default value. It calculates the percentage of records containing the default value. It compares the result of this calculation to the historical mean of past measurements and calculates a difference. It then compares the difference to a threshold based on three standard deviations from the historical mean to determine whether the difference is statistically significant and sets an indicator. It notifies staff if the threshold is exceeded.

Support Processes and Skills

Staff in the target data store must be in place to respond to alerts that a threshold has been exceeded. Staff must be able to perform analysis of the defaulted records to detect any patterns that might indicate a problem or unexpected condition. Staff must also be assigned to periodically review trend data. How often trend data is reviewed depends on the frequency with which the data store is updated. Source system staff must also be available to contribute to analysis.

Measurement Logical Data Model

The metric definition table for Measurement Type #15 contains the following attributes (as defined under #6): Measurement Type Number, Specific Metric Number, Dataset Name, Dataset Source, Dataset Type, Data Quality Threshold Type, Data Quality Threshold (if threshold is set manually). In addition it contains the attributes listed in Table 16.6.

The Results table for Measurement Type #15 contains Measurement Type Number, Specific Metric Number, Measurement Date, and Notification Sent Indicator (as defined in #6), and the attributes listed in Table 16.7.

Table 16.6 Metric Definition for Measurement Type #15

Attribute Name	Attribute Definition
Target Column 1	This field indicates which field or Target Column is being measured. Target Column fields may be numbered, if more than one is required for a measurement. For the sake of consistency, even on those measurements that involve only one Target Column, the field can be named Target Column 1. For some measurement types, such as those specific to dates or amount fields, the first Target Column field must represent a specific type of data. In cases where two elements are measured by creating a ratio, Target Column 1 should be identified as the numerator and Target Column 2 as the denominator.
Default Value	This field contains the specific value that represents the default for a field being measured. For example, if the default for ZIP code is 00000, then the value for measuring defaulted ZIP codes is 00000.

Table 16.7 Measurement Results for Measurement Type #15

Attribute Name	Attribute Definition
Dataset Total Record Count	This field contains the number of records present in the dataset being measured (see #10).
Measurement Record Count	The number of records that meet the condition being measured (see #14)
Record Count Percentage	(Measurement record count/Dataset total record count)*100) (see #14)
Historical Mean Record Count Percentage	Calculated historical mean (see #14)
Difference from the Historical Mean Percentage of Defaulted Records	Historical mean percentage minus the percentage of the current measurement
Threshold Exceeded Indicator for difference from the Historical Mean Percentage of Defaulted Records	Records whether or not a specific measurement is greater than the established data quality threshold (see #6)

Measurement Type #16: Dataset Completeness Based on Date Criteria
Definition

Description: Ensure that minimum and maximum dates on critical dates fields conform to a defined range identified parameters for loading data.
Object of Measurement: Condition of data upon receipt
Assessment Category: Process control
Cross Reference: 1, 17

Business Concerns

Dates are often critical data elements in relation to data processing as well as to content. In situations governed by date criteria, date fields can provide a means of confirming expectations related to data content (i.e., data loaded in February as part of a monthly process might be expected to contain records largely from January) or completeness (the database must contain at least three years' worth of data) or consistency (e.g., the amount of data related to one month's transactions should be of similar size to that of another month's transactions).

The purpose of this process control is to confirm that the data meets specific criteria and to stop processing or rejecting records if the data does not meet the criteria. For example, it can be used as a means of rejecting records that meet certain conditions, such as those with future dates.

Measurement Methodology

This control checks the content of date fields and compares it to rules or other criteria. It determines whether data meets specific date criteria and sends notifications, rejects records, or stops data processing if they do not meet the criteria.

Programming

This control requires metadata documenting criteria against which date fields will be compared. It also requires programming to interrogate date fields and detect where content does not meet criteria. The control may be set up to reject records or to stop a job or prevent further processing and alert staff to this situation. If so, the process must notify staff about the condition of the data.

Support Processes and Skills

Staff in the target data store must be in place to respond to alerts that a process has been stopped. Staff must be able to analyze the records to detect patterns in records that have not met date criteria. Source system staff must also be available to contribute to analysis, since any non-derived and non-system-generated dates will be traceable to a source system. Pattern analysis is required if the measure is used as a reasonability check.

Measurement Type #17: Dataset Reasonability Based on Date Criteria
Definition

Description: Ensure that minimum and maximum dates on critical date fields conform to a reasonability rule.
Object of Measurement: Condition of data upon receipt
Assessment Category: In-line measurement
Cross Reference: 1, 16

Business Concerns

As noted under Measurement Type #16: Dataset Completeness Based on Date Criteria, dates are often critical data elements in relation to processing as well as to content. In situations governed by date criteria, date fields can provide a means of confirming expectations related to data content or completeness and consistency.

This in-line reasonability test measures the degree to which data meets expectations by identifying the proportion of records that do not meet specific criteria and comparing this result to past measurements.

Measurement Methodology

This measurement type checks the content of date fields and compares it to rules or other criteria in order to identify the portion of records that do not meet the criteria. It compares this result to a threshold based on past measurement results or otherwise defined by SMEs to determine whether the proportion is unexpectedly large or small. It is unlikely that results from this measurement type will require that data processing be stopped. If dates are highly critical, then the related process control should be put in place to stop processing if defined criteria are met.

Programming

As input, this measurement type requires metadata documenting criteria against which date fields will be compared. It also requires past measurements so that the historical mean or median can be calculated. Programming must interrogate date fields and detect where content does not meet criteria. It must count the total number of records in the dataset and the number of records that do not meet date criteria in order to calculate the proportion of records that do not meet date criteria. It must compare these results to the history of past measurements and calculate the differences. It then compares the difference to a threshold to determine whether the difference is significant and notify staff if the threshold is exceeded.

Support Processes and Skills

Staff must be able to perform analysis to identify patterns in data content and to determine whether changes are business-expected. Source system staff must also be available to contribute to analysis.

Measurement Logical Data Model

The metric definition table for Measurement Type #17 contains the following attributes (as defined under #6): Measurement Type Number, Specific Metric Number, Dataset Name, Dataset Source,

Dataset Type, Data Quality Threshold Type, Data Quality Threshold (if threshold is set manually), Range Minimum, and Range Maximum. In addition, it contains Target Column 1 as defined in #15. For #17, Target Column 1 must be a date field.

The Results table for Measurement Type #17 contains Measurement Type Number, Specific Metric Number, Measurement Date, and Notification Sent Indicator (as defined in #6), and the attributes listed in Table 16.8.

Table 16.8 Measurement Results for Measurement Type #17

Attribute Name	Attribute Definition
Dataset Total Record Count	This field contains the number of records present in the dataset being measured (see #10).
Less-than-range-minimum Record Count	Record count for all records that are less than the minimum defined by the range—in this case, less than the oldest date in the range.
Greater-than-range-maximum Record Count	Record count for all records that are greater than the maximum value defined by the range—in this case, newer than the most recent date in the range.
Out-of-range Record Count	Combined record count for all out-of-range records; includes those less than the minimum and greater than the maximum in the range.
Percentage Less-than-range-minimum Record Count	(Less-than-date-range-minimum record count/Total record count)*100
Percentage Greater-than-range-maximum Record Count	(Greater-than-date-range-maximum record count/Total Record data set count)*100
Percentage Out-of-range Record Count	(Record count for all out-of-range records/Total dataset record count)*100
Historical Mean of Percentage of Less-than-range-minimum Record Count	Calculated historical mean (see #14)
Historical Mean of Percentage of Greater-than-range-maximum Record Count	Calculated historical mean (see #14)
Historical Mean Percentage of Out-of-range Record Count	Calculated historical mean (see #14)
Difference from historical mean percentage of less-than-range-minimum record count	Historical mean percentage minus the percentage of the current measurement
Difference from historical mean percentage of greater-than-range-maximum record count	Historical mean percentage minus the percentage of the current measurement
Difference from historical percentage out-of-range record count	Historical mean percentage minus the percentage of the current measurement
Threshold Exceeded Indicator for difference from the Historical Mean Percentage of Less-than-range-minimum Record Count	Records whether or not a specific measurement is greater than the established data quality threshold (see #6)
Threshold Exceeded Indicator for difference from the Historical Mean Percentage of Greater-than-range-maximum Record Count	Records whether or not a specific measurement is greater than the established data quality threshold (see #6)
Threshold Exceeded Indicator for difference from the Historical Mean Percentage of Out-of-range Record Count	Records whether or not a specific measurement is greater than the established data quality threshold (see #6)

Measurement Type #18: Field Content Completeness—Received Data is Missing Fields Critical to Processing
Definition

Description: Inspect population of critical fields before processing records.
Object of Measurement: Condition of data upon receipt
Assessment Category: Process control
Cross Reference: 1, 11, 12, 14, 20, 30

Business Concerns

Records are rejected when they meet conditions stipulated in exclusion rules or when they fail to meet conditions stipulated in selection rules. The most efficient way to reject records is upon initial inspection rather than while data is being processed. If conditions can be tested when data is received, and records can be rejected before processing begins, then those records do not impact later processing. Any record rejected is rejected for a specific reason. Reject reasons can be codified and codes can be used in analysis of reasons why records are rejected.

The purpose of this process control is to inspect data on arrival and ensure that critical fields are populated as expected and to remove records that are incomplete. This data can be used as input to data quality improvement efforts in source systems. In a stable process, with consistent and acceptable patterns for rejecting records, the measure can be used to identify any unexpected changes in those patterns.

Measurement Methodology

This measurement type compares the proportion of rejected records in an instance of a dataset to the proportion in past instances of the same dataset. It uses a threshold based on past measurement results or otherwise defined by SMEs to determine whether the proportion is unexpectedly large or small. Its focus is on data critical to processing. It can be executed in conjunction with Measurement Type #12: Field Completeness—Non-nullable Fields.

Programming

This measurement type counts the total number of records in the dataset and the number of records initially rejected. It calculates the percentage of records rejected. It compares the result of this calculation to the historical mean or median of past measurements and calculates a difference. Next it compares the difference to a threshold to determine whether the difference is significant, and it notifies staff if the threshold is exceeded.

Support Processes and Skills

Staff in the target data store must be in place to respond to alerts that a threshold has been exceeded. Staff must be able to perform analysis of the rejected records to detect any patterns that might indicate a problem or an unexpected condition. Source system staff must also be available to contribute to analysis since problems may originate in source systems.

Measurement Type #19: Dataset Completeness—Balance Record Counts Through a Process

Definition

Description: Balance record counts through data processing, account for rejected records, including duplicates; for exact balance situations.
Object of Measurement: Data processing
Assessment Category: Process control
Cross Reference: 8, 13, 14

Business Concerns

A basic function of data management is to account for records moving within or between systems. In complex data processing, records can be dropped unexpectedly or because they meet conditions for rejection. In exact balance situations, those that require accounting for each and every record, record balancing can be applied as a control. Records can be balanced at the end of a process by comparing input counts to output counts and accounting for rejected records. If records do not balance, the loading of data to tables can be prevented until the reasons for the imbalance are determined and remediated. Balancing can also be taken at intermediate steps within a process.

The purpose of this control is to ensure that all records are accounted for when data is processed. It balances records between predetermined points in a process to detect when record counts are not in balance. This type of measure works when there an expectation for balance. In situations where records are combined or split, the measure may be taken more effectively as a consistency check with a ratio (see Measurement Type #21: Dataset Completeness Through a Process—Ratio of Input to Output).

Measurement Methodology

This control counts records at the beginning of data processing and at predetermined checkpoints within a sequence of data processing jobs and compares the results from consecutive points in order to detect out-of-balance situations. In its simplest form, it counts only at the beginning and end of a defined process.

Programming

As input, this control requires metadata that defines the points at which records will be counted and the relation of these points to each other. It requires counting the records at those points and comparing the results to each other to determine whether they differ. If the process accounts for rejected records, then rejects must also be counted in the check points. Depending on data processing requirements, the control may also stop a job or prevent further processing. If so, the process must alert staff about the condition of the data. Because it requires an initial record count, this control can be built in conjunction with Measurement Type #8: Dataset Completeness—Record Counts to Control Record.

Support Processes and Skills

Staff in the target data store must be in place to respond to alerts that a process has been stopped. Staff must be able to analyze the sequence of jobs in order to detect where records have been dropped.

Measurement Type #20: Dataset Completeness—Reasons for Rejecting Records
Definition

Description: Reasonability check, compare number and percentage of records dropped for specific reasons with a defined threshold or historical number and percentage.
Object of Measurement: Data processing
Assessment Category: In-line measurement
Cross Reference: 1, 11, 12, 14, 18, 24, 27

Business Concerns

As noted under Measurement Type #18: Field Content Completeness—Received Data Is Missing Fields Critical to Processing, records are rejected when they meet conditions stipulated in exclusion rules or they fail to meet conditions stipulated in selection rules. To the extent possible, these conditions should be identified so that records can be rejected before processing begins. However, it is not always possible to do so because some rules do not pertain to the initial condition of data. Some records may be rejected as they are being processed. As part of processing, a code can be assigned to each record, capturing the reason why it was rejected. These codes can be used in analysis of reasons explaining why records are rejected.

The purpose of this in-line measurement is to collect data on the reasons for rejecting records. This data can be used as input to data quality improvement efforts in the source system and in the target database. In a stable process, with consistent and acceptable patterns for rejecting records, the measure can be used to identify any unexpected changes in those patterns.

Other Facets

See Measurement Type #18.

Measurement Logical Data Model

The metric definition table for Measurement Type #20 contains the following attributes (as defined under #6): Measurement Type Number, Specific Metric Number, Dataset Name, Dataset Source, and Dataset Type.

The Results table for Measurement Type #20 contains Measurement Type Number, Specific Metric Number, Measurement Date, and Notification Sent Indicator (as defined in #6), and the attributes listed in Table 16.9.

Table 16.9 Measurement Results for Measurement Type #20

Attribute Name	Attribute Definition
Dataset Total Record Count	This field contains the number of records present in the dataset being measured (see #10).
Data Value 1 (from reject codes)	This field contains the value present on the data being measured in the column being measured. Values from Target Column 1 are stored in Data value 1, those from Target Column 2 in Data Value 2, etc. In the case of #20, the data values represent the reject codes.
Measurement Record Count	The number of records that meet the condition being measured (see #14)
Record Count Percentage	(Measurement record count/Dataset total record count)*100 (see #14).
Historical Mean Percentage of Records Associated with Each Data Value	Calculated historical mean (see #14)
Difference from the Historical Mean Percentage of Records Associated with the Code Value	Historical mean percentage minus the percentage of the current measurement
Threshold Exceeded Indicator for difference from the Historical Mean Percentage of Records Associated with the Data Value	Records whether or not a specific measurement is greater than the established data quality threshold (see #6)

Measurement Type #21: Dataset Completeness Through a Process—Ratio of Input to Output

Definition

Description: Reasonability check, compare the ratio of process input/output to the ratio in previous instances of dataset.

Object of Measurement: Data processing

Assessment Category: In-line measurement

Cross Reference: 8, 19

Business Concerns

As noted under Measurement Type #19: Dataset Completeness—Balance Record Counts Through a Process, a fundamental function of data management is to account for records moving within or between systems. But some data processing involves combining or splitting records, so exact balance by record count is not expected.

The purpose of this in-line measure is to provide a degree of assurance about the reasonability of results in situations where exact balance is not expected. This measure addresses the risk of failing to detect that a file has unusual content.

Measurement Methodology

This in-line reasonability test compares the proportion of input records to output records in an instance of an individual dataset to past instances of input/output for the same dataset. It uses a threshold based on past measurement results or otherwise defined by SMEs to determine whether the proportion is unexpectedly large or small. This measurement works for processes where there is a reasonable expectation for consistency between records-in and records-out.

Programming

This measure requires metadata that defines the points at which records will be counted and their relation to each other. It also requires access to past measurements so that the historical mean or median can be calculated. The process of measuring involves counting the records at the designated points and calculating the ratio between records-in and records-out. It compares the result of this calculation to the historical mean or median of past measurements and calculates a difference. It then compares the difference to a threshold to determine whether the difference is significant and notifies staff if the threshold is exceeded. It can also include other calculations, such as a ratio between the measurement being taken and the median or mean of past measures (as opposed to a difference from the historical median or mean).

Support Processes and Skills

Staff in the target data store must be in place to respond to alerts that a process has been stopped. Staff must be able to analyze the sequence of jobs in order to detect where records have been dropped.

Measurement Logical Data Model

The metric definition table for Measurement Type #21 contains the following attributes (as defined under #6): Measurement Type Number, Specific Metric Number, Dataset Name, Dataset Source, Dataset Type, Data Quality Threshold Type, and Data Quality Threshold.

The Results table for Measurement Type #21 contains Measurement Type Number, Specific Metric Number, Measurement Date, and Notification Sent Indicator (as defined in #6), and the attributes listed in Table 16.10.

Measurement Type #22: Dataset Completeness Through a Process—Balance Amount Fields
Definition

Description: Balance amount field content throughout a process, for exact balance situations.
Object of Measurement: Data processing
Assessment Category: Process control
Cross Reference: 9, 23

Table 16.10 Measurement Results for Measurement Type #21

Attribute Name	Attribute Definition
Dataset Total Record Count (at process initiation)	This field contains the number of records present in the dataset being measured. It serves as the denominator in percentage calculations. For some measurement types, it may also contribute in other ways as a measurement of consistency.
Dataset Total Record Count (at process completion)	This field contains the number of records present in the dataset being measured. It serves as the denominator in percentage calculations. For some measurement types, it may also contribute in other ways as a measurement of consistency.
Ratio (input/output ratio)	Dataset total record count (at process initiation) divided by dataset total record count (at process completion)
Historical Mean of Input/Output Ratios	Calculated historical mean (see #14)
Difference from the Historical Mean of Ratios	Historical mean of ratio minus the current measurement
Threshold Exceeded Indicator for difference from the Historical Mean of Input/Output Ratio	Records whether or not a specific measurement is greater than the established data quality threshold (see #6)

Business Concerns

As noted under Measurement Type #19: Dataset Completeness—Balance Record Counts Through a Process, a fundamental function of data management is to account for data moving within or between systems. In complex data processing, data can be dropped unexpectedly. In addition to using record counts as a control, missing data can also be detected by summing critical numeric columns. Amount fields can be balanced at the end of a process by comparing input summary to output summary and accounting for amounts associated with rejected records. If summed fields do not balance, loading of data to tables can be prevented until the reasons for the imbalance are determined and remediated. Balancing can also be taken at intermediate steps within a process.

The purpose of this control is to ensure that all data is accounted for by balancing summed amount fields between predetermined points in a process and to detect any out-of balance situation. This type of measure works when there an expectation for balance. In situations where records are combined or split, the measure may be taken more effectively as a consistency check with a ratio. (See Measurement Type #23: Field Content Completeness—Ratio of Summed Amount Fields.)

Measurement Methodology

This control sums an amount column at the beginning of data processing and at predetermined points within a sequence of data processing jobs. It compares the results at each point in order to detect out-of-balance situations. In its simplest form, it balances only at the beginning and end of a defined process. The check can be used in conjunction with measures of process timing.

Programming

This control requires metadata that defines the column that will be summed and the points at which summation will occur and their relation to each other. It requires functionality to sum records at those points, accounting for rejected records, and comparing the results to each other to determine whether they differ. Depending on data processing requirements, the control may also stop a job or prevent further processing. If so, the process must notify staff about the condition of the data. Because it requires an initial summation, this control can be built in conjunction with Measurement Type #9: Dataset Completeness—Summarized Amount Field.

Support Processes and Skills

Staff in the target data store must be in place to respond to alerts when data does not reconcile. Staff must be able to perform analysis of the data chain to identify where records may have been dropped or duplicated or where the population of amount fields is different from what is expected. Source system staff must also be available to contribute to this analysis in the event that the problem or unexpected condition originates in the source system.

Measurement Type #23: Field Content Completeness—Ratio of Summed Amount Fields
Definition

> **Description**: Amount field reasonability check, compare ratio of summed amount field input and output to ratio of previous instances of a dataset, for nonexact balance situations.
> **Object of Measurement**: Content/Amount fields
> **Assessment Category**: In-line measurement
> **Cross Reference**: 9, 22

Business Concerns

As noted under Measurement Types #19 and 22, a fundamental function of data management is to account for data moving within or between systems. This accounting can be achieved at the record level or through summing critical numeric columns, such as currency amount fields in financial data. But some data processing involves combining or splitting records, so exact balance by amount is not expected.

The purpose of this in-line measure is to provide a degree of assurance about the reasonability of results in situations where exact balance is not expected. This measure addresses the risks of failing to detect that a file has unusual content or failing to detect that data content has been dropped during processing.

Measurement Methodology

This in-line reasonability test confirms the proportion of input in an amount field to output in an amount field for a given process is similar to the proportion in past instances of the same process for the same dataset. This measurement works for processes where there is a reasonable expectation for consistency between amounts-in and amounts-out.

This measurement type compares the proportion of input for an amount field to output for an amount field in the processing of an instance of a dataset to past instances of input/output for the same dataset. It uses a threshold based on past measurement results or otherwise defined by SMEs to determine whether the proportion is unexpectedly large or small.

Programming

This control requires metadata that defines the column that will be summed and the points at which the column will be summed and their relation to each other. It also requires access to past measurements so that the historical mean or median can be calculated. The process of measuring involves summing a column at both designated points and calculating the ratio between amount-in and amount-out. It compares the result of this calculation to the historical mean or median of past measurements and calculates a difference. It then compares the difference to a threshold to determine whether the difference is significant, and it notifies staff if the threshold is exceeded. It can also include other calculations, such as a ratio between the measurement being taken and the median or mean of past measures (as opposed to a difference from the historical median or mean).

Support Processes and Skills

Staff in the target data store must be in place to respond to alerts that a process has been stopped. Staff must be able to analyze the sequence of jobs in order to detect where records have been dropped or where fields are not populated as expected.

Table 16.11 Metric Definition for Measurement Type #23	
Attribute Name	**Attribute Definition**
Target Column 1 (numerator)	This field indicates which field or Target Column is being measured (see #15).
Target Column 2 (denominator)	This field indicates which field or Target Column is being measured. Target Column fields may be numbered, if more than one is required for a measurement. For the sake of consistency, even on those measurements that involve only one Target Column, the field can be named Target Column 1. For some measurement types, such as those specific to dates or amount fields, the first Target Column field must represent a specific type of data. In cases where two elements are measured by creating a ratio, Target Column 1 should be identified as the numerator and Target Column 2 as the denominator.
Data Quality Threshold Type	Data quality thresholds are numeric representations of the acceptable limit of a measurement. They can be established in different ways (see #6).
Data Quality Threshold (if threshold is set manually)	This field contains the data quality threshold number for thresholds that are set manually. This field is populated only if the type is manual.

Table 16.12 Measurement Results for Measurement Type #23

Attribute Name	Attribute Definition
Amount Total Target Column 1 (numerator)	Sum of values (total amount) of the first field being measured (numerator)
Amount Total Target Column 2 (denominator)	Sum of values (total amount) of the second field being measured (denominator)
Ratio (of amount fields)	Ratio between the two fields being measured. In this case, Amount Total Target Column 1/Amount Total Target Column 2
Historical Mean of Ratios	Calculated historical mean (see #14). The historical mean of a ratio sums the value of the previous measurements for a specific metric and divides by the number of measurements to establish the mean.
Difference from the Historical Mean of Ratios	Historical mean of ratio minus the current measurement
Threshold Exceeded Indicator for difference from the Historical Mean of Ratios	Records whether or not a specific measurement is greater than the established data quality threshold (see #6)

Measurement Logical Data Model

The Metric Definition table for Measurement Type #23 contains the following attributes (as defined under #6): Measurement Type Number, Specific Metric Number, Dataset Name, Dataset Source, Dataset Type, and the attributes listed in Table 16.11.

The Results table for Measurement Type #23 contains Measurement Type Number, Specific Metric Number, Measurement Date, and Notification Sent Indicator (as defined in #6), and the attributes listed in Table 16.12. If median is used instead of mean, attributes related to mean should be replaced with median.

Measurement Type #24: Field Content Completeness—Defaults from Derivation
Definition

Description: Reasonability check, compare the number and percentage of records defaulted for derived fields to a defined threshold or historical number and percentage (subtype of Measurement Type #33: Multicolumn Profile).
Object of Measurement: Data processing
Assessment Category: In-line measurement
Cross Reference: 1, 15, 33

Business Concerns

This measurement works in the same manner as Measurement Type #15: Field Content Completeness—Defaults from Source. There are two important differences. First, the measurements are taken at different places in the data flow (measurements of source data should be taken as part of initial inspection; derived defaults need to be measured after the derivation has been completed). Second, they measure different risks.

Data can be derived in a database based on defined rules. Because such rules must account for all possible conditions of the data, they usually contain a final clause that allows for the possibility that the data meets none of the stipulated conditions. In such a case, a default value is assigned. The presence of the default signifies that requirements of the rule have not been met. When other conditions are similar, derived fields can be expected to default in a consistent proportion for individual instances of the same dataset.

The purpose of this in-line measurement is to detect changes in the levels of defaulted records on derived fields. Doing so confirms the success or failure of derivations. As was explained under Measurement Type #15, changes in the levels of defaults may have different causes (data is missing, business or technical processes have changed). For derived fields, changes in default levels may also indicate changes to processes within the database that have an effect on the derivation rules. This measurement type can detect both significant changes (spikes or drops) and trends.

Measurement Methodology

As does Measurement Type #15, this measure compares the proportion of defaulted records in an individual column in an instance of a dataset to the proportion in past instances of the same dataset. It uses a threshold based on past measurement results or otherwise defined by SMEs to determine whether the proportion is unexpectedly large or small. See #33 Multicolumn Profile.

Programming

This measurement type requires metadata identifying the fields that will be measured and the value that represents the default. The measure counts the total number of records in the dataset and the number of records for which an identified column contains a defaulted value. It calculates the percentage of records containing the default value. It compares the result of this calculation to the historical mean or median of past measurements and calculates a difference. It then compares the difference to a threshold to determine whether the difference is significant and notifies staff if the threshold is exceeded.

Support Processes and Skills

Staff in the target data store must be in place to respond to alerts that a threshold has been exceeded. Staff must be able to perform analysis of the defaulted records to detect any patterns that might indicate a problem. Source system staff must also be available to contribute to analysis since problems may originate in source systems. Derived data often relies on input from multiple sources, any one of which may contribute to the root cause of the problem that prevented the derivation from working correctly.

Measurement Logical Data Model

See Measurement Type #15.

Measurement Type #25: Data Processing Duration
Definition

Description: Reasonability check, compare process duration to a schedule, a historical process duration, or a defined time limit.

Object of Measurement: Data processing

Assessment Category: In-line measurement

Cross Reference: 6, 35

Business Concerns

Data processing includes a series of jobs that format, de-duplicate, combine, aggregate, and otherwise prepare data files that can be loaded into tables. Jobs take different amounts of time to execute depending on their complexity, the size of the data files that are being processed, and the other processing work going on in the system. Other factors being similar, the duration of any instance of a job should be similar to the duration of other instances of the same job. In other words, the duration of any specific job should be predictable.

Significant differences in processing time may indicate a problem with the data or a problem with the job itself. Whatever the cause, processing that takes longer than expected can adversely affect the entire system, since subsequent jobs may be dependent on the execution of the job that is incomplete. Jobs running a significantly shorter time than expected can also indicate a problem, such as missing data.

The purpose of this in-line measurement is to detect significant changes in the duration of data processing jobs so that these can be investigated and the overall efficiency of processing can be maintained. When changes represent problems with the data or with the construction of the processing work, these should be remediated. Results of the measurement can also provide input for analysis to identify process improvements (Nadkarni, 2006).

Measurement Methodology

This in-line reasonability test determines whether data processing time is significantly longer or shorter than expected for any instance of processing where an input dataset is of a size similar to past instances of the same dataset. This measurement compares an instance of the duration of a data processing job to historical instances of processing for the same job. It detects instances that are unexpectedly long or unexpectedly short compared to the historical median.

Job schedules in a data processing environment are rarely simple. Their structure depends in part on what scheduling tool they are created in. Any scheduling tool will allow for parent jobs with child jobs, predecessor and dependent jobs, and even sibling predecessor or dependent jobs. These can be arranged in different ways, depending on the work to be done and the effects of sequence on that work. In order to measure timeliness and to leverage the results of such measures, one will need to be very clear about the beginning and end points of any process measured, as well as the relation between processes within the specific environment being measured.

Knowledge of such details is also required to leverage these measurements to make design and process improvements.[3]

Programming

This assessment requires metadata describing where, within the job stream, the measurements will be taken. The measurement process must collect the start time and end time of jobs to be measured. From these it will calculate job duration. It requires data from past measurements of job duration for comparisons. It must identify the median of past measurements and compare the current instance to the median, by subtracting the median from the current instance. Additionally, it can compare the current instance to the median by creating a ratio between the two. The result of either calculation can be used to establish a threshold that can be calculated through automation. Or a threshold can be established based on SME recommendations. The measurement process can then compare the difference to a threshold to determine whether the difference is significant and notify staff if the threshold is exceeded.

Support Processes and Skills

Taking this measure allows for an understanding of data delivery and processing patterns. Staff must have the time and ability to assess those patterns and identify changes that indicate risks or problems.

Measurement Logical Data Model

The Metric Definition table for Measurement Type #25 contains the following attributes (as defined under #6): Measurement Type Number, Specific Metric Number, Data Quality Threshold Type, and Data Quality Threshold. In addition, it must contain the name of the process being measured. This name is usually an ETL or other data processing job. Depending on how processing is organized, it may also include a dataset name, source, and type.

The Results table for Measurement Type #25 contains Measurement Type Number, Specific Metric Number, Measurement Date, and Notification Sent Indicator (as defined in #6), and the attributes listed in Table 16.13.

---

[3]My discussion on process measures is highly influenced by Pravin Nadkarni's paper, "Delivering Data on Time: The Assurant Health Case," delivered at MIT's 2006 International Conference on Information Quality. Nadkarni describes how timeliness measures were applied in the ETL environment in Assurant's enterprise data warehouse. He applies duration measurements and critical path methodology to identify opportunities to improve the structure and relation between processing jobs.

Table **16.13** Measurement Results for Measurement Type #25

Attribute Name	Attribute Definition
Process Start Time	The time at which the process being measured begins
Process End Time	The time at which the process being measured stops
Process Duration	Absolute value of the difference between process start time and process end time. (A process duration cannot be a negative number).
Historical Median of Process Duration	Calculated historical median (see #10)
Difference from historical median of past process duration	Historical median minus current measurement
Threshold Exceeded Indicator for difference from the Historical Median of Process Duration	Records whether or not a specific measurement is greater than the established data quality threshold (see #6)

Measurement Type #26: Timely Availability of Data for Access
Definition

Description: Compare actual time data is available for data consumers' access to scheduled time of data availability.
Object of Measurement: Process/Adherence to schedule
Assessment Category: In-line measurement
Cross Reference: 6, 25

Business Concerns

In order for data to be used, it must be made accessible to data consumers. If data has been delivered according to schedule, and if data processing jobs have run within expected durations, then data need only be loaded to tables to be accessible to data consumers. However, sometimes these schedules are not met. In addition, loading tables can sometimes be delayed due to a technical challenge or the size of load files. Either situation can result in delays to data consumers. In some data stores, no data will be available until all data is loaded. In others, tables are made available as they are loaded.

The purpose of this measurement is to ensure that all required data has been made available to data consumers within specified time frames by comparing actual availability to expected availability and to detect differences, especially delays. The check can be taken at the table, domain, or database level. This kind of check can be used to measure adherence to service level agreements. It can also be used in combination with other process measures to identify opportunities for process improvements.

Measurement Methodology

This process control collects data about the actual availability of data in a data store and compares it to the scheduled availability. It then calculates a difference from a schedule. It can also include a comparison of any instance of a measurement to the past measurement results on availability. This measurement may be applied to the overall availability of the data store or to the availability of specific tables.

Programming

As input, this process control uses metadata describing the scheduled accessibility of a data store or of particular tables in a data store. It collects the time of actual availability and calculates a difference from scheduled availability.

It also requires past measurement results on availability. A comparison can be made between any individual instance of the measurement (the time difference between actual and scheduled accessibility) and the mean or the median of past differences. If one of these measures of central tendency is adopted as the point of comparison, then an automated threshold can be established which identifies instances that are more than three standard deviations from it. The process can include a notification to staff if the threshold is exceeded.

For a measurement like this, however, it makes sense to notify data consumers if data will not be available on schedule. A set threshold can be established based on data consumer requirements for how soon they want to know that data may not be available.

Support Processes and Skills

Taking this measure allows for an understanding of data delivery and processing patterns. Staff must have the time and ability to assess those patterns and to identify changes that indicate risks or problems.

Measurement Logical Data Model

The Metric Definition table for Measurement Type #26 contains the following attributes (as defined under #6): Measurement Type Number, Specific Metric Number, Dataset Name, Dataset Source, Dataset Type, Data Quality Threshold Type, Data Quality Threshold (if threshold is set manually), Range Minimum, and Range Maximum. In the case of #26 range minimum and maximum refer to the timeframes for making data accessible to data consumers.

The Results table for Measurement Type #26 contains Measurement Type Number, Specific Metric Number, Measurement Date, and Notification Sent Indicator (as defined in #6), and the attributes listed in Table 16.14.

Table 16.14 Measurement Results for Measurement Type #26

Attribute Name	Attribute Definition
Dataset Availability Time	This field records the actual time that scheduled data arrives.
Difference from Expected Availability Time	This field records the difference between the range minimum for data accessibility and the actual time data was made accessible.
Threshold Exceeded Indicator	Records whether or not a specific measurement is greater than the established data quality threshold (see #6)

Measurement Type #27: Validity Check, Single Field, Detailed Results
Definition

Description: Compare values on incoming data to valid values in a defined domain (reference table, range, or mathematical rule).
Object of Measurement: Content/Row counts
Assessment Category: In-line measurement
Cross Reference: 1, 20, 28, 29, 31, 39

Business Concerns

Assuring that data is valid, that actual data values adhere to a defined domain of values, is fundamental to data quality assurance. Domains of valid values may be established within reference tables, defined as ranges, or they may be defined through a mathematical formula or algorithm. In all cases, they represent a basic expectation about the data: specifically, that data values on incoming records will correspond to valid values in the domain; and that the actual values will thereby be comprehensible to data consumers. Validity checks mitigate the risk of having sets of values in the database that are not defined within the value domain. Because such checks detect new values in core data, they can also serve as a prompt to update reference data that may have changed over time.

The results of validity checks come in two forms: details and roll-ups. Detailed results present the counts and percentages of records associated with each specific value (see Measurement Type #30: Consistent Column Profile), along with indicators as to whether or not values are valid. Roll-ups present the overall numbers of and overall percentages of valid and invalid records.

The purpose of this in-line measurement is to identify the levels of specific invalid values within the fields measured. Once these are identified, support work is required to determine why they are present and to make updates or process improvements that reduce the overall incidence of invalids. The measure also provides the raw data needed for validity roll-ups representing the overall percentages of valid and invalid values.

It is not likely that a change in the level of validity for any particular value or even the overall level of validity for a single column will be critical enough to require a database stoppage. If there is data whose validity is highly critical, it is best to identify it as part of an intake check such as the one described under Measurement Type #17.

Measurement Methodology

This in-line reasonability measure identifies distinct values within a field and calculates a percentage distribution of those values. It compares the values to those in the defined data domain in order to identify which values are valid and which are invalid. The percentage of any individual value can then be compared to past percentages of that value in order to detect changes in the patterns of incremental data. Automation of this capability is especially important in data domains with a high number of distinct values. High cardinality can be prohibitive to analysis of trends.

In addition, because the result set will include multiple rows, a single threshold for investigation cannot be applied; nor is it realistic to manage multiple thresholds through a manual process. Instead, an automated threshold should be applied: for example, three standard deviations from the mean of past percentages of rows associated with a particular value. Setting an indicator on measurement

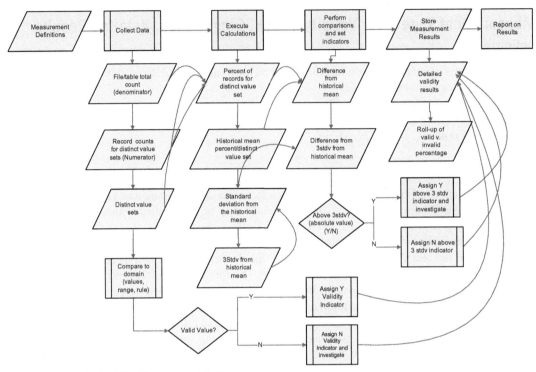

Figure 16.2 In-line Validity Measurement Pattern

The process to confirm data validity is similar regardless of how the domain of valid values is defined (set of valid values, range of values, or rule). First, the data that will be validated must be identified and its domain defined. Next, record counts for the distinct value set must be collected from the core data. Then the distinct values can be compared to the domain, and validity indicators can be assigned. The results of the comparisons constitute the detailed measurements. These can be compared to past measurements to identify statistically significant changes in the percentage distributions. For reporting purposes, these results can be rolled up to an overall percentage of valid and invalid values. These can also be compared to past results. If the measurements produce unexpected results, notifications will be sent and response protocols initiated. All results will be stored in results tables for reporting purposes.

results for which in percentage of records exceed three standard deviations from the mean of past percentages enables analysts to home in on potential anomalies. This measurement does not generally require notifications (see Figure 16.2).

Programming

Input for this measurement type includes metadata that identifies the fields that will be tested for validity as well as the domains against which they will be tested. It also requires past measurement results. The process must count the overall number of records in the dataset as well as the number of records associated with each distinct value for the field being measured. From these two counts, it must calculate the percentage of records associated with each distinct value. Having obtained the distinct values, the process must compare them with the valid values as defined by the domain rule and assign an indicator, designating each value as either valid (contained in the domain) or invalid (not contained within the domain). With each run of the measurement, for each distinct value, the process should compare the percentage of records to the historical mean percentage from past runs. Calculate the difference between the current percentage and the historical percentage. Calculate the standard deviation from the mean of past runs and three standard deviations from the mean of past runs. Assign an indicator to each distinct value showing whether the current percentage is more than three standard deviations from the mean of percentages of past runs.

Support Processes and Skills

Since it is not likely that a change in the level of validity will require a database stoppage, this measurement is not likely to require notifications to alert staff to urgent problems. Instead, staff is required to review both the roll-ups and the detailed results to identify invalid values and research their presence in the database. From initial assessment and profiling, knowledge should be captured related to business-expected patterns in the distribution of values. Since the measure detects changes in patterns, support staff should also investigate changes in trend to determine whether these are business-expected. Any findings should be added to the metadata.

Measurement Logical Data Model

The Metric Definition table for Measurement Type #27 contains the following attributes (as defined under #6): Measurement Type Number, Specific Metric Number, Dataset Name, Dataset Source, Dataset Type, Data Quality Threshold Type, Data Quality Threshold (if threshold is set manually), and the attributes contained in Table 16.15.

Table 16.15 Metric Definition for Measurement Type #27

Attribute Name	Attribute Definition
Target Column 1	This field indicates which field or Target Column is being measured (see #15).
Validity type	This field defines how validity will be established (through comparison to reference data, through a defined range, or through a rule). Other fields within the validity table will be populated based on which type of validity is measured.
Reference Data Table	For validity tests based on reference data, this field contains the name of the table that contains the values against which validity will be tested.
Reference Data Column 1	For validity tests based on reference data, this field contains the name of the column on the reference table that contains the values against which the validity of Target Column 1 will be tested.
Range Minimum	For any measurement based on a range of values, this field represents the lowest value in that range (see #6).
Range Maximum	For any measurement based on a range of values, this field represents the highest value in that range (see #6).
Validity Business Rule	For any measurement based on a business rule, this field contains the rule (in this case, a validity rule).

Table 16.16 Measurement Results for Measurement Type #27

Attribute Name	Attribute Definition
Dataset Total Record Count	This field contains the number of records present in the dataset being measured (see #10).
Data Value 1 (Target Column 1)	This field contains the value present on the data being measured in the column being measured. Values from Target Column 1 are stored in Data Value 1, those from Target Column 2 in Data Value 2, etc.
Validity Indicator	Y—Value is valid; N—Value is invalid
Measurement Record Count	The number of records that meet the condition being measured (see #14)
Percentage of Records Associated with the Data Value	(Measurement Record Count/Dataset Total Record Count) *100
Historical Mean Percentage of Records Associated with Each Data Value	Calculated historical mean (see #14)
Difference from the Historical Mean Percentage of Records Associated with the Data Value	Historical mean percentage minus the percentage of the current measurement
Threshold Exceeded Indicator for difference from the Historical Mean Percentage of Records Associated with the Data Value	Records whether or not a specific measurement is greater than the established data quality threshold (see #6)

The Results table for Measurement Type #27 contains Measurement Type Number, Specific Metric Number, Measurement Date, and Notification Sent Indicator (as defined in #6), and the attributes listed in Table 16.16.

Measurement Type #28: Validity Check, Roll-up
Definition

Description: Summarize results of detailed validity check; compare roll-up counts and percentage of valid/invalid values to historical levels.
Object of Measurement: Content summary
Assessment Category: In-line measurement
Cross Reference: 1, 27, 29, 30, 41

Business Concerns

As noted under Measurement Type #27: Validity Check—Detailed Results, the relation of validity to quality can be understood at both the detailed and rolled-up levels. Detailed results present the counts and percentages of records associated with each value (see Measurement Type #30: Consistent

Column Profile), along with indicators as to whether or not values are valid. Detailed results often contain a significant number of distinct values, making it challenging to analyze and characterize the overall condition of the data. Roll-ups summarize the overall number of records and the overall percentages of valid and invalid records. Roll-ups work first at the field level and can also be used to characterize the condition of a table or even of a database overall.

The purpose of this in-line measurement is to summarize the results of a detailed validity check in order to detect and analyze trends in the data. The validity check roll-up works the same way regardless of how the domain of valid values is defined and regardless of whether that validity is measured in a single column or across multiple columns or across tables.

Measurement Methodology

This measurement type summarizes the results of a detailed validity check by calculating the overall number and percentage of records that are valid and invalid. It compares the overall percentage of invalid values to the historical percentages in order to detect changes in the overall level of invalid values. This measurement does not generally require notifications.

Programming

This measurement type uses output from the detailed validity check to calculate the total number and overall percentages of valid and invalid values. It uses data from past measurements to calculate the historical mean of the overall percentage for valid and invalid records and compares the two. With each run of the measurement, the process should compare the percentages of valid and invalid records to the historical mean percentages from past runs. Calculate the difference between the current percentage and the historical percentage. Calculate the standard deviation from the mean of past runs and three standard deviations from the mean of past runs. Assign an indicator showing whether the current percentage is more than three standard deviations from the mean of percentages of past runs.

Support Processes and Skills

As noted, it is not likely that a change in the level of validity will require a database stoppage, so this measure does not include notifications to staff. Instead, staff are required to review both the roll-ups and the detailed results to identify invalid values and to research their presence in the database, as well as to review any patterns in the distribution of values to determine whether or not they are business-expected.

Measurement Logical Data Model

The validity roll-up measurement type uses output from the detailed validity measurement. It does not require a separate metric definition table. In addition to Measurement Type Number, Specific Metric Number, Measurement Date, and Notification Sent Indicator, it includes the attributes listed in Table 16.17.

Table 16.17 Measurement Results for Measurement Type #28

Attribute Name	Attribute Definition
Dataset Total Record Count	This field contains the number of records present in the dataset being measured (see #10).
Total Count Valid Records	This field contains the total number of records associated with valid data values (where validity indicator = Y on the detailed results table).
Percentage Valid Records	(Total count valid records/Dataset total record count) *100
Total Count Invalid Records	This field contains the total number of records associated with invalid data values (where validity indicator = Y on the detailed results table).
Percentage Invalid Records	(Total count invalid records/Dataset total record count) *100
Historical Mean Percentage of Invalid Records	Calculated historical mean (see #14)
Difference from the Historical Mean Percentage of Invalid Record	Historical mean percentage minus the percentage of the current measurement
Threshold Exceeded Indicator for difference from the Historical Mean Percentage of Invalid Records	Records whether or not a specific measurement is greater than the established data quality threshold (see #6)

Measurement Type #29: Validity Check, Multiple Columns within a Table, Detailed Results

Definition

Description: Compare values in related columns on the same table to values in a mapped relationship or business rule.
Object of Measurement: Content/Row counts
Assessment Category: In-line measurement
Cross Reference: 1, 27, 28, 41

Business Concerns

As noted under Measurement Type #27: Validity Check—Detailed Results, assuring that data is valid, that actual data values adhere to a defined domain of values, is fundamental to data quality assurance. While validity is thought of first in terms of individual columns, domains of values also have relationships with each other. Therefore the validity of the relationship between values in related columns can also be tested. Validity may be based on a direct mapped relationship. For example, any valid ZIP code is associated with one-and-only-one valid State Abbreviation Code. All ZIP codes could be valid and all State Abbreviation Codes could be valid, but the relationship between individual ZIP codes and State Abbreviation Codes may not be valid. ZIP 06085 is a Connecticut code and should not be on records with addresses elsewhere.

The purpose of this in-line measurement is to identify the levels of invalid relationships between columns within one table, determine why they are present, and make updates or process improvements that reduce the overall incidence. The measure also provides the raw data needed for validity roll-ups representing the overall percentages of valid and invalid values. See Measurement Type #28.

Measurement Methodology

This in-line reasonability measure identifies distinct value sets associated with the columns defined by a mapped relationship or business rule and calculates a percentage distribution of those values. It compares the value sets to those in defined data domain in order to identify which value sets are valid and which are invalid. The percentage of any value set can then be compared to historical percentages of that value set in order to detect changes in the patterns of incremental data. As with Measurement Type #27, automation of the capability to compare to past percentages is especially important in high cardinality value sets.

Programming

Input to this measurement type includes metadata that identifies the sets of fields that will be tested for validity as well as the domains against which they will be tested. It also requires past measurement results. The process of taking the measurement is the same as described in Measurement Type #27, except that the value set returned will include combinations of values instead of individual values. Assignment of the validity indicator will be based on the combinations of values.

Support Processes and Skills

See Measurement Type #27.

Measurement Logical Data Model

The Metric Definition table for Measurement Type #29 contains all the attributes in Type #27 and extends the concept to include additional Target and Reference Data columns.

The Results table for Measurement Type #29 contains all the attributes present in Type #27; in addition, it contains fields needed to accommodate the additional values produced when the validity is being measured across columns. See Table 16.19.

Measurement Type #30: Consistent Column Profile
Definition

Description: Reasonability check, compare record count distribution of values (column profile) to past instances of data populating the same field.
Object of Measurement: Content/Row counts
Assessment Category: In-line measurement
Cross Reference: 27

Table 16.18 Metric Definition for Measurement Type #29

Attribute Name	Attribute Definition
Target Column 1	This field indicates which field or Target Column is being measured (see #15).
Target Column 2	This field indicates which field or Target Column is being measured (see #23).
Target Column N	This field indicates which field or Target Column is being measured (see #23).
Validity Type	This field defines how validity will be established (through comparison to reference data, through a defined range, or through a rule). Other fields within the validity table will be populated based on which type of validity is measured.
Reference Data Table	For validity tests based on reference data, this field contains the name of the table that contains the values against which validity will be tested.
Reference Data Column 1	For validity tests based on reference data, this field contains the name of the column on the reference table that contains the values against which the validity of Target Column 1 will be tested.
Reference Data Column 2	For validity tests based on reference data, this field contains the name of the column on the reference table that contains the values against which the validity of Target Column 2 will be tested.
Reference Data Column N	For validity tests based on reference data, this field contains the name of the column on the reference table that contains the values against which the validity of Target Column N will be tested.
Validity business rule	For any measurement based on a business rule, this field contains the rule (in this case, a validity rule).

Table 16.19 Measurement Results for Measurement Type #29

Attribute Name	Attribute Definition
Data Value 1 (Target Column 1)	This field contains the value present on the data being measured in the column being measured (see #27).
Data Value 2 (Target Column 2)	This field contains the value present on the data being measured in the column being measured. Values from Target Column 1 are stored in Data value 1, those from Target Column 2 in Data Value 2, etc.
Data Value N (Target Column N)	This field contains the value present on the data being measured in the column being measured. Values from Target Column 1 are stored in Data value 1, those from Target Column 2 in Data Value 2, etc.
Validity indicator	Y—Value set combination is valid; N—Value set combination is invalid
Measurement Record Count	The number of records that meet the condition being measured (see #14)
Percentage of Records Associated with Each Data Value Set	(Measurement Record Count/Dataset Total Record Count)*100
Historical Mean Percentage of Records Associated with Each Data Value Set	Calculated historical mean (see #14)
Difference from the Historical Mean Percentage of Records Associated with Each Data Value Set	Historical mean percentage minus the percentage of the current measurement
Threshold Exceeded Indicator for difference from the Historical Mean Percentage of Records Associated with Each Data Value Set	Records whether or not a specific measurement is greater than the established data quality threshold (see #6)

Business Concerns

Organizations that create large data stores, such as data warehouses, often have large sets of similar data that need to be processed in the same way over time. Organizations use this data to understand how well they are executing their business and to make decisions about how to improve it. Consistency measures are based on the assumption that a stable process (the same process executed in the same manner) with similar input should produce similar results with each execution. Within such a process there will be some variation—common cause or normal variation—that can itself be measured. Therefore data consistency measures depend on establishing expected tolerances for normal variation and monitoring to ensure these tolerances are not crossed. Consistency measures can be simple (focusing on one data element or one step in a process) or complex (incorporating multiple data elements and relationships between them). Applied to critical data and monitored closely on incremental loads, these checks can detect changes that might have a negative effect on the business uses of the data.

The most basic consistency check is a column profile. A column profile is a reasonability check that compares record count and percentage distribution of distinct values to past instances of data populating the same field. It includes calculations of variations in both record counts and percentages. For fields with a specified data domain, it can also be combined with a validity check since it depends on exactly the same data collection (see Measurement Type #27: Validity Check—Detailed Results).

The purpose of this in-line measurement is to detect changes in the distribution of values in critical fields, so that these changes can be investigated and their causes identified. As was described in the discussion on validity, detailed results often contain a significant number of distinct values, making it challenging to analyze and characterize the overall condition of the data. A pure column profile without a validity component does not have inherent criteria for summarizing. Therefore it is important that the comparison to past results be automated. In addition, as was explained in relation to Measurement Type #27, because the result set will include multiple rows, a single threshold for investigation cannot be applied. An automated threshold of three standard deviations from the mean of past percentages of rows associated with each particular value will serve to surface potential anomalies (See Figure 16.3).

Measurement Methodology

This in-line reasonability measure identifies distinct values within a field and calculates a percentage distribution of those values and a comparison to past values, as described under Measurement Type #27.

Programming

Column Profiling works the same way as basic validity (Measurement #27) but is slightly simpler because it does not require comparisons with a standard for validity.

Support Processes and Skills

Since it is not likely that a change in the distribution of values will require a database stoppage, this measurement will not require notifications to alert staff to urgent problems. Instead, staff is required to review the detailed results to identify patterns in the distribution of values to determine whether or not they are business-expected. If the distributions do conform to business expectations, then review

Table 16.20 Measurement Results for Measurement Type #30

Attribute Name	Attribute Definition
Data Value 1 (Target Column 1)	This field contains the value present on the data being measured in the column being measured (see #27).
Measurement Record Count	The number of records that meet the condition being measured (see #14)
Percentage of Records Associated with the Data Value	(Measurement Record Count/Dataset Total Record Count) *100
Historical Mean Percentage of Records Associated with Each Data Value	Calculated historical mean (see #14)
Difference from the Historical Mean Percentage of Records Associated with the Data Value	Historical mean percentage minus the percentage of the current measurement
Threshold Exceeded Indicator for difference from the Historical Mean Percentage of Records Associated with the Data Value	Records whether or not a specific measurement is greater than the established data quality threshold (see #6)

can focus largely on the values whose percentages cross the threshold of more than three standard deviations from the mean of past percentages.

Measurement Logical Data Model

The Metric Definition table for Measurement Type #30 contains the following attributes (as defined under #6): Measurement Type Number, Specific Metric Number, Dataset Name, Dataset Source, Dataset Type, Data Quality Threshold Type, Data Quality Threshold (if threshold is set manually), Range Minimum, and Range Maximum. In addition, it contains Target Column 1 as defined in #15.

The Results table for Measurement Type #30 contains Measurement Type Number, Specific Metric Number, Measurement Date, and Notification Sent Indicator (as defined in #6), and the attributes listed in Table 16.20.

Measurement Type #31: Consistent Dataset Content, Distinct Count of Represented Entity, with Ratios to Record Counts
Definition

Description: Reasonability check, compare distinct counts of entities represented within a dataset (e.g., the distinct number of customers represented in sales data) to threshold, historical counts, or total records.

Object of Measurement: Content summary

Assessment Category: In-line measurement

Cross Reference: 1, 32

Business Concerns

As noted under Measurement Type #30: Consistent Column Profile, organizations that create large data stores, such as data warehouses, often have large sets of similar data that need to be processed in the same way over time. Consistency measures are based on the assumption that a stable process (the same process executed in the same manner) with similar input should produce similar results with each execution. The concept of consistency in relation to past input can be applied at the dataset level as well as at the column level. For example, each month's worth of data might be expected to contain transactions from a similar percentage of the overall customer base or from a minimum number of customers.

The purpose of this in-line measurement is to provide reasonability checks about incoming data content based on distinct counts of a particular entity represented within a dataset—for example, a count of the distinct number of customers represented in sales data or the distinct number of insured persons (members) represented in medical claim data. Reasonability is based on the degree of consistency with past instances of the same dataset. This type of measure is best applied to transactional data for which transactional activities are expected to have a degree of consistency. It does not apply to reference or dimensional data. It can be used as a completeness or sufficiency test, if a criterion for completeness or sufficiency is the presence of a minimum number of a particular entity in a dataset.

Measurement Methodology

This in-line reasonability measure applies rules or sets of attributes required to represent a distinct entity (such as a customer or a product) in a dataset. From these it counts the distinct number of the entity represented in an instance of the dataset. It then compares this result to past instances of the same dataset. Comparisons can be made through raw counts against the past average or as a percentage of the median of past measures or as a ratio between the number of the distinct attribute and the total number of records in the dataset (resulting in the number of records per distinct entity). Or comparisons can be made in all three ways.

Programming

Input to this measurement type includes metadata that defines the rules or sets of attributes required to represent a distinct entity within a dataset. It also requires past measurement results to determine the median. The measurement process queries the dataset to count the distinct number of entities present in the dataset and compares this result to the number present in past instances of the measurement. Comparisons include raw numbers to the past average, percentage of median, or a ratio of distinct number of entities to overall number of records. Thresholds can be established based on the historical variation (three standard deviations from the median) or based on other criteria established by SMEs. Depending on these criteria, the measurement can be executed as a process control. If the data does not contain the minimum number of the entity, then notifications need to be sent to support staff.

Table 16.21 Measurement Results for Measurement Type #31

Attribute Name	Attribute Definition
Dataset Total Record Count	This field contains the number of records present in the dataset being measured (see #10)
Distinct Count of Represented Entity	This field contains the result of application of the rule to define a represented entity.
Average Records per Represented Entity	(Dataset Total Record Count/Distinct Count of Represented Entity) *100
Historical Mean of Average Records per Represented Entity	Calculated historical mean (see #14)
Difference from the Historical Mean of the Average of Records per Represented Entity	Historical mean of average minus the current measurement
Threshold Exceeded Indicator for difference from the Historical Mean of the Average of Records per Represented Entity	Records whether or not a specific measurement is greater than the established data quality threshold. (see #6)

Support Processes and Skills

Staff in the target data store must be able to perform analysis to identify patterns in data content and to determine whether changes in the ratios are business-expected. Source system staff must also be available to contribute to analysis. Staff in the target data store must be in place to respond to alerts that a process has been stopped, if that functionality is put in place.

Measurement Logical Data Model

The Metric Definition table for Measurement Type #31 contains the following attributes (as defined under #6): Measurement Type Number, Specific Metric Number, Dataset Name, Dataset Source, Dataset Type, Data Quality Threshold Type, and Data Quality Threshold (if threshold is set manually). In addition, it must include a name of the represented entity to be measured and the rule needed to define the represented entity.

The Results table for Measurement Type #31 contains Measurement Type Number, Specific Metric Number, Measurement Date, and Notification Sent Indicator (as defined in #6), and the attributes listed in Table 16.21.

Measurement Type #32 Consistent Dataset Content, Ratio of Distinct Counts of Two Represented Entities
Definition

Description: Reasonability check, compare ratio between distinct counts of important fields/ entities (e.g., customers/sales office, claims/insured person) to threshold or historical ratio.

Object of Measurement: Content summary
Assessment Category: In-line measurement
Cross Reference: 1, 31

Business Concerns

The concept of consistency in relation to past input applied at the dataset level can be extended beyond distinct counts of a particular entity to relationships between entities—for example, in medical claims data, the relationship between the distinct number of patients and the distinct number of medical providers represented in a dataset. Results from the measurements of distinct counts can be used as input for these additional comparisons. As with the ratio of records per entity described under Measurement Type #31, a ratio between distinct counts of two entities provides a high-level measure of data consistency.

The purpose of this in-line measurement is to provide a reasonability check about incoming data content based on a ratio of distinct counts of two types of entity represented within a dataset, and to detect significant changes in that content. Reasonability is based on the consistency with past instances of the same dataset.

Measurement Methodology

For each of the entities that are part of the ratio, this in-line reasonability measure applies rules or sets of attributes required to represent a distinct entity in a dataset (as was described under Measurement Type #31). It then creates a ratio between distinct counts of two entities and compares this result to past instances of the same dataset as a raw number and as a percentage of the mean to identify instances that exceed an established threshold.

Programming

Input to this measurement type includes metadata that identifies the fields that will be measured, along with results from Measurement Type #31 and past measurement results. The process should create a ratio between the two distinct counts. Calculate the difference between the current ratio and the historical ratio. Calculate the standard deviation from the mean of past runs and three standard deviations from the mean of past runs. Assign an indicator to each distinct value set showing whether the current percentage is more than three standard deviations from the mean of percentages of past runs.

Support Processes and Skills

Staff in the target data store must be able to perform analysis to identify patterns in data content and to determine whether changes are business-expected. Source system staff must also be available to contribute to analysis. Staff in the target data store must be in place to respond to alerts that a process has been stopped, if that functionality is put in place.

Measurement Logical Data Model

The Metric Definition table for Measurement Type #32 contains all the attributes contained in Type #31. But it includes names and rules for two represented entities instead of just one.

Table 16.22 Measurement Results for Measurement Type #32

Attribute Name	Attribute Definition
Dataset Total Record Count	This field contains the number of records present in the dataset being measured (see #10).
Distinct Count of Represented Entity 1	This field contains the result of application of the rule to define a represented entity.
Distinct Count of Represented Entity 2	This field contains the result of application of the rule to define a represented entity.
Ratio (distinct count 1/distinct count 2)	Distinct count of represented entity 1/Distinct count of represented entity 2
Historical Mean of Ratios	Calculated historical mean (see #14 and #23)
Difference from the Historical Mean of Ratios	Historical mean of ratio minus the current measurement
Threshold Exceeded Indicator for difference from the Historical Mean of Ratios	Records whether or not a specific measurement is greater than the established data quality threshold (see #6)

The Results table for Measurement Type #32 contains Measurement Type Number, Specific Metric Number, Measurement Date, and Notification Sent Indicator (as defined in #6), and the attributes listed in Table 16.22.

Measurement Type #33: Consistent Multicolumn Profile
Definition

Description: Reasonability check, compare record count distribution of values across multiple fields to historical percentages, in order to test business rules (multicolumn profile with qualifiers).
Object of Measurement: Content/Row counts
Assessment Category: In-line measurement
Cross Reference: 24, 27, 30, 34

Business Concerns

The concept of a column profile (a basic consistency check accomplished in-line through a distribution of values) described under Measurement Type #30 can be extended across multiple columns. Related columns embed business rules and relationships. Once identified and defined, these rules can be expressed in terms of the relationship between columns in a table (lateral relationship). Rules are often expressed as conditions and results (If /Then statements) that stipulate either a positive or negative relation. For example, If condition A exists, then result A must exist (If a person is married, then he or she has a spouse). Or If condition A exists, then result B cannot exist (If a person is not married, then he or she does not have a spouse). From the perspective of business rules, If/Then statements can also identify possible conditions. For example, If condition C exists, then result D can exist, but it does not have to (If a person is an aunt, then she may or may not have a niece. She may have a nephew and no nieces).

The consistency of these rules can be evaluated through analysis of how sets of values distribute. Repeated execution of such a distribution of value sets can be used to identify changes in data populations across columns. If rules can be strictly defined as sets of domain values, a multicolumn profile amounts to the same thing as a multicolumn validity test. If rules are less strictly defined, then measurements depend on establishing the degree of consistency between sets of values in multiple instances of the same dataset. Because some business rules can be defined in a targeted fashion and because distributions of values with large cardinality are difficult to manage, this type of measurement works best when the conditions of business rules can be narrowed through qualifiers. For example, if a single rule could be established to define all records that meet an unacceptable condition, then application of such a rule would produce one measurement result row.

The purpose of this in-line measurement is to detect changes in the distribution of values across sets of related fields that embody business rules, so that these changes can be investigated and their causes identified. As was described in the discussions on validity and column profiling, detailed results can contain a significant number of distinct values, making it challenging to analyze and characterize the overall condition of the data. Even if results for some specific measurements are narrowed through qualifiers, it is important that the comparison to past results be automated. Because the result set may include multiple rows, it is not possible to establish a single threshold for investigation. In such cases, an automated threshold of three standard deviations from the mean of past percentages of rows associated with a particular value should be applied.

Measurement Methodology

This in-line reasonability measure identifies distinct values within a set of related fields and calculates a percentage distribution of those values. The percentage of any value set can then be compared to past percentages of that value set in order to detect changes in the patterns of incremental data. As described under Measurement Type #27, automation of comparisons to past percentages and of thresholds is especially important for high cardinality value sets. When such measurements are targeted to critical business rules, the measurement process should include the option to stop data processing and notify staff if thresholds are exceeded (see Figure 16.3).

Programming

Input to this measurement type includes metadata that identifies the fields that will be measured, as well as past measurement results. The programming then follows the same pattern described in Measurement Types 27 and 30.

Support Processes and Skills

Staff in the target data store must be able to perform analysis to identify patterns in data content and to determine whether changes are business-expected. Source system staff must also be available to

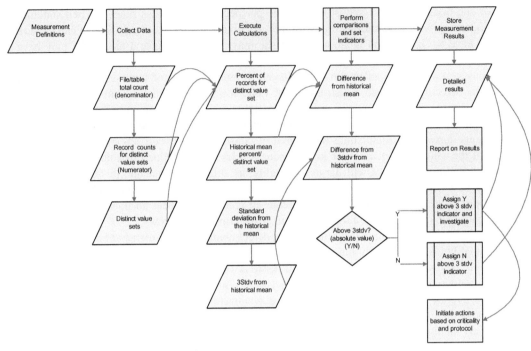

Figure 16.3 Consistent Multicolumn Profile

The process of measuring consistency compared with past instances of the same dataset follows a similar pattern, regardless of how many data elements are included in the comparison. First the data that will be measured must be identified. Next record counts for the distinct value set must be collected from the core data, so that the percentage of records associated with each value can be calculated. Then the percentage of each distinct value set can be compared to the percentage in past instances of the dataset, and a difference can be calculated. If this difference is significant, notifications should be sent so that analysts can review the data and determine whether the difference indicates a problem with the data and can initiate actions based on defined protocols. The results of the comparisons constitute the detailed measurements. These can be used to report on data quality.

contribute to analysis. Staff in the target data store must be in place to respond to alerts that a process has been stopped, if that functionality is put in place.

Measurement Logical Data Model

The Metric Definition table for Measurement Type #33 contains the following attributes (as defined under #6): Measurement Type Number, Specific Metric Number, Dataset Name, Dataset Source, Dataset Type, Data Quality Threshold Type, and the attributes listed in Table 16.23.

The Results table for Measurement Type #33 contains Measurement Type Number, Specific Metric Number, Measurement Date, and Notification Sent Indicator (as defined in #6), and the attributes listed in Table 16.24.

Table 16.23 Metric Definition for Measurement Type #33

Attribute Name	Attribute Definition
Target Column 1	This field indicates which field or Target Column is being measured (see #15).
Target Column 2	This field indicates which field or Target Column is being measured (see #23).
Target Column N	This field indicates which field or Target Column is being measured (see #23).
Condition Column 1	This field identifies a column to which a filter or other condition will be applied to narrow the measurement. In a SQL statement, it is part of the "where" clause. Note: The changes under Condition Column 1 are to ensure that the terms refer to the attributes listed later in the table. Condition column 1 identifies the first column for which a condition is applied. It is associated with Function Column 1 and Filter Condition Text 1. For example, if a condition for a measurement was: measure all claim records where Provider Identifier = 999-99-9999, then Provider Identifier is the Condition Column=is the Function and 999-99-9999 is the Filter Condition Text.
Condition Column 2	This field identifies a second column to which a filter or other condition will be applied to narrow the measurement. See Condition Column 1.
Condition Column N	This field identifies any additional column to which a filter or other condition will be applied to narrow the measurement. See Condition Column 1.
Function Column 1	This field identifies the type of condition being applied. In an SQL statement, it defines the mathematical function applied to the where clause (=,>,<, etc.)
Function Column 2	This field identifies the type of condition being applied. In an SQL statement it defines the mathematical function applied to the where clause (=,>,<, etc.)
Function Column N	This field identifies the type of condition being applied. In an SQL statement, it defines the mathematical function applied to the where clause (=,>,<, etc.)
Filter Condition Text 1	This field specifies the filter or other condition being applied to narrow the measurement.
Filter Condition Text 2	This field specifies the filter or other condition being applied to narrow the measurement.
Filter Condition Text N	This field specifies the filter or other condition being applied to narrow the measurement.

Measurement Type #34: Chronology Consistent with Business Rules within a Table

Definition

Description: Reasonability check, compare date values to business rule for chronology (subtype of Measurement Type #33 Multicolumn Profile).
Object of Measurement: Content/Date content
Assessment Category: In-line measurement
Cross Reference: 1, 16, 17, 33, 35

Table 16.24 Measurement Results for Measurement Type #33

Attribute Name	Attribute Definition
Dataset Total Record Count	This field contains the number of records present in the dataset being measured (see #10).
Data Value 1 (Target Column 1)	This field contains the value present on the data being measured in the column being measured (see #27).
Data Value 2 (Target Column 2)	This field contains the value present on the data being measured in the column being measured (see #29).
Data Value N (Target Column N)	This field contains the value present on the data being measured in the column being measured (see #29).
Measurement Record Count	The number of records that meet the condition being measured (see #14)
Percentage of Records Associated with each Data Value Set	(Measurement record count/Dataset total record count)*100
Historical Mean Percentage of Records Associated with Each Data Value Set	Calculated historical mean (see #14)
Difference from the Historical Mean Percentage of Records Associated with Each Data Value Set	Historical mean percentage minus the percentage of the current measurement
Threshold Exceeded Indicator for difference from the Historical Mean Percentage of Records Associated with Each Data Value Set	Records whether or not a specific measurement is greater than the established data quality threshold (see #6)

Business Concerns

As noted under Measurement Type #15 and 16, dates are often critical data elements in relation to processing and content. Date fields within a dataset often represent related points in a business process and imply business rules. For example, within a sale process, an order received date must come before an order shipped date. Or, in medical claims, date of service must come before adjudication date.

This measurement type is a subtype of the multicolumn profile that focuses on dates and implied chronology. Its purpose is to enable understanding of the adherence of related date data to chronological business rules and to detect significant changes in the consistency of that adherence. It identifies the level of records that are illogical based on date relationships and monitors changes in those levels. The subtype is called out because date content differs from codified content. While a consistent portion of records may have an illogical relationship between dates (death date before birth date, for example), it would not be expected that specific dates on incrementally loaded records would be consistent. Date measurements need to be formulated to account for this characteristic of date data.

Other Facets

For measurement methodology, programming, support processes, and a measurement logical data model, see Measurement Type #33: Consistent Multicolumn Profile

Measurement Type #35: Consistent Time Elapsed (hours, days, months, etc.)

Definition

Description: Reasonability check, compare consistency of time elapsed to past instances of data populating the same fields.
Object of Measurement: Content/Date content
Assessment Category: In-line measurement
Cross Reference: 1, 16, 17, 25, 34

Business Concerns

As noted under Measurement Type #15 and 16, dates are often critical data elements in relation to processing and content. Date fields often represent related points in a business process and imply business rules. Dates may be tested for logical adherence to rules (see Measurement Type #34) and for consistency. However, testing consistency requires a roll-up because date content differs from codified content. Consistency is expected at the relationship between date fields, not at the level of specific dates. Date measurements need to be formulated to account for this characteristic of date data. Date measurements can detect changes in business processes or changes in data delivery processes that may affect data availability.

The purpose of this measurement type is to apply a reasonability check between important date fields expressed as time elapsed. For example, the number of days elapsed between when an order is placed and when a product is shipped is expected to be consistent (but the specific dates are not expected to be the same). Changes in population can be analyzed to determine whether they represent problems or are business-expected.

Measurement Methodology

This measurement type calculates a difference between two date fields, expresses this difference in time elapsed (hours, days, months), and compares the result to past instances of the same measurement, calculates differences, and compares these to historical differences or to a threshold established by SMEs. This measurement type is very similar in structure to Measurement Type #25: Data Processing Duration. When such measurements are be targeted to critical business rules, the measurement process should include the option to stop data processing and notify staff if thresholds are exceeded.

Programming

This measurement type can use input from Measurement Type #34: Chronology Consistent with Business Rules to calculate the time elapsed between date fields. Or data collection can be set up separately. The measurement process collects data based on two identified date fields. It then summarizes the data associated with each value of time elapsed and calculates a percentage for each of the different values of elapsed time. For example, the percentage of records associated with one day elapsed, the percentage of records associated with two days elapsed, and so on. It compares those percentages to the historical percentages for those values and calculates a difference. It then compares the difference to a threshold to determine whether the difference is significant and notifies staff if the threshold is exceeded.

Support Processes and Skills

Staff in the target data store must be able to perform analysis to identify patterns in data content and to determine whether changes are business-expected. Source system staff must also be available to contribute to analysis. Staff in the target data store must be in place to respond to alerts that a process has been stopped, if that functionality is put in place.

Measurement Logical Data Model

The Metric Definition table for Measurement Type #35 contains the following attributes (as defined under #6): Measurement Type Number, Specific Metric Number, Dataset Name, Dataset Source, Dataset Type, Data Quality Threshold Type, and Data Quality Threshold (if threshold is set manually). In addition, it contains two target columns (Target Column 1 and Target Column 2), to identify the date fields being measured.

The Intermediate Results table for Measurement Type #35 contains Measurement Type Number, Specific Metric Number, Measurement Date, (as defined in #6), and the attributes listed in Table 16.25. This table is needed capture the detail required to calculate time elapsed. The Measurement Results table contains the standard attributes and Notification Sent Indicator, plus those listed in Table 16.26.

Table 16.25 Intermediate Measurement Results for Measurement Type #35

Attribute Name	Attribute Definition
Dataset Total Record Count	This field contains the number of records present in the dataset being measured (see #10).
Data Value 1 (Target Column 1)	This field contains the value present on the data being measured in the column being measured (see #27).
Data Value 2 (Target Column 2)	This field contains the value present on the data being measured in the column being measured (see #29).
Time Elapsed Value	This field represents the difference between Data Value 1 and Data Value 2 in the unit of measure appropriate to the data being measured.
Measurement Record Count	The number of records that meet the condition being measured (see #14)

Table 16.26 Measurement Results for Measurement Type #35

Attribute Name	Attribute Definition
Dataset Total Record Count	This field contains the number of records present in the dataset being measured (see #10).
Distinct Time Elapsed Value	This field represents the distinct set of time elapsed values from the intermediate measurement. For example, on the intermediate table, there may be several date combinations that have three days elapsed time. Only one row on the results table would represent three days elapsed time so that all row counts with that value can be rolled up into one measurement record count.
Measurement Record Count	The number of records that meet the condition being measured (see #14)
Percentage of Records Associated with Each Time Elapsed Value	(Measurement record count/Dataset total record count) *100
Historical Mean Percentage of Records Associated with each Time Elapsed Value	Calculated historical mean (see #14)
Difference from the Historical Mean Percentage of Records Associated with each Time Elapsed Value	Historical mean percentage minus the percentage of the current measurement
Threshold Exceeded Indicator for difference from the Historical Mean Percentage of Records Associated with Each Time Elapsed Value	Records whether or not a specific measurement is greater than the established data quality threshold (see #6)

Measurement Type #36: Consistent Amount Field Calculations Across Secondary Fields
Definition

Description: Reasonability check, compare amount column calculations, sum (total) amount, percentage of total amount, and average amount across a secondary field or fields to historical counts and percentages, with qualifiers to narrow results.
Object of Measurement: Content/Amount fields
Assessment Category: In-line measurement
Cross Reference: 1, 23, 33

Business Concerns

As noted under Measurement Type #23, amount fields often contain data that is critical to understanding an organization's success. They provide a means, in addition to record counts, of assessing the consistency of data content. Between incremental loads of similar data, there is usually an expectation that amount fields will contain similar data. For example, that net sales will be similar month-to-month. In addition to being taken at the dataset level, such measurements can be taken across other fields, for example, net sales per customer.

The purpose of this in-line measurement is to understand the degree to which amount field data is consistent and to identify unexpected changes.

Measurement Methodology

This in-line reasonability measure identifies a distinct value set based on a group of related fields, one of which is an amount field, such as a currency amount field for financial data (dollar, euro, etc.). It sums the total amount field as well as the amounts associated with each value set. The total amount sum serves as the denominator in calculations of percent of total amount (amount for distinct value set/total column amount). The sum associated with each value set serves as the numerator for calculations of average amount (amount for distinct value set/number of rows associated with distinct value set). The percentage of and averages of any value set can then be compared to historical percentages and averages of that value set in order to detect changes in the patterns of incremental data. As noted under Measurement #27, automation of historical comparisons and thresholds is especially important in data domains with a high number of distinct values (see Figure 16.4).

Programming

Input to this measurement type includes metadata that identifies the fields that will be measured and past measurement results. As is done with Measurement Type #33: Multicolumn Consistency, the process must count the overall number of records in the dataset as well as the number of records associated with each distinct value set for the fields being measured. From these two counts, it must calculate the percentage of records associated with each distinct value set. In addition, it must sum the total of the amount column and sum the records associated with each distinct set of values in order to calculate the percent of total amount (amount for distinct value set/total column amount) and average amount (amount for distinct value set/number of rows associated with distinct value set). With each run of the measurement, for each distinct value set, the process should compare the percentage of records to the historical mean percentage from past runs. Calculate the difference between the current percentage and the historical percentage. Calculate the standard deviation from the mean of past runs and three standard deviations from the mean of past runs. Assign an indicator to each distinct value set showing whether the current percentage is more than three standard deviations from the mean of percentages of past runs. It must perform these same calculations in relation to total amount, percentage of total amount, and average amount, except that average amount does not require a percentage of historical average.

Support Processes and Skills

Staff in the target data store must be able to perform analysis to identify patterns in data content and to determine whether changes are business-expected. Source system staff must also be available to contribute to analysis. Staff in the target data store must be in place to respond to alerts that a process has been stopped, if that functionality is put in place.

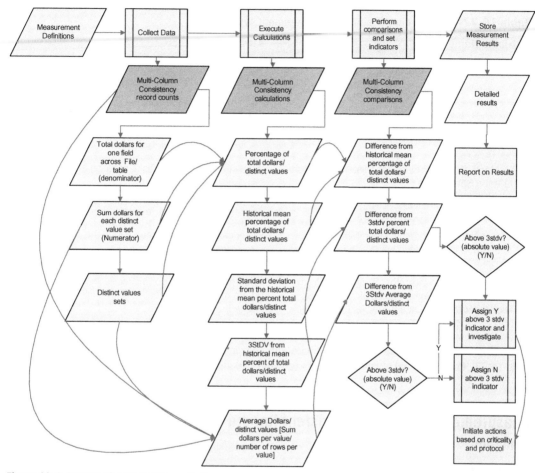

Figure 16.4 Amount Field Consistency Pattern:

The process of measuring amount field consistency depends on input from the Consistent Multicolumn Profile measurement (#33). Comparing results with past instances of the same dataset follows the similar pattern, regardless of how many data elements are included in the comparison. In addition to collecting distinct counts for each value set, the measurement requires summing the value of the amount field to be measured and the amount associated with each distinct set of values so that the percentage of total amount and average amount can be calculated and compared with past measurements. When significant differences are identified, notifications should be sent and actions initiated based on defined protocols. Detailed results can be used to report on data quality.

Measurement Logical Data Model

The Metric Definition table for Measurement #36 is structured identically to that of #33. The only difference is that Target Column 1 must be an amount field.

Table 16.27 Measurement Results for Measurement Type #36

Attribute Name	Attribute Definition
Total Amount (Target Column 1)	This field records the summed amount of the amount column being measured.
Measurement Amount	This field records the summed amount associated with each set of data values in the target columns.
Average Amount Associated with Each Data Value Set	Measurement Amount/Measurement record count
Percentage of Total Amount Associated with Each Data Value Set	(Measurement amount/Total amount) *100
Historical Mean Percentage of Total Amount Associated with Each Data Value Set	Calculated historical mean (see #14)
Difference from the Historical Mean Percentage of Total Amount Associated with Each Data Value Set	Historical mean percentage minus the percentage of the current measurement
Threshold Exceeded Indicator for difference from the Historical Mean Percentage of Total Amount Associated with Each Data Value Set (fields 2-N)	Records whether or not a specific measurement is greater than the established data quality threshold (see #6)

The Results table for Measurement #36 contains the same attributes as #33 and those contained in Table 16.27. The additional attributes contain raw and calculated data related to amount fields.

Measurement Type #37: Consistent Record Counts by Aggregated Date

Definition

Description: Reasonability check, compare record counts and percentage of record counts associated an aggregated date, such as a month, quarter, or year, to historical counts and percentages.
Object of Measurement: Content/Aggregated date
Assessment Category: Periodic measurement
Cross Reference: 30

Business Concerns

As noted under Measurement Type #15 and #16, dates are often critical data elements in relation to processing and content. Date fields can provide a means of confirming expectations related to data content or completeness and consistency. However, date content differs from codified content because the dates themselves change. In addition, date data input is usually at a finer level of grain than is desirable for analysis. Most date input contains day/month/year, creating hundreds of different dates per year. While comparisons between data related to specific dates do take place (think of weather data), comparisons based on aggregated dates (weekly, monthly, quarterly or annual) are more common and more comprehensible. Reasonableness depends on the expected volatility of the data. For most transactional business processes, newer date categories (the most recent month, or the current quarter) are more volatile than older date categories (three-year-old data).

This measure depends on choosing dates that are pertinent to the business processes represented by the data. For example, aggregating records based on order received date allows for both a data consistency measure and a business consistency measure; whereas backorder date would not be expected to be consistent, since it introduces the variable of the supplier. Choosing the level at which to aggregate also depends on expectations related to business processes. Some businesses measure goals monthly, others quarterly. In addition, business cycles can also influence choices for comparisons. Comparisons month-over-month may be less meaningful than comparisons between the same month year-over-year. For example, retail sales figures increase significantly at the end of the calendar year. Comparisons between sales figures in December of two different years may be more important than comparisons between January and February in a single year.

Such observations point to the close connection between data quality measurements and business measurements. Significant changes between content in the aggregate can indicate missing or duplicated data or changes in business process that should be accounted for when monitoring data quality.

The purpose of this measure is to provide a degree of assurance about the consistency of data content (record counts) aggregated by date. The measure should detect significant changes in content so that they can be investigated and explained or remediated.

Measurement Methodology

This measurement type is defined as periodic based on the assumption that most data stores load data incrementally. It cannot be taken incrementally because incremental datasets will not contain all the records needed to make comparisons at the aggregate level.

This measurement type periodically summarizes record counts based on aggregated dates (month, quarter, year). It compares results to past aggregations of the data, identifies differences, and compares these to a threshold, such as a percentage of total records from the previous instance of the measurement, or other measure established by SMEs. Reasonableness depends on the expected volatility of the data.

Programming

This measurement type uses record counts from a table as input. Based on the identified date field and the level of aggregation (month, quarter, year), it summarizes record counts by aggregate date and calculates the percentage of total for each date. It compares this percentage to past percentages for the same aggregate date and calculates the difference. If required, it can compare the difference to a threshold based on age of data and expected volatility or established by SMEs and send notifications if the threshold is exceeded.

Support Processes and Skills

Staff in the target data store must be able to perform analysis to identify patterns in data content and to determine whether changes are business-expected. Analysis must account for different degrees of volatility based on the age of aggregated data. Source system staff must also be available to contribute to analysis.

Table 16.28 Measurement Results for Measurement Type #37

Attribute Name	Attribute Definition
Aggregated Date Value	This field represents the distinct set of aggregated date values. For example, if data were aggregated by month-year, values might include 01-2010, 01-2010, etc.
Measurement Record Count	The number of records that meet the condition being measured (see #14)
Percentage of Records Associated with Each Aggregated Date Value	(Measurement record count/Dataset total Record Count) *100
Historical Mean Percentage of Records Associated with each Aggregated Date Value	Calculated historical mean (see #14)
Difference from the Historical Mean Percentage of Records Associated with Each Aggregated Date Value	Historical mean percentage minus the percentage of the current measurement
Threshold Exceeded Indicator for difference from the Historical Mean Percentage of Records Associated with Each Aggregated Date Value	Records whether or not a specific measurement is greater than the established data quality threshold (see #6)

Measurement Logical Data Model

The Metric Definition table for Measurement Type #37 contains the following attributes (as defined under #6): Measurement Type Number, Specific Metric Number, Dataset Name, Dataset Source, Dataset Type, Data Quality Threshold Type, and Data Quality Threshold (if threshold is set manually). In addition, it must include an aggregation type, which describes the time period used in the aggregation (weekly, monthly, quarterly, annually). Target Column 1 must be a date field.

The Results table for Measurement Type #37 contains Measurement Type Number, Specific Metric Number, Measurement Date, and Notification Sent Indicator (as defined in #6), and the attributes listed in Table 16.28.

Measurement Type #38: Consistent Amount Field Data by Aggregated Date

Definition

Description: Reasonability check, compare amount field data (total amount, percentage of total amount) aggregated by date (month, quarter, or year) to historical total and percentage.

Object of Measurement: Content/Aggregated date

Assessment Category: Periodic measurement

Cross Reference: 36, 37

Business Concerns

The concepts described under Measurement Type #36: Consistent Amount Column Calculations (total, percent of total, average)" and #37: Consistent Record Counts by Aggregated Date also apply when amount field data is aggregated by date. Amount fields often contain data that is critical to understanding an organization's success. They provide a means, in addition to record counts, of assessing the consistency of data content. There may be an expectation, for example, that quarter-over-quarter sales numbers will be consistent. Significant changes between content in the aggregate can indicate missing or duplicated data or changes in the business process that should be accounted for when monitoring data quality.

The purpose of this in-line measure is to provide a degree of assurance about the consistency of data content aggregated by date. The measure should detect significant changes in content so that they can be investigated and explained or remediated.

Measurement Methodology

This measurement type is defined as periodic based on the assumption that most data stores load data incrementally. Incremental datasets will not contain all the records needed to make comparisons at the aggregate level.

This measurement type periodically aggregates data from amount fields to calculate total amount and percentage of total amount. With each periodic run of the measurement, it compares these results to past aggregations of the data, identifies differences, and compares these to a threshold, such as a percentage of total records from the previous instance of the measurement, or other measure established by SMEs. Reasonableness depends on the expected volatility of the data. The measurement process can include the assignment of indicators when differences from past measurements exceed thresholds. Since the measurement is against data that is already loaded, differences will not be a cause to stop data processing, such as a table load. However, the measurements will help identify data that requires additional investigation and should include notifications and the assignment of indicators.

Programming

This measurement type uses amount field data from a table as input. Based on the identified amount field, the identified date field, and the level of aggregation (month, quarter, year), it summarizes amount counts by aggregate date and calculates the percentage of total for each date. It compares this percentage to past percentages for the same aggregate date and calculates the difference. If required, it can compare the difference to a threshold based on age of data and expected volatility or established by SMEs and send notifications if the threshold is exceeded.

Support Processes and Skills

Staff in the target data store must be able to perform analysis to identify patterns in data content and to determine whether changes are business-expected. Analysis must account for different degrees of volatility based on the age of aggregated data. Source system staff must also be available to contribute to analysis.

Table 16.29 Measurement Results for Measurement Type #38

Attribute Name	Attribute Definition
Total Amount (Target Column 2)	This field records the summed amount of the amount column being measured.
Measurement Amount	This field records the summed amount associated with each set of data values in the target columns.
Average Amount Associated with Each Aggregated Date	Measurement amount/Measurement record count
Percentage of Total Amount Associated with Each Aggregated Date	(Measurement amount/Total amount) *100
Historical Mean Percentage of Total Amount Associated with Each Aggregated Date	Calculated historical mean (see #14)
Difference from the Historical Mean Percentage of Total Amount Associated with Each Aggregated Date	Historical mean percentage minus the percentage of the current measurement
Threshold Exceeded Indicator for difference from the Historical Mean Percentage of Total Amount Associated with Each Aggregated Date	Records whether or not a specific measurement is greater than the established data quality threshold (see #6)
Notification Sent Indicator	Y = notification was sent. N = notification was not sent (see #6)

Measurement Logical Data Model

The Metric Definition table for Measurement Type #38 contains the same attributes as are required for #37. As with #37, Target Column 1 must be a date field. Target Column 2 must be an amount field. Additional target columns can be included if there is a need to aggregate by secondary attributes.

The Results table for Measurement Type #38 contains all the attributes required for #37, plus those listed in Table 16.29. The additional attributes store calculations related to amount fields.

Measurement Type #39: Parent/Child Referential Integrity
Definition

Description: Confirm record level (parent/child) referential integrity between tables to identify parentless child records, (i.e., "orphan") records.
Object of Measurement: Cross-table content
Assessment Category: Periodic measurement
Cross Reference: 1, 27, 28, 40

Business Concerns

Referential integrity is defined as the degree to which data in two or more tables related through a foreign key relationship is complete. Referential integrity is often explained through parent/child table relationships. Within a relational database, all values that are present on a child table should also be present on its parent table (the child inherits values from the parent). If a child table has values that are not on its parent table, it does not have referential integrity with the parent table. These records represent parentless children, or "orphans." There are many reasons why a value on a child table might be absent from a parent table. A lack of data entry controls can allow values to be entered without any reference to their validity. Two systems processing similar data may not be synchronized. Or there may be differences in the update schedules of parent tables and child tables within one database.

Referential integrity is most often illustrated in relation to reference data. If a value on a fact or core table (which is a child to a reference table) is not present in a reference table, then the two will not have referential integrity. However, referential integrity also applies to the relationship between fact tables, such as between header and detail records. For example, if someone who purchases goods from a business does not have a record on the customer table but does have a record in the order table, then the record in the order table will be an orphan.

The purpose of this periodic assessment is to test the level of referential integrity in critical fields throughout a database. It mitigates the risks associated with having incomplete relationships between related datasets. Summarized results from the assessment can be used as a way to characterize the overall quality of data in a warehouse or other database.

Measurement Methodology

The measurement of referential integrity related to reference data works in the same way as the detailed validity measure. Values identified as invalid in the validity check are missing from their parent (reference) tables. Across fact tables, the check can be executed as a multicolumn profile. In databases that include cross-table match processes, the referential integrity check can be accomplished by reviewing the success of those match processes and then performing manual queries to determine whether the match processes may be impacted by timing issues or other factors that reduce the level of referential integrity between tables. Once stable levels of orphan records are established, measurements should identify significant changes to these, using a threshold established through historical calculations or by SMEs. Finally, referential integrity checks can be executed periodically across a database for relationships that might not be measurable as part of data processing. Such measurement would consist of joining the parent and child tables using a left outer join to identify orphan records and measuring their level as a percentage of total records.

Programming

This measurement type requires metadata identifying the foreign key relationships that need to be tested. All those involving reference data should be measured through the detailed validity measurement type. Those that involve the relationship between fact tables should be measured through the cross-table multicolumn profile, with rules specified to identify orphan records. Or they can be measured as a left outer join between parent and child tables to identify the level of orphan records.

Support Processes and Skills

Staff in the target data store must be able to perform analysis to identify patterns in orphan records that might point to root causes for their presence in the data store. Source system staff must also be available to contribute to analysis.

Measurement Type #40: Child/Parent Referential Integrity
Definition

> **Description**: Confirm record level (child/parent) referential integrity between fact tables to identify "childless" parent records.
> **Object of Measurement**: Cross-table content
> **Assessment Category**: Periodic measurement
> **Cross Reference**: 1, 27, 28, 39, 41

Business Concerns

As noted under Measurement Type #39, referential integrity is defined as the degree to which data in two or more tables related through a foreign key relationship is complete. The term is often explained through parent child table relationships, where there is a concern about "orphan" records. In some cases, however, there is also an expectation that each parent record will have at least one child record. The purpose of this periodic assessment is to test the level of referential integrity in critical fields throughout a database in order to identify childless parent records when there is a rule that such records should exist. This type of measurement can detect failures in complex processing that may result in missing records. It can also confirm that the data has followed business rules.

Measurement Methodology

The measurement of child/parent referential integrity requires a comparison between tables based on business rules that enable the identification of childless parent records. This type of integrity does not usually apply to reference data because there is not usually an expectation that all values in a reference dataset need to be present in fact data. Across fact tables, the check can be executed as a multicolumn profile or a periodic integrity check that joins parent and child tables to identify parent records that do not have child records.

Programming

This measurement type requires metadata identifying the relationships that need to be tested. Those that involve the relationship between fact tables should be measured through the cross-table multicolumn profile or full table join, with rules specified to identify childless parent records.

Support Processes and Skills

Staff in the target data store must be able to perform analysis to identify patterns in childless parent records that might point to root causes for their presence in the data store. Source system staff must also be available to contribute to analysis.

Measurement Type #41: Validity Check, Cross Table, Detailed Results
Definition

> **Description**: Compare values in a mapped or business rule relationship across tables to ensure data is associated consistently.
>
> **Object of Measurement**: Cross-table content
>
> **Assessment Category**: Periodic measurement
>
> **Cross Reference**: 1, 27, 28, 29

Business Concerns

As noted under Measurement Type #27, assuring that data is valid, that actual data values adhere to a defined domain of values, is fundamental to data quality assurance. The cross-table validity check works in a manner similar to other validity checks. It differs in the degree of complexity by which the domain of valid values is identified. It addresses the risk that data is identified as valid but is still incorrect. To identify such situations, it compares the results of validity checks for the fields related to the same represented entity, but existing on two different tables, and confirms whether the sets of data values are the same across both tables. For example, a customer may be associated with a specific market on a demographic table, and that market may be valid. The same customer may be associated with a different market on a table recording sales, and that market may also be valid. If both markets exist in the same state, they may also be valid in relation to a State Abbreviation Code. However, if there is a rule that a customer should be associated with one-and-only-one market at a time, then at least one of the records has incorrect (albeit valid) data. This purpose of this periodic measurement is to identify instances where the integrity of data is absent between records in a database.

Measurement Methodology

The cross-table validity check works in a manner similar to other validity checks. It compares two sets of values that are supposed to be in a valid relationship and identifies instances where the value sets do not align. It includes marking all such values with a validity indicator.

Programming

The cross-table validity check should be run after the levels of validity have been established for the fields involved on the tables being compared. If there are high levels of invalid relationships on either table, that situation should be addressed before executing this more complex periodic measurement. The check compares the values or value sets associated with a represented entity (such as a customer) on two tables to ensure that these correspond. It identifies instances where there are different values associated with the same represented entity.

Support Processes and Skills

If the attributes being measured correspond exactly to each other, then there should not be differences between tables. Therefore, staff in the target data store must be able to perform analysis to identify patterns in data content and to determine why there are discrepancies between the data. Source system staff must also be available to contribute to analysis.

Measurement Type #42: Consistent Cross-table Multicolumn Profile
Definition

Description: Cross-table reasonability check, compare record count distribution of values across fields on related tables to historical percentages, in order to test adherence to business rules (multicolumn profile with qualifiers).
Object of Measurement: Cross-table content
Assessment Category: Periodic measurement
Cross Reference: 33

Business Concerns

The concepts described under Measurement Type #33: Consistent Multicolumn Profile can be extended to include comparisons between two tables or two systems. The purpose of this measurement is to provide a reasonability check based on a record count distribution of values across a set of tables or between files. The measure can include calculated variations in record counts and percentage of record counts. Cross-table comparisons can result in very large, unmanageable results sets. Ideally, this kind of measurement should include qualifiers that enable precise definition of expectations and rules.

Measurement Methodology

This measurement type is defined as periodic based on the assumption that most data stores load data incrementally. Incremental datasets will not contain all the records needed to make comparisons at the aggregate level.

This measurement type periodically compares the distribution of values from queries joining tables. With each periodic run of the measurement, it calculates the percentage of records associated with each value set and compares the results to past instances of the measurement, identifying differences in the percentage distributions. Reasonableness is defined based on the expected relation between the datasets. The measurement process can include the assignment of indicators when differences from past measurements exceed thresholds. Since the measurement is against data that is already loaded, differences will not be used to stop data processing. However, they will help identify data that requires additional investigation and can include notifications and the assignment of indicators.

Programming

Input to this measurement type includes metadata that identifies the tables and columns that will be included in the measurement, along with past measurement results. It joins the tables and counts the records associated with each set of distinct values across the fields. The process uses the overall number of records in the returned dataset as the denominator in calculations. From these two counts, it calculates the percentage of records associated with each distinct value set. As with the multicolumn profile within one table, with each run of this cross-table measure, the process should compare the percentage of records to the historical mean percentage from past runs for each distinct value set and execute the set of calculations described in #27.

Support Processes and Skills

Staff in the target data store must be able to perform analysis to identify patterns in data content and to determine whether changes are business-expected. Source system staff must also be available to contribute to analysis.

Measurement Type #43: Chronology Consistent with Business Rules Across-tables
Definition

> **Description**: Cross-table reasonability based on business rules for chronology on related tables.
> **Object of Measurement**: Content/Chronology/Cross-table
> **Assessment Category**: Periodic measurement
> **Cross Reference**: 34

Business Concerns

The concepts described under Measurement Type #34: Chronology Consistent with Business rules within a Table can be extended to include comparisons between two tables or two systems. The purpose of this measure is to test the consistency between related date fields across-tables, based on business rules for chronology (e.g., birth date must be less than death date, even if records for these events are stored in different tables)

Measurement Methodology and Programming

See Measurement Type #33: Consistent Multicolumn Profile.

Support Processes and Skills

Staff in the target data store must be able to perform analysis to identify patterns in data content and to determine whether changes are business-expected. Source system staff must also be available to contribute to analysis.

Measurement Type #44: Consistent Cross-table Amount Column Calculations
Definition

> **Description**: Cross-table reasonability check, compare summed amount calculations (total, percentage of total, average or ratios between these) on related tables.
> **Object of Measurement**: Cross-table content/Amount fields
> **Assessment Category**: Periodic measurement
> **Cross Reference**: 36

Business Concerns

The concepts described under Measurement Type #36: Consistent Amount Column Calculations (total, percent of total, average) can be extended to include comparisons between two tables or two systems.

Measurement Methodology

This measurement type is defined as periodic based on the need to summarize data from two different tables to make comparisons. While the measurement and the comparison of results can be automated, it cannot be accomplished in-line in data stores where loads are incremental.

This measurement type periodically aggregates data in amount fields from two tables. With each periodic run of the measurement, it calculates total amount and percentage of total amount in both tables and compares these to each other. Comparisons can include differences between total amounts, differences in percentages of total amount, or ratios between total amounts on the two tables. Reasonableness is defined based on the expected relation between the datasets. The measurement process can include the assignment of indicators when differences from past measurements exceed thresholds. Differences will not be used to stop data processing. However, they will help identify data that requires additional investigation.

Programming

This measurement type uses amount field data from two tables as input. It sums the amounts content in both fields and compares the two. Comparisons can include simple difference or ratios between them. If required, it can compare the difference to a threshold based on historical measurements or established by SMEs and send notifications if the threshold is exceeded.

Support Processes and Skills

Staff in the target data store must be able to perform analysis to identify patterns in data content and to determine whether changes are business-expected. Source system staff must also be available to contribute to analysis.

Measurement Type #45: Consistent Cross-Table Amount Columns by Aggregated Dates
Definition

Description: Cross-table reasonability check, compare amount field data (total amount, percentage of total amount) associated with an aggregated date (month, quarter, or year) on related tables.
Object of Measurement: Cross-table content/Aggregated date
Assessment Category: Periodic measurement
Cross Reference: 38

Business Concerns

The concepts described under Measurement Type #38. Consistent Total Amount by Aggregated Date can be extended to include comparisons between two tables or two systems.

Measurement Methodology

This periodic reasonability measure determines the consistency of content between two related datasets (i.e., two tables) and detects significant changes in that content, based amount fields aggregated by date (monthly, quarterly, annually). This measurement type is defined as periodic based on the need to summarize data from two different tables to make comparisons. While the measurement and the comparison of results can be automated, it cannot be accomplished in-line in data stores where loads are incremental.

This measurement type periodically aggregates data in amount fields from two tables based on an aggregated date (month, quarter, year). With each periodic run of the measurement, it calculates total amount and percentage of total amount in both tables, summarizes these based on the date field, and compares the results to each other. Comparisons can include differences between total amounts, differences in percentages of total amount, or ratios between total amounts on the two tables. Reasonableness is defined based on the expected relation between the datasets. The measurement process can include the assignment of indicators when differences from past measurements exceed thresholds. As is the case with other periodic measurements, it can be used to detect data that requires investigation.

Programming

This measurement type uses amount field data from two tables as input. Based on the identified amount fields, the identified date fields, and the level of aggregation (month, quarter, year), it summarizes amounts content by aggregate date and calculates the percentage of total for each date. It compares the results from the two tables and calculates differences or constructs ratios between them. If required, it can compare the difference to a threshold based on age of data and expected volatility or established by SMEs and send notifications if the threshold is exceeded.

Support Processes and Skills

Staff must be able to perform analysis to identify patterns in data content and to determine whether changes are business-expected. Analysis must account for business rules that govern the relationship between the two systems being compared, as well as for different degrees of volatility based on the age of aggregated data. Source system staff must also be available to contribute to analysis.

Measurement Type #46: Consistency Compared to External Benchmarks
Definition

Description: Compare data quality measurement results to a set of benchmarks, such as external industry or nationally established measurements for similar data.

Object of Measurement: Overall database content

Assessment Category: Periodic measurement

Cross Reference: Potentially all

Business Concerns

Many of the consistency measures depend on comparing any given instance of a dataset to past instances of the same dataset. This measurement type extends that concept by comparing a dataset to an external benchmark. Benchmark data usually contains a large sample or has been tested in a range of ways to confirm that it can serve as a reliable standard against which other data can be evaluated. Input to comparisons with benchmarks can come directly from column or multicolumn profiles. The purpose of such comparisons is to identify differences from the benchmark and to determine whether or not these are business-expected.

Measurement Methodology

This periodic assessment compares column profile and multicolumn profile results from datasets to be tested with benchmark data obtained from a standards organization or other source that confirms its reliability. This type of measure will not require notifications. However, automated comparisons can include indicators that identify any measurements exceeding thresholds established in relation to the benchmarks.

Programming

This periodic assessment requires output from other measurements as input to the comparisons. Measurements will need to be mapped to their corresponding measures in the benchmark data. Differences will need to be calculated. If past measurement results are available, comparisons can be made to the historical mean or median for individual values and aggregates.

Support Processes and Skills

Staff in the target data store need a high degree of business knowledge or access to business SMEs who can review findings and determine whether differences from benchmarks are business-expected.

Measurement Type #47: Dataset Completeness—Overall Sufficiency for Defined Purposes

Definition

Description: Compare macro database content (e.g., data domains, sources, number of records, historical breadth of data, represented entities) to requirements for specific uses of the data.
Object of Measurement: Overall database content
Assessment Category: Periodic assessment
Cross Reference: Potentially all

Business Concerns

Data completeness is understood not only at the field or dataset level but also across a database. Completeness will first be understood in terms of the macro content of the database: what data domains are represented, the number of months or years of historical data present, the level of granularity of data represented in the data model. Completeness may also be assessed in relation to the number of records present, the time frame represented in the data, and the number of real-world entities (e.g., customers, members, sales) represented in the data or by other macro content requirements.

The purpose of this assessment is to ensure that actual data content is documented and understood so that data consumers can determine whether a database meets their needs and to identify gaps that can be addressed. This kind of assessment should be undertaken periodically because most data stores undergo numerous changes as business processes evolve and new uses of data emerge. It is difficult to understand the breadth of data contained in a data store without periodically taking an inventory of it.

Measurement Methodology

Periodic assessment to confirm data meets macro content requirements. This periodic assessment inventories high-level content and compares it to documented requirements. It includes review of metadata as well as detailed data content.

Programming

This periodic assessment of data content can be executed using a profiling tool or through ad hoc queries.

Support Processes and Skills

Staff in the target data store need access to business SMEs who can define and confirm requirements and contribute to the assessment by confirming findings and identifying gaps.

Measurement Type #48: Dataset Completeness—Overall Sufficiency of Measures and Controls
Definition

> **Description**: Assess specific data quality metrics for effectiveness and comprehensiveness in relation to critical data.
> **Object of Measurement**: Data environment
> **Assessment Category**: Periodic measurement
> **Cross Reference**: Potentially all

Business Concerns

The establishment of a program of automated data quality measurement will produce a set of metadata (definitions of the metrics) and data (measurement results) that need to be managed and periodically assessed for their effectiveness.

The purpose of this measurement type is to ensure that the specific metrics developed to measure data quality are effective at managing risk and provide insight about the most critical data. The question the assessment should answer is whether the metrics provide an optimal set of measures. If they do not, then new metrics may need to be established or existing ones removed.

Measurement Methodology

This periodic assessment reviews each metric and assesses its effectiveness based on agree-to criteria, such as its business criticality and the appropriateness of the measurement to the data content and data process. Results from the assessment should be used to revise existing measurements and response protocols and to establish new ones.

Programming

This assessment does not require programming to automate any processes. It takes as its input metadata describing the metrics and results from the measurements. It requires that analysts apply their knowledge and judgement.

Support Processes and Skills

Staff in the target data store need a high degree of business knowledge as well as knowledge about the goals and structure of the measurements. They also need access to business SMEs who can provide input on the effectiveness of the measurements.

Concluding Thoughts: Know Your Data

"The greatest enemy of knowledge is not ignorance; it is the illusion of knowledge."
—Stephen Hawking, British Physicist

I was privileged to be a participant on the closing panel of the 2012 DGIQ (Data Governance Information Quality Conference). It is always good to be prepared for such events, and I spent some time thinking through my experience at the conference in order to formulate responses to the prompts. However, when the question came up as to what advice I would give conference attendees, the response I gave was different from what I had prepared. It was simply this: Know your data. I had attended several sessions on metadata and had many conversations with attendees about the challenges we all face in our organizations around definitions, policies, and projects. The experience made me realize: There is no substitute for knowledge.

In today's world, data is complex, technology is constantly developing, and organizations continuously evolve. In 1988, Peter Drucker wrote of the emerging need for knowledge workers. He compared the organization of the future to a symphony orchestra, in which each player is an expert on his or her instrument, but each also has a full understanding of how music works and how all members of orchestra must work together to perform well. I think we should take his metaphor seriously.

As I was writing this book, I told myself I would not use the word "intuitive" except when quoting other people. My irritation with the word stems from its usage as a synonym for "easy." The question "Can you make it more intuitive?" Often means, "I don't understand you. Make things simple for me." The challenge is, whatever efforts we make to simplify, one person's "intuitive" is still often another's "I don't get it." In researching this book, I was pleased to discover Emanuel Derman's characterization of intuition (based on that of the insights of seventeenth-century philosopher Baruch Spinoza): "Intuition may sound casual, but it emerges only from intimate knowledge acquired after careful observation and painstaking effort. Before you can move one level higher in the pyramid of understanding, before you can attain intuition in some domain, you have to struggle with the particulars of that domain until knowledge of its details is second nature to you" (Derman, 2011, p. 96). Data won't be intuitive unless we learn about it.

Measurement is a form of knowledge. To manage a thing, you need to know what it is or how many of it you have and what you expect it to do. To understand its quality, you need a means of characterizing its condition. I hope that the DQAF can help people in the process of learning about their data.

Glossary

Accessibility Data Quality Accessibility data quality is understood as the extent to which data is available to or obtainable by data consumers. Dimensions include accessibility, access security (from the Wang & Strong framework, 1996).

Accuracy Accuracy is the quality or state of being correct or precise; accurate information is correct in all details (*NOAD*). When used as a dimension of data quality, accuracy can be measured against the real-world objects it represents or against a surrogate—an acknowledged, authorized source—that serves as a standard (English, 1999).

Amount Field An amount field is a field that contains data in numeric form representing amounts of objects that can be counted (such as number of products ordered) or representing currency amounts (such as net sales amount). Synonyms include: dollar fields, financial fields, numeric fields.

Assessment Assessment is the process of evaluating or estimating the nature, ability, or quality of a thing. As a synonym for *measurement, assessment* implies the need to compare one thing to another in order to understand it. Assessment implies drawing a conclusion—evaluating—the object of the assessment (*NOAD*) whereas measurement does not always imply so. ASQ defines assessment as "A systematic evaluation process of collecting and analyzing data to determine the current, historical or projected compliance of an organization to a standard" (ASQ).

Assessment Category In the DQAF, an assessment category is a way of grouping measurement types based on where in the data life cycle the assessment is likely to be taken. Assessment categories pertain to both the frequency of the measurement (periodic or in-line) and the type of assessment involved (control, measurement, assessment). They correspond closely to assessment scenarios and include: initial assessment, process control, in-line measurement, periodic measurement, and periodic assessment.

Assessment Scenario In the DQAF, an assessment scenario is a setting and process for particular kinds of data assessment. These are connected with the information life cycle. Assessment scenarios include: initial, one-time assessment of data for purposes of data discovery and understanding; measurement of data within improvement projects to ensure that improvements have had the desired effects; in-line measurement and control of data to sustain and improve data quality; and periodic measurement of data quality, also to sustain and improve it.

Assignable Cause Assignable cause is a name for the source of variation in a process that is not due to chance and therefore can be identified and eliminated. Also called "special cause" (ASQ).

Atomicity Atomicity is the state or fact of being composed of individual units (*NOAD*). With regard to data, atomicity refers to what constitutes a unit. In modeling, as data is normalized, each attribute is expected to represent one thing, not a set of things. One system may define a name as one thing. Another may define it as three things (first name, middle initial, last name). Atomicity results from decisions about how to structure data.

Attribute In modeling, an attribute represents a characteristic of an entity. Because of this use, attribute is sometimes understood as a *data element* (which is a component piece of a data used to represent an entity), or a *field* (which is part of a system used to display or intake data), or a *column* (which is a place in a table to store a defined characteristic of a represented entity, that is, to store values associated with data elements).

Baseline Measurement A baseline measurement is taken to serve as a point of comparison for subsequent measurement. ASQ it as "The beginning point, based on an evaluation of output over a period of time, used to determine the process parameters prior to any improvement effort; the basis against which change is measured."

Benchmarking Benchmarking is the process of measuring against a known standard for purposes of determining how to improve toward that standard. For example, many companies benchmark their success against their competitors or against organizations that are considered best-in-class. Data can also be measured against benchmarks. In health care, this technique is used to determine the reasonability of data, as well as to identify areas for improvement in the delivery of health care services.

The Business The business is a term, usually used by information technology professionals, to refer to people within an organization whose work is focused on the primary mission of the organization, as opposed to being focused on developing or maintaining information systems. *Businesspeople* is a synonym.

Business Process A business process is a series of steps required to execute a function that is important to an organization. Business processes include things like taking an order or setting up an account or paying a claim. In process analysis, business processes are the focus of opportunities for improvement. Organizations usually have a set of key processes that require support from other areas, like information technology. (See also Technical Process.)

Cardinality Cardinality is a term from mathematics that refers to "the number of elements in a set or other grouping as a property of that grouping" (*NOAD*). In data management, cardinality is used to refer to two things: the number of distinct values in a specific field and the relationship between entities (one-to-one, one-to-many, etc.).

Column/Field/Attribute A column is a component part of a table in a database. Tables are made up of rows, each representing one instance of an entity represented by the table and columns, containing characteristics of the represented entity. *Field* and *attribute* are usually understood as synonyms for columns, because they also contain characteristics of a represented entity. But columns are specific to tables.

Column Profile (column profiling) A column profile is a means of assessing data that populates one field in a dataset. Column profiling usually includes a distribution of the values in the column, as well as an assessment of the number of formatting patterns and the level of null or defaulted values.

Common Cause Variation In statistical process control, common causes are sources of variation that are inherent in a process, part of its normal operation. They are contrasted with special causes, which exist outside of the process but have an impact on it.

Completeness Completeness is a dimension of data quality. As used in the DQAF, completeness implies having all the necessary or appropriate parts; being entire, finished, total. A dataset is complete to the degree that it contains required attributes and a sufficient number of records, and to the degree that attributes are populated in accord with data consumer expectations. For data to be complete, at least three conditions must be met: the dataset must be defined so that it includes all the attributes desired (width); the dataset must contain the desired amount of data (depth); and the attributes must be populated to the extent desired (density). Each of these secondary dimensions of completeness can be measured differently.

Conceptual Data Models Conceptual data models represent entities (ideas or logical concepts) but contain little if any detail about the attributes of these entities. Conceptual data models are usually created as a starting point for modeling to ensure that the relation between high-level concepts is understood.

Consistency Consistency is a dimension of data quality. As used in the DQAF, consistency can be thought of as the absence of variety or change. Consistency is the degree to which data conform to an equivalent set of data, usually a set produced under similar conditions or a set produced by the same process over time.

Contextual Data Quality Contextual data quality considers the extent to which data are applicable (pertinent) to the task of the data user, not to the context of representation itself. Contextually appropriate data must be relevant to the consumer, in terms of timeliness and completeness. Dimensions include: value-added, relevancy, timeliness, completeness, and appropriate amount of data (from the Wang & Strong framework.)

Control A control is a form of feedback built into a system to keep it stable. A control has the ability to detect conditions that indicate a lack of stability (most often in the form of a measurement) and initiate action based on this observation. With automated controls, action may involve stopping the system or taking action that mitigates the condition (such as adjusting another variable within the system),

Control Chart A control chart is a time sequence graph with additional features that identify data out of expected limits. In a typical individual/moving range statistical process control chart, the upper and lower control limits (UCL and LCL) are three standard deviations from the historical mean of the set of readings. If the measurement remains within the upper and lower controls limits, then the process is in control. *In control* means that any differences between the readings are affected only by *normal* or *common cause* variation (variation inherent in the process being measured). A process is in control when measurement points fall within the upper and lower control limits, and the points graphed on a control chart do not display any non-random patterns

Conventions of Data Representation Conventions of representation include the set of decisions required to create or store data. These include the data structure of the model, as well as details about the physical presentation of data. If we know and agree on the conventions by which data represents reality (how it effects its representation), then we have the tools to measure its quality: the rules or standards by which associated with these conventions.

Cost of Poor Quality (COPQ) Cost of poor quality is the cost associated with providing poor-quality products or services. There are four categories: internal failure costs (costs associated with defects found before the customer receives the product or service), external failure costs (costs associated with defects found after the customer receives the product or service), appraisal costs (costs incurred to determine the degree of conformance to quality requirements), and prevention costs (costs incurred to keep failure and appraisal costs to a minimum). (From ASQ)

Cost/Benefit Analysis A cost/benefit analysis (CBA; also called benefit-cost analysis) is a comparison of the costs of implementing a change and the expected benefits of implementing the change. Cost/benefit analysis accounts for hard numbers (direct measurable costs) and soft numbers (expected effects on people's behavior and attitudes). Data quality improvement efforts should include a CBA.

Critical Data Critical data includes data that is necessary to run an enterprise, is the subject of reporting, or is essential for input for other business processes. Criticality is relative and must be defined in the context of the needs of a specific organization. Data that is critical for one process may not be critical for another. Still, many organizations can identify data that is critical to multiple processes. For example, customer data is generally critical to many processes within an enterprise (Loshin, 2001).

Data Data are abstract representations of selected characteristics of real-world objects, events, and concepts, expressed and understood through explicitly definable conventions related to their meaning, collection, and storage. We also use the term *data* to refer to pieces of information, electronically captured, stored (usually in databases), and capable of being shared and used for a range of organizational purposes. ASQ defines *data* as "A set of collected facts. There are two basic kinds of numerical data: measured or variable data … and counted or attribute data." ISO defines *data* as "re-interpretable representation of information in a formalized manner suitable for communication, interpretation, or processing" (ISO 11179).

Data assessment See Data Quality Assessment.

Data Asset The term *data asset* refers generically to organizational data, or to any transactional system, data storage system, or application that contains data required for business functions. Any of these systems might be involved in the production and use of data and therefore may affect its quality. Treating data as an asset enables organizations to manage and increase its value. The quality of the data in a system has direct effects on the successful execution of business functions and therefore the success of the enterprise as a whole.

Data Chain The data chain refers to the movement of data from one system to another; an instance of data moving through a part of its life cycle. Also called the Information Chain.

Data Brokers Data brokers do not produce data, but they enable others to consume it. They are similar to distributors of manufactured goods. It is important to recognize brokers because they are part of the information chain and can influence data content and the formal structure of data, as well as its availability and timeliness.

Data Consumers Data consumers are those people and systems that use data at any point in the information chain. Data consumers have requirements for data.

Data Environment The data environment is a broad term for the collection of factors that influence the creation and use of data: the business processes through which data is produced, the technical systems through which it is produced and stored, the data itself, metadata (including data standards, definitions, specifications), technical architecture (including data access tools), and data uses. All of these have implications for understanding data quality.

Data Flow Data flow refers to the movement of data from one purpose to another; also the movement of data through a set of systems, or through a set of transformations within one system; it is a nontechnical description of how data is processed. See also Data Chain.

Data Governance "Data Governance is a system of decision rights and accountabilities for information-related processes, executed according to agreed-upon models which describe who can take what actions with what information, and when, under what circumstances, using what methods" (from Gwen Thomas).

Data Lag Data lag is the time between when data is updated in its source and when it is made available to data consumers. Data lag influences the perception of data currency and timeliness.

Data Life Cycle The data life cycle is the set of processes a dataset goes through from its origin through its use(s) to its retirement. Data that moves through multiple systems and multiple uses has a complex life cycle. Danette McGilvray's POSMAD formulation identifies the phases of the life cycle as: planning for, obtaining, storing and sharing, maintaining, applying, and disposing of data. Also called the Information Life Cycle.

Data Lineage Data lineage refers to a set of identifiable points that can be used to understand details of data movement and transformation (e.g., transactional source field names, file names, data processing job names, programming rules, target table fields). Lineage describes the movement of data through systems from its origin or provenance to its use in a particular application. Lineage is related to both the data chain and the information life cycle. Most people concerned with the lineage of data want to understand two aspects of it: the data's origin and the ways in which the data has changed since it was originally created. Change can take place within one system or between systems.

Data Model A data model is a visual representation of data content and the relationships, created for purposes of understanding how data is or might be organized, and for ensuring the comprehensibility and usability of that way of organizing data. Different kinds of models are created for different purposes and present different levels of detail about data and relationships. Modeling for a data store generally begins with a conceptual model and progresses to logical and physical models. (See also Conceptual Data Model, Logical Data Model, and Physical Data Model.)

Data Producers Data producers include people and systems that create, store, or otherwise make available data used by data consumers

Data Profiling Data profiling is a specific kind of data analysis used to discover and characterize important features of datasets. Profiling provides a picture of data structure, content, rules, and relationships by applying statistical methodologies to return a set of standard characteristics about data—data types, field lengths, and cardinality of columns, granularity, value sets, format patterns, content patterns, implied rules, and cross-column and cross-file data relationships, and cardinality of those relationships.

Data Quality The level of quality of data represents the degree to which data meets the expectations of data consumers, based on their intended use of the data. Data quality is thus directly related to the perceived or established purpose of the data. Purpose is usually associated with how data consumers intend to use data ("fitness for use"). However, because data also serves a semiotic function (it serves as a sign of something other than itself), data quality is also directly related to the perception of how well data effects this representation. High-quality data meets expectations for use and for representational effectiveness to a greater degree than low-quality data. Measuring the quality of data requires understanding those expectations and determining the degree to which the data meets them.

Data Quality Assessment Data quality assessment is the process of evaluating data to identify errors and understand their implications (Maydanchik, 2007). Most often, data quality assessment understands the condition of data in relation to particular expectations, requirements, or purposes in order to draw a conclusion about whether it is suitable for those expectations, requirements, or purposes. This process always implies the need also to understand how effectively data represent the objects, events, and concepts it is designed to represent.

Data Quality Issue A data quality issue is a condition of data that is an obstacle to a data consumer's use of that data—regardless of who discovered the issue, where/when it was discovered, what its root causes are determined to be, or what the options are for remediation. Data that has quality issues does not meet consumer expectations or is not fit for its intended use. Root causes of data issues can range from incorrect, inconsistent, or incomplete data brought into a system or created by a system; incorrect, inconsistent, or incomplete data processing or choices in storing data; or incorrect, inconsistent, or incomplete assumptions on the part of data consumers. Data issues can emerge at any point in a data life cycle and at any point in a data chain. Issues introduced upstream have cumulative impacts and costs down the information chain. Issues that are not addressed at their root causes will continue to impose costs on the information chain.

Data Quality Issue Management Data issue management is the process of removing or reducing the impact of obstacles that prevent effective use of data. Issue management includes identification, definition, quantification, prioritization, tracking, reporting, and resolution of issues. Prioritization and resolution depend on data governance. To resolve a problem means to find a solution and implement that solution. A resolution is a solution to a problem. Issue resolution refers to the process of bringing an issue to closure through a solution or through the decision not to implement a solution. Any individual issue will have a specific definition of what constitutes its "resolution."

Data Quality Program A data quality program is a set of projects and tasks directed at improving data quality within an organization. Data quality programs should be driven by a data quality strategy aimed at creating a culture focused on quality. This driver is why data quality programs usually include education and training on data quality, in addition to projects focused on data and process assessment, issue remediation, and improvement efforts. Sustaining data quality requires some level of ongoing measurement and control.

Data Quality Program Team The data quality program team refers to people charged with implementing a data quality strategy, either directly as hands-on analysts or indirectly as propagators and subject matter experts in the data quality methodology.

Data Quality Requirement Data quality requirements describe characteristics of data necessary for it to be of high quality. Data quality content requirements define the expected condition of data in terms of quality characteristics, such as completeness, validity, and consistency. Data quality measurement requirements define how a particular characteristic should be measured.

Data Quality Standards Data quality standards are assertions about the expected condition of the data that relate directly to quality dimensions: how complete the data is, how well it conforms to defined rules for validity, integrity, and consistency, as well as how it adheres to defined expectations for presentation.

Data Quality Threshold A data quality threshold is a numeric representation of the acceptable limit of a data quality measurement.

Data Standards Data standards are assertions about how data should be created, presented, transformed, or conformed for purposes of consistency in presentation and meaning and to enable more efficient use. Data standards can be defined at the value (column) or structure (table) or database levels. They have an impact on technical processing and storage of data, as well as on data consumer access to and use of data.

Data Steward The term s*tewardship* is "the management or care of another person's property" (*NOAD*). *Data stewards* are individuals who are responsible for the care and management of data. This function is carried out in different ways based on the needs of particular organizations.

Data Structure Data structure is a general term referring to how data is organized. In modeling, it refers more specifically to the model itself. Tables are referred to as "structures."

Database A database is a structured set of data that is held in a computer, especially one that is accessible in various ways (*NOAD*).

Dataset Dataset is a general term for referring to a collection of data; most often I have used it to refer to a collection of data that will be measured.

Derivation Derivation or transformation is a manner of processing data to populate a field or fields. Derivations execute rules that can result in the creation of new data or the modification of existing data. The data used in the derivation may or may not be stored. *Derivation* is a synonym for *transformation*.

Distribution Analysis Distribution analysis is a form of data analysis used to determine the reasonability of a set of values by assessing the relative proportion of any individual value and the relation of individual values to each other in one field of the dataset. As input, distribution analysis entails counting all the records associated with each value (the numerator for each calculation) and dividing these by the total number of records in the dataset (the denominator for all the calculations) so that the number of records associated with any individual value is represented as a percentage of the whole set. Percentages provide a more comprehensible way than raw numbers to understand relative size of the subset of data associated with any individual value. Percentage calculations also help in identifying other relationships within the data. Columns that have similar distributions may be related to each other logically, for example.

Distribution of Values Distribution of values is a way of displaying data as part of distribution analysis.

Direct Source System The direct source system is the system from which the data warehouse or other store actually receives the data. It may or may not be a system of record or a system of origin.

DMAIC DMAIC is an acronym for Define, Measure, Analyze, Improve, and Control, the Six Sigma approach to quality improvement.

DQAF The Data Quality Assessment Framework is a descriptive taxonomy that enables a common understanding of data quality measurement and assessment. It defines generic patterns of measurement related to the dimensions of completeness, timeliness, validity, consistency, and integrity. These patterns can be used to define specific metrics.

Edit Controls Edit controls are controls put in place on data creation to prevent errors from entering a system.

Enterprise The term *enterprise* refers to a business or other organization that produces and uses data to accomplish its goals. (In today's world, that includes nearly every business, large or small, along with nonprofits and government agencies.) *Enterprise* is a synonym for *organization*.

Enterprise System Sourcing Strategy ESSS is an approach to systems planning that identifies enterprise systems of record to source a central data warehouse and makes those systems accountable for the data they produce (Couture, 2012).

Entity In the process of entity resolution, an *entity* is "a real world person, place, or thing that has a unique identity that distinguishes it from all other entities of the same type" (Talburt, 2011, p. 205). In the process of modeling, an *entity* is a concept being modeled and is sometimes used as a synonym for *table*.

ETL (Extract, Transform, Load) ETL is an acronym for data processing used to prepare data to be loaded to a database or data warehouse.

Expectations To *expect* something is to regard it as likely to happen, or likely to do or be something; an *expectation* is "a strong belief that something will happen or be the case in the future" (*NOAD*). The term *data quality expectation* refers to data consumers' assumptions related to the condition of the data. Expectations may be based on very little knowledge or thorough understanding of data content, structure, and limitations. Expectations are usually connected to intended uses of data and to what the data is supposed to represent. They may be well articulated and even documented (for example, a simple data definition may imply a set of expectations) or they may not have even been identified.

Explicit Knowledge Explicit knowledge is information that is captured in a way that it can be shared. People can learn it without having to rely directly on other people. In knowledge management practice, explicit knowledge is contrasted with tacit knowledge, which is knowledge that is inside people's heads.

Grain The grain of data refers to the meaning of a single row in a fact table. The level of grain (or detail) in a table is determined as part of the modeling process.

Historical Mean The mean is a statistical measure of variation. It is most easily understood as the mathematical average. It is calculated by summing the value of a set of measurements and dividing by the number of measurements taken. The historical mean uses the data from past measurements to calculate the mean of past measurements.

Historical Median The median is a statistical measure of variation. It represents the middle measurement when a set of measurements are collected in ascending order: 50% of the measurements are above the median and 50% are below it. The historical median uses past measurements as input to determine the middle point.

In-Control Process The in-control process is the process in which the statistical measure being evaluated is in a state of statistical control; in other words, the variations among the observed sampling results can be attributed to a constant system of chance causes. Also see Out-of-Control Process (ASQ).

Individual Measurement See Specific Metric.

Information Chain See Data Chain.

Information Float Information float refers to the time between when a fact becomes known and when it is available for use. Information float influences the perception of data currency and timeliness.

Information Life Cycle See Data Life Cycle.

In-line Measurement In-line measurement refers to measurement that takes place in conjunction with the processing of data within a data store or other application—for example, measurements that are taken as part of an extract, transform, and load (ETL) process. Synonyms include *in-process measurement, in-line data quality monitoring, and per load or run-over-run data quality monitoring.*

Integrity Integrity is a dimension of data quality. As used in the DQAF, integrity refers to the state of being whole and undivided or the condition of being unified. Integrity is the degree to which data conform to data relationship rules (as defined by the data model) that are intended to ensure the complete, consistent, and valid presentation of data representing the same concepts. Integrity represents the internal consistency of a dataset.

Intrinsic Data Quality Intrinsic data quality denotes that data have quality in their own right; it is understood largely as the extent to which data values are in conformance with the actual or true values. Intrinsically good data is accurate, correct, and objective, and comes from a reputable source. Dimensions include: accuracy objectivity, believability, and reputation (from the Wang & Strong framework).

Knowledge Management Knowledge management is a set of practices related to how organizations learn from their own experiences. Many of these practices focus on ensuring that what employees know and learn is captured in a shareable form (explicit knowledge).

Logical Data Model A logical data model is more detailed than a conceptual model, but not as detailed as a physical data model. Logical data models include detail about attributes (characteristics in columns) needed to represent a concept, such as key structure (the attributes needed to define a unique instance of an entity), and they define details about the relationships within and between data entities.

Mean The mean is a statistical measure of central tendency. It is most easily understood as the mathematical average. It is calculated by summing the value of a set of measurements and dividing by the number of measurements taken.

Measurement The process of measurement is the act of ascertaining the size, amount, or degree of something. Measurements are the results of the process of measuring.

Measurement Logical Data Model The measurement logical data model is the model of DQAF measurement types. There are two types of table in the model: metric definition tables that store the specific measurements to be taken by the type and measurement results tables.

Measurement Type Within the DQAF, a measurement type is a subcategory of a dimension of data quality that allows for a repeatable pattern of measurement to be executed against any data that fits the criteria required by the type, regardless of specific data content. For example, any measurement of data validity for a single column, the domain of which is defined as a range of values, follows the same pattern as any other measurement of validity for a single column whose domain is defined as a range. The measurement results of a particular measurement type can be stored in the same data structure regardless of the data content.

Median The median is a statistical measure of variation. It represents the middle measurement when a set of measurements are collected in ascending order: 50% of the measurements are above the median and 50% are below it.

Metadata Metadata is usually defined as "data about data," but it would be better defined as explicit knowledge, documented to enable a common understanding of an organization's data, including what the data is intended to represent (definition of terms and business rules), how it effects this representation (conventions of representation, data definition, system design, system processes), the limits of that representation (what it does not represent), what happens to it as it moves through processes and systems (provenance, lineage, information chain and information life cycle), how data is used and can be used, and how it should not be used.

Mode The *mode* is a statistical measure of central tendency. It refers to the value that occurs most frequently in a dataset.

Model A model is a representation of another thing or of a proposed structure or system. In mathematics, models are simplified descriptions of a system or process to assist with calculations and predictions.

Monitor To monitor something is to observe or check its progress over time (*NOAD*). Data quality monitoring involves processes (measurements and controls) that observe the data for purposes of ensuring that it does not change unexpectedly.

Normal Variation See Common Cause Variation.

Objective Measures Objective measures (or measurements) measure the task-independent characteristics of data. Objective measurements can be taken without knowledge of how the data is being or will be applied (that is, without information about the context of its use).

Object of Measurement In the DQAF, objects of measurement are groupings of measurement types based on whether types focus on process or content, or on a particular part of a process (e.g., receipt of data) or kind of content (e.g., the data model). Content-related objects of measurement include: the data model, content based on row counts, content of amount fields, date content, aggregated date content, summarized content, cross-table content (row counts, aggregated dates, amount fields, chronology), overall database content. Process-related objects of measurement include: receipt of data, condition of data upon receipt, adherence to schedule, and data processing

Ongoing Measurement Ongoing measurement is a measurement that is conducted more than once, usually as part of an overall program to sustain data quality. Forms of ongoing measurement include: in-line measurements, process controls, and periodic measurement or assessment.

Out-of-Control Process An out-of-control process is a process in which the statistical measure being evaluated is not in a state of statistical control. In other words, the variations among the observed sampling results cannot be attributed to a constant system of chance causes. See also In-Control Process (ASQ).

Physical Characteristics of Data While data are not "physical" in the sense that manufactured goods are, in order to be stored and accessed, they need to be defined in terms of data type, length, format, and so on.

Physical Data Models Physical data models represent the way that data are physically stored in a database. They describe the physical characteristics of tables and columns that are required to set up and store actual data about the entities represented.

Plan, Do, Check, Act Also Plan, Do, Study, Act the Shewhart Cycle or Deming Cycle. All refer to the process of improving quality through a defined series of steps.

Process Management Process management refers to the pertinent techniques and tools applied to a process to implement and improve process effectiveness, hold the gains, and ensure process integrity in fulfilling customer requirements (ASQ).

Reasonability Check A reasonability check provides a means of drawing a conclusion about data based on knowledge of data content rather than on a strictly numeric measurement. Reasonability checks can take many forms, many of which use numeric measurement as input, but they all answer a simple question: Does this data make sense, based on what we know about it? The basis for judging "reasonability" ranges from simple common sense to deep understanding of what the data represents. A synonym (and metaphor) for reasonability is a "smell test."

Referential Integrity (RI) Referential integrity is the degree to which data in two or more tables related through a foreign key relationship is complete. Referential integrity is often explained through parent/child table relationships. Within a database, all values that are present on a child table should also be present on its parent table. If a child table has values that are not on its parent table (orphan values), it does not have referential integrity with the parent table.

Representational Data Quality Representational data quality indicates that the system must present data in such a way that it is easy to understand (represented concisely and consistently) so that the consumer is able to interpret the data; understood as the extent to which data is presented in an intelligible and clear manner. Dimensions include: interpretability, ease of understanding, representational consistency, and concise representation (rom the Wang & Strong framework).

Represented Entity Data are representations of real-world objects, referred to as entities. An entity may have numerous references (records) in a dataset. A distinct count of entities represented in a dataset determines how many individual entities the data contains references to, regardless of how many references there are. For example, a library may have 10 books (records) by Mark Twain, but Mark Twain is only one entity (author).

Requirements Requirements are the things that a system must supply or the functionality that it must provide. Business requirements are statements describing what a system must have or do. They provide the basis for the work accomplished by software engineers and other technical personnel.

Risk Risk is the possibility that something unpleasant or unwelcome will happen (*NOAD*). Risk to data is the possibility that something will negatively affect its quality and make it less fit for use.

Risk Management Risk management is using managerial resources to integrate risk identification, risk assessment, risk prioritization, development of risk-handling strategies, and mitigation of risk to acceptable levels (ASQ).

Root Cause The root cause of a problem is the fundamental reason the problem exists.

SIPOC Diagram A SIPOC diagram is a tool for understanding opportunities for improvement. SIPOC stands for suppliers, inputs, process, outputs, and customers. The tool works by facilitating analysis regarding the effects each of these has on the quality of a product.

Source System A source system is an information technology system that provides data to another system or provides data for a business process. See also Transactional system.

Special Cause Variation In statistical process control, special cause variation refers to causes outside of a process that might negatively affect it, such as the weather interfering with a supplier. Special cause variation is contrasted with common cause variation, which is inherent in a process.

Specific Metric In the DQAF, a specific metric describes the particular data that will be measured. Definitions of specific metrics are stored in Metric Definition tables. Synonyms include: *individual measurement, data quality measurement.*

Standard A standard is something considered by an authority or by general consent as a basis of comparison; an approved model. Or it is a rule or principle that is used as a basis for judgment. Standards embody expectations in a formal manner. To *standardize* something means to cause it to conform to a standard; or to choose or establish a standard for something. ASQ defines standard as "the metric, specification, gauge, statement, category, segment, grouping, behavior, event or physical product sample against which the outputs of a process are compared and declared acceptable or unacceptable."

Statistical Process Control Statistical process control is an approach to measurement that was developed by Walter Shewhart in the 1920s, when he applied principles derived from statistics to the measurement of product quality. He recognized that variation exists within any process and that variation can be measured. Common cause variation is inherent in the process. Special cause variation comes from outside the process. Special causes can be identified and eliminated to produce a more predictable outcome from a process.

Statistics Statistics is the practice or science of collecting and analyzing numerical data in large quantities, especially for the purpose of inferring proportions in a whole from those in a representative sample (*NOAD*). ASQ defines statistics as "a field that involves tabulating, depicting, and describing datasets; a formalized body of techniques characteristically involving attempts to infer the properties of a large collection of data from inspection of a sample of the collection." Statistics are also the results of this kind of activity.

Subject Matter Expert SME is an acronym used to refer to people who understand and can explain information related to a knowledge domain. SMEs may be technically or business-oriented.

Subjective Measures Subjective measures (or measurements) focus on dimensions of quality (for example, believability, relevancy, etc.) that require input from data consumers (via a survey or other instrument) who have specific uses of data in mind. Subjective data assessments "reflect the needs and experiences" of data consumers (Wang, et al., 2002).

Sufficiency Sufficiency is a variation on the data quality dimension of completeness; it refers to "the condition of being adequate" (*NOAD*). If you have a sufficient amount of something, then you have enough. With respect to data quality, sufficiency can be measured against the requirements of a particular use of data.

Suitability Suitability pertains to how well data meets requirements; it refers to "being right or appropriate for a person, purpose, or situation" (*NOAD*). A data sample might be sufficient (of the right size, representing a sufficient percentage of a population) but still not be suitable.

SWOT Analysis A SWOT analysis is an approach to developing strategy that begins by identifying an organization's strengths, weaknesses, opportunities, and threats (hence SWOT). From these categories, an organization can identify ways to build on its strengths, improve its weaknesses, take advantage of opportunities, and minimize the potential impact of threats.

System A system is a set of connected things forming a complex whole (*NOAD*). Systems are often understood as mechanisms, but they can also comprise a set of principles or a method for doing things. In modern organizations, the term *system* is used to refer to information technology applications that carry out work needed by an organization. An example is a system for processing claims or one for inventorying products.

System of Origin The system of origin is the technical system in which data was first created or captured. The concept of a system of origin is important when tracing data lineage. The system of origin marks the data's provenance—the earliest instance of the data. The system of origin may or may not be the system of record. For any given data store, the system of origin may or may not be the direct source system.

System of Record The system of record is a system that is charged with keeping the most complete or trustworthy representation of a set of entities. Within the practice of master data management, such representations are referred to as *golden records* and the system of record can also be called the *system of truth*. Master data management refers to "control over master data values to enable consistent, shared, contextual use across systems of the most accurate, timely, and relevant version of the truth about essential business entities" (Loshin, 2010).

Table A two-dimensional collection of data consisting of rows in which instances of entities are represented and columns in which characteristics of those entities are associated with data values (Hay, 2006).

Tacit Knowledge Tacit knowledge is sometimes referred to as knowledge inside people's heads. It includes the skills and intuition that experienced people apply as a matter of course in their work. Tacit knowledge is contrasted with explicit knowledge, which is knowledge that is documented in a sharable form. One of the goals of knowledge management is to enable tacit knowledge to be shared by making it explicit knowledge.

Technical Process Technical processes are those whose goal is management of the internal workings of a system or the movement of data, without regard to the content of the system or its data. Technical processes are usually contrasted with business processes. Business processes should be directly related to the goals of the organization, whereas technical processes should be executed in support of business processes.

Timeliness Timeliness is a dimension of data quality related to the availability and currency of data. As used in the DQAF, timeliness is associated with data delivery, availability, and processing. Timeliness is the degree to which data conforms to a schedule for being updated and made available. For data to be timely, it must be delivered according to schedule.

Transactional System A transactional system is an application that is used to carry out the everyday operations of a business (for example, placing orders, processing claims). Transactional systems are contrasted with data stores (data warehouses, data marts, etc.), the purpose of which is to store data so that it can be used for analysis. There is not always a hard and fast line between system types (some transactional systems store data and some data consumers use data stored in transactional systems), but the conceptual distinction is important. Transactional systems have historically produced data as a by-product of other processes. To produce better data requires planning between transactional systems and data consumers of data storage systems.

Validity Validity is a dimension of data quality, defined as the degree to which data conforms to stated rules. As used in the DQAF, validity is differentiated from both accuracy and correctness. Validity is the degree to which data conform to a set of business rules, sometimes expressed as a standard or represented within a defined data domain.

Volatility The degree to which data is likely to change over time. Volatility influences the perception of data currency and timeliness.

Bibliography

"Some books are to be tasted, others to be swallowed, and some few to be chewed and digested."
—Francis Bacon, *Essays* (1625)

Ackoff, R. L. (1967, December). Management misinformation systems. *Management Science, (14.4)*, B147–B156.

Adelman, S., Moss, L., & Abai, M. (2005). *Data strategy*. Indianapolis, IN: Addison-Wesley Professional.

Al-Hakim, L. (2007). *Challenges of managing information quality in service organizations*. Hershey, PA: Idea Group Publishing.

Allee, V. (1997). *The knowledge evolution: Expanding organizational intelligence*. Newton, MA: Butterworth-Heinemann.

Allemann, G. (2011-10-07). DQ Metrics—don't blow up the whale! Retrieved from <http://dataqualitymatters.wordpress.com/2011/10/07/dq-metrics-dont-blow-up-the-whale/> Accessed 2011-10-12.

Andrei, N. (2005). *Modern control theory—a historical perspective*. Bucharest, Romania: Research Institute for Informatics.

ASQ. ASQ Knowledge Center. Retrieved from <http://asq.org/knowledge-center/> Accessed May–August 2012.

Baskarada, S. (2009). *Information quality management capability maturity model*. Weisbaden: Vieweg & Teubner.

Baudrillard, J. (1988). *Selected writings*. Stanford, CA: Stanford University Press.

Bellinger, G., Durval, C., & Mills, A. (2004). Data, information, knowledge, and wisdom. Retrieved from <http://www.systems-thinking.org/dikw/dikw.htm> Accessed 2012-08-25.

Bellis, M. History of the thermometer. *About.com*. Retrieved from <http://inventors.about.com/od/tstartinventions/a/History-Of-The-Thermometer.htm> Accessed 2011-10-11.

Bernholz, L. (2011-12). The data ecosystem. *Philanthropy 2173*. Blog. Retrieved from <http://philanthropy.blogspot.com/2011/12/data-ecosystem.html> Accessed 2012-07-12.

Bibel, D. (2010). Crime data as a 'Worst Case' IQ example. In *Proceedings of the fourth MIT information quality industry symposium*. 494.

Boslaugh, S., & Watters, P. A. (2008). *Statistics in a Nutshell: A desktop quick reference*. Sebastopol, CA: O'Reilly.

Bradshaw, T. (2006). The quality threshold. *Information Age*. (2006-05-19). Retrieved from <http://www.information-age.com/channels/information-management/perspectives-and-trends/277086/the-quality-threshold.thtml> Accessed 2011-10-30.

Bridges, W. (2009). *Managing transitions: Making the most of change* (3rd ed.). New York: Da Capo Press.

Brooking, A. (1999). *Corporate memory: Strategies for knowledge management*. London: International Thomson Business Press.

Bugajski, J. (2009-08-24). *Foundations of data Governance [G00203828]*. Stamford, CT: Gartner Burton IT1 Research.

Business Requirements. (2012). *Wikipedia*. Retrieved from <http://en.wikipedia.org/wiki/Business_requirements> Accessed 2012-03-01.

Chandler, D. (2009). Semiotics for beginners. Retrieved from <http://www.aber.ac.uk/media/Documents/S4B/sem0a.html> Accessed 2012-07-12.

Chen, P. P. S. (1980). English sentence structure and entity-relationship diagrams: *Proceedings of the first international conference on the entity-relationship approach to systems analysis and design*. New York: Elsevier Science Publishing Co.

Chisholm, M. D. (2010). *Definitions in information management: A guide to the fundamental semantic metadata.* Canada: Design Media.

Chisholm, M. D. (2004). *How to build a business rules engine: Extending application functionality through metadata engineering.* Boston, MA: Morgan Kaufmann.

Chisholm, M. D. (2012-08-16). Data quality is not fitness for use. *Information Management* Retrieved from <http://www.information-management.com/news/data-quality-is-not-fitness-for-use-10023022-1.html> Accessed 2012-08-17.

Churchman, C. W., & Ratoosh, P. (Eds.). (1962). *Measurement: Definitions and theories.* New York: John Wiley and Sons.

Codd, E. F. (1970). A relational model of data for large shared data banks. *Communications of the ACM (13.6),* 377–387.

Committee on Innovation in Computing and Communications: Lessons from history, National Research Council. (1999). *Funding a Revolution: Government Support for Computing Research.* Washington, DC: The National Academies Press (Retrieved from) <http://www.nap.edu/openbook.php?record_id=6323&page=1>.

Crease, R. P. (2011). *World in the balance: The historic quest for an absolute system of measurement.* New York: W. W. Norton.

Couture, N. (2012, Quarter 1). Reducing data management complexity in the enterprise. *The Business Intelligence Journal (17.1),* 31–37.

Cummings, T. G., & Worley, C. G. (1993). *Organizational development and change* (5th ed.). Minneapolis/St. Paul, MN: West Publishing Company.

Database Design Tutorial. (2012). *Tekstenuitleg.* Retrieved from <http://en.tekstenuitleg.net/articles/software/database-design-tutorial/intro.html> Accessed 2012-08-25.

Das, S. (2007-10-18). DIKW model. *Knowledge Management [Blog]* Retrieved from <http://knowmgt.blogspot.com/2007/10/dikw-model.html> Accessed 2012-08-25.

Davenport, T. H., & Prusak, L. (1998). *Working knowledge: How organizations manage what they know.* Cambridge, MA: Harvard.

Deming, W. E. (1994). *The new economics for industry, government, education* (2nd ed.). Cambridge, MA: MIT Press.

Derman, E. (2011). *Models. behaving. badly: Why confusing illusion with reality can lead to disaster on wall street and in life.* New York: Free Press.

Dodge, Y. (2006). *The Oxford dictionary of statistical terms* (6th ed.). Oxford: Oxford University Press.

Drucker, P. (1988, January–February). The coming of the new organization: *Harvard business review. Reprinted in Harvard business review on knowledge management. (1998).* Boston, MA: Harvard Business School Publishing. 1–19.

Early, S. (Ed.). (2011). *The DAMA dictionary of data management* (2nd ed.). Bradley Beach, NJ: Technics Publications, LLC.

Ellis, K. (2012). The executive briefing on the issues surrounding getting business requirements right. *Scribd* Retrieved from <http://www.scribd.com/doc/6766319/Business-Requirements> Accessed 2012-03-13.

English, L. P. (1999). *Improving data warehouse and business information quality.* Indianapolis, IN: John Wiley and Sons.

English, L. P. (2009). *Information quality applied.* Indianapolis, IN: John Wiley.

English, L. P. (2008). Information quality management: Job position roles. *IDQ Newsletter (4.2)* Retrieved from <http://iaidq.org/members/doc/english-2008-04.shtml> Accessed 2012-01-30.

Few, S. (2006). *Information dashboard design: The effective visual communication of data.* Sebastopol, CA: O'Reilly.

Fisher, C., Eitel, L., Chengalur-Smith, S., & Wang, R. (2006). *Introduction to information quality.* Cambridge, MA: MIT Information Quality Program.

Fisher, T. (2009). *The data asset: How smart companies govern their data for business success*. Hoboken, NJ: John Wiley and Sons.

Gackowski, Z. (2007). A formal definition of operation quality factors: A focus on data and information. *International Journal of Information Quality. (1.2)*, 225–249.

Gartner. (2011-06-27). Gartner says solving "Big Data" challenge involves more than just managing volumes of data. Gartner special report examines how to leverage pattern-based strategy to gain value in big data. Retrieved from <http://www.gartner.com/it/page.jsp?id=1731916> Accessed 2011-10-20.

Garvin, D. (1993, July–August). Building a learning organization: *Harvard business review. Reprinted in Harvard business review on knowledge management*. (1998). Boston, MA: Harvard Business School Publishing. 47–80.

Glazer, I. (2011-06-16). *Protecting privacy by using data labels [G00212150]*. Stamford, CT: Gartner Burton IT1 Research.

Glazer, I., & Henry, T. (2012-06-05). *The story of information sprawl [G00229277]*. Stamford, CT: Gartner Burton IT1 Research.

Gould, S. J. (1996). *The mismeasure of man*. New York: W. W. Norton.

Haines, M. (2010). Information quality research from the healthcare point of view. In *Proceedings of the fourth MIT information quality industry symposium*. 451–453.

Harris, J. (2012-03-19). What is weighing down your data? *Obsessive Compulsive Data Quality Blog* Retrieved from <http://www.ocdqblog.com/home/what-is-weighing-down-your-data.html>.

Harris, J. (2012-07-12). Quality is the Higgs field of data. *Obsessive Compulsive Data Quality Blog* Retrieved from <http://www.ocdqblog.com/home/quality-is-the-higgs-field-of-data.html>.

Harris, J. (2012-07-17). The five stages of data quality. *Obsessive Compulsive Data Quality Blog* Retrieved from <http://www.ocdqblog.com/home/dq-view-the-five-stages-of-data-quality.html?goback=%2Egde_41393_member_135175504> Accessed 2012-07-23.

Hay, D. (2006). *Data model patterns: A metadata map*. New York: Morgan Kaufmann.

Hubbard, D. W. (2010). *How to measure anything: Finding the value of "Intangibles" in business*. Hoboken, NJ: John Wiley and Sons.

Huff, D. (1954). *How to lie with statistics*. New York: W. W. Norton.

Inmon, W., O'Neil, B., & Fryman, L. (2008). *Business metadata: Capturing enterprise knowledge*. Boston, MA: Morgan Kaufmann.

International Association for Information and Data Quality (IAIDQ). *IQ/DQ glossary*. Retrieved from <http://iaidq.org/main/glossary.shtml> Accessed October 2011 through August 2012.

International Association for Information and Data Quality (IAIDQ). *Publications*. Retrieved from <http://iaidq.org/publications> Accessed October 2011 through August 2012.

International Standards Organization, (1993). *ANSI/ISO/ASQ A3534, Statistics—Vocabulary and Symbols*.

International Standards Organization. (2004-07-15). *ISO/IEC 11179-4 information technology–metadata registries (MDR) Part 4 formulation of data definitions* (2nd ed.).

Ivanov, K. (1972). *Quality-control of information: On the concept of accuracy of information in data-banks and in management information systems*. Stockholm, Sweden: The Royal Institute of Technology and the University of Stockholm Sweden.

Joffe-Walt, C. (2011-12-07). Can eurozone countries actually follow their own rules this time? National Public Radio. Retrieved from <http://www.npr.org/blogs/money/2011/12/07/143274540/can-eurozone-countries-actually-follow-their-own-rules-this-time?print=1> Accessed 2011-12-10.

Jones, D. (2012-07-12). 5 tips for overcoming data quality growing pains. *Data Quality Pro Journal* Retrieved from <http://www.dataqualitypro.com/blogpost/703684/Data-Quality-Pro-Journal> Accessed 2012-08-12.

Jones, D. (2012-08-15). Data quality metrics: Are you adopting the Dilbert approach?: *Data quality pro journal* Retrieved from <http://www.dataqualitypro.com/blogpost/703684/Data-Quality-Pro-Journal> Accessed 2012-08-25.

Kent, W. (2000). *Data and reality*. Bloomington, IN: 1st Books Library.

Kimball, R. (1996). *The data warehouse toolkit: Practical techniques for building dimensional data warehouses*. New York: John Wiley and Sons.

Kimball, R., Reeves, L., Ross, M., & Thronthwaite, W. (1998). *The data warehouse lifecycle toolkit: Expert methods for designing, developing, and deploying data warehouses*. Indianapolis, IN: John Wiley and Sons.

Kimball, R. (2004). The surprising value of data profiling. Retrieved <http://www.kimballgroup.com/html/designtipsPDF/DesignTips2004/KimballDT59SurprisingValue.pdf>Accessed 2012-03-01.

Kircher, P. (1962). Measurement and managerial decisions. In C. W. Churchman & P. Ratoosh (Eds.), *Measurement: Definitions and theories* (pp. 64–82). New York: John Wiley and Sons.

Klein, B. D., & Callahan, T. J. (2007). A comparison of information technology professionals' and data consumers' perceptions of the importance of the dimensions of information quality. *International Journal of Information Quality (1.4)*, 392–411.

Konnikova, M. (2012). Humanities aren't a science. stop treating them like one. *Scientific American. Blog post* Retrieved from <http://blogs.scientificamerican.com/literally-psyched/2012/08/10/humanities-arent-a-science-stop-treating-them-like-one/> Accessed 2012-08-16.

Lee, Y., Pipino, L., Funk, J. D., & Wang, R. (2006). *Journey to data quality*. Cambridge, MA: MIT Press.

Litwin, P. (1994). Fundamentals of relational database design. Retrieved from <http://www.deeptraining.com/litwin/dbdesign/FundamentalsOfRelationalDatabaseDesign.aspx> Accessed 2012-02-01.

Loshin, D. (2007-01-18). Developing a data quality strategy. *B*Eye Business Intelligence Network* [e-newsletter].

Loshin, D. (2001). *Enterprise knowledge management: The data quality approach*. Boston, MA: Morgan Kaufmann.

Loshin, D. (2008). *Master data management*. Boston, MA: Morgan Kaufmann.

Loshin, D. (2011). *The practitioner's guide to data quality improvement*. Boston, MA: Morgan Kaufmann.

Maydanchik, A. (2007). *Data quality assessment*. Bradley Beach, NJ: Technics Publications, LLC.

Maydanchik, A. (2012). Data quality monitoring—faster or better: The ultimate choice. *Data Quality Pro Journal* Retrieved from <http://www.dataqualitypro.com/blogpost/703684/Data-Quality-Pro-Journal?tag=data+quality+monitoring> Accessed 2012-03-30.

McGilvray, D. (2008). *Executing data quality projects: Ten steps to quality data and trusted information.*™. Boston, MA: Morgan Kaufmann.

McKean, E. (Ed.). (2005). *The new Oxford American dictionary* (2nd ed.). New York: Oxford University Press.

Measurement. (2012). History world. Retrieved from <http://www.historyworld.net/wrldhis/plaintexthistories.asp?historyid=ac07> Accessed 2012-08-25.

Mitra, A. (1993). *Fundamentals of quality control and improvement*. New York: Macmillan Publishing Company.

Moen, R., & Norman, C. Evolution of the PDCA cycle. [Academic paper] Retrieved from <http://pkpinc.com/files/NA01MoenNormanFullpaper.pdf> Accessed 2012-08-10.

Molloy, C. (2012-04-15). The data ecosystem in R&D. *Genetic Engineering & Biotech News. (32.8)* Retrieved from <http://www.genengnews.com/gen-articles/the-data-ecosystem-in-r-d/4080/?page=1> Accessed 2012-05-10.

Mosely, M., Brackett, M., Early, S., & Henderson, D. (Eds.), (2009). *The data management body of knowledge (DAMA-DMBOK Guide)*. Bradley Beach, NJ: Technics Publications, LLC.

Nadkarni, P. (2006). Delivering data on time: The Assurant Health case: *Proceedings of the eleventh international conference on information quality (ICIQ-06)*. Cambridge, MA: MIT Press.

NASA. (2005). A brief history of measurement systems. Retrieved from <https://standards.nasa.gov/history_metric.pdf> Accessed 2012-07-12.

National Committee for Quality Assurance (NCQA). Retrieved from <http://www.ncqa.org/> Accessed August 2012.

National Information Standards Organization [NISO], (2007). *Understanding metadata.* NISO Press.

Nonaka, I. (1991, November–December). The knowledge-creating company: *Harvard business review. Reprinted in Harvard business review on knowledge management.* (1998). Boston, MA: Harvard Business School Publishing. 21–46.

Olson, J. (2003). *Data quality: The accuracy dimension.* Boston, MA: Morgan Kaufmann.

O'Neal, K. (2012-03). Practical formulas for estimating the value of quality data. *IAIDQ.org.* Retrieved from <http://iaidq.org/publications/doc2/oneal-2012-03.shtml> Accessed May 2012.

Orr, K. (1998, February). Data quality and systems theory. *Communications of the ACM (41.2),* 66–71.

Ott, E. R., & Schilling, E. G. (1990). *Process quality control: Troubleshooting and interpretation of data* (2nd ed.). New York: McGraw-Hill.

Pearce, J. M. S. (2002, April). A brief history of the clinical thermometer. *QJM: An International Journal of Medicine (95.4),* 251–252.

Peirce, C. (1955). In J. Buchler (Ed.), *Philosophical writings of Peirce.* New York: Dover Publications.

Pierce, E. (2004). Developing, implementing and monitoring an information product quality strategy: *Proceedings of the Ninth International Conference on Information Quality (ICIQ-04).* Cambridge, MA: MIT Press. 13–26.

Pierce, E. (2003). Pursuing a career in information quality: The job of the data quality analyst: *Proceedings of the Eighth International Conference on Information Quality.* Cambridge, MA: MIT Press.

Pinker, S. (1999). *Words and rules: The ingredients of language.* New York: Basic Books.

Pipino, L., Lee, Y., & Wang, R. (2002, April). Data quality assessment. *Communications of the ACM (45.4),* 211–218.

Pollock, R. (2011-10-31). Scaling the open data ecosystem. *Open Knowledge Foundation Blog* Retrieved from <http://blog.okfn.org/2011/10/31/scaling-the-open-data-ecosystem/> Accessed 2012-05-10.

Prusak, L. (Ed.). (1997). *Knowledge in organizations.* Boston, MA: Butterworth-Heinemann.

Redman, T. C. (2007). The body has a heart and soul: Roles and responsibilities of the chief data officer. *IDQ Newsletter (3.1)* Retrieved from <http://iaidq.org/publications/doc2/redman-2007-01.shtml> Accessed 2012-01-30.

Redman, T. C. (2008). *Data driven: Profiting from your most important business asset.* Boston, MA: Harvard Business Press.

Redman, T. C. (1994). *Data quality management and technology.* New York: Bantam.

Redman, T. C. (2001). *Data quality: The field guide.* Boston, MA: Digital Press.

Redman, T. C. (1996). *Data quality for the information age.* Boston, MA: Artech House.

Redman, T. C. (2010, October). Ten habits for data quality: Focus on preventing errors at the source. *The Information and Data Quality Newsletter [IAIDQ], (6.4)*

Redman, T. C. (2005, July). Understanding the Rancor between IT and "The Business." *The Information and Data Quality Newsletter [IAIDQ] (1.3),* 12–13.

Requirements Analysis. (2012). *Wikipedia.* Retrieved from <http://en.wikipedia.org/wiki/Requirements_analysis> Accessed 2012-01-03.

Rumsey, D. (2011). *Statistics for dummies.* Indianapolis, IN: John Wiley and Sons.

Salkind, N. (2011). *Statistics for people who (think they) hate statistics.* Thousand Oaks, CA: Sage.

Salsburg, D. (2001). *The lady tasting tea: How statistics revolutionized science in the twentieth century.* New York: Holt.

Senge, P. (2006). *The fifth discipline: The art and practice of the learning organization.* New York: Doubleday.

Shannon, C. E. (1948, July and October). A mathematical theory of communication. *The Bell System Technical Journal, 27*, 379–423. 623–656.

Simon, A. R. (1997). *Data warehousing for dummies*. Foster City, CA: IDG Books Worldwide.

Simon, P. (Ed.). (2011). *101 lightbulb moments in data management: Tales from the data roundtable*. Las Vegas, NV: Motion.

Smith, A. M. (2001). Business requirements gathering–an overview. *TDAN.com* Retrieved from <http://www.tdan.com/view-articles/4842> Accessed 2012-03-01.

Stewart, T. (1999). *Intellectual capital: The new wealth of organizations*. New York: Doubleday.

Stigler, S. (1986). *The history of statistics: The measurement of uncertainty before 1900*. Cambridge, MA: Harvard University Press.

Tague, N. R. (2005). *The quality toolbox*. Milwaukee, WI: ASQ Quality Press.

Talburt, J. R. (2011). *Entity resolution and information quality*. Boston, MA: Morgan Kaufmann.

Taleb, N. N. (2007). *The black swan: The impact of the highly improbable*. New York: Random House.

Thomas, G. (2011-11-1). Goals and principles for data governance. *The Data Governance Institute [web site]* Retrieved from <http://www.datagovernance.com/gbg_data_governance_goals.html> Accessed 2011-11-01.

Tufte, E. R. (1983). *The visual display of quantitative information*. Cheshire, CT: Graphics Press.

Wang, R. (1998, February). A product perspective on total data quality management. *Communications of the AMC*, 58–65.

Wang, R., Lee, Y., & Pipino, L. (1998, Summer). Manage your information as a product. *Sloan Management Review*, 95–105.

Wang, R., & Strong, D. (1996, Spring). Beyond accuracy: What data quality means to customers. *Journal of Management Information Systems*, 5–33.

Wang, R. Y., Story, V. C., & Firth, C. (1995, August). A framework for analysis of data quality research. *IEEE Transactions on Knowledge and Data Engineering*, 623–639.

Wand, Y., & Wang, R. Y. (1996, November). Anchoring data quality dimensions in ontological foundations. *Communications of the AMC, 39*(11), 86–95.

Webber, L., & Wallace, M. (2007). *Quality control for dummies*. Hoboken, NJ: John Wiley & Sons.

Weinberg, G. M. (2001). *An introduction to general systems thinking*. New York: Dorset House.

Well, D., & Duncan, K. (1999). *Rule based data cleansing*. Info-Centric. [PowerPpoint presentation, privately shared].

West, M. (2003). *Developing high quality data models*. EPISTLE. (2.1).

West, M. (2011). *Developing high quality data models*. Boston, MA: Morgan Kaufmann.

West, M. (2009). ISO 8000—the emerging standard for data quality. *IDQ Newsletter (5.3)* Retrieved from <http://iaidq.org/members/doc/west-2009-07.shtml>.

Woods, D. (2009). Why data quality matters. *Forbes* Retrieved from <http://www.forbes.com/2009/08/31/software-engineers-enterprise-technology-cio-network-data.html> Accessed 2011-10-12.

Wurman, R. S. (2001). *Information anxiety 2*. Indianapolis, IN: QUE.

Yeager, S. (2011). Data governance: Quality reports and more. *Information Management* Retrieved from <http://www.information-management.com/newsletters/governance-data-quality-MDM-data-model-10021394-1.html?ET=informationmgmt:e2678:1071662a:&st=email&utm_source=editorial&utm_medium=email&utm_campaign=IM_Daily_102811> Accessed 2011-11-10.

Yonke, C. L., Walenta, C., & Talburt, J. R. (Eds.), (2011). *The job of the information/data quality professional*. IAIDQ. Retrieved from <http://iaidq.org/members/doc/yonke-2011-02-job-analysis-report.pdf> Accessed 2012-06-10.

Zhu, J., Alon, T., Arkus, G., Duran, R., Haber, M., & Liebke, R., et al. (2011). *Metadata management with IBM Infosphere Information Server*. IBM Technical Support Organization.

Zins, C. (2007). Conceptual approaches for defining data, information, and knowledge. *Journal of the America Society for Information Science and Technology (58.4)*, 479–493.

Index

Note: Page numbers followed by "*f*" and "*t*" refer to figures and tables, respectively; "*e*" followed by page number refers to appendices which are available only at online.

A

Accessibility DQ, e6
Accuracy, 63–64, e9
Adjudication, 37
Alternate Identifier, e17
American Society for Quality (ASQ), 3
Amount field, 199
ASQ, *see* American Society for Quality
Assessment category, 65–66
Assessment scenarios, 94*t*, 95
Asset, 177
Attribute, 30–31

B

The business, 18
Business requirements, 133–136
By-product, 12

C

Cardinality, 103, *see also* Relationship cardinality
Cause and effect diagram, e30
"Characteristics,", e9
Column, 30–31
Column property profiling, 100–105
  column population, 102–105
    cardinality different from expected, 103–104
    cardinality of one, 103
    invalid values, presence of, 102–103
    less-than-complete population, 104
    multiple data patterns, 104–105
    valid values, absence of, 103
  date data, 101–102
  high-frequency values, 101
  low-frequency values, 101
Communications model of information quality, e22–23
Completeness, 62, e9, e13*t*
Conceptual data models, 31, 158
Condition of data upon receipt, 65, 72–74
Consistency, 63, e13*t*
Contextual clarity, e10
Contextual DQ, e5, e6
Control, definition of, 52
Control chart, 205–206, e28–29
Controls and measurements, 83, 124–125

Crosby, Philip, e30
Cross-table content, 66, 81–82

D

DAMA, *see* Data Management Association
DAMA Body of Knowledge (DAMA-BOK), 28
Data
  analysis of, 12
  definition of, 3–4
  and expectations, 13–14
  as facts, 11
  and information, 14–15
  as knowledge, e37
  measuring value of, e1
  physical characteristics of, 32
  poor-quality data, e1, e2, e3
    hard and soft costs of, e2
    in organization's financial performance, e1
  as product, 11–12
  as product redux, e37–38
  as representation, 4–11, e37
  semiotic function, 6–8
  and systems, e38
  uniqueness of, e1, e1–2
Data assessment, *see* Data Quality Assessment
Data asset, 28–29
Data banks, 28, e25
Data brokers, 20
Data chain, 36, 181
Data consumers, 19–20
Data content, 65–66
  consistency, 66, 76–78
  validity, 65, 74–75
Data criticality, 123
  factors influencing, 140–141
Data ecosystem, 118–119
Data element, 30–31
Data governance, 21–22
  and data quality strategy, 168
Data issue management, 49
Data lag, 62
Data lineage, 37
Data management, 27–28, 58–60
  strategy, 167

Related Titles from Morgan Kaufman

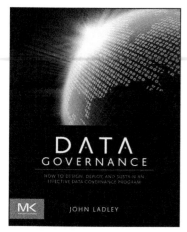

Data Governance
How to Design, Deploy and Sustain an Effective Data Governance Program
John Ladley
978-0-12-415829-0

Writing Effective Business Rules
Graham Witt
978-0-12-385051-5

The Practitioner's Guide to Data Quality Improvement
David Loshin
978-0-12-373717-5

Executing Data Quality Projects
Ten Steps to Quality Data and Trusted Information™
Danette McGilvray
978-0-12-374369-5

Data Quality
The Field Guide
Thomas Redman
978-1-55558-251-7

Data Quality
The Accuracy Dimension
Jack Olson
978-1-55860-891-7

mkp.com